LONGSTREET HIGHROAD GUIDE
——— TO THE ———

GEORGIA
COAST & OKEFENOKEE

BY RICHARD J. LENZ

FOREWORD BY THE GEORGIA CONSERVANCY

D0945605

LONGSTREET
ATLANTA, GEORGIA

Published by
LONGSTREET PRESS, INC.
a subsidiary of Cox Newspapers,
a subsidiary of Cox Enterprises, Inc.
2140 Newmarket Parkway
Suite 122
Marietta, Georgia 30067

Great efforts have been made to make the information in this book as accurate as possible. However, over time, trails are rerouted, beaches erode, towns are developed, and signs and landmarks may change. If you find a change has occurred to a beach, island, or trail in the book, please let us know so we can correct future editions. *A word of caution:* Outdoor recreation by its nature is potentially hazardous. All participants in such activities must assume all responsibility for their own actions and safety. The scope of this book does not cover all potential hazards and risks involved in outdoor recreation activities.

Printed by RR Donnelley & Sons, Harrisonburg, VA

1ˢᵗ printing 1999

Library of Congress Catalog Number 98-89179

ISBN: 1-56352-542-9

Book editing, design, and cartography
by Lenz Design & Communications, Inc., Decatur, Georgia

Cover illustration by Alfred R. Waud, *Picturesque America*, 1872

Cover design by Richard J. Lenz, Decatur, Georgia

Illustrations by Danny Woodard, Loganville, Georgia

"I really don't know why it is that all of us are so committed to the sea,
except I think it's because in addition to the fact that the sea changes, and
the light changes, and ships change, it's because we all came from the sea.
And it is an interesting biological fact that all of us have, in our veins
the exact same percentage of salt in our blood that exists in the ocean,
and therefore, we have salt in our blood, in our sweat, in our tears.
We are tied to the ocean. And when we go back to the sea—
whether it is to sail or to watch it—
we are going back from whence we came."

—John F. Kennedy, *Remarks in Newport, R.I., at the Australian Ambassa-
dor's Dinner for the America's Cup Crews, September 14, 1962*

Contents

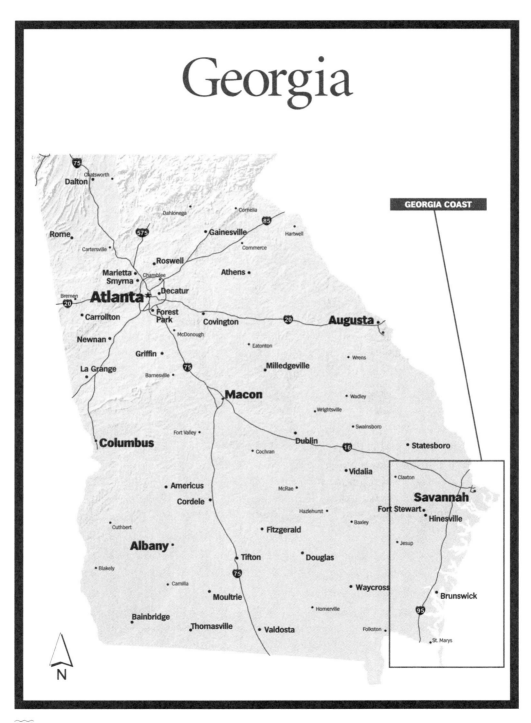

Georgia

Legend

Amphitheater	Camping	Misc. Special Areas
Parking	Bathroom	Town or City
Telephone	Wheelchair Accessible	Physiographic Region/ Misc. Boundary
Information	First Aid Station	
Picnicking	Picnic Shelter	Regular Trail
Dumping Station	Shower	State Boundary
Swimming	Biking	70 Interstate
Fishing	Comfort/Rest Station	522 U.S. Route
Interpretive Trail	Park Boundary	643 State Highway

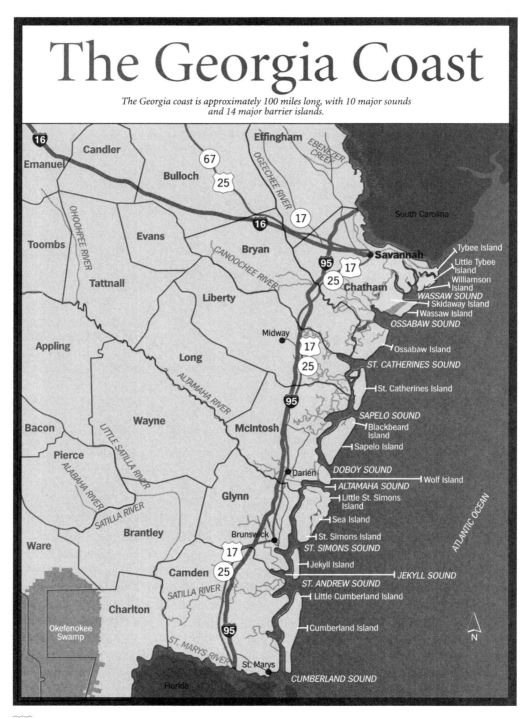

The Georgia Coast

*The Georgia coast is approximately 100 miles long, with 10 major sounds
and 14 major barrier islands.*

How to Use Your Longstreet Highroad Guide

The *Longstreet Highroad Guide to the Georgia Coast and Okefenokee* offers detailed information about the best places on the Georgia coast to pursue your favorite outdoor activities, including hiking, camping, fishing, boating, biking, wildlife watching, and touring of historic sites. The book also includes distinctive restaurant, lodging, and night life information. These attractions are known to change over time, altering their operating hours, quality of food and service, and ownership, so it is wise to call ahead before making a long drive to visit an establishment profiled here. Also, there is detailed information on the natural and human history of most areas, which can add dimension and depth to any outdoor pursuit.

The book is divided into three sections; the northern coast, central coast, and southern coast. Each division covers two counties. An additional chapter covers the coast's natural history. While the book is focused on natural qualities and outdoor recreation of the coast, it also features Savannah, a beautiful city with tremendous appeal and well worth the coastal traveler's attention. The Okefenokee Swamp is another highlighted natural area that receives special treatment.

In the directions and maps, two highway exit numbers are given. As this book went to press, the numbering system of all of Georgia's interstates was in the process of being changed to reflect mileage. This book has the current and future exit numbers. Also, all phone numbers are area code 912 unless otherwise indicated.

As the book was going to press, the state of Georgia was establishing the Colonial Coast Birding Trail, based on successful models in Texas and other states. These sites were selected for their abundance of bird life and ease of access. In the future, brochures will be available and signs will be posted at the sites on the trail. Selected sites are indicated in this book. For more information, contact the Department of Natural Resources, Wildlife Resources Division, 116 Rum Creek Drive, Forsyth, GA 31029. Phone (912) 994-1438. Also, county officials on the

WEST INDIAN MANATEE
(Trichechus manatus)
Most manatee sightings in Georgia take place in Camden, Glynn, and McIntosh counties from May through October.

coast are working on preliminary plans for a 450-mile Coastal Georgia Greenway, which would be a biking and pedestrian path linking the six coastal counties.

The Georgia coast is a sensitive and valuable area. Many of the natural communities profiled here are fragile and should be treated with great respect. Stay off sand dunes. Too many people walk on dunes without understanding the destruction this brings to the dune ecosystems of our barrier islands. Refrain from collecting live plants such as sea oats and carnivorous pitcher plants, which perform important tasks in their ecosystems. Live animals, such as sand dollars, snakes, and sea turtles, should be left alone so they can continue their species as well as be enjoyed by future generations. Many a time I've witnessed tourists on the beach filling their buckets with live sand dollars. Even these creatures can be depleted.

A word of caution: For the most enjoyment, visitors to wilderness areas should prepare themselves for heat and insects. Bring water for drinking, use insect repellant, and wear a hat, long sleeves, and pants. Coastal waters can be dangerous for swimming, fishing, and boating as Georgia has powerful and frequently changing tides. Be very aware of your surroundings and make safe decisions. If boating, use common sense and a personal floatation device. Many a Georgia boat has been stranded on a sand bar by low tides and was forced to wait many hours for the tide to lift it back out.

BROWN PELICAN
(Pelecanus occidentalis)
The brown pelican, with a wingspan up to 6 and a half feet, dives headfirst into the ocean to catch fish in its large gular pouch.

Foreword

Water, sky, and land meet in ultimate triumph on the Georgia coast. Tides roll back and forth, and dunes increase and diminish at the whim of sea and air. On a sultry morning, herons and cranes work the blue mud at the marsh's edge. Hot afternoon sun melts into golden evening, followed by a lonely moonlit night. On a nearby beach, a loggerhead turtle pulls herself to shore, deposits her eggs, and returns to sea. These and other traces of life catch your eye—while others remain unnoticed.

Experiences such as these have a way of changing who you are. Once you experience a sunrise on a Georgia beach, you are more aware of the dynamic forces of life that depend on the natural rhythms of our coastal environment. Once you understand these subtle rhythms, the more questionable man-made disturbances to the natural order become. The Georgia Conservancy was founded in 1967 by people who understood this link: the link between the appreciation and enjoyment of nature and the reasons people become inspired to stand up in defense of it.

Over the years, The Georgia Conservancy has worked hard to protect the resources that make the Georgia coast unique. Through education and advocacy, the Conservancy has helped secure protection for beaches and dunes, marshlands, endangered species, the Okefenokee Swamp, Cumberland Island National Seashore and Wilderness Area, Sapelo Island National Estuarine Sanctuary, the Ogeechee River, Blackbeard Island National Wildlife Refuge and Wilderness Area, Gray's Reef National Marine Sanctuary, and Harris Neck National Wildlife Refuge. Our work continues to reflect a deep respect for nature and a solutions-oriented approach toward conserving resources and protecting sensitive ecosystems.

Guidebooks, like this excellent guide by Richard J. Lenz, provide a multitude of opportunities to cultivate a relationship with our natural world. I encourage all who come across the *Longstreet Highroad Guide to the Georgia Coast and Okefenokee* to use it immediately to become personally acquainted with the vast treasures that constitute our beloved coast and prized marshlands. Spread word of your discoveries to friends and family, as well as those in your communities and places of work. Encourage all to tread gently in their travels, so the beauty they experience may be preserved for future generations.

As Richard writes, "The environment doesn't have a vote at the General Assembly of Georgia or in the U.S. Congress, unless someone represents it." Let us actively instill in our leaders a sense that a sunrise on a Georgia beach, and all that falls under its domain, is of importance and worthy of our watchful protection.

—John Sibley, President, The Georgia Conservancy

Preface

Let's go to the beach! These words around the family table generate excitement and sometimes shouting as the thrilling thought of visiting the coast awakens our dulled urban senses. Many think of the Florida coast as ideal, or perhaps more exotic locales in the Bahamas or Virgin Islands. I have spent time in these areas and for me, the Georgia coast is as beautiful and fascinating as any stretch in tourist-mad Florida or the Caribbean.

Unfortunately, there was no definitive guide to the Georgia coast. I mean until now. There were guides to Savannah and guides to some of the natural attractions, and guides to certain islands, but there were no guides that comprehensively treated the area's natural features, outdoor recreation, restaurants, and lodging. Some people are surprised to learn that Georgia even has a coast.

My goal was to create a book that I wished I had when I first started exploring the Georgia shore. I have worked very hard to produce such a volume and hope it brings an additional awareness of Georgia's great resource that is the coast.

One of the reasons that the Georgia coast is so special is its untamed nature. Of the 14 major barrier islands, only four are developed: Tybee, St. Simons, Sea Island, and Jekyll. The rest are under various degrees of private, state, and federal protection, a testament to the generosity of island owners and foundations, the political will of commendable government officials, and the visionary work of conservationists and scientists. Because of them, there remains a vibrant, fascinating, and inspiring coast to explore. We remain in their debt.

This is not to say the coast isn't facing some daunting issues. The depletion of the coastal aquifer, the dredging of rivers, the loss of beach, the overfishing of certain marine species, and the potential for mining the edge of the Okefenokee Swamp are just a few of the problems that must be solved. Also, it appears that where the coast can be developed, it will be developed. The path of "progress" on developed islands and the coastal mainland is being hotly debated between islanders and developers, who face off at rowdy public meetings. Residents who "got theirs" are hostile to newcomers who have just discovered the area. Property taxes are on the rise as services are increased to meet the demands of a swelling coastal population that is predicted to grow 40 percent in the next 20 years, and is straining outdated infrastructures and choking roads. Tourism has boomed as well. To longtime residents, their home is forever changed and the good old days are gone for good.

There is a generous helping of history between these covers, which is intentional. I believe it is important to understand the past so we can perhaps guide our future activities with more wisdom in an area as special as the Georgia coast. All of the motivations driving human history today can be found in the hoary fables that are hundreds, if not thousands, of years old. Whether about greedy pirates, rapacious land barons, visionary planters, freedom-loving slaves, or awestruck naturalists, this book tries to tell some of the true tales of the Georgia coast.

A guidebook could be written just on Savannah—indeed, many have. While the highlights of Savannah have been included, a more pene-trating focus has been saved for the other interesting and lesser-known natural and historic features of the Georgia coast in order to illuminate the off-the-beaten-track places that may be new to readers.

I've included attractions, lodging, and restaurants that I believe are worth experiencing. It is very possible that some of my recommendations aren't to your liking. This may be because our tastes are different, or because an attraction has changed owners and the quality is not what it once was. My apologies for leading anyone astray.

One final note: If you visit the coast, please treat it with care.

GREAT WHITE EGRET
(Casmerodius albus)
One of the most common wading birds on the coast, this bird was almost hunted to extinction for its beautiful plumes before 1900. It is recognized by its yellow bill and black legs and feet.

Many of these natural areas are relatively fragile, are important to man, and deserve respect. Also, become a member of a conservation organization and support the cause of careful use and protection of our valuable natural resources. The environment doesn't have a vote at the General Assembly of Georgia or U.S. Congress, unless someone represents it. While one developer may not get his or her way on a single project, every day we benefit from the naturally occurring processes supplied free of charge by healthy ecosystems. Enough preaching. Whatever your reason for visiting the Georgia coast, I hope you will love it as much as I do.

So…*let's go to the beach!*

—Richard J. Lenz

Acknowledgments

I must first thank Steve Gracie and Chuck Perry of Longstreet Press for having the vision and business guts to commit to the Longstreet Highroad Guide series. In today's ultracompetitive world of publishing, it takes leadership and courage to produce a book series as ambitious as this one. Thank you, gentlemen.

Second, I must thank Marge McDonald, project director of the series. She found and hired me. Her energy, creativity, and spirit are second to no one's.

Sir Isaac Newton wrote to a colleague, "If I have seen further it is by standing upon the shoulders of giants." As author of this book, I owe an incalculable debt to the scientists, conservationists, and government researchers who spent many years examining and writing on the complex natural relationships of the Georgia coast. Much of the work of these giants is incorporated here. Thank you Dr. Charles Wharton, Dr. Eugene Odum, Dr. John Bozeman, and Mildred and John Teal. A special thanks to Buddy Sullivan, the manager of Sapelo Island and the extraordinary historian of the Georgia coast. And a sincere thanks to Mike Harris, of the Georgia Department of Natural Resources, for sharing his tremendous expertise.

I received a lot of help all along the coast as I labored to produce a comprehensive and accurate book. Many gave generously of their time and resources. I must thank the following for pointing me in the right direction and untangling my fictions from my facts: Penn Myrick, Dennie McNeely, Sally Keller, Michael Bart, Cullen Chambers, Walter Parker, Marsha Kevill, James Mack Adams, Susan Brockway, Melanie Hoffman,

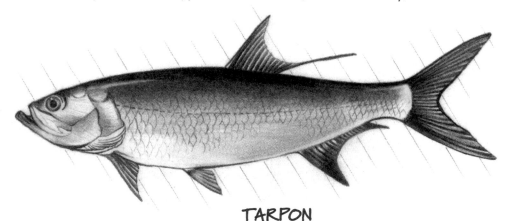

TARPON
(Megalops atlanticus)
The tarpon is a powerful swimmer that is famous for its spectacular leaps when hooked by sport fishermen

Cliff Kevill, Amy Blackburn, Lance Hatten, Sue Cole, Connie Bazemore, Edith Schmidt, Greg Starbuck, Bobby Moulis, Gerald Williamson, Raymond Thomas, Carl Hall, Jack Hoyt, Bob Monroe, Eleanor Torrey West, Elizabeth DuBose, Joann Clark, Arthur Edgar; Laura, Don, and Meredith Devendorf; Sandy Bray, Deborah Stone, Jane Bozza, Debbie and Kevin McIntyre, Patrick R. Saylor, Dennis Davis, Hans Neuhauser, Brad Winn, Duane Harris, Barbara Zoodsma, Lea King, Steve Moore, Buzzy Pickren, Chris Trowell, and Terry Johnson. Thank you to Clyde "Doc" Partin who kept an eye on Berlin while I was away, and Betty Partin, for keeping an eye on Doc. A special thanks to Pat Metz of the Savannah Coastal Wildlife Refuges and to Taylor Schoettle, an excellent naturalist and educator of all things coastal.

The Georgia Conservancy was very generous in opening its files to me and I owe the organization a big thank you, especially John Sibley and Michael Halicki. Everyone owes The Georgia Conservancy a debt of gratitude for its excellent conservation work on the coast. Anyone who reads this book will discover the exceptional land preservation work The Nature Conservancy of Georgia has performed as well. The Georgia Wildlife Federation also supported the production of this volume and continues to be a positive force across the state. Anyone who cares about the coast should join all three of these organizations.

"If you see a turtle on a fencepost, you know someone put him there." I think I first heard this from former Gov. Zell Miller. This turtle must thank renowned educator Conrad Fink and legendary newspaperman Dink NeSmith. No one has had finer role models. Mr. NeSmith gave me my first real introduction to the Georgia coast and supported my first book project. Additional credit should go to Jerry McCollum and Jim Wilson of the Georgia Wildlife Federation for a decade of support and encouragement of *my* professional efforts in the area of conservation, which I hope have had the effect of supporting all *their* efforts in the same field.

Pam Holliday did a first-rate job of editing my sloppy prose. She's incredibly gifted and one of the best in the field. I owe John Lenz a debt of gratitude for his business skill in keeping the ship afloat and pointed in the right direction while I was on a mini-sabbatical researching and writing this book, and for doing such a great job on the layout. Barbara Keenlyside's skill with words made a significant contribution to the ultimate quality of the book. Illustrator Danny Woodard is a brilliant designer whose tremendous talent knows no limits.

Finally, this book never would have or could have been produced by me without Sheila Jones Lenz. What is it they said about Ginger Rogers? She did everything Fred did, but did it backward and in high heels. Not only did Sheila help with every part of this book (including the indexing), she did it while taking care of Claire Jacquelyne.

Sheila is by far the best decision I ever made, and this book is dedicated to *her*— and to my parents, *Roger and Jacquelyne Lenz.*

—Richard J. Lenz

Streams of the Coastal Plain

Alluvial and blackwater streams flow through Georgia's Coastal Plain.

1. Tuckassee King Landing
2. New Ebenezer
3. Fort Argyle
4. Fort Barrington and Barrington County Park
5. Satilla River Waterfront Park

The Natural History
of the Georgia Coast

A s you sit in your beach chair and waves lap your bare feet with reassuring
regularity, you, the lover of sea, salt, and sun, feel connected to the infinite. To
the poetic soul, the Georgia coast seems like eternity itself, with the natural
rhythms of tides and seasons keeping tempo in the ceaseless flow of time. The miles
and miles of pungent, sun-baked salt marsh, the intense heat and light of the sand
dunes, and the flickering green canopy of the live oak forest make an indelible impres-
sion upon the senses. Surely this is the way it has always been and will always be.

Geologists are not so impressed. They know that the coast is quite young and always
changing. Sixty million years ago, all this property was under water and the coastline was
much farther inland. During the height of the last Ice Age approximately 18,000 years ago,
sea level was 400 feet lower and the coastline was 95 miles east of its current position. And
as average sea level continues to rise, the current coastline may once again be submerged.

[*Above:* Sea oats help stabilize and build dunes by trapping blowing sands]

Geologic Time Scale

Era	System & Period	Series & Epoch	Some Distinctive Features	Years Before Present
CENOZOIC	Quaternary	Recent	Modern man.	11,000
		Pleistocene	Early man; northern glaciation.	1/2 to 2 million
	Tertiary	Pliocene	Large carnivores.	13 ± 1 million
		Miocene	First abundant grazing mammals.	25 ± 1 million
		Oligocene	Large running mammals.	36 ± 2 million
		Eocene	Many modern types of mammals.	58 ± 2 million
		Paleocene	First placental mammals.	63 ± 2 million
MESOZOIC	Cretaceous		First flowering plants; climax of dinosaurs and ammonites, followed by Cretaceous-Tertiary extinction.	135 ± 5 million
	Jurassic		First birds, first mammals; dinosaurs and ammonites abundant.	181 ± 5 million
	Triassic		First dinosaurs. Abundant cycads and conifers.	230 ± 10 million
PALEOZOIC	Permian		Extinction of most kinds of marine animals, including trilobites. Southern glaciation.	280 ± 10 million
	Carboniferous	Pennsylvanian	Great coal forests, conifers. First reptiles.	310 ± 10 million
		Mississippian	Sharks and amphibians abundant. Large and numerous scale trees and seed ferns.	345 ± 10 million
	Devonian		First amphibians; ammonites; Fishes abundant.	405 ± 10 million
	Silurian		First terrestrial plants and animals.	425 ± 10 million
	Ordovician		First fishes; invertebrates dominant.	500 ± 10 million
	Cambrian		First abundant record of marine life; trilobites dominant.	600 ± 50 million
	Precambrian		Fossils extremely rare, consisting of primitive aquatic plants. Evidence of glaciation. Oldest dated algae, over 2,600 million years; oldest dated meteorites 4,500 million years.	

In fact, Georgia's bluffs, marshes, and barrier islands are just the beautiful results of a lucky convergence of natural forces.

Georgia's coast is in the physiographic region known as the Lower Coastal Plain, and is made up of sediments washed down over millions of years from the Blue Ridge and Piedmont physiographic regions. During the end of the Cretaceous Era 65 to 70 million years ago, when dinosaurs last roamed the earth, the world experienced its greatest period of inundation, and the coastline was located at the present-day Fall Line that stretches from the towns of Columbus through Macon to Augusta. Sediments such as clays and sands washed down from the highlands and were deposited at this shoreline. At the dawn of the mammalian age, or Cenozoic Era 63 million years ago, the seas started to slowly drop. As you drive from Macon to Savannah, you pass by younger and younger soils of the Coastal Plain that were deposited as the sea receded. Mining operations in the Coastal Plain frequently uncover fossilized bones of prehistoric whales, sharks, and other marine creatures, more evidence of the Coastal Plain's past as an ocean floor.

The Lower Coastal Plain physiographic region begins at the shoreline and runs inland for 60 miles. Its soils are Plio-Pleistocene and only 3 million years old. During the Pleistocene Epoch that began 2 million years ago, the repeated freezing and thawing of the polar ice caps raised and lowered sea levels, which formed successive shorelines and barrier islands that today appear as a series of inland sand ridges.

Barrier islands, common on the Atlantic and Gulf coasts, are globally rare. Barrier island chains front only 2.2 percent of the world's coastlines. Most of them are found where the Coastal Plain slopes gently, where there is abundant sand, and where waves supply enough energy to transport the sand.

Georgia's salt marshes are also a fortuitous result of having the right natural conditions: barrier islands to the east and rivers to the west. When sea levels rose, shoreline dunes became barrier islands, and the protected areas between the islands and the mainland became lagoons, which filled with trapped river sediments. As salinity was reduced from freshwater rivers, the right conditions were created for the formation of salt marshes.

Geologists have identified six strands of inland sand ridges of varying ages, each a little higher as one travels west from the coast. Because of their elevation and north to south orientation, these ridges have served as game trails, Indian trails, and highways. They also were popular sites for Indian, Spanish, and English settlements. The towns of Savannah, Darien, Brunswick, and St. Marys are located on the ancient barrier islands of the Princess Anne and Pamlico series that were formed when sea level was 15 to 25 feet higher. Trail Ridge is an ancient barrier island of the Wicomico shoreline that runs from Starke, Florida to near Jesup, Georgia, and disrupts drainage in this portion of the state and plays a crucial role in the formation of the Okefenokee Swamp.

During the Wisconsin Ice Age of 20,000 years ago, the shoreline was at least 50 miles to the east of its current position. As the earth warmed and the ice melted, sea levels rose and wrapped around sand dunes or ridges, which became barrier islands. As the sea level kept rising, some islands eroded and rolled backward over themselves. Approximately

4,500 years ago, sea level rise paused, leaving Georgia's barrier islands in their current positions. Some of the younger, Holocene islands have rolled all the way back to join an older, earlier series of sand ridges that were created in the Pleistocene Epoch 25,000 to 35,000 years ago. Some barrier islands, such as St. Catherines, Sapelo, St. Simons, and Cumberland, are composed mainly of Pleistocene soils in their cores on their western sides and Holocene soils on their eastern sides. Tybee and Wassaw islands are composed of young, Holocene soils and have not rolled back to meet their older, western Pleistocene neighbors of Wilmington and Skidaway islands. Scientists believe this is because Tybee and Wassaw islands are close to major river mouths and have been suppled with large inputs of sediment. Little St. Simons has grown tremendously over the last 100 years from Altamaha River sediments.

Salt marshes have been located both west and east of their current location on the Georgia coast. Behind the inland sand ridges or ancient barrier islands were salt marshes and tidal creeks, which today are timberlands and river swamps. Clay deposits exposed by eroding dunes fronting island beaches are evidence that marshes once were found in front of Georgia's coastal islands.

In the past century, global sea level has been rising at a rate of 6 inches a century. Because of global warming, United Nations scientists believe the rate will increase to 18 inches in the next century, which would push back the shoreline nearly 2 miles in places where the Coastal Plain slopes very gently.

Natural Processes of the Georgia Coast

CLIMATE AND WEATHER

The Georgia coast has a moderate climate, with subtropical temperatures. During summer, a high pressure system called the Bermuda high settles in the Southeast and with its clockwise-rotating winds deflects most fronts moving across the area from the west. This produces occasional droughts.

Where the sea meets land at the coastline, daily temperature changes result in predictable ocean breezes. The sea maintains a more constant temperature, while landmasses heat up and cool down between day and night. During the day, the air above the land heats and rises, which draws wind toward land from the sea. At night, the land cools, and wind is drawn toward the warmer sea.

This cycle produces convection storms during the summer. As the sun rises, it heats the land, which heats the air above it, and as heated air rises, it draws in cooler, moisture-laden air from the coast. This air heats and rises as well, creating storm clouds as it rises and condenses. By noon, a thunderhead may have been created and by the afternoon, the coast may be drenched by a short-lived rainstorm, depositing the moisture back on the coast.

HURRICANES

Occasionally, the Georgia coast is walloped by a hurricane. Hurricanes can be devastating, with winds up to 200 miles an hour, spawning deadly tornadoes and floods. On average, 1.6 hurricanes make landfall each year in the U.S. The Georgia coast has a 5 percent risk of being hit by a hurricane annually, with August, September, and October being the most common months for the storms. The origin of hurricanes is not entirely clear, but they are formed in tropical oceans when there is a large body of warm, moist air that develops into a counterclockwise-rotating storm with winds over 74 miles per hour.

Because of its geographic position, Georgia is one of the safest-rated areas on the Atlantic and Gulf coasts. But that doesn't mean don't worry if there's a hurricane warning. The Georgia coast experienced five major hurricanes in the 1800s, including one that put Tybee Island completely under water, but has been mostly spared in the 1900s. Hurricane Hugo was headed for Tybee in 1989, but veered north to Charleston, South Carolina, where it killed 86 people and did $7 billion worth of damage. Hurricane Andrew in 1992 hit Miami and killed 61 people, destroyed $26.5 billion worth of property, and made 160,000 people homeless. The most deadly hurricane of the 1900s landed in Galveston, Texas, in 1900 and killed 8,000 people.

NOR'EASTERS

These seasonal storms, first recognized by Benjamin Franklin, merit significant mention because of the erosion they cause on the Georgia coast. Occurring every fall to spring, nor'easters feature strong frontal winds created by a low-pressure cell that accompanies cold fronts that sweep through the area. Nor'easter winds swirl in a counter-clockwise fashion, with steady winds blowing from the northeast at 25 miles an hour, which can continue for several days. The wind pushes tides higher, makes the surf and longshore currents rougher and stronger, and blows a lot of sand. A long season of strong nor'easters can lead to significant erosion.

TIDES, CURRENTS, AND WAVES

Tides are the effect of the gravitational pull of the moon and sun. Currents are the effect of tides, wind, rain, rivers, evaporation, and ocean topography. Waves are created by open ocean winds. Combined, they are an overpowering and defining force on all coasts, and on the Georgia shore, life is defined and dependent on them.

The moon's gravity pulls a bulge of water toward it. On the opposite side of Earth, another bulge is created due to centrifugal forces from the earth's rotation. As the water is stretched into an oblong, the sea between these two opposite bulges is lessened in volume, creating low, or ebb tides. As the moon circles the earth every 24 hours and 50 minutes, the water bulge follows it, creating a high tide on the shoreline below the moon. With every complete orbit around a specific piece of landscape, there is a different tide every quarter of the cycle, or every 6 hours and 12.5 minutes. First a high or flood tide (the bulge below the moon), then 6 hours and 12.5 minutes later a low tide, then 6 hours

Form and Growth of a Recurved Spit

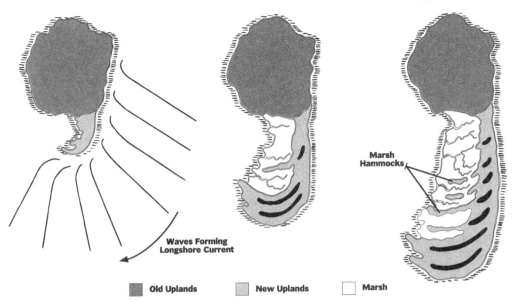

Marsh Hammocks

Waves Forming
Longshore Current

▮ Old Uplands   ▮ New Uplands   ▢ Marsh

The ends of islands are constantly changing because of the tidal influences. Waves and longshore currents push sediments southward along an island. When the longshore current reaches the end of the island, it bends or is refracted, and deposits sand that begins to form a recurved shape. Over time, these sand deposits can build into dunes, and marshes can develop behind the protected barrier.

and 12.5 minutes later the second high tide (the bulge opposite the moon), then 6 hours and 12.5 minutes later the second low tide, and 6 hours and 12.5 minutes later the high tide again that completes the cycle. Because it takes the moon 24 hours and 50 minutes to cycle around the earth, tides are 50 minutes later each day.

The sun also has a gravitational pull, but being much farther away, it only has roughly half the effect. When the sun and moon are in the alignment called syzygy (when the moon is directly between the earth and sun, indicated by a new moon, or is directly behind the earth, indicated by a full moon), gravitational forces are combined to create the highest and lowest tides on earth called spring tides. Neap tides occur when the moon, earth, and sun create a 45-degree angle to each other, indicated by a quarter moon phase, which has a canceling effect that produces small differences between high and low tides. Two spring tides and two neap tides occur every month.

The degree of sea level change between high and low tides is greatly affected by the slope and shape of underwater geography. The world's biggest tides are in the Bay of Fundy, located between New Brunswick and Nova Scotia, which rises 45 feet, while Lake Superior only has a tide of 2 inches. Every 24 hours, the Atlantic coast has two high tides and low tides, the Gulf of Mexico coast has one high tide and low tide, and the Pacific coast has two high and low tides of mixed heights.

The Georgia coast is the most western coastline on the Atlantic seaboard, putting Georgia at the center of a giant funnel called the Georgia bight. At high tide, water is pushed by the shape of the coastline from North Carolina and Florida, forcing water to gather on top of itself, creating a 6- to 8-foot tidal change on the Georgia coast at the center of the funnel. The sides of the funnel on the central Florida and North Carolina coasts have 3-foot tides.

On some coasts, like North Carolina, the dominant force is wave energy. On the Georgia coast, the dominant natural force is the tide. Like a heart pumping blood through the body's vital organs, Georgia's tides pump a tremendous volume of water in and around the barrier island, into the sounds (the area between barrier islands), and the marshlands. Life has adapted to and become dependent on this natural process in ways great and small. Without the pulsing of tides, Georgia's *Spartina* marshes would disappear. When tides are high, mollusks like clams and oysters open and feed. When tides drop and expose

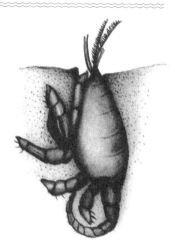

MOLE CRAB
(*Emerita talpoida*)
These small burrowing crabs are filter feeders that live in the intertidal area of the beach.

the bivalves, they close and retain sea water inside their shells, waiting for the next tide to come. Juvenile fish and other life feed on the nutrients circulated through the marsh and estuary by tides. The tides carry dead *Spartina* out of the estuary on outgoing tides, then deposit the stalks on beaches during high tides. The *Spartina* traps blowing sands and becomes the foundation of dunes, laying the groundwork for other plants to come. When tides are low, many birds and mammals know food sources are more exposed in the intertidal zone and come to the beaches and mud flats to feed.

To humans, knowledge of the tides can be an asset. When Julius Caesar attacked the English coast in 54 B.C. during a full moon (which creates the greatest tidal range), he was unaware of the 20-foot tide, which stranded his fleet, then destroyed it when the tides changed. Closer to home, beach lovers have drowned on the Georgia coast when they have been stranded on sandbars and underestimated the strength, direction, and dura-tion of tidal forces. Tidewater plantations harnessed the power of tides for growing rice, and sawmills in Darien used the action of tides to power machinery.

The Georgia shore is greatly affected by tidal currents pulsing in and out of sounds and longshore currents running north to south and close to barrier islands. Having a much smaller effect on the Georgia coast is the Gulf Stream, which is located 80 to 120 miles offshore and flows south to north.

Because of tides, longshore currents, waves, and winds, barrier islands in Georgia tend to be shaped like a turkey drumstick with a bulbous northern end and narrower southern end. Fast-running tidal currents, which flow in and out of sounds found between barrier islands, carry nutrients and sediments from marshes and rivers. When they reach the longshore current, they are deflected south and drop much of their sediment load. Here sandbars or shoals can build up to become barrier islands.

Wave energy on the Georgia coast is relatively low, because of the long distance waves must travel over the Continental shelf before reaching the shoreline. Waves are created by open ocean winds and may travel hundreds of miles. Waves break when water on top of the wave moves faster than water on the bottom of the wave, which is generally caused by the bottom of the wave dragging or tripping on underwater shoals, causing the peak to topple over.

SALT AND FRESH WATER

At the coast, fresh water from rivers and precipitation runoff mixes with salty sea water to create the estuarine ecosystem. Sea water averages 3.5 percent salt, or roughly one teaspoon of table salt in a glass of fresh water. When we taste the salt of our tears, sweat, or blood, we are being reminded of our origins. In our bodies the salt content is 0.9 percent, but the elements sodium, potassium, and calcium are combined in almost the same proportions as in sea water, an inheritance from remote ancestors from millions and millions of years ago when the first primitive circulatory systems consisted of sea water.

If our systems were as salty as the ocean, we would be able to drink sea water. But, when we drink salt water we are actually dehydrating ourselves because of a process called osmosis. Living cells must be wet to function and all life processes occur in water solutions or mixtures. Osmosis is the physical process in which a living cell tries to balance the concentration of minerals on either side of a membrane. Water passes through a membrane from the less to the more concentrated solution in an attempt to make concentrations equal. So when one drinks sea water, fresh water is absorbed by the sea water due to osmosis, dehydrating the parched drinker. This fact of life has a dominating effect on the plants of the salt marsh. The concentration of salts in most plants is lower than salt water, so when most plants are immersed in sea water, they lose fresh water through their membranes, which kills the cells. So only plants that have developed strategies for dealing with salt water can survive in the salt marsh, such as smooth cordgrass (*Spartina*), needle rush, salt grass, glasswort, salt meadow cordgrass, and sea oxeye.

Fauna of the estuary and inshore waters must adapt to a brackish environment. The saline content of the water drops as one moves from the coastal waters (32 parts of salt per thousand parts [ppt] of water) up a river (less than 1 ppt). Generally, freshwater organisms do not descend far down a river estuary, but marine creatures, with different degrees of tolerance, can penetrate far upstream. Oysters can tolerate less than 5 ppt, but their predator the oyster drill can tolerate no less than 9 ppt, resulting in an oyster "line" that marks a safe zone for oysters.

The degree of salinity in a particular zone of the coast plays a role in the chemistry of the sea, affecting the natural cycles of elements that provide the foundation of life for sea creatures. From sea water, marine animals extract mineral salts and use them in many ways. Mollusks and crustaceans extract calcium from the water for their shells and skeletons.

Natural Communities of the Georgia Coast

Quite simply, the coast is defined as where the land meets the sea. How flora and fauna adapt to this region of abruptly different realms has fascinated naturalists for thousands of years. In order to study relationships in the natural world, scientists group plants and animals into ecosystems. Ecosystems can be as small as a drop of water or as large as the Northern Hemisphere. The Georgia coast is frequently divided into the following ecosystems: coastal marine, barrier island, estuaries and sounds, mainland upland, rivers, and swamps.

COASTAL MARINE

East of Georgia's shoreline is the continental shelf, which is 70 to 80 miles wide with a gentle slope of about 2 feet per mile, varying in depth from the shallows of the shoreline to 600 feet deep. It is covered by sediments deposited during low stands of the sea. Approximately 80 miles offshore, the continental shelf abruptly increases in slope of descent known as the continental slope. Seaward of the continental shelf is the Blake Plateau, an intermediate plateau between the continental shelf and the ocean basin that averages 2,300 to 3,300 feet in depth.

Georgia's continental shelf consists primarily of two natural communities: sandy bottoms and live bottoms. Sandy bottoms are virtual aquatic deserts, with shifting sands preventing the establishment of large plant and animal communities. Live or "hard" bottoms, such as Gray's Reef National Marine Sanctuary, consist of limestone outcrops anchored on ancient shorelines that serve as reefs where flora and fauna can flourish. Smaller organisms are food for small fish, which in turn are eaten by larger fish such as Spanish and king mackerel, gag and scamp grouper, sea bass, cobia, wahoo, dolphin, and amberjack. The live bottoms are well documented and can be easily located with modern equipment, and saltwater fishermen make long boat trips to fish them, including Savannah Snapper Banks, Grand Banks, and Brunswick Snapper Banks. The Coastal Department of Natural Resources and saltwater fishing organizations, in an effort to increase habitat for fish, have created at least 13 artificial reefs by sinking bridges, barges, and Liberty ships. A series of eight offshore Navy towers are also popular fishing sites.

The sea serves as critical habitat for many migratory oceanic birds, sea turtles, and marine mammals, including the endangered right whale that calves in Georgia waters

December through February. Only 300 of these tremendous creatures remain, and the future of the species is being determined off Georgia's shore. For more information on coastal marine environments, see Gray's Reef National Marine Sanctuary, page 196, or the Georgia Department of Resources.

BARRIER ISLAND

Because they are composed of unstable sand, barrier islands are fickle geologic entities that are constantly on the move from the action of tides, waves, winds, and storms. Relatively young and fragile, barrier islands are always losing and gaining sand, but in different places and at different rates. In the last 100 years, Tybee Island has lost 2,000 feet of beach, while Little St. Simons has gained at least that much. In essence, barrier islands are built-up sandbars with dunes where plants have gained a vulnerable foothold.

Off the Georgia coast, where the tidal range is high and wave energy is low, islands are relatively short. Along the Florida and North Carolina coasts, a low tidal range and high wave energy have produced long, narrow barrier islands.

Scientists divide barrier islands into several natural zones: sandbars, beach, dunes, interdune meadows, freshwater and brackish sloughs, and maritime forest.

SANDBARS

Offshore toward inlets are extensive sandbars or shoals that play a role in the formation of islands as well as support marine life and shorebirds. Since the beginning of colonization, Georgia's inlets have been notorious among sailors for their tricky and ever-changing shoals that have trapped many an ancient and modern mariner.

Sandbars form from sands that have been transported from rivers, other barrier islands, or offshore areas. Currents and tides are continually moving and shaping complexes of sandbars that may be here today and gone tomorrow. Exposed at low tide, sandbar complexes are evidence of tidal influences and can be excellent areas to look for marine life such as sand dollars, worms, crabs, and other creatures. Be careful to not get stranded on them as the tide changes, as swimming back to shore against tidal currents can exhaust even good swimmers and result in drowning.

Shorebirds and seabirds use these sandbars for resting and feeding, and if sandbars build up to remain exposed during high tides, some birds may use them for nesting. A lack of established vegetation generally means an absence of mammalian predators that eat bird eggs. All of Georgia's barrier islands have sandbars to examine, but some of the easiest to see are on St. Simons and Tybee islands. On East Beach on St. Simons Island, one can examine sandbar formation and observe the many shorebirds that use the shoals of Gould's Inlet. The south end of Tybee Island is an excellent area to study shoals formed in a typical manner.

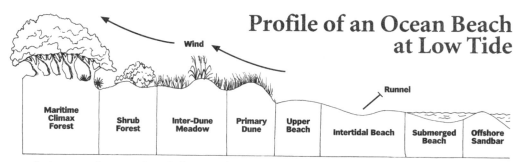

Profile of an Ocean Beach at Low Tide

Wind

Runnel

Maritime Climax Forest | Shrub Forest | Inter-Dune Meadow | Primary Dune | Upper Beach | Intertidal Beach | Submerged Beach | Offshore Sandbar

In its natural state, a Georgia barrier island has at least eight distinctive areas that range from maritime climax forest to offshore sandbars. Each has its own assemblage of plants and animals.

BEACH

The Georgia beach is composed mainly of mineral sand eroded from the Piedmont and Appalachian highlands. Georgia's sand has less shell content and is finer than what is found on many higher energy beaches of the Atlantic. The majority is quartz sand with many other minerals present, including ilmenite, a heavier, black mineral. When winds blow across the beach, the lighter quartz gets pushed to the top, and the black sand rolls to the bottom, producing beautiful black and white patterns.

The beach is subdivided into two main areas: the intertidal beach and the upper beach. The intertidal area is defined as the portion submerged at high tide and exposed at low tide. In Georgia, this area is hard-packed and inhabited by a variety of life adapted to the pounding of the surf and an alternating wet and dry environment. Flourishing in these harsh conditions are burrowing filter-feeders, including echinoderms such as sand dollars (*Mellita* sp.) and brittle stars, polychaete worms, mole crabs, razor clams, and ghost shrimp (*Callianassa* sp.). Ghost shrimp live in pencil-size burrows identified by fecal pellets that look like chocolate sprinkles. These fecal pellets give the beach some of its color and add to the nutrient cycle of the beach. Straining beach sand will reveal small, whitish creatures known as amphipods that live between grains of sand. Hungry shore-birds are aware of these burrowing forms and are seen probing the sands with their sensitive beaks.

Newcomers to Georgia's beaches wonder why there aren't more shells. Shells are generally the skeletons of dead mollusks. Mollusks live far off the Georgia shoreline and with low surf energy, not as many are washed to the beach. The best time to find shells is after a storm at low tide, when one might come across cockles, letter olives, whelks, oyster drills (*Urosalpinx cineraea*), and Atlantic moon snails (*Polinices duplicatus*). A dramatic find on the beach is the horseshoe crab, a primitive form that can grow its helmet-looking shell to more than a foot long. The horseshoe crab feeds along muddy estuarine bottoms and comes ashore during spring tides to lay over 500 eggs. The shells found on the beach are frequently empty exoskeletons that have been shed by growing horseshoe crabs. The animal is related to scorpions, ticks, and sea spiders, and its larval form is very similar to 400-million-year-old trilobites. The tail is not a weapon but is used to flip the crab over. Horseshoes once were used for fertilizer and chicken feed in the northeast, and for eel bait in Georgia, but today are important in medicine. Their copper-rich, blue blood is used in cancer research and as an indicator of spinal meningitis.

Occasionally, beachcombers discover jellyfish stranded on the beach. The more common species are the moon jelly (*Aurelia aurita*), a translucent animal identified by a magenta sunburst and four U-shaped gonads, and cannonball jellyfish (*Stomolophus meleagris*), a thick, half-egg-shaped coelenterate with a reddish-purple band. Both of these are nonstinging and relatively safe to touch. Stinging forms to worry about include the sea wasp, which is found in coastal waters April to July and recognized by its tentacles that dangle from the four corners of its boxlike body; sea nettles (*Chrysaora quiquecirrha*), which are common in August as young hatch in 80-degree Fahrenheit waters; and Portuguese man-of-war (*Physalia physalis*), a severely stinging jellyfish identified by its sail-like, blue colored gas bag that floats above the surface of the water. These jellyfish can sting after they have washed up on the beach, so do not touch!

Sometimes the Georgia surf creates brown foam that is misidentified as water pollution. Actually, because Georgia waters are rich with plankton and detritus, the stirring of the surf produces bubbles because microscopic creatures act to coagulate the water, not unlike what happens when soap is added to dishwater to produce bubbles. Other misidentified but natural elements of the Georgia coast are greenish and yellowish smears seen on the beach. These are algae that live between grains of sand along with amphipods, diatoms, and worms, and are another sign of the living beach.

The upper beach is defined as the area above the high tide line. Here you find a great variety of insects, amphipods, sea wrack, and most conspicuously, ghost crabs. Ghost crabs live in burrows that are recognized by penny to half-dollar size holes. These fleet-footed arthropods are evolving from life in the water to life on land. While adults have lost their swimming legs and remain out of the sea, they periodically must wet their gill chambers with sea water to keep breathing, and females release their young into the ocean as plankton. Ghost crabs are great scavengers of the nighttime beach and are easily seen with a flashlight.

The upper beach is used as nesting grounds by a variety of birds, including oystercatchers, terns, and plovers, as well as loggerhead sea turtles, a signature animal of the Georgia coast. Loggerheads are the only marine turtle that regularly nests on Georgia beaches. Females, weighing between 150–300 pounds, crawl ashore at night from late May to early August and bury an average of 120 eggs that look remarkably like ping-pong balls. Approximately two months later, the eggs hatch and the sand-dollar-size hatchlings race to the sea. Raccoons and feral hogs will come to the shore to feed on the eggs.

Those interested in Georgia's sea turtles should see Jekyll Island, page 255, and Wassaw Island, page 119, for volunteer opportunities.

During spring tides, beach wrack is deposited on the upper beach. Beach wrack is a mixture of cordgrass and other natural flotsam, which serves as an important mini-ecosystem for a wide variety of insects, amphipods, and microorganisms. The cordgrass traps blowing sand and as it decays, becomes a starter kit for new dunes on the beach.

DUNES AND INTERDUNE MEADOWS

Dunes are the front lines of island building. At some point, all barrier islands started as sand dunes that were colonized by hardy plants. For a plant to survive on a dune, it must adapt to many harsh conditions such as erosion from shifting sands, hot winds, salt spray, quick water drainage, and solar radiation. Plants are extremely important for dune formation. This is why beach lovers should always use boardwalks or paths instead of running over dune vegetation, which if killed results in the erosion of beach. Cumberland's feral horses, while popular with tourists, are unpopular with some environmentalists who worry about the damage caused by these animals that trample on the dunes as they graze on sand-trapping grasses.

The closer to the beach, the hardier the dune plants. These are called pioneer plants because they move in first. Typical species are seaside orache, croton, and spurge. Sea oats are the kings of dune building plants and are protected by law. Using excellent sand-trapping strategies, sea oats can live on the tops of dunes and stay ahead of migrating sands as other plants are buried.

As one moves away from the beach, species diversity increases. Dunes located behind the first set of dunes, called the secondary dunes, are older and have had a longer time to build up richer soils that support more kinds of plants. Between dune peaks in the swales are the greatest variety of plants because the conditions are more favorable: less wind, more water, and richer soil. Interdune meadows may support thorny plants such as yucca, sandspur, hercules club, and Russian thistle, as well as thick-leafed succulent species such as sea rocket, saltwort, seabeach sandwort, and prickly pear cactus. Farther back from the beach, woody species such as wax myrtle, and yaupon holly become more common. A variety of grasses flourishes from the primary dunes to the interdune meadows, including nutgrass, bitter panic grass, and common broomsedge, along with creeping vines such as beach pennywort, morning glory, and *Smilax*. Small mammals, including mice, rice rats, moles, and rabbits, are found in dune meadows, and they are preyed on by snakes, including the Eastern diamondback rattlesnake. Deer and feral hogs are common on Ossabaw, St. Catherines, and Cumberland islands.

Finding extensive interdune meadows is less and less easy on all coasts as beachfront developers gobble this property up. On the Georgia coast, however, interdune meadows can still be found, with the best examples on undeveloped islands.

FRESHWATER AND BRACKISH SLOUGHS

An extremely important natural feature of Georgia's barrier islands is its freshwater and brackish sloughs or ponds. These can be naturally formed or man-made, but either way, they add appreciably to an island's diversity. They serve as important

How to Catch a Blue Crab

If you want to participate in one of the timeless forms of recreation on the Georgia coast—one that has gone on for thousands of years—you must catch, cook, and eat some Georgia blue crabs. All along the coast there are thousands of places and opportunities to catch *Callinectes sapidus*—or "beautiful swimmer"—for supper. It has to be the easiest fishing on the coast and it is great family fun. Children are fascinated by these clawed creatures, which are raised from the murky depths of the estuary.

Many become fans of crabbing, which has a high rate of success with the application of rudimentary equipment and skill. The most basic is the "chicken neck" technique. You need a long-handled dip net—available at convenience stores or bait shops—and a short pole. Get a bucket and put a wet rag in the bottom. Tie a piece of line on the pole long enough to match the handle. Tie a chicken neck on the end of the line. Now all you need to do is find a place—creek bank, dock, bridge, pier or even surf—to crab.

Drop the chicken neck into the water and let it sink deep enough to where it disappears. Watch the line. When the line begins to move or jerk, you probably have a crab working on your chicken neck. Slowly raise the bait and swing the crab toward your dip net. More likely than not, a blue crab will hang onto the chicken neck long enough for you to put him in the net. Release the crab into the bucket. Be careful how you handle it because a crab's pinchers can really hurt. Sport crabbers may catch a bushel of crabs a day, but crabs must be 5 inches long from spike to spike to keep. Crabs can survive for hours if shaded from the sun and if you keep the rag in the bucket moist. A popular fishing equipment alternative—good for use off a dock or pier—is hoop nets or collapsible traps known as crab pots. These are sold in convenience stores and bait shops.

freshwater sources and habitat for a variety of island life, including wading birds, reptiles, and amphibians. Migrating and wintering waterfowl use ponds as resting and feeding areas during winter. In the spring, many wading birds such as herons and egrets congregate around ponds to form rookeries where they build nests and raise their young. Frogs, fish, water snakes, crustaceans, and insects also use ponds for reproduction and become food for larger animals on the island. In early summer, alligators build nests of their own here.

Many of the freshwater sloughs appear in times of rainfall and disappear in dry periods. Opportunistic species have adapted to these fluctuations. Treefrogs will remain scattered about an island and go months without breeding until a torrential downpour creates temporary freshwater pools suitable for breeding. Then the frogs will gather at these pools in dense breeding congregations, which produce huge numbers of tadpoles that ensure the survival of their species. The temporary pools have naturally fewer predators than a year-round pond.

Wood storks (*Mycteria americana*) are so inefficient at catching fish that they depend

How to Cook and Clean a Blue Crab

To cook your crabs, use a large pot. Some like to steam their crabs, whereas others prefer to boil them. Choose a method, add water to your pot, and bring it to a boil. Some people add crab boil, found in grocery stores. I prefer Old Bay seasoning, a red, Maryland-style mix that adds some spice to the crabs. Carefully add your crabs to the pot and dust them with the Old Bay. Remember: Dead crabs should never be cooked. When they turn bright orange-red, they are ready to eat.

Catching crabs is easy. Cooking crabs is easy. Cleaning crabs takes some effort and a tolerance for marine biology. With practice you will gain speed and efficiency. Your reward will be one of the most delicious seafood experiences you will ever have. You will need a table that can tolerate a wet mess such as a picnic table. Spread out newspapers and find a tool to crack the hard pincer shell, such as a nutcracker or hammer.

After cooking the crabs, drain them and let them cool for several minutes. Turn them over and examine their breastplate or apron. This part of the crab is hinged and easy to pull back. If it is long and narrow, you are eating a male crab. If it is much broader, it is a female. After lifting the plate, pry the top main shell part of the crustacean off and throw it away. Twist off the pincers and save them for cracking. Pull off and throw away the smaller pointy legs. Leave the last pair of flat appendages known as the backfins.

You may notice yellowish gunk in the center of the crab. This is part of the crab's reproductive structure. Some crab lovers consider this material a delicacy and others are repulsed by the notion and throw it away. On either side of the bottom half of the shell are feathery structures known as the "dead man." These are the crab's gills and absolutely should not be eaten. Pull them off and throw them away.

Break the remaining shell in half, exposing the body and white backfin meat. With a pointed knife or your fingers, pick out your crab meat. If you are talented or experienced, you may be able to pull out the backfin meat by carefully pulling out the backfin appendages. If you are successful, you will have a large lump of crab meat dangling deliciously on the end of a leg, which you can use to dip into butter or cocktail sauce. When you clean the meat, be careful not to include the clear plastic-like divisions of the body, which are part of the crab's skeleton.

Using your cracking tool, break the crab's pinchers and enjoy the darker, firm claw meat. Now that you've picked one crab, you can reflect on the effort it took to produce several bites of yummy crab meat—and a mound of crab remains. Time for crab No. 2!

on drier periods that shrink ponds and concentrate aquatic prey. Stork nesting cycles are timed with periods of falling water so sufficient food supplies are available for hatchlings.

Freshwater ponds can be observed on the northern ends of Blackbeard and Cumberland islands, as well as Little St. Simons and Wassaw islands. On the southern interior of Jekyll Island is a freshwater slough that's worth examining.

❧ MARITIME FOREST

Maritime forests, the climax community of barrier islands, are an association of plants and shrubs that are well adapted to the harsh conditions of the island environment. Forming the forest canopy are live oaks, laurel oaks, Southern yellow pines, cabbage palms, red cedars, and magnolias that shelter the interior. Adding to the forest's beauty are the numerous vines, ferns, lichens, and mosses that grow on branches and trunks, including muscadine grape, *Smilax*, Spanish moss, and resurrection fern. A natural indicator of humidity, resurrection ferns are green and luxuriant after a rain and inconspicuous and brown during dry spells. Spanish moss (*Tillandsia usneoides*), a characteristic plant of the Georgia coast, is neither a parasite of trees nor a moss; it is a member of the pineapple family that survives by deriving its moisture and nutrients from rain and airborne dust. Seeing moss on dead branches, some people erroneously conclude that Spanish moss is harmful to trees. Actually, the Spanish moss thrives on dead branches because of a lack of competition from the tree's leaves.

In the understory are shrubs and smaller trees such as yaupon, wax myrtle, red bay, sparkleberry, and cherry laurel. Saw palmettos, a characteristic plant of a live oak maritime forest, grow along the ground and shoot up distinctive, fan-shaped fronds that give the forest a jungle appearance.

As trees grow higher than protective dunes and shrubs on the eastern side of an island, they adapt to the damaging salt-laden winds that blow in from the shoreline. Trees located near the shore form a gradual sloping shape in response to upward-angled winds. The trees here may be dwarfed and wind-sheared, an effect of salt pruning. Salt spray kills plants' terminal buds that extend beyond the protective canopy of the forest, resulting in thicker lateral growth below called the shrubbing effect. The end result is a protected, interior forest where little light reaches the forest floor.

The maritime forest provides a protected environment used by a wide variety of animals, including white-tailed deer, gray squirrels, and raccoons. Bird life is diverse, with warblers and songbirds flitting about in the canopy and wild turkeys strutting on the forest floor. Treefrogs and lizards can be found hiding on palmetto fronds.

Excellent extensive examples of maritime forest can be examined on Cumberland, Wassaw, Sapelo, Blackbeard, Jekyll islands.

❧ SOUNDS AND ESTUARIES

Between the mainland and barrier islands are the sounds and estuaries where Georgia's rivers and the sea meet. Here one finds the salt marsh, the most prominent and characteristic feature of the Georgia coast, totaling approximately 378,000 acres in a band roughly 4 to 6 miles wide. Georgia has 10 sounds, each with its own unique attributes determined by tidal action, surrounding marshes, and the inputs of rivers of varying qualities. If the estuary is equated to the human body, the tides are the heartbeat, tidal waters are the blood stream, tidal creeks are the circulatory system, and salt marshes are the living tissue.

The brownish-green waters of southeastern coastal waters are not an indication of pollution but a sign of vitality. Tidal waters are rich with plankton, detritus, and sediments that support life processes on the Georgia coast. While many love the beautiful blue water of the Caribbean, this clear water is a virtual desert of microscopic life.

Plankton is a group consisting of plants (phytoplankton) and animals (zooplankton) that drift with the currents and tides. Plankton is the most abundant, basic, and important food in the ocean. Phytoplankton, such as one-celled diatoms, consists of fast-reproducing marine plants that make up 80 percent of the earth's vegetative population and are most responsible for producing the earth's oxygen. They give Georgia water its greenish hue. Zooplankton is a group of animals at the mercy of currents and tides, including larval forms of marine creatures, tiny crustaceans known as copepods, and jellyfish.

The brownish color comes from decaying plants and animals called detritus, a protein-rich mixture of 95 percent decaying *Spartina* and 5 percent algae, bacteria, fungi, and wastes.

▨ SALT MARSH

Salt marshes in Georgia began as lagoons behind the barrier islands, which filled with rich alluvial sediments deposited by mainland rivers. After the lagoons have developed suitable soils and water salinities, emergent vegetation can survive and thrive in the estuarine zone. The dominant species in a particular area of the marsh is determined primarily by the elevation, which determines frequency, depth, and duration of salt water inundation and soil salinity.

Approximately 70 percent of the marsh is *Spartina alterniflora*, or smooth cordgrass. This plant has developed mechanisms that permit it to survive both the salinities and tidal fluctuations of the low tidal marsh. While *Spartina* grows even better in fresh water, it is unable to compete with more vigorous species, so it has claimed the salt marsh where it can thrive without much competition, growing to 10 feet tall in places. In higher areas with infrequent inundation and relatively low salinities, darker needlerush thrives in almost pure stands and makes up nearly 18 percent of the Georgia salt marsh. In these areas grow other salt-tolerant plans such as marsh elder, sea oxeye, and glasswexists. Some areas in the marsh, called salt or sand pans, lack vegetation because of very high salinities that are too harsh for plants to survive.

Marshes produce biomass measuring nearly 20 tons to the acre, making them four times more productive than the most productive farmland. Georgia's salt marshes produce more food energy than any estuarine zone on the Eastern seaboard. Marsh plants and other tiny plants trap the sun's energy and covert it to food. As marsh plants die and decompose, they provide basic nutrients that benefit minute creatures in the estuary, which in turn are fed upon by larval forms of marine creatures such as crabs, oysters, and fish, which develop and support even larger marine animals. Coastal rivers add nutrients to the estuarine system where they are trapped by marsh. Tidal action plays an important role in this nursery by

Profile of a Salt Marsh

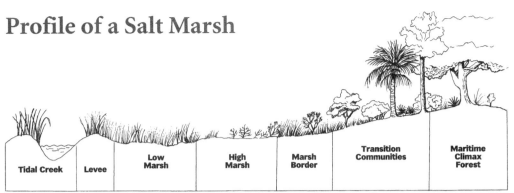

| Tidal Creek | Levee | Low Marsh | High Marsh | Marsh Border | Transition Communities | Maritime Climax Forest |

At first glance, the salt marsh may appear to be one uniform natural area, but it actually can be divided into several ecological zones relative to the time and depth of tidal inundation. Each zone has its own assemblage of predominant species.

stirring nutrients and introducing planktonic plants and animals to the marsh. The rotten egg smell of the marsh is hydrogen sulfide (H_2S), which is naturally released from the decaying action of anaerobic bacteria. Red streaks in marsh mud reveal the presence of oxidized iron, a common and important element in the marsh.

The marsh also provides shelter and food for a wide variety of coastal fauna. As coastal visitors soon learn, insects are very common residents of the marsh. While some are annoying to the tourist, insects are extremely important links in the food chain of the Georgia coast. Their larval and adult forms support a wide variety of fauna including fish, frogs, birds, and larger insects like damselflies. Some insects feed on vegetation and detritus, while others require the blood of mammals. Small insects and mites preying on man include no-see-ums (six species of midges), mosquitos, deerflies, horseflies, chiggers, and ticks.

No-see-ums are midges that are so small they can crawl through most screen mesh. They swirl around the face and inflict stabbing bites. They can breed in almost any damp area and are encountered everywhere on the coast. Another annoyance on the coast are chiggers, also known as red bugs. The larval form preys on humans. This mite, found in pine straw, leaves, and pine bark, crawls up human hosts to areas where body heat is high, then digs into the pores and sucks blood until a week later it's ready to drop off and mature into an adult. Ticks are also common on the coast. The adult forms hang off of grass stems and grab your clothing as you brush by. Then they climb to a soft spot on your body and shove their pronged beak into your skin. Ticks transmit potentially deadly diseases such as Rocky Mountain spotted fever and Lyme disease, so they should be carefully removed from your body once discovered. Apply alcohol to the tick then remove the anesthetized tick with a pair of tweezers, being careful to get the entire insect.

There are dozens of mosquito species on the coast. The females are the biters, as they quest for blood used in reproduction. The mosquito's anticoagulant saliva causes irritation of the skin. Mosquitoes also transmit diseases such as malaria and yellow fever. Deerflies and horseflies have the worst bites of the coastal insects and will swirl around

Southern Yellow Pines

Pines are the most abundant vegetation on Georgia's Coastal Plain and can be confusing to identify due to their similarities of appearance. Georgia has six native Coastal Plain species and each has a different preferred habitat. Longleaf pines (*Pinus palustris*) have the longest needles (10–15 inches) and largest cones (6–10 inches) of any Eastern pines, and mostly three needles per sheath. The young pine is called a bottlebrush because of its appearance. Longleafs prefer well-drained sandy soil. Slash pines (*Pinus elliottii*) are identified by gray bark, usually two needles per sheath, and shiny, egg-shaped cones from 2.5 to 6 inches long on short stalks. Popular with foresters because it is fast-growing, the species thrives in poorly drained sandy soil and swampy areas or "slashes." Loblolly pine (*Pinus taeda*) are the most popular commercial pine in the southeast U.S. and the most abundant on the coast. Loblolly is another name for a wet depression, which is the preferred habitat of the water-loving species. Identify this pine by its thick, reddish bark; dull brown, stalkless cones; and three needles per sheath. Pond pines (*Pinus serotina*) are medium-sized trees that thrive on marsh borders, with three or four needles in bundles and small, yellowish cones that remain closed for several years. Spruce pines (*Pinus glabra*) prefer moist lowland soils and salt marsh side bluffs, and are identified by their two needles per sheath, smooth gray bark, and 2.5-inch, reddish-brown cones that point backward or downward. Shortleaf pines (*Pinus echinata*), not common in the coastal plain, prefer the sand and silt loams of floodplains. Needles are 2.75 to 4.5 inches long and are arranged two or three to a sheath. Bark is reddish-brown with large, flat, scaly plates. Cones are 1.5 to 2.5 inches long, dull-brown in color, and short-stalked.

your head and literally chase you down a barrier island path. All of these insects are most common from May to September, during which the visitor should be prepared to combat these nuisances by using insect repellant and wearing a floppy hat, long sleeves, and pants.

The marsh killifish (*Fundulus confluentus*) is one of the only fish species that spends its entire life in the salt marsh. It breeds and deposits eggs at the highest water levels in the salt marsh. When the waters recede, the eggs will remain stranded but will hatch in 15 minutes upon reflooding. A salt marsh mosquito (*Aedes taeniorhynchus*) also deposits its eggs, which hatch upon reflooding. The fish's behavior results in protection of its eggs from aquatic predators and provides its young with a food supply of mosquito larvae, which become available at the right time and the right place for killifish during reflooding.

Periwinkle (*Littorina* sp.) and saltmarsh (*Melampus lineatus*) snails are seen climbing marsh stalks and serve as easy prey for mammals and birds. Saltmarsh snails lack a protective covering for their foot opening, so are susceptible to dessication and must remain close to water. The snail moves up and down *Spartina* stalks with the tides. Its biological clock is timed to tidal movements and the snail begins its climb up the stalks before the tidal water arrives.

White ibis (Eudocimus albus) have long, decurved bills that turn brilliant red during breeding season.

Armies of fiddler and square-backed crabs, perhaps the most common animals in the salt marsh, are observed scuttling across the muddy floor of the marsh. Crabs are fed on by raccoons, mink, rice rats, and birds, which make their homes on higher and drier ground in the marsh. Birds that live in the marsh include the clapper rail or marsh hen (*Rallus longirostris*), the long-billed marsh wren (*Telmatodytes palustris*), willets, and seaside sparrow. The clapper rail is a game animal and is approximately the size of a small chicken with a grayish color and a long, slightly down-curved bill. The long-billed marsh wren is a medium-sized bird with white stripes on a reddish-brown back, a white breast, and a prominent white line over the eyes.

Diamondback terrapins inhabit the marsh throughout the year. Alligators are occasionally observed in tidal creeks when they move between freshwater and brackish marshes. Feeding in the shallower areas of the marsh are wading birds including egrets, herons, ibis, and storks.

Freshwater marshes, such as the Savannah National Wildlife Refuge, support a greater diversity of aquatic plants than saltwater marshes, and are important nesting and resting habitat for migrating waterfowl. Except on Blackbeard Island, most coastal waterfowl management occurs in old rice field impoundments and newly diked marsh in brackish water areas. Alligators, frogs, turtles, and snakes are abundant residents of the freshwater marsh.

On the Georgia coast, you can study the salt marsh in many areas including Fort Pulaski National Monument (page 83), Earth Day Nature Trail (page 216), Harris Neck National Wildlife Refuge (page 166), and Jekyll Island State Park (page 255).

SOUNDS AND TIDAL CREEKS

The sounds and tidal creeks, the subtidal zones of the estuary, are important natural areas that teem with life. The murky water is a veritable organic soup abounding with creatures, which support larger and larger animals. High tides flood the sounds and tidal creeks, stir up bottom nutrients, and introduce oceanic fish and plankton to the estuary. Low tides and currents pump nutrients and plankton outside the estuary into offshore areas where they support other marine animals.

It has been estimated that the salt marsh and surrounding waters serve as feeding and nursery grounds for 70 percent of all commercially important fish and crustaceans. In 1997, the commercial fisheries of fish, shrimp, and crab caught in Georgia sounds were worth $28 million. The most valuable commercial product was shrimp, with 4,543,631 pounds caught worth $22.2 million. Blue crab ranks a distant second, with 6,808,290 pounds caught worth $3.8 million.

Recreational fisheries are also dependent on the marshes and sounds, which serve as nurseries and feeding grounds for many inshore game fish, including red drum (also known as channel or spottail bass), spotted seatrout, flounder, croaker, black drum, sheepshead, and whiting. Tarpon (*Tarpon atlanticus*) is another popular game fish because of its fighting tendencies and size. Fish that are 6 feet in length and 100 pounds are common. Of all the game fish sought on the Georgia coast, the tarpon is the most primitive.

A prominent animal of tidal creeks and sounds is the Atlantic bottle-nosed dolphin, a beloved marine mammal known for its playfulness and intelligence. Manatees are also occasionally seen in subtidal areas during summer when the water is warmer.

MAINLAND UPLAND

Georgia's mainland upland may be the most significantly altered ecosystem on the Georgia coast. Much of the land is in cultivation for Southern yellow pine, the most commercially valuable agricultural product in Georgia.

Vegetative communities change over time in a natural process known as succession. Given enough time, a forest matures and changes until it reaches a stage where it becomes a stable, self-reproducing natural community. In Georgia, a cleared field eventually becomes a grassy meadow, which then becomes a pine forest. Pines are fast-growing and love sunlight. Below the pines, shade-tolerant hardwoods will start to grow, and eventually will shade out younger pines and dominate the forest. In this example, the hardwood forest is the climax community, which will exist indefinitely unless there is a major natural or man-made disaster that kills the hardwoods and starts the process over again.

Researchers believe the climax forest on the mainland upland of Georgia, before the arrival of the Europeans, was a diverse southern mixed hardwood forest, consisting of live oak, southern magnolia, American holly, American beech, white oak, pignut hickory, dogwood, saw palmetto, redbay, and pawpaw. Today, only a few examples of this forest remain. The southern mixed hardwood forest was not the only forest community found on the Coastal Plain. The Coastal Plain has a variety of natural communities, conditions, and soil types including sand ridges, bottomlands, and bluffs, which produce a great variety of forest types.

Also, fire was a natural influence on the Coastal Plain that kept large areas in perpetual youth, preventing them from reaching a climax form. Forest fires would kill hardwoods but spare fire-adapted pines. Much of the Coastal Plain was pine flatwoods consisting of longleaf and slash pine, with wiregrass growing in the understory. These pines were clear cut in the late 1800s to early 1900s, and today unspoiled examples of this forest community are very rare.

▨ ALLUVIAL, BLACKWATER, AND TIDEWATER RIVERS

The Georgia coast would not be what it is today without its rivers. They deliver fresh water and nutrients that are vital to the estuarine system, and over the millennia, rivers have carried sediment loads that helped to create our barrier islands. Georgia's rivers are great places to observe a wide variety of wildlife, each with its preferred type of river habitat. In the river are many reptiles, including the alligators, snakes, and alligator snapping, mud, musk, and river turtles. A variety of fish also inhabit the waterways such as shad, crappie, bluegill, sunfish, catfish, and largemouth bass. River swamps are home to many species of amphibians, including the bird-voiced treefrog, green treefrog, and leopard and cricket frogs. Bird life is plentiful, and the quiet observer may see the rare swallow-tailed kite or bald eagle cruising the river. In tidal impoundments will be a wide variety of waterfowl such as wood ducks, pintails, mallards, geese, and wading birds such as herons, egrets, and ibis. Seen in the water and on the banks are shy otters, minks, and beavers, and more frequently heard are songbirds, woodpeckers, and owls hidden in the trees. In the bottomland forest may be white-tailed deer, raccoons, armadillos, bobcats, opossums, and wild turkeys. Near the Okefenokee Swamp one may catch sight of a Florida black bear.

Three distinctive types of rivers meet the Georgia coast: alluvial, blackwater, and tidewater. Alluvial rivers, such as the Savannah and Altamaha, originate in the Georgia mountains and Piedmont. Typically, alluvial rivers in Georgia carry a high sediment load and have a broad floodplain from 3 to 12 miles wide. In the 1700s and 1800s, rice plantations were established along these rivers in tidally influenced areas. Blackwater rivers originate in the Coastal Plain, carry low nutrients and low sediment loads, and have narrow floodplains. Blackwater rivers get their name from the tannin-stained color and reflective quality of their waters. The Satilla, St. Marys, and Suwannee rivers are blackwater rivers. The Ogeechee River is considered a mix of alluvial and blackwater characteristics. Tidewater rivers are located near the coastline and have short lengths and are greatly influenced by the tides. The Medway and Turtle rivers are examples of tidewater rivers.

Floodplains and river swamps should be considered part of the river and are extremely important

WHITE OAK
(Quercus alba)
Its high-grade wood was used for whiskey barrels and shipbuilding.

to the health of the environment. During periods of high water, according to Dr. Charles Wharton, author of *Southern River Swamp: A Multiple Use Environment*, water overflows into these river swamps or floodplains, dissipating its energy over a wide area and depositing sediments and minerals that help the swamp ecosystem. Also, organic materials accumulated on the forest floor of the floodplain get swept up and carried into the river, helping to support detritus feeders in the river and eventually contributing nutrients to the coastal marine ecosystem. River swamps, sometimes called bottomland forests, also perform as highly efficient water treatment plants that naturally filter industrial, agricultural, and urban wastes at no cost, and help buffer downstream areas from flooding by holding and absorbing flood waters. The flood cycle is important to young fish, tadpoles, insects, and other organisms that mature and feed in freshwater sloughs and ponds, which serve as protected nursery areas. As development chews up natural areas across the state, it pushes wildlife into smaller patches of natural habitat. The river serves as a natural greenway that links wild areas such as river swamps together, providing natural travel corridors between havens for wildlife. A much greater abundance and diversity of wildlife is found in river swamps, compared with pine plantations found dominating much of Georgia's landscape.

During winter and early spring, rivers flow higher due to frequent rains. Flora and fauna of the river swamps and coastal estuaries have adapted and become dependent on these pulses of water and nutrients. In the estuaries, for example, oysters rely on the nutritional and freshwater inputs during spring for their development. If natural flows are interrupted (by dams), it can be disastrous to the survival of the species. Fresh water keeps the oyster predator, the saline dependent oysterdrill, out of the estuary when salinity is sufficiently lowered.

There are two types of river swamps: cypress-gum forests and bottomland hardwood forests. The cypress-gum swamp is more frequently inundated with water, and here you will find baldcypress, tupelo gum, and overcup oaks. In the less frequently inundated bottomland hardwood forest, indicator species are water hickory, diamond-leaf oak, cherrybark oak, and green ash.

Across Georgia, man has drained the bottomlands to harvest the trees and farm the rich soil. While this has produced timber and agricultural products, it has also destroyed many naturally occurring benefits of the river swamp, including the cycling of nutrients for swamp flora and fauna, flood buffering, and natural treatment of agricultural, industrial, and human wastes. It also has eliminated important wildlife habitat.

Man has tried to tame the river by channelizing and damming. Impoundments, built to provide a growing population with hydroelectric power and waterfront property, interrupt the natural pulses of water and sediment to downstream areas. Impoundments eliminate ecologically diverse whitewater areas upstream and replaced them with man-made lakes stocked with gamefish and surrounded by lake homes. Pollution, silt, and watercraft fill these impoundment lakes, where once existed a diversity of freshwater fish and mussels (the most endangered faunal group in the U.S.).

Alligators are common sights in freshwater areas of the coast, including barrier island ponds, coastal rivers, and swamps.

Man has built many channels, dikes, and levees to prevent the river from flooding. In some cases, it is believed floods are much worse because the river is not allowed into natural river swamps that would absorb the energy and waters of the flood.

SWAMPS

Swamp, like the word wetland, is used to describe many types of wet areas. Here it refers to a depressed freshwater wetland (river swamps are discussed in the previous section). Across the Coastal Plain there are several types of swamps, ranging from 1-acre cypress ponds to the vast American treasure that is the Okefenokee Swamp. All forms of swamps are less and less common as massive agricultural operations drain and fill the depressions that make the swamps in order to grow Southern yellow pine.

The cypress-gum swamp is recognized by its arched form known as a cypress dome or head. Many of these are found in the depressed, former areas of marshes west of ancient shorelines. The ancient lagoons left behind clayey soils that resist draining, thus keeping water tables high, allowing cypress and blackgum to grow. These swamps serve as important water sources, as well as feeding and breeding grounds for a variety of amphibians, reptiles, birds, and mammals.

Another type is the bay swamp, a rare evergreen forest consisting of sweetbay, loblolly bay, swamp red bay, and myrtle. This natural type has a wet, peaty soil and is rarely flooded.

The Carolina bay is another wetland form that is common on the Coastal Plain, with approximately 1,000 identified in Georgia. Carolina bays are tear-drop shaped ponds that are typically inundated and circled by cypress and blackgum, with typical swamp vegetation in the interior. Scientists believe Carolina bays may have been scoured out by gale-force Pleistocene winds or a shower of nonmetallic meteors.

Two more types are savanna and herb bogs, which are wet grassland communities that depend on frequent fires. Fire keeps shrubs and hardwoods from invading the area. Wildflowers here are the most beautiful in coastal Georgia, including lilies, meadow beauty, hatpins, and a variety of orchids. Most fascinating about these bogs are the insectivorous plants that thrive in the low-nutrient acidic soils. These plants, such as the trumpet, hooded, and parrot pitchers, have adapted to poor conditions by developing various strategies for trapping and consuming insects.

Okefenokee is a vast mosaic of different vegetative communities, including bay swamp, herb bog, cypress-gum, and prairie. The swamp is profiled in detail in this book (*see* Okefenokee Swamp, page 295).

BARRED OWL
(Strix varia)
This owl is seen in the Okefenokee Swamp and is recognized by its round head with no ear tufts, barred throat, and streaked underparts.

Chatham and Bryan Counties

Chatham County has the greatest population of any coastal county in Georgia, with approximately 250,000 citizens. Bryan County has become a fast-growing bedroom community of Savannah, a fact recognized by its inclusion into the statistical metropolitan area of Savannah. It is predicted to double its 1980 population of 10,000 residents to 20,000 by the year 2000.

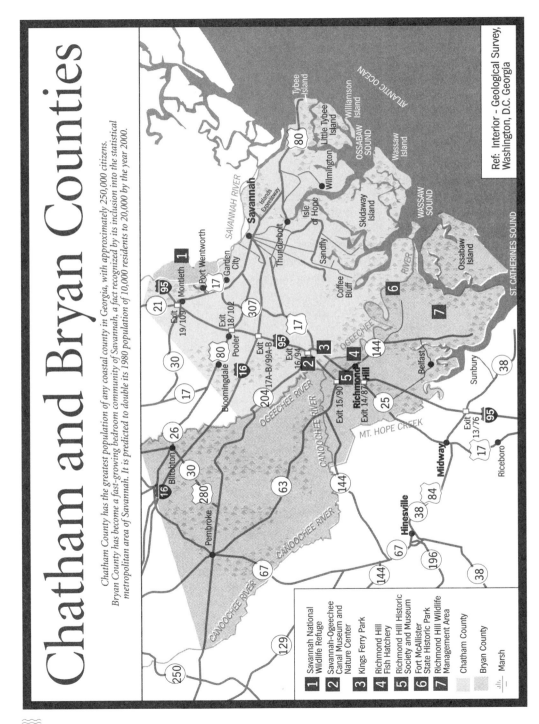

Ref: Interior – Geological Survey, Washington, D.C. Georgia

1 Savannah National Wildlife Refuge
2 Savannah-Ogeechee Canal Museum and Nature Center
3 Kings Ferry Park
4 Richmond Hill Fish Hatchery
5 Richmond Hill Historic Society and Museum
6 Fort McAllister State Historic Park
7 Richmond Hill Wildlife Management Area

Chatham County
Bryan County
Marsh

The Northern Coast:
Chatham & Bryan Counties

The Northern Coast offers the most attractions to tour of any division of this book, because of the town of Savannah, the developed barrier islands of Tybee, Wilmington, and Skidaway, as well as the wildlife preserves of Wassaw and Ossabaw islands.

Chatham County by far has the greatest population of any coastal county in Georgia, with approximately 250,000 citizens. Because of this and the charms of Savannah, the attractions in Chatham County receive the highest number of visitors of any on the Georgia coast. Besides Savannah, visitors can tour Fort Jackson, Savannah-Ogeechee Canal Museum, Wormsloe Historic Site, Skidaway Island State Park, Skidaway Institute of Oceanography and Marine Extension Center, Savannah National Wildlife Refuge, Oatland Island Education Center, and Fort Pulaski National Monument. On Tybee Island, there is Fort Screven Historic District, Tybee Lighthouse, Tybee Island Museum, and Tybee Island Marine Science Center. With a

[*Above:* The Waving Girl Statue welcomes ships to Savannah]

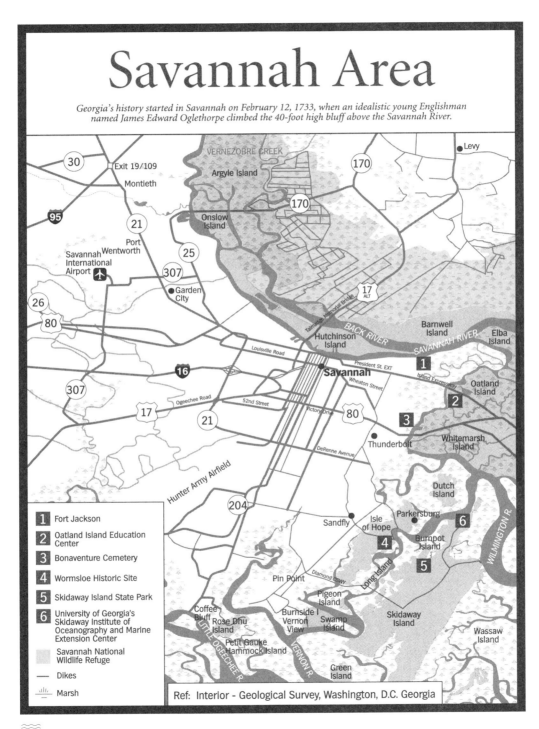

Savannah Area

Georgia's history started in Savannah on February 12, 1733, when an idealistic young Englishman named James Edward Oglethorpe climbed the 40-foot high bluff above the Savannah River.

Legend:

1. Fort Jackson
2. Oatland Island Education Center
3. Bonaventure Cemetery
4. Wormsloe Historic Site
5. Skidaway Island State Park
6. University of Georgia's Skidaway Institute of Oceanography and Marine Extension Center

Savannah National Wildlife Refuge

— Dikes

Marsh

Ref: Interior - Geological Survey, Washington, D.C. Georgia

boat, the adventurous can reach Wassaw National Wildlife Refuge, Little Tybee Island, and, with permission and transportation, Ossabaw Island Heritage Preserve.

Savannah

[Fig. 6] With its cobblestone streets, historic squares, opulent mansions, and spreading live oaks dripping with Spanish moss, Savannah is one of the most distinctive cities in the United States, ranking with New Orleans, San Francisco, and Charleston, South Carolina. The town has a lazy, genteel feel, accentuated by the humid southern climate and laid-back nature of its citizens. There is much to see and do in Savannah, and it serves as a good home base for excursions to other, wilder areas of the Georgia coast.

Georgia's history, for the most part, started in Savannah on February 12, 1733, when an idealistic young Englishman named James Edward Oglethorpe climbed the 40-foot-high bluff above the Savannah River. Oglethorpe had arrived from England with the goal of establishing a new colony where England's poor could get a chance to work their way out of debt. With Oglethorpe were 114 colonists, who were eager to carve a new town out of the virgin pine forests that grew on the sandy bluff. The English general had already negotiated a deal with Tomochichi, the mico of the Yamacraw Indians, which permitted the colonists to establish their new town in peace. With the help of engineers, Oglethorpe marked off a planned city of wards, squares, trust lots, tything (residential) lots, streets, and avenues, creating a layout that continues to influence Savannah to this day. The town was named for the Savannah River, which took its name from an immigrant band of Shawnee Indians known as the *Savana*, who settled near the site of present day Augusta in 1681.

Oglethorpe's conscience led him to Georgia. Years earlier, a friend of his died in a debtor's prison, which convinced Oglethorpe that a new approach was needed for dealing with debtors. After pushing for reforms, Oglethorpe engineered a plan that would help the poor and the King of England. His idea was to give the poor some basic means of support and transport them to the new colonies, where they could work and ship back valuable crops and natural resources while at the same time help to expand the empire of England. The King agreed, and Oglethorpe sailed across the ocean to establish the 13th American colony, which he named for his benefactor King George II.

Most of the settlers were not debtors, however, but skilled craftsmen and working class Britons who had talents to lend to the new colony. Over the next 10 years, thousands of colonists from many different countries and faiths came to Georgia to start a new life, including Jewish refugees from Spain and Portugal, Moravians and Salzburgers from Germany, Scottish Highlanders, French Huguenots, Irish Catholics, Italians, Greeks, and Swiss. They all played a role in helping Oglethorpe establish forts and settlements on the Georgia coast as well as defeat the Spanish at the Battle of Bloody Marsh, thus securing Georgia for England. After 10 years of work in the colony, Oglethorpe sailed home to England.

Trustees' Rules For The Colony Of Georgia 1735

Imagine how different Georgia would be today if Oglethorpe's original rules had continued to be observed:

Labor, clear, and fence the land
Guard against the enemy
Set self up with craft
Plant mulberry trees upon 50 acres and other such crops
Hard liquor, such as rum, is forbidden
No slavery
No unlicensed trading with the Indians
No lawyers in the Georgia Land

Savannah, like other Southern coastal towns, struggled for survival as it was ravaged by wars, epidemics, fires, and economic depression. One of the great battles of the American Revolutionary War was the Siege of Savannah. Early in the war, the British had seized Savannah with little trouble. American Patriots, with help from French allies, decided to attack the entrenched redcoats on October 9, 1779. After a fierce struggle, the British maintained their hold on Savannah. The battle was the second bloodiest of the war, with 264 British losses, 600 French losses, and 600 American losses. Savannah remained under British control until 1783.

A decade later, a tutor named Eli Whitney invented the cotton gin at Mulberry Grove, a Savannah plantation owned by American Revolutionary War hero Nathanael Greene. The invention revolutionized the cotton industry, and cotton became king in the South. The seaport of Savannah became very important for cities located upriver. Shipping merchants in Savannah got rich and built huge mansions.

During the Civil War, Savannah became the goal of Union General William Tecumseh Sherman, who burned Atlanta and went on his March to the Sea. When Sherman reached the city, an entrenched Savannah surrendered after the fall of Fort McAllister as Confederate forces slipped across the river into South Carolina. Luckily, Sherman did not lay Savannah to waste as he did Atlanta.

The Civil War, the boll weevil, and destructive agricultural practices put an end to the South's prosperity from "white gold." The advent of railroads reduced the importance of Savannah as a seaport, and the town went through a period of stagnation and slumber, which it was not to awaken from until the early twentieth century. During this period, development was farther south in Savannah, as citizens turned their backs to the river and their ancestors' historic neighborhoods. From the 1920s to the 1960s, the historic district deteriorated and declined. Between 1960 and 1970, the city lost 20 percent of its population, as citizens moved away from urban areas to suburbs and bedroom communities.

When developers decided to demolish historic City Market to build a parking garage, preservationists organized to oppose their plans. While the preservationists lost this battle, the seeds of the preservation movement were sown. When developers eyed the historic Isaiah Davenport House, a group of committed and influential citizens organized the Historic Savannah Foundation and prevented the demolition of the building. The foundation went on to lay the groundwork for preservation activities for the entire 2.5-square-mile Historic Landmark District, which today is the largest in the U.S. In the 1970s, millions of dollars were pumped into the historic riverfront, which became a preservation success story.

Another tremendous boost to Savannah was the founding and success of the Savannah College of Art and Design in 1978, which lead to the preservation of more than 40 buildings in the historic district. With 4,000 art students, the college contributed significantly to the culture of Savannah, while expanding the local economy and making the downtown area more attractive. Also contributing to Savannah's economic stability is Savannah's continuing role as a major shipping harbor, which ranks as the tenth busiest container port in the nation, and large corporations such as Gulfstream and Union Camp.

Despite Savannah's new investments and renovations in its historic district, it was not that well known on the national stage. Its neighbor 100 miles to the north, Charleston, was a much more popular tourist destination. More like an eccentric small town, Savannah remained relatively unknown, a hidden jewel. But that was all about to change with the publishing of *the book* in 1994.

John Berendt's phenomenally selling *Midnight in the Garden of Good and Evil* drew back the curtain on Savannah's quirky Southern charms. The book strings together a series of slightly exaggerated but essentially true humorous vignettes about Savannah's more unusual characters and social traditions, with the murder trial of a prominent antiques dealer taking center stage. The book was made into a movie that was filmed in Savannah, spreading the town's image across the silver screen. It may be that no book in the history of publishing has had a greater single effect on an American city. Since the success of the book, tourists have flocked to the city in droves, looking for the city portrayed in the book. While upsetting some locals who preferred a more isolated, less-crowded Savannah, the book has nonetheless added many millions of dollars to the local economy and spurred renovation work in other historic neighborhoods. An estimated 6 million people visit Savannah a year with an economic impact of more than $800 million. To accommodate and spur additional visitors, the city is building a new $175-million, 345,000-square-foot convention center on Hutchinson Island, across the river from Riverfront Plaza.

WAX MYRTLE
(*Myrica cerifera*)

▒ TOURING SAVANNAH

Savannah is ranked in the top 10 best walking cities in the U.S. by *Walking Magazine*. Most tourists sites are concentrated around River Street, City Market, and the Historic District. River Street and City Market are thriving tourist areas within walking distance of each other that feature a collection of restaurants, clubs, art galleries, and souvenir shops housed in the historic buildings of Savannah's waterfront and City Market.

While these two areas have much to offer, visitors should not leave Savannah without spending some time in the 2.5-square-mile National Historic Landmark District. To capture the essence of Savannah, visitors should stroll through some of the historic district's beautiful squares, where they will find more than 1,700 restored homes, museums, galleries, and shops worth their attention. Officially, the district is defined by the Savannah River and Gaston Street (Forsyth Park) and bordered by East Street and Martin Luther King Jr. Boulevard. The Victorian Historic District, which stretches south from Forsyth Park for approximately 1 square mile, is undergoing renovation and development that has already swept through the neighborhoods to the north. Some beautiful lodging and delicious dining are found in this area as well.

It is recommended that visitors start their sojourn in Savannah at the Savannah Visitors Center. From here, tourists can get oriented to the town's charms by taking a tour or picking up maps and helpful information. Annual events to be aware of start with St. Patrick's Day. For more than 160 years, this riotous event has celebrated the Irish heritage of the city. The St. Patrick's Day parade is the second largest in the U.S., behind New York, and the celebration is the third oldest, behind New York and Boston. Other events to look out for are annual tours of homes and gardens, which allow a peek into some of Savannah's finer homes that usually are closed to the public. See Appendix D, Annual Events.

▒ SAVANNAH VISITORS CENTER/SAVANNAH HISTORY MUSEUM

[Fig. 7] Located in the 1860 Central of Georgia Railroad Building, visitors starting here can get information on lodging, restaurants, and attractions that make Savannah distinctive. Walking, driving, or carriage tours are booked here. The Savannah History Museum offers an excellent introduction to the area's history. Exhibits feature Forrest Gump's bench and the *Bird Girl* statue on the cover of *Midnight in the Garden of Good and Evil*, discuss the Siege of Savannah, Savannah-born songwriter Johnny Mercer, and Savannah's railroad history.

Directions: I-16 to Martin Luther King Jr. Boulevard Exit 37A/167. At light, go left. Visitors Center is on left.

Activities: Historical touring.

Facilities: Restrooms, gift shop, snack bar.

Dates: Open 7 days a week, 9–5.

Fees: A small fee is charged for the museum.

For more information: Savannah Visitors Center/Savannah History Museum, 301 Martin Luther King Jr. Boulevard, Savannah, GA 31499. Visitors Center: Phone 944-0455. History Museum: Phone 238-1779.

City Market

[Fig. 7] The former Ellis Square, one of the oldest squares in Savannah, was the site of Old City Market, established in the eighteenth century. In the 1950s, developers decided to demolish the market and build a parking lot. Preservation forces rose up and fought the plan, but lost the battle. This started a long and ultimately successful effort by activists to save the remainder of the area, which today is four blocks of bustling restaurants, nightclubs, shops, and art galleries that capture the atmosphere and character of the eighteenth century marketplace.

The City Market Art Center, located in the upstairs level of the market, contains the working studios of 35 of the area's finest artists, including sculptors, potters, painters, photographers, wood carvers, and glass designers. A fine selection of restaurants is found here offering everything from pizza to French cuisine, with indoor and outdoor seating. Dance clubs are located between here and River Street two blocks away. A vibrant strip of night life options, including restaurants, pubs, live music venues, dance clubs, and a billiard hall, is located on the south side of City Market along Congress Street, Savannah's former red-light district. Events are held in City Market throughout the year.

Directions: Located between Franklin Square and Johnson Square on W. St. Julian St.

For more information: Phone 232-4903.

CITY MARKET AREA RESTAURANTS

Sapphire Grill. 110 W. Congress Street. Seafood is acclaimed in this popular newcomer, but steaks and lamb entrees are very good. Dinner. *Moderate. 443-9962.*

Trattoria Rivazza. 116 W. Congress Street. This Italian restaurant has a strong local following. Delicious pizzas, pastas, and appetizers. Lunch and dinner. *Moderate. 234-7300.*

Garabaldi's. 315 W. Congress Street. Delicious Northern Italian cuisine in a lively restaurant. Great place to take a date. Dinner. *Moderate. 232-7118.* **Bistro Savannah.** 302 W. Congress Street. Gourmet, inventive entrees with a Southern flair, such as pecan-crusted chicken and tasso ham. Fine dining and casual dress make this one of Savannah's most popular restaurants. *Moderate. 233-6266.* **Vinnie Van Go-Go's**. 317 W. Bryan Street. A pizza joint that's popular with the younger, hangout crowd. Lunch and dinner. *Inexpensive. 233-6394.* **Seasons**. 315 W. St. Julian. A hot restaurant with delicious seafood creations, lamb, and other options. Highly recommended crab cakes. Lunch and dinner. *Moderate. 233-2626.*

▨ CITY MARKET AREA NIGHTLIFE

Malone's. 27 Barnard. This City Market mainstay has three levels to explore, where one may watch sports on TV, grab a bite to eat, drink a frozen daiquiri, play pool, or meet a member of the opposite sex and tear up the dance floor. *234-3059*. **Velvet Elvis**. 127 W. Congress Street. Savannah's best live music club. Open 5 p.m. to 3 a.m. *236-0665*. **The Zoo**. 121 W. Congress Street. With three floors of dancing action, if you can't dance here, you can't dance. *236-6266*. **Cross Roads**. 411 W. Congress Street. Savannah's live blues club. *234-3636*. **The Rail Pub**. 405 W. Congress, once a bordello in Savannah's red-light district, this is a good place to grab a beer and talk to some locals. *238-1311*.

River Street

[Fig. 7] On the bluff facing the Savannah River are nine blocks of renovated cotton warehouses that house about 80 restaurants, pubs, night spots, hotels, shops, galleries, and boutiques. Adding to the sight-seeing is a working harbor of huge, building-size cargo ships, tug boats, and sailing ships that are seen plowing the murky waters of the Savannah River. During the day, families stroll alongside the river, eating ice cream cones and browsing in gift shops. At suppertime, people are seen feasting on seafood and steaks in some of Savannah's best restaurants. Come sundown, Savannah's night life kicks in, and couples amble through the streets as live music reverberates out of pubs and nightclubs.

Historic River Street features many of Savannah's most popular hotels, restaurants, clubs, and small shops.

On River Street, there are several good options for lodging that offer a view of Savannah's main natural attraction (the river), along with quick walking access to River Street, City Market, and the historic squares of the city.

It hasn't always been this way. The city had turned its back on the historic waterfront, which was abandoned and deteriorating when a wide-ranging group of civic leaders joined forces in the early 1970s to create the River Street Urban Renewal Project. When the work was finished in 1977, approximately 80,000 square feet of abandoned warehouse space on the historic waterfront had been transformed into Savannah's most popular tourist attraction. Additional improvements have produced an attractive city park that hosts many festivals and special events.

The ambiance of the waterfront is an atmospheric fusion of nineteenth century old-world charm and twentieth century tourist potpourri. Stony ramps that connect Bay

Street with River Street are made of English ballast stones, which gave schooners added stability for their trips from Europe, only to be thrown out and replaced with cotton bales in Georgia. The stones were used in buildings and walkways, and became the foundation of ballast stone islands found today in river channels.

Along the waterfront are two memorials worth closer examination. One is the *Waving Girl*, a 1971 statue by Felix De Weldon that honors Florence Martus, a Savannahian who greeted every ship entering the port from 1887 to 1931 by waving a cloth from her home on Elba Island (*see* Cockspur Beacon, page 89). The other is a memorial to the 1996 Olympics, during which Savannah hosted the yachting event.

On the bluff next to Bay Street are the gold-domed City Hall, Factors Walk, and Emmet Park (*see* Historic Parks and Cemeteries, page 44). City Hall was built in 1905 on the site of the Old City Exchange. Notice the bench commemorating Oglethorpe's landing on February 12, 1733. Factors Walk once housed the offices of nineteenth century cotton merchants. Today, a variety of businesses call it home. Of interest to the historian are the Washington Guns, presented by George Washington when he visited Savannah in 1791. The bronze cannons were captured from the British at Yorktown.

Directions: River Street is located north of Bay Street. River Street can be driven, but walking is strongly recommended.

For more information: Savannah Waterfront Association. Phone 234-0295.

RIVER STREET LODGING

Old Harbour Inn. 508 E. Factors Walk. A former factory built in 1892, this modernized inn features suites with kitchens, living rooms, and balconies where one can watch ships navigating the Savannah River. Full continental breakfast, evening cordials, and turndown service are part of the inn's charm. *Moderate to expensive. (800) 553-6533.* **River Street Inn**. 115 E. River Street. Built circa 1853, this cotton warehouse serves as a beautifully furnished inn and offers "the charm of an inn with the convenience of a full-service hotel." Can't disagree. Huey's is located here (*see* below). *Moderate to expensive. (800) 253-4229.* **Hyatt**. 2 W. Bay Street. If you are looking for a totally modern hotel with all the amenities, this is your best choice. Rising seven stories, some rooms have views of the river. Restaurant, lounge, and indoor pool are part of the building. *Moderate to expensive. (800) 233-1234.* **Mulberry Inn**. 601 E. Bay Street. Across the street from Factors Walk and River Street, this sumptuous inn, with eighteenth century paintings, crystal chandeliers, and a lush courtyard, features first-class Southern hospitality. *Moderate to expensive. (800) 465-4329.*

RIVER STREET RESTAURANTS

Huey's. 115 E. River Street. This Cajun/Creole restaurant is one of Savannah's most popular breakfast spots, offering rich coffee, beignets, omelets, and pancakes. Lunch and dinner offer traditional New Orleans fare such as étouffé and jambalaya. Breakfast, lunch, dinner. *Moderate. 234-7385.* **River House**. 125 W. River Street. Seafood creations and a

Savannah Historic District

Savannah is one of the best walking cities in the U.S. Most tourist sights are concentrated around River Street, City Market, and the Historic District.

stylish, fine dining atmosphere in an 1810 cotton warehouse. Mesquite grilled fish, fresh from the Atlantic. Extensive wine list. Lunch and dinner. *Moderate to expensive. 234-1900.* **The Shrimp Factory**. 313 E. River Street. Pine Bark Stew is one signature item, as well as large cocktails, chargrilled fish and steaks, and, oh yeah, great shrimp dishes. Lunch and dinner. *Moderate. 236-4229.* **W.G. Shuckers**. 225 W. River Street. This locals' favorite, a mainstay on River Street, is a great place for fresh oysters, cold beer, she-crab soup, and a full menu of seafood specials. Lunch and dinner. *Moderate. 443-0054.*

🌊 RIVER STREET NIGHT LIFE

Billy Bob's. 21 E. River Street. Newcomer on the street features bar food with a Western twang. Barbecue, steaks, and burgers. Bluegrass music. Lunch and dinner. *234-5588.* **Kevin Barry's**. 117 W. River Street. This friendly Irish pub has food, live Irish music sing-alongs, a deck for watching River Street action, and is ground-zero on St. Patrick's Day. *233-9626.* **The Warehouse**. 18 E. River Street. Live music, drink specials, pool, and darts. *234-6003.* **Wet Willie's**. 101 E. River Street. Frozen daiquiris and bar food basics. *233-5650.*

Historic District: Squares, Homes, Museums, and Churches

[Fig. 7] The most defining feature of Savannah is its eighteenth century design, following an extraordinary urban plan created in 1733 by the founder of Georgia, Gen. James Edward Oglethorpe. Today, visitors should stroll through Savannah's 24 historic squares, some of which were paced off by Oglethorpe himself, and see that his pattern is still in use. The sun-dappled squares, called Savannah's jewels, serve as tranquil city parks, beautifully landscaped with live oaks, magnolias, azaleas, oleanders, and crape myrtle. Located around these squares are the majority of Savannah's historic inns and museums, as well as beautiful churches and parks (*see* Historic Parks and Cemeteries, page 44).

Oglethorpe originally divided the city into four wards. In the center of the wards were public squares, and on the east-west axis of the squares, four large trust lots were reserved for public buildings such as churches or markets. On each side of the north-south axis of the squares, Oglethorpe marked off 40, 60- by -90-foot residence lots, in two rows separated by alleys, said to accommodate the number of families that first arrived on the *Anne*.

Whitaker Street was the centrally located road, dividing four symmetrically placed squares—Ellis (now a parking garage), Johnson, Telfair, and Wright. By 1839, the city had grown to 18 squares and shifted slightly eastward, with Bull Street, and a series of squares, being the spine of the city. As the city grew into the 1850s, the final set of squares was marked off using Oglethorpe's pattern, reaching all the way to Gaston Street and the centrally placed Forsyth Park. South of Gaston Street, the system of squares was abandoned, allowing Forsyth Park to serve as that area's central park.

One confusing feature of Savannah is that the squares and monuments don't match. The Oglethorpe Monument is in Chippewa rather than Oglethorpe Square, the Pulaski Monument is in Monterey rather than Pulaski Square, and the Greene Monument is in Johnson instead of Greene Square. (*See* Fig. 7 for location of the following squares and attractions.)

Calhoun Square. Laid out in 1851, this shady square was named for the South Carolina Southern-rights firebrand John C. Calhoun. On the square is Wesley Monumental United Methodist Church, whose congregation organized in 1875. The Gothic-revival church was built in 1890 as a memorial to John and Charles Wesley, founders of the Methodist movement, through national fund-raising.

Chatham Square. Named in 1851 after William Pitt, the Earl of Chatham, this square was laid out in 1847. **Ralph Mark Gilbert Civil Rights Museum**. 460 Martin Luther King Jr. Boulevard. Opened in 1996, this museum features 15 exhibits showcasing Savannah's African-American history from the Emancipation Proclamation to the Civil Rights movement. Located three blocks west of Chatham Square. Open Monday through Saturday 9–5, Sunday 1–5. A small fee charged. *231-8900.*

Chippewa Square. A beautiful bronze figure by Daniel Chester French, the sculptor of the Lincoln Memorial, immortalizes General James Edward Oglethorpe, who looms over the square named for the American victory in the Battle of Chippewa during the War of 1812. This is where Forrest Gump's bench was placed, at Bull and Hull streets, during the filming of that popular movie. Two blocks north of the square is Independent Presbyterian Church, which was founded in 1755. The current church is an 1891 replica of the 1819 church, and is considered a notable example of American church architecture. Woodrow Wilson married Ellen Axon in a room in the manse in 1885.

Columbia Square. This marks the eastern limit of Savannah when it was a walled city between 1757-90. Bethesda gate, one of six city gates, was on this square. Today it is a tranquil spot away from the busy commercial district. The fountain in the center is from Wormsloe. Located on the square is Isaiah Davenport House Museum, perhaps the most significant structure in Savannah, as it launched the historic preservation effort that revived the city. **Isaiah Davenport House Museum**. 324 E. State Street. Anyone who loves Savannah should pay tribute to this museum. Threatened with demolition in the 1950s, this classic Federal-style home became a catalyst for the formation of the Historic Savannah Foundation, a group of seven influential women who stayed the wrecker's hand less than 24 hours before demolition was to begin. Built in 1820, this fine home features Hepplewhite, Chippendale, and Sheraton furnishings. Open daily 10–4. A small fee is charged. *236-8097.*

Crawford Square. Laid out in 1841 and named for former Georgia Governor and Senator William Harris Crawford, the centerpiece today is a busy basketball court. Crawford ran for U.S. president in 1824 but finished third to winner John Quincy Adams and second-place finisher Andrew Jackson.

Elbert Square. Located on Montgomery Street between Hull and Perry streets, this square was created and named in 1801 for Governor Henry Ellis. One of Savannah's obliterated squares, it is covered with pavement and open to through traffic.

Ellis Square. Located on Barnard Street between Bryan and Congress streets, this is one of the original four squares laid out by Oglethorpe in 1733. It is named for Henry Ellis, who in 1758 became the second royal governor of Georgia. It was the site of Old City Market, a covered market built in

Isaiah Davenport House Museum.

1870 that was torn down and replaced by a parking garage in 1954.

Franklin Square. Laid out in 1790 and named for Benjamin Franklin, the famous American statesman and agent for the Colony of Georgia from 1768–1775. **First African Baptist Church**. 23 Montgomery Street. This is reportedly the first brick building built by African-Americans for their own use, erected in 1859. Church membership was derived from the oldest black congregation in the U.S. (1777) from nearby Brampton Plantation. Runaway slaves were hidden under the sanctuary floor during the Civil War. Open daily 10–5. Donations accepted. *233-2244*. **Ships of the Sea Museum/Scarbrough House**. 41 Martin Luther King Jr. Boulevard. The Scarbrough House, designed in the Greek Revival style by William Jay, was built in 1819 for Savannah cotton merchant Prince William Scarbrough, who was a major investor in the steamship *Savannah*, the first to cross the Atlantic. The restored home is one of Savannah's top 10 historic buildings. Inside the house is the Ships of the Sea Museum, which highlights Savannah's and the country's maritime history with scale models of ships. Open Tuesday to Sunday, 10–5. A small fee is charged. *232-1511*.

Greene Square. Named in honor of American Revolutionary War General Nathanael Greene, who had a Savannah River plantation at Mulberry Grove.

Johnson Square. The first square laid out by Oglethorpe in 1733, it was the center of life in the earliest days of the colony. It is named for Robert Johnson, the friend of Oglethorpe and governor of South Carolina who helped the Georgia colony. In the center is the monument and grave of General Nathanael Greene. The original drawing of Savannah called for a church on the lot where Christ Episcopal Church now stands. Savannah's original settlers were members of the Church of England, and their church in the new colony was Christ Church, the first church established in the new colony. John Wesley preached at this location from 1736–1737. The influence of the church was such that the parish was called Christ Church Parish. Its ministers were loyalists to England, so after the Revolutionary War, the church fell into decline. The church reformed as Christ Episcopal Church, and the current structure dates back to 1838.

Lafayette Square. Laid out in 1837, and named for the Marquis de Lafayette, who visited Savannah in 1825 and spoke to the crowd from the balcony of the Owens-Thomas house located on Oglethorpe Square. On this square are the Andrew Low House, Hamilton Turner Mansion and Museum, and a few steps west, the Flannery O'Connor House. She was a member of Cathedral of St. John the Baptist, the oldest Roman Catholic church in Georgia, and a glorious example of French-Gothic church design. In the early days of the colony, Catholicism was banned and Irish Catholics entered the colony as indentured servants. Prejudices against Catholics changed during the American Revolution when the French allied with American Patriots against England. Today, the St. Patrick's Day celebration in Savannah is the second largest in the country. **Andrew Low House**. 329 Abercorn St. This home was built in 1848 by one of Savannah's wealthier merchants, Andrew Low. His son William later owned the house, and he married Juliette Gordon, who founded the Girl Scouts here on March 12, 1912. Robert E. Lee and William Thackeray dined here. Closed Thursdays. Open 10:30–4. A small fee is charged. *233-6854.* **Hamilton-Turner Mansion and Museum**. 330 Abercorn. A Second-Empire styled mansion built circa 1873, this home belongs to Nancy Hillis, the "Mandy" of *Midnight in the Garden of Good and Evil*, who sometimes leads tours. Open daily 10–4. A small fee is charged. *233-4800.* **Flannery O'Connor House**. 207 E. Charlton Street. The birthplace and childhood home of one of America's greatest writers today serves as a shrine to her life and work. Open Saturdays and Sundays 1–4. Donation requested. *233-6014.*

Liberty Square. Montgomery Street between State and York streets. One of Savannah's effaced squares, it was laid out in May 1799 and named to honor the "Sons of Liberty" who fought the British during the Revolutionary War. Now paved over and open to through traffic.

Madison Square. Named for the fourth U.S. President James Madison, the 15.5-foot bronze statue in the center commemorates Sgt. William Jasper, who fell in the Siege of Savannah in 1779 as he planted the colors on a British entrenchment. A granite marker cites the southernmost line in the British defense during the American Revolution. Sherman stayed in the Green-Meldrim house, which is open to tours. **Green-Meldrim House**. 14 W. Macon Street. General Sherman's Civil War headquarters, this mansion is an excellent example of neo-Gothic architecture and one of the most expensive mansions ever built in Savannah. Designed by John Norris and built in 1853, today it serves as the parish house for St. John's Episcopal Church, but thankfully it is open to tours. From here, Sherman sent his famous message to President Lincoln, reprinted in many newspapers of the day: "I beg to present to you as a Christmas gift, the City of Savannah with 140 heavy guns and plenty of ammunition and also about 25,000 bales of cotton." After the war, Sherman returned to Savannah and stayed again at Green's home. Open Tuesday and Thursday through Saturday 10–4. A small fee is charged. *233-3845.*

Monterey Square. Some consider this square to be Savannah's loveliest. The Mercer House, the setting for the murder featured in *Midnight in the Garden of Good and Evil*, is located on this square. Named for the capture of Monterey, Mexico in 1846 by Gen. Zachary Taylor during the Mexican War, the monument in the center commemorates

Count Casimir Pulaski, a Polish nobleman mortally wounded in the Siege of Savannah in 1779. He was the highest ranking foreign officer killed in the American Revolution. Built in 1878, Temple Mickve Israel serves the third oldest Jewish congregation in America, established in 1733. The temple houses the oldest Torah in America, and a museum is home to many historically valuable books, along with letters from Presidents Washington, Jefferson, and Madison to the congregation. **Mercer House**. 429 Bull Street. Designed by John S. Norris before the Civil War, it wasn't finished until 1871, after the bloody conflict. Built for Gen. Hugh W. Mercer, the home was abandoned in the 1960s, and later restored in the 1970s and furnished with antiques by Jim Williams, who was featured in the book *Midnight in the Garden of Good and Evil*. In this house, Williams shot his lover, Danny Hansford. In 1990, Williams died near the spot where Hansford was killed. Mercer is a relative of songwriter Johnny Mercer. Not open to tours.

Oglethorpe Square. Laid out in 1742 and named for Georgia's founder, this is a popular spot to take a shady break or picnic lunch. **Owens-Thomas House Museum**. 124 Abercorn Street. Built in 1819 and designed by William Jay, this house may be the finest example of Regency architecture in the U.S. Marquis de Lafayette spoke for two hours from the balcony. Closed Monday. Open 10–4. A small fee is charged. *233-9743*.

Orleans Square. This square was laid out in 1815 to honor the heroes of the Battle of New Orleans during the War of 1812. The fountain in the center was dedicated in 1989 by Savannah's German Societies to commemorate the contributions to Savannah of early German immigrants.

Pulaski Square. This square, featuring some of Savannah's most beautiful live oaks, is named for the Polish nobleman who died during the Siege of Savannah in 1779.

Reynolds Square. Originally called Lower New Square, this square was home to the Filature, where silk was woven from silkworm cocoons during the colony's failed experiment to establish the silk industry in Georgia. The square is named for Captain John Reynolds, governor of Georgia in 1754, and the statue of John Wesley was erected in 1969.

Telfair Square. One of the original four squares when Savannah was laid out in 1733, it was originally called St. James, then renamed Telfair in 1883 in honor of three-time governor Edward Telfair. It also has a Girl Scout tribute. Trinity United Methodist Church, built circa 1848, resembles the design of Wesley Chapel of London, and is the oldest Methodist Church in Savannah. **Telfair Academy of Arts and Sciences**. 121 Barnard Street. The former home of Alexander Telfair is a museum itself, built in 1819 and designed by William Jay. Inside is an outstanding permanent collection of impressionist paintings and classic sculptures. Closed Monday. Open Tuesday through Saturday 10–5. Sunday 2–5. A small fee is charged. *232-1177*.

Troup Square. This square is named for Governor George Michael Troup and was laid out in 1851. In the center is Armillary Sphere, an astronomical centerpiece made of iron that is supported by small metal turtles.

Warren Square. Laid out in 1791, this square was named for Revolutionary War hero General Joseph Warren, president of the Third Provincial Congress.

Washington Square. Formerly called Eastern Commons, this square once bordered the original Trustees' Garden, where colonists grew a variety of experimental crops. It was established in 1790 and named for the first U.S. President.

Whitefield Square. This square was laid out in 1851 and named for George Whitefield, early Savannah minister, nationally famous preacher, and founder of Bethesda Orphanage. The white gazebo has hosted countless marriages.

Wright Square. A large boulder in this square marks the grave of Tomochichi, the mico of the Yamacraws who helped Oglethorpe settle the Georgia coast. One of Savannah's original four squares, it was first called Percival Square, then later renamed for Sir James Wright, the third and last colonial governor. A monument honors William Washington Gordon, the early mayor of Savannah who established the Central of Georgia Railroad. The current Lutheran Church of the Ascension was constructed from 1843 to 1878 by the congregation organized by the Salzburgers in 1741. The original church of 1772 burned. **Juliette Gordon Low Birthplace/Girl Scout National Center**. 142 Bull Street. Savannah's first National Historic Landmark is the 1860 birthplace of the founder of the Girl Scouts, who own and operate the museum. Built in 1820, the design is attributed to William Jay. The home is furnished with antiques from the period of Juliette Gordon's youth in the 1870s and 1880s. A mecca for Girl Scouts, this the reason you see so many of the uniformed pilgrims in Savannah. Closed Wednesday. Open Monday through Tuesday and Thursday through Saturday 10–4. Sunday 12:30–4:30. A small fee is charged. *233-4501.*

✺ LODGING IN HISTORIC DISTRICT

The Historic District and the Victorian District offer more than three dozen options for historic lodging. Here are some of the more popular choices. **Ballastone Inn**. 14 E. Oglethorpe Avenue. Located near Chippewa Square, this 1838 antebellum mansion once served as a bordello. Today, the beautiful inn features rooms and suites with private baths and period antiques. Most have fireplaces and guests can exercise for free at First City Club. *Moderate to expensive. (800) 822-4553.* **Bed & Breakfast Inn**. 117 W. Gordon Street. Built in 1853, this B&B is located a few blocks away from Forsyth Park and is an excellent choice for visitors on a budget. Some guest rooms have shared baths. *Inexpensive to moderate. 238-0518.* **Eliza Thompson House**. 5 W. Jones Street. Two blocks north of Monterey Square is this 1847 townhouse, which has been one of the most popular B&Bs in Savannah. *Moderate to expensive. (800) 348-9378.* **Foley House Inn**. 14 W. Hull Street. Located on Chippewa Square, this nineteenth century Victorian townhouse is full of period antiques and reproductions that create a sumptuous Savannah ambiance. Five of the 19 rooms have whirlpool tubs. *Moderate to expensive. (800) 647-3708.* **The Kehoe House**. 123 Habersham Street. One of the most luxurious B&Bs in Savannah, if not the South, this magnificent Victorian mansion overlooks Columbia Square in the heart of the historic district. *Expensive. (800) 820-1020.* **The Gastonian**. 220 E. Gaston Street. A beautifully furnished, 1868 inn features 16 rooms furnished with Georgian and Regency antiques and working fireplaces, and most have whirlpool tubs. *Moderate to expensive. (800) 322-6603.*

RESTAURANTS IN HISTORIC DISTRICT

Clary's Café. Corner of Jones and Abercorn. Profiled in *Midnight in the Garden of Good and Evil*, this neighborhood eatery on Lafayette Square not only has good food but also loads of character. Open 7 days a week for breakfast, lunch, and dinner. *Inexpensive. 233-0402.*

Elizabeth on 37th. 105 E. 37th Street. Sparking a new appreciation of Southern culinary arts is Elizabeth's, one of the most famous restaurants in the South. Chef Elizabeth Terry's original creations using regional seafood, meats, and ingredients are delicious discoveries for the fine diner. The restaurant is located in an elegant, turn-of-the-century mansion in the Victorian District, which adds to the experience. Open Monday through Saturday. Reservations recommended. Dinner. *Expensive. 236-5547.*

Il Pasticcio. 2 E. Broughton Street. An excellent, visionary Italian restaurant that has become part of Savannah's preservation history. When Savannahians took their business to malls and shopping centers located farther out in the suburbs, Broughton, the former commercial district of department stores and dress shops, underwent serious decline. By 1993 Broughton Street had become a mostly deserted strip of boarded up shops when the Venetico family purchased the former Lerner Shop and designed a beautiful new restaurant. Il Pasticcio won many loyal followers for its Italian cuisine that some believe is the best in Savannah, if not the Georgia coast. And Broughton Street is experiencing a resurgence. Open 7 days a week. Dinner. *Moderate. 231-8888.*

Mrs. Wilkes Boarding House. 107 W. Jones. Crowds line up down the sidewalk to wait for a table at this family-style sit-down Southern restaurant, featuring fresh vegetables and meats. The fried chicken is legendary. Open Monday through Friday for breakfast 8–9, and lunch 11:30–3. No credit cards. *Inexpensive. 232-5997.*

Olde Pink House. 23 Abercorn Street. Built in 1771, this is one of the oldest buildings in Savannah, which today is an elegant restaurant on Reynolds Square. Heart of pine floors, eighteenth century antiques, and an excellent wine cellar create a colonial ambiance that original owner, wealthy James Habersham must have enjoyed. The piano bar in the basement is a Savannah institution. Open 7 days a week for dinner. *Moderate. 232-4286.*

Pirate's House. 20 E. Broad. This family seafood restaurant, in Trustees' Garden near Washington Square, is popular with tourists, and is worth a visit for its nautical ambiance and creaky charm. Built in 1794, the structure first served as a tavern for sailors. Robert Louis Stevenson is said to have set part of his classic *Treasure Island* here. One frequently repeated tale is that Captain Flint died in an upstairs room and his angry ghost still can be heard roaming the halls. Of special note is the "Herb House," a room in the restaurant that may have been built in 1734, making it the oldest structure in Georgia. Lunch and dinner, Sunday brunch. *Moderate. 233-5757.*

Located upstairs at the Pirate's House is Hannah's East, a jazz nightclub that features legendary Ben Tucker, as well as Emma Kelley, "Lady of 6,000 Songs," who was featured in *Midnight in the Garden of Good and Evil*. Open 5 p.m. until 2 a.m. *233-2225.*

Walls' BBQ. 515 E. York Lane (Off Oglethorpe Avenue between E. Houston Street and W. Price Street). Opened in 1968, Walls' has become a local legend, with some zealots declaring that Walls' barbecue is the best on the southeastern coast. The sauce is mustard-tangy, and is served on delicious open-pit cooked ribs and chicken. The pork sandwich is a monster. Lunch Wednesday, lunch and dinner Thursday through Saturday. *Inexpensive. 232-9754.*

🁣 NIGHT LIFE IN HISTORIC DISTRICT

Appropriately, Savannah has some great English-flavored pubs that serve good food to accompany your microbrew of choice. A great place for a sandwich and beer is **Churchill's Pub**, 9 Drayton St. (one block east of Johnson Square). It's British owned and operated, with darts, fish 'n' chips, and Yorkshire pudding. *232-8501.* Also worth your drinking dollars are **Six Pence Pub**, 245 Bull St. (North of Liberty near Chippewa Square), *233-3156*, and **McDonough's**, 21 E. McDonough St. (one block east of Chippewa Square). Food and drinks served early (8 a.m.) and late (2 a.m.) 7 days a week. *233-6136.* **J.J. Cagney's**. 17 W. Bay Street. This section of Bay Street, between City Market and River Street, is becoming a nightlife strip, with Cagney's leading the way, featuring live rhythm and blues. *233-2444.*

Historic Parks and Cemeteries

Visitors should take a stroll through some of Savannah's historic parks and cemeteries, which are notable for their beauty, tranquility, and history.

Trustees' Garden. E. Broad Street. One of Oglethorpe's activities was to establish a 10-acre experimental garden on the outskirts of the settlement, which he named Trustees' Garden in honor of the men in England who supported the colony. As Georgia has the longest growing season of any of the colonies, the plan was to find crops that thrived in the New World that could help support the other colonies. Grapes were grown to produce wine, and mulberry trees were cultivated to produce silk, but both efforts failed. Cotton succeeded, however, and went on to become the most important crop in Georgia. When the garden was no longer needed, the area was converted to residential and commercial buildings. One building was a tavern, which was built in 1794 to serve the needs of sailors who visited the growing seaport. This tavern became the Pirate's House, an eccentric-looking family restaurant (*see* page 43).

Within walking distance is Fort Wayne, known as "The Fort" during the American Revolution when the British captured Savannah. In 1784, it was renamed Fort Wayne for "Mad"Anthony Wayne, and was improved for the War of 1812.

Emmet Park. Bordering E. Bay Street is a beautiful, tree-shaded park named for Irish patriot and orator Robert Emmet. Found here is a Vietnam Veterans Memorial and historic Harbor Light (1858), a gas-powered light erected as a navigational aid to vessels in the Savannah River. The light stands 77 feet above the river and helped ships avoid the hulls of ships scuttled by British forces during the siege of 1779 in an effort to prevent French warships from using the harbor.

Colonial Park Cemetery. Oglethorpe and Abercorn streets. Between 1750 and 1853, Savannahians were buried here in this shaded, moss-draped cemetery. Victims of the 1820 yellow fever epidemic that claimed 700 lives were interred here. Historical plaques mark graves of important early colonists, including Button Gwinnett, a signer of the Declaration of Independence. During the Civil War, encamped Union soldiers vandalized the cemetery. Later, the broken headstones were cemented to the rear wall. Today, the cemetery is a public park. Open daily from 9–5. Free.

Forsyth Park.

Forsyth Park. Bull Street between Gaston Street and Park Avenue. This 20-acre park features one of the most beautiful fountains in America, in a breathtakingly beautiful setting of azaleas, flowering trees, and live oaks. During the Civil War, Union soldiers encamped here. The lovely white fountain was built 1858 and restored in 1988. Memorials in other parts of the park honor Civil War and Spanish-American War dead. Lighted tennis and basketball courts are always in use, and joggers and cyclists will enjoy the 1.5-mile perimeter path.

Georgia Historical Society. 501 Whitaker Street. Located across the street from Forsyth Park is Hodgson Hall, the headquarters for the Georgia Historical Society. Built in 1875, the Italianate-Greek Revival building is open to the public and is a treasure trove of manuscripts, records, and artifacts relating to Savannah and Georgia's history. Open Tuesday through Friday 10–5. Saturday 9–3. Free. *651-2128.*

King-Tisdale Cottage. 514 E. Huntingdon Street. Located four and a half blocks east of the park on E. Huntingdon is a quaint Victorian cottage built in 1896 and dedicated to preserving African-American history and culture. Open Tuesday to Friday, noon–4:30. Weekends 1–4. Small fee charged. *234-8000.*

Laurel Grove Cemetery. Established in 1852, beautiful Laurel Grove has thousands of graves that give silent testimony to Savannah's rich history in a natural setting of dogwoods, magnolias, live oak, and pine. Divided into north and south sections by a highway, visitors will find in the north section Girl Scout founder Juliette Gordon Low, "waving girl" Florence Martus, and 1,500 Confederate graves (101 of whom died at Gettysburg), including eight generals. In the south section are many African-American graves, including two Confederate veterans. To find the cemetery, drive south from the visitors center on Martin Luther King Jr. Boulevard. Turn right on Anderson Street and drive straight to the gate. Open daily 8–5. Free. *236-8097.*

BONAVENTURE CEMETERY

[Fig.6(3)] Many believe Bonaventure is the most beautiful cemetery in the world. The attractive plants, sweet smells, and beautiful views of the Wilmington River make for a peaceful final resting site—and a tranquil site to visit. Recently, it has received worldwide fame from being featured on the cover and in the text of writer John Berendt's hugely popular bestseller *Midnight in the Garden of Good and Evil*. Benches have been installed on the perimeter roadway to allow enjoyment of peaceful views of the golden marsh, or one can stroll the cemetery among the live oaks, red cedars, southern magnolias, and azaleas.

Gifted naturalist, explorer, and politician John Muir spent five days camping on the grounds in September of 1867 on his famous 1,000-mile walk from Louisville, Kentucky to Cedar Key, Florida. Down to his last 25 cents, he waited for funds from his brother at Bonaventure Cemetery, where he became impressed with the plant and animal communities he found. Muir was a Scotsman who went on to found the Sierra Club and influenced the U.S. Congress to establish Yosemite and Sequoia national parks, along with the national forest system. His words were posthumously published in the book *Thousand-Mile Walk to the Gulf*. He wrote that he discovered at Bonaventure "one of the most impressive assemblages of animal and plant creatures I have ever met…Bonaventure is called a graveyard, a town of the dead, but the few graves are powerless in such depth of life…The rippling of living waters, the song of birds, the joyous confidence of flowers, the calm undisturbed grandeur of the oaks, mark this place of graves as one of the Lord's most favored abodes of life and death."

Other famous people buried in the cemetery include the Noble Jones family descendants, the Tattnalls, Edward Telfair, songwriter Johnny Mercer, poet Conrad Aiken (whose memorial is a bench overlooking the Wilmington River inscribed with "Cosmos Mariner, Destination Unknown"), and Danny Hansford of *Midnight in the Garden of Good and Evil* fame. Visitors who wander the cemetery in search of the enigmatic statue that graces the cover of *Midnight in the Garden of Good and Evil* are wasting their time. The Bird Girl, as it is called, was moved to the Savannah History Museum after the book and the statue became so popular.

Famous Civil War Confederate generals found here include Robert J. Anderson, who commanded cavalry under Wheeler in the Atlanta Campaign; Henry R. Jackson, who served in western Virginia and Georgia; Hugh Mercer, who commanded in the Atlanta Campaign; and Claudius C. Wilson, who commanded at Chickamauga and Chattanooga and died of disease in Ringgold 13 days after Missionary Ridge. Also buried here is Alexander R. Lawton, a West Point graduate who was president of the Augusta and Savannah Railroad, and commanded the Lawton-Gordon-Evans brigade under Stonewall Jackson, considered to be one of the hardest fighting units in the Civil War. Wounded at Sharpsburg, he recovered to become the quartermaster of the Confederate Army until the end of the war. He later became president of the American Bar Association and was U.S. minister to Austria.

Bonaventure was first settled by an English colonel named John Mulryne, who came to Savannah from Charleston around 1760. He named it by combining the Italian words *buono ventura*, meaning "good fortune." His daughter married Josiah Tattnall, and to mark the event he planted avenues of live oaks in the form of a monogram combining the letters M and T. These Spanish-moss draped oaks, which so impressed John Muir, are still found in the cemetery today. The eighteenth century plantation home of Josiah and Mary Mulryne Tattnall no longer stands on the property, having burned to the ground. Mrs. Tattnall is believed to be the first buried at Bonaventure in 1794.

During the Revolutionary War, Savannah citizens were divided between their loyalties for England and America. Josiah, a Tory, wouldn't fight for either side, and he had Bonaventure confiscated by the local patriots. He and his two sons, John and Josiah Jr., left for England. John fought on the English side, but Josiah Jr. fought on the American side with Gen. Nathanael Greene. He distinguished himself so well that the state let him buy back Bonaventure. He eventually became a member of U.S. Congress and Governor of Georgia. When he died in 1804 at the age of 38, he was buried next to his wife in Bonaventure, leaving behind an orphaned son, Josiah Tattnall III, who was raised in England by his grandfather, the original Josiah Tattnall. The son returned to America and later joined the U.S. Navy. He felt a strong allegiance to England as well, and on one occasion he breached American neutrality by coming to the aid of the British fleet, which was fighting in Chinese waters. His famous defense when he was reprimanded was "blood is thicker than water," which helped mend some of the bad feelings that remained between the British and Americans from the War of 1812. Josiah III went on to serve as commodore for the Confederate Navy during the Civil War, and was involved in the naval defense of Savannah and the burning of the ironclad C.S.S. *Virginia* or *Merrimack*. Josiah III was buried in the family plot at Bonaventure.

Bonaventure became a cemetery in 1850, when Captain Peter Wiltberger, owner of the Pulaski Hotel, purchased the property. In July 1907, the property transferred to the City of Savannah, which owns it today. Since Berendt's book, many city tours have included a tour of Bonaventure on their must-see list.

Directions: From the city of Savannah where Bull Street and US 80 (Victory Drive) meet, go approximately 3 miles east on US 80 (Victory Drive) to Thunderbolt. Take a left on Whatley Avenue. Go approximately 0.75 mile on Whatley, which becomes Bonaventure Road, to the entrance of the cemetery.

Activities: Historic touring, nature hiking.

Facilities: Museum, bookstore, bathrooms, hiking trails, handicapped-accessible facilities, boat ramp, picnic area.

Dates: Monday through Friday 8-5. Saturday noon–2. Sunday 2–4.

Fees: None.

Closest town: Thunderbolt.

For more information: Bonaventure Cemetery, City of Savannah, 330 Bonaventure Road, Savannah, GA 31404. Phone 235-4227.

Near Savannah

FORT JACKSON

[Fig. 6(1)] Fort Jackson is Georgia's oldest standing fort and important to understanding the shipping and military history of the Georgia coast. Here visitors will enrich their knowledge of Savannah's Civil War and maritime history with a backdrop of the Savannah River and huge cargo ships, in a serene setting of coastal marsh.

SAW PALMETTO
(Serenoa repens)
The shrub palm of the coast is recognized by the sharp saw spikes that grow on the stem of the plant.

Fort Jackson is located on the strategically important Salters Island. During the Revolutionary War, War of 1812, and Civil War, all ships wishing to approach Savannah had to pass by this piece of real estate. Even today, all merchant ships still must pass by Fort Jackson. Geography is the reason. The different channels of the Savannah River and inland waterway approaches to Savannah converge at Fort Jackson. Attacking naval forces could go around Savannah's other guardian Fort Pulaski (*see* page 83) by using the Wilmington River to the south or navigating around Daufuskie Island to the north—but all still had to pass by Fort Jackson to attack Savannah from the water. The fort also had the advantage of being protected by marshes from a land attack, and a deep-water anchorage at the fort's dock on the Savannah River eased shipment of supplies and troops.

Salters Island was first the site of a brickyard belonging to Thomas Salter in 1741. During the eighteenth and nineteenth centuries, this high spot was surrounded by rice fields and marsh, which sometimes would be submerged during spring tides. The river here was called "five fathom hole" and was a popular anchorage site for cargo vessels. Salters Island's strategic value was recognized early in American history and during the 1770s was the site of an earthen battery called Mud Fort that was used during the Revolutionary War. Later, President Thomas Jefferson decided that a national system of coastal fortification was needed to protect the young nation. The original brick fort on Salters Island was begun in 1808 by the U.S. Army Corps of Engineers under Captain William McRee and was used by local militia and federal troops as a signal station during the War of 1812.

Named for James Jackson, a governor of Georgia and a hero of the American Revolution, the fort was enlarged and strengthened between 1845 and 1860, when engineers built the moat and drawbridge, brick barracks, privies, rear wall, and powder magazine. A close look at the brick wall near the drawbridge reveals three distinct layers of bricks. The first layer of brown and red bricks was laid between May 1808 and June 1812. The topmost brown bricks were added between 1845 and 1860. The fort has 20-foot-high walls, and a 9-foot-deep moat. It held nine cannons: five 32-pound smooth bore, one 32-pound rifled, two 8-inch Columbiads, and one mountain howitzer. A 32-pounder is still fired in demonstrations; it is the largest black powder cannon still fired in the United States.

Although the surrounding marsh protected Fort Jackson from land attack, it also brought the threat of the mosquito-borne diseases of yellow fever and malaria. The fort was described in 1819 as "the most distempered spot in the universe." Consequently, the Fort Jackson garrison was housed in Savannah from May to November. The fort was abandoned during the Revolutionary War due to malaria, thereby allowing the British to sail up the river and capture Savannah with ease. The fort was also used as a quarantine station during years of epidemic diseases.

During the Civil War, Fort Jackson became the Confederate headquarters for the Savannah River defenses. Robert E. Lee, Jefferson Davis, and P.G.T. Beauregard all visited this fort. This inner line of defense consisted of Fort Jackson, the Savannah River Squadron, and a network of earthen batteries and signal stations along the marsh and waterways between Savannah and Wilmington rivers, as well as river obstructions and underwater mines.

Despite as many as 40,000 Union troops on nearby Hilton Head and the fall of Fort Pulaski on Cockspur Island to Union troops on April 11, 1861, the Savannah River defenses kept Savannah safe from Federal forces attacking from the sea. Savannah was not surrendered until December 21, 1864, when Union Gen. William Tecumseh Sherman, on his famous March to the Sea, captured Fort McAllister on the Ogeechee River and poised his huge army outside the city. However, the 18,000-man Confederate garrison was able to sneak out of the city unharmed, something that Sherman was much criticized for by his superiors. On the night of December 20, 1864, the garrisons of Causton Bluff, Thunderbolt, and the Savannah River batteries gathered at Fort Jackson and evacuated across the Savannah River by steamer and on makeshift bridges, successfully eluding capture. The army and naval forces joined up with North and South Carolina forces and continued to fight Sherman's army until they surrendered at Durham Station, North Carolina on April 26, 1865—17 days after Lee surrendered to Grant at Appomattox Court House, Virginia.

Three hundred yards away from Fort Jackson, a red buoy in the Savannah River can be seen marking a historic remnant of the Savannah River Squadron. The Savannah-made C.S.S. *Georgia* lies under water, scuttled by her crew the night of Savannah's evacuation to prevent it from falling into Union hands. Built from funds from the Georgia Ladies Gunboat Association, it was Georgia's first ironclad, launched May 19, 1862, and stationed downstream from Fort Jackson as a floating battery with its ten heavy guns. The C.S.S. *Georgia* is an internationally significant naval relic as it was one of the few ironclads that was engineered and built as an ironclad and today remains largely intact under the water with all her armament and stores. (Most of the other ironclads were re-engineered and retro-fitted steamers.) The ship awaits a Herculean and expensive effort to raise it from the river.

When troops under Sherman seized Fort Jackson, they raised the American flag over the fort. A member of the Savannah Squadron, the ironclad C.S.S. *Savannah*, displeased with this display, fired on the Federal troops from the river. This gunboat was commissioned in July 1863 as the flagship of the squadron and was 174 feet long and 45 feet wide and had five rifled guns. The C.S.S. *Savannah* was blown up by rebel troops on December 21, 1864, to prevent it from falling into Union hands. Following the Civil War, Fort Jackson was modified and then abandoned by the Army in 1905.

Fort Jackson has excellent living history demonstrations that feature cannon firing, musketry, blacksmithing, and other programs. Fort Jackson's museum features the naval history of the area and houses artifacts from the C.S.S. *Georgia* brought to the surface by divers.

The self-guided tour of the 8-acre site takes approximately one hour. The entrance and gift shop to Fort Jackson is the former pre-World War I Tybee Train Depot. The depot, which was barged to the site in 1988, was the departure point for train rides to Tybee Island between 1887 and 1933.

Directions: From Savannah downtown, go east on Bay Street to the President Street extension to Island Expressway. Head east toward Tybee Island approximately 2.5 miles. Turn left at sign for Fort Jackson.

Activities: Historic touring. Special events and programs are offered during the year. Group tours, cannon firings, lunch and dinner programs, and student programs may be arranged. Cannon firing programs during the summer months. Phone 232-3945 for details.

Facilities: Museum, bathrooms, trails, gift shop, exhibits.

Dates: Open 7 days a week from 9–5.

Fees: Admission is charged.

Closest town: Savannah.

For more information: Old Fort Jackson, 1 Fort Jackson Road, Savannah, GA 31404. Email: ofj@g-net.net Phone 232-3945.

SAVANNAH-OGEECHEE CANAL MUSEUM AND NATURE CENTER

[Fig. 5(2)] From 1830 to 1890, a canal operated between the Ogeechee and Savannah rivers. Put out of business by economic and natural disasters in the late 1800s, sections of the canal still exist. The canal is owned by the City of Savannah and currently under a long-term lease to Chatham County for the purposes of establishing a linear park. One of the most preserved sections of the canal is found at the Ogeechee River end located 2.3 miles west on Highway 204 west of Exit 16/94 on I-95. This section lies adjacent to the 184-acre tract owned and operated by the Savannah-Ogeechee Canal Society Inc., a nonprofit organization dedicated to preserving the canal's history and appreciating the natural communities found on the property. This is a good site for a hike through an interesting and rare sandhill community as well as a beautiful lowland hardwood river swamp, consisting of baldcypress and tupelo gum. The nature preserve is on the Colonial Coast Birding Trail established by the Georgia Department of Natural Resources.

Adjoining the property is the Ogeechee Natural Area that features a river dune ridge ecosystem community, which consists of a dwarf oak-evergreen shrub forest with a lichen floor. Georgia-threatened gopher tortoises (*Gopherus polyphemus*), Eastern diamondback rattlesnakes (*Crotalus adamanteus*), and Eastern kingsnakes (*Lampropeltis getula getula*) inhabit the sand ridge.

This ecosystem, according to Dr. Charles Wharton in *The Natural Environments of Georgia*, is "one of Georgia's most exceptional, picturesque, and unique." A larger section of river dune ridge ecosystem is found on the northern and eastern banks of the Ohoopee River. The Ohoopee River dune system stretches 35 miles and covers approximately 40,000 acres and is a registered State Natural Area and a National Natural Landmark. The Nature Conservancy of Georgia has preserved a 267-acre tract of the dunes in Emanuel County near Swainsboro. The Ohoopee Dunes Preserve is open to those who have an interest in this fascinating natural community, but must make prior arrangements with The Nature Conservancy of Georgia. Call (404) 873-6946.

The dunes, found only on the eastern side of rivers, are believed to have been created by strong winds during the late Pleistocene era 20,000 years ago and formed of deep, coarse, riverine alluvial sand. Similar dunes are found east of the Canoochee River. The impoverished soil produces dwarfed versions of native trees such as live oaks, with a 6-inch diameter tree being approximately 140 years old. Other interesting indicator flora found in this ecosystem include trees such as turkey oak and longleaf pine; shrubs such as rosemary (*Ceratiola ericoides*), red basil (*Calamintha coccinea*), shrub goldenrod (*Chrysoma pauciflosculosa*), and jointweed (*Polygonella polygama*); along with the lichen commonly known as British soldiers. Fauna consists of sandhill-adapted animals, or animals that burrow, such as gopher tortoise (*Gopherus polyphemus*) and pocket gopher (*Geomys pinetis*), and burrowing insects. With cypress ponds nearby, the following vertebrates have been recorded: canebrake rattlesnake; smooth earth, coral, pine, and copperhead snakes; green, pinewoods, squirrel, and barking treefrogs, and oak toad. Some scientists believe that this unusual ecological community has been in existence long enough to have evolved endemic species. More study and protection of this unique environment is needed.

The canal began in 1824 as a venture by Ebenezer Jenckes, a local turnpike owner. He obtained a charter from the state to build a canal that would connect the Savannah and Ogeechee rivers, and eventually the Ogeechee and Altamaha rivers. When he failed to raise enough capital, several Savannah citizens took control of the project in 1826. By 1830, the work had been completed on 16.5 miles of canal, built by hundreds of slaves and Irishmen at the cost of $190,000. The canal, which had four lift locks and two tidal locks, was operated much like the Erie Canal, with flat-bottomed barges pulled by horses on the banks. Problems plagued the operation, including decay of the wooden locks and erosion of the embankments, and by November of 1836, the company was foreclosed and the property sold. In 1837, Amos Scudder, who was a major contractor for the construction of the canal, believed the canal could be successful and purchased the stock owned by the City of Savannah and State of Georgia. During the late 1830s and early 1840s, he replaced the wooden locks with the brick, which you can still see today. He improved the embankments and towpath and widened the downtown channel, ushering in an era of prosperity for the canal company from the 1840s to 1860s.

In 1864, the canal was the scene of several skirmishes and was damaged by Confederate forces hoping to slow Sherman's army during his March to the Sea. Union forces repaired it and used it to supply their operations against Savannah and Fort McAllister.

After the Civil War, with the continued rise of railroads, the canal continued operation, but with declining profits. On September 11, 1892, a storm broke the summit level dam and the canal company lacked the funds to repair it. The Central of Georgia Railroad bought the Canal Company property, planning to use it as a rail route, but never did. The City of Savannah acquired the canal in 1916, which was leased by Chatham County in 1992 to be developed into a linear recreational facility.

The museum and nature center are located on 184 acres where the canal meets the Ogeechee River. Several trails take you through the lowland hardwood swamp. The 0.4-mile Heel Path, which follows the canal to the Ogeechee River, is accessed by crossing Lock #5 located by the museum and picnic pavilion. The Tow Path is on the eastern side, and is also a 0.4-mile walk to the river and Lock #6. On the grounds just west of the canal, U.S. Gen. William T. Sherman's army encamped. They crossed the canal and followed Jenckes Road. This 0.5-mile road is now a nature trail that leads to the Ogeechee River, crossing bridges and boardwalks. The easternmost route over the Ogeechee, Dillon Bridge, was located here. Confederates burned it to delay Sherman, but Union engineers quickly repaired it and marched on to Fort McAllister, where they overran the Confederate fort on December 13 before the evacuation and fall of Savannah on December 21. The 0.15-mile Ridge Trail leads off of Jenckes Road to the Holly Trail, which connects to an old logging road for access to the river dune community. The Popcorn Trail is a 0.2-mile loop off of Jenckes Road.

Other remains of the canal are visible nearby. Bush Road, located opposite the museum off Fort Argyle Road, takes you 3 miles to Half Moon Lake. The lake was the primary source of water that fed the canal. It was constructed by an impoundment on the Little Ogeechee River. On your way to the lake, look for Lock #4 on your left. Lock #3 is found near Tom Triplett Park in Pooler.

The museum and nature center feature exhibits on the history of the canal, various canal artifacts, and live reptiles and amphibians native to the area. Lectures concerning the flora and fauna of the area and canal history, and guided nature walks are available to groups at a nominal charge. Please call for further details, prices, and reservations.

Trail: Several 1-mile and shorter nature trails are found near the Savannah-Ogeechee Canal and Ogeechee River.

Directions: Located 2.5 miles west on Fort Argyle Road (204) from I-95 Exit 16/94.

Activities: Historic touring, nature hiking, picnicking. Special lectures and guided nature walks can be arranged for groups. Call for details and reservations.

Facilities: Museum, bathrooms, hiking trails, picnic pavilion and grills, Boy Scout campground.

Dates: Open 7 days a week from 9–5.

Fees: None but donations are encouraged.

Closest town: Savannah.

For more information: Savannah-Ogeechee Canal Society, 681 Fort Argyle Road, Savannah, GA 31419-9239. Email: socm@csam.net Phone 748-8068.

Thunderbolt, Isle of Hope, and Skidaway Area

THUNDERBOLT

Located on a bluff overlooking the intracoastal waterway at the Wilmington River, Thunderbolt is the home of a large, busy marina. A picturesque drive along the waterfront's high bluff leads visitors past million-dollar yachts to several excellent restaurants that retain the flavor of a maritime community.

Essentially as old as Savannah, Thunderbolt was settled when Gen. James Edward Oglethorpe determined the bluff was of military strategic importance when he arrived in 1733. Thunderbolt has one of the more memorable names of any town in Georgia. According to Oglethorpe, the town was named after "a rock which was here shattered by a thunderbolt, causing a spring to gush from the ground, which continued ever afterward to emit the odor of brimstone." Oglethorpe built a settlement and fort here, the first of several through the years. By 1734, Thunderbolt was ready to defend Savannah with a hexagonal palisade and a battery of four cannons. During the Revolutionary War, the leader of the French forces, Charles-Henri Comte d'Estaing, used Thunderbolt as his base of operations during the unsuccessful siege of Savannah. During the Civil War it was the site of a battery and a garrison.

A casino, built in 1875 on the land bordering the river, became one of the most popular recreation spots in the Savannah area. It burned in 1930, and today Thunderbolt Marina operates in the former location.

For many years, Thunderbolt was home to fishing families, who worked the coastal waters and moored their fishing and shrimp boats at the river. Today, the fishing-supported Thunderbolt community is disappearing as gentrification pushes through the area, and million-dollar yachts are much more common than shrimp boats.

River Road, which follows the banks of the Wilmington River between Bonaventure Cemetery and Thunderbolt, is a scenic route on the southern side of US 80 (Victory Drive) that features the marsh, yachts, shrimp boats, and marina toward the water and some locally famous restaurants on the other side. Locals appreciate their live oaks enough to build their road around a huge one as you enter the town.

FISHING, MARINAS, AND CHARTERS IN THUNDERBOLT

Palmer-Johnson Marina. 3124 River Road, Thunderbolt. If you love big, expensive yachts, you will find the biggest and most expensive on the Georgia coast right here. Nearby, the luxury vessels are bought and sold, built and rebuilt, furnished and refurbished to the tune of thousands, if not millions, of dollars in what is considered the premier repair yard in the southeast. *356-3875*. Downstream and on the other side of the river is **Savannah Bend Marina**, a full-service marina offering wet and dry storage, gas and diesel fuel, hoists and docks, bait and tackle, indoor boat storage, and a restaurant. *897-4956*.

RESTAURANTS IN THUNDERBOLT

The view of the Wilmington River and ready access to daily fresh seafood traditionally made Thunderbolt a great location for seafood restaurants.

Teeple's. 2917 River Drive, Thunderbolt. This is reputably the oldest "shell-your-own" restaurant in the Savannah area, featuring local blue crab, shrimp, oysters, and clams. Charlie Teeple started Teeple's in 1976, and the third-generation Thunderbolt family still runs it today. The restaurant is such a fixture in the community that when it had a fire a few years back, locals still were dropping by to pick up steamed crabs to go. Some say this place invented the hole-in-the-middle-where-you-dump-your-shells table, but no one can prove it. Best when the seafood is in season. Nice view of the marsh and river. Open Monday through Thursday for dinner and Friday through Saturday for lunch and dinner. *Moderate. 354-1157*.

The River's End Restaurant and Lounge. 3122 River Drive, Thunderbolt. For a classier dining experience in Thunderbolt, The River's End located near the Palmer-Johnson Marina is an excellent choice. A local favorite for more than 30 years, the restaurant overlooks the intracoastal waterway and features local seafood and charbroiled steaks. Open at 5 p.m. for dinner only. Closed Sundays. *Moderate. 354-2973*.

ISLE OF HOPE

The Isle of Hope National Historic District, with its expansive live oaks, magnolias, and azaleas, is as charming as its name implies. But it is somewhat false advertising because Isle of Hope is not really an island, but a sandy peninsula with a high bluff looking over to Skidaway Island across the intracoastal waterway at Skidaway Narrows and the Isle of Hope River. Whether on foot, bike, or car, visitors can view Isle of Hope's beautiful antebellum homes and old summer cottages in this picturesque community, which has been used many times as a setting for movies.

The Isle of Hope Methodist Church, located 412 Parkersburg Road, was built in 1859 prior to the start of the Civil War. The grounds were used as a Confederate battery, consisting of two 8-inch Columbiads and two 32-pound cannon. The church was used as a Confederate hospital during the Union occupation of the area in 1864, and the pews, still in existence, were used as beds. Carvings in the pews made by patients are still visible today. General Sherman, who didn't have much respect for organized religion, melted the church bell for cannonballs. A gallery in the back was for slaves. The historic cemetery holds the graves of 33 Confederates from Effingham County.

First settled in 1736 by Noble Jones, John Fallowfield, and Henry Parker, the area was recognized as an important defensive outpost on the young colony's inland waterway south from Savannah. Noble Jones's Wormsloe Plantation was the site of a fort that defended Savannah from Spanish attack until 1742. During the 1800s, the area attracted more residents and a small community known as Parkersburg was established. The area was fortified during the Civil War, but saw little action. After the Civil War, Isle of Hope became a popular resort community, with daily train service in the 1870s. Where the river met the railroad was Barbee's Pavilion, which became world renowned in the 1920s.

Historic Wormsloe Plantation (*see* below); Bethesda, the oldest still-operating orphanage in America; and the Isle of Hope Marina are located on Isle of Hope. All these attractions are located a few miles away from each other and can be reached by car or bike.

Bethesda Orphanage was conceived by Charles Wesley and James Oglethorpe, and the idea was made reality by the Reverend George Whitefield, who arrived in Georgia in 1738. He received a grant of 500 acres in 1739, and in 1740 he opened the first orphanage in the New World. The name is Biblical in origin and means "house of mercy." Governor John Milledge and Gen. Lachlan McIntosh both were raised by the orphanage. The Rev. Whitefield was famous for his fund-raising sermons, working tirelessly for 32 years to raise funds for the orphanage, and preaching over 18,000 times. One sermon even moved the penny-pinching Ben Franklin to give money to the orphanage, which Franklin wrote about in his famous autobiography. Whitefield Square in the Savannah Historic District is named in his honor.

Wormsloe features a grand entrance to one of the state's last architectural remnants from the Oglethorpe era.

The orphanage is still in operation today. Bethesda's main support comes from The Union Society, which was originally formed in 1750 by a "union" of a Catholic, Protestant, and a Jew. Some claim that it is the oldest charitable organization in America. Bethesda is located at 9520 Ferguson Avenue. Phone 351-2040.

The Isle of Hope Marina, 50 Bluff Drive, is a good place to book a ride to Wassaw National Wildlife Refuge. Phone 354-8187.

Directions: Isle of Hope is located southeast of Savannah where Laroche Avenue meets Bluff Drive.

WORMSLOE HISTORIC SITE

[Fig. 6(4)] The most breathtaking driveway in the entire state belongs to Wormsloe Plantation, which features an impressive 1.5-mile avenue lined with approximately 400 live oaks. A state-operated historic site, Wormsloe Historic Site features hiking trails through the maritime forest, the oldest estate in Georgia, one of the last architectural remnants of Savannah from the Oglethorpe era, Confederate fortifications, and an excellent museum telling the history of colonial Georgia.

The hiking trail takes one down to the tabby ruins of Wormsloe, which sits on a bluff overlooking Jones Narrows. A short spur trail takes the hiker to the Jones Narrows and the original gravesite of Noble Jones, his wife Sarah, and their youngest son, Inigo. Today, they are buried in Bonaventure Cemetery. In colonial days, this channel was the main inland water route between Savannah and settlements to the south. Dredging for the Atlantic Coastal Waterway altered the flow in the marsh, clogging the channel with silt. *Spartina* marsh now fills much of the waterway.

Jones's Fort was built in a strategic location to control shipping traffic and defend against possible attacks by the Spanish from the south. It was one in a series of forts built by Oglethorpe to protect the 13th colony from the Spanish. Other forts included Fort Argyle where the Ogeechee and Canoochee rivers meet; Mount Venture on the Altamaha River; Fort Darien and Barrington in McIntosh County; Bachelors Redoubt; Fort Frederica and Fort Saint Simons on St. Simons Island; Carrs Fort in Brunswick; Fort Saint Andrews and Fort Prince William on Cumberland; and Amelia Fort on Amelia Island. These forts were put to use during the War of Jenkins' Ear (1739–1743) when Spaniards invaded Georgia before being beaten by Oglethorpe in the Battle of Bloody Marsh on St. Simons in 1742.

On the 1-mile long, interpretive hiking trail, you will see cabbage palm, red cedar, live oak, and pines. Spanish bayonet, dogwood, azaleas, and ferns are abundant. Deer are very frequently spotted on the Wormsloe property. More careful and quiet observation is needed to see raccoons, opossums, and possibly bobcats. Small bridges cross tidal creeks, where you may see wading birds such as egrets, herons, and ibis in the marsh. During the right season, migratory songbirds are found in the forest. Plaques display reproductions done by eighteenth century naturalist and artist Mark Catesby. Insect repellant is recommended.

Massive old-growth pines that dominated Wormsloe were destroyed in 1974 when a southern pine beetle epidemic swept through the property. The Georgia Forestry Commission successfully fought the pine beetles by removing the trees, but the insect effectively changed the forest, allowing more sunlight to reach the forest floor, prompting dense understory growth.

The museum has artifacts, exhibits, and an audiovisual presentation that tells the story of the coastal colonial plantation of Noble Jones and his family. Jones, a physician, carpenter, surveyor, and military man, was one of the original settlers of Georgia, coming with Gen. James Edward Oglethorpe in 1733. In 1736, Jones leased from royal trustees 500 acres on the Isle of Hope approximately 10 miles south of Savannah. In 1739, he started building a five-room, fortified tabby house incorporated into a rectangular tabby wall with four bastions. Construction was interrupted twice during the War of Jenkins' Ear. By 1745, Jones returned and completed his home. He received the property in 1756 by a royal grant conveying ownership.

The 750-acre plantation became well known for its experimental horticultural efforts in the young colony, with rice, indigo, cotton, and silk grown here. The silk-production effort—silk worms on mulberry trees—is the source of the plantation's original name: Wormslow. In 1765, famed naturalists John and son William Bartram visited Wormslow to learn about Jones's plant experimentation, and William wrote in his famous book *Travels* about the unusual fruits he found growing here such as oranges, figs, pomegranates, peaches, and apricots.

Jones was a renaissance man. He helped found the colony of Georgia. He commanded a company of Marines who patrolled the inland water route in a guard boat to defend Savannah from any attack from the Spanish. A middle-class carpenter from England, he served as soldier, constable, Indian agent, physician, and treasurer of the colony, Royal Council member, and Justice of the Province. He built the first lighthouse on Tybee Island, and as surveyor he laid out the towns of New Ebenezer and Augusta.

Noble Jones, a Tory, died in 1775 before the American Revolution. Surviving him was his son, Noble Wimberly Jones, who supported the Patriot cause and was captured by the British. Noble Wimberly Jones was 10 when he arrived with his father aboard the *Anne* in 1733. After the war, he practiced medicine in Savannah until his death in 1805. Surviving him was his son, George Jones, who was an excellent businessman and enlarged the family fortune. George Jones abandoned the tabby home and built a new one in 1828, where he lived until he died in 1838. His son, George Frederick Tilghman Jones, changed his name to George Wymberley Jones DeRenne to avoid confusion with another prominent George Jones in Savannah. He also changed the name of Wormslow to its current spelling of Wormsloe. It is believed he was the richest man in Savannah.

Wormsloe was the site of Confederate earthworks known as Fort Wimberly during the Civil War. The breastworks and the large earthen battery are still visible. Union troops arrived at the fort after the fall of Savannah and vandalized the house.

Eventually, the property fell into decay, and in 1972, Jones's descendants donated 822 acres to The Nature Conservancy, which transferred the property to the State of Georgia. The 1828 house and 65.5 acres are still owned by the family.

A colonial life area is located just off the nature and interpretive trails. Structures here simulate the small wattle and daub huts that served as quarters for Jones's Marines, indentured servants, and slaves. Living history programs are held here, where costumed staff display skills and crafts necessary to early settlers of coastal Georgia.

Directions: From I-95, take Exit 16/94 toward

RACCOON
(*Procyon lotor*)
This highly adaptable animal feeds on crabs in Georgia's salt marsh.

Savannah for 12 miles on GA 204. Turn right onto Montgomery Cross Road and drive 3.2 miles until the road dead-ends. Turn right onto Skidaway Road and proceed 0.8 mile to entrance. Drive through the large arch that says Wormsloe.

Activities: Historic touring, living history programs, nature hiking.

Facilities: Museum, bookstore, bathrooms, hiking trails, picnic tables, handicapped-accessible facilities.

Dates: Tuesday through Saturday 9–5; Sunday 2–5:30.

Fees: $2 parking fee.

Closest town: Isle of Hope.

For more information: Wormsloe State Historic Site, 7601 Skidaway Road, Savannah, GA 31406. Phone 353-3023.

Skidaway Island

[Fig. 6] Skidaway Island, an interior barrier island fronted by Wassaw Island, is home to Skidaway Island State Park, the world-renowned Skidaway Institute of Oceanography and the University of Georgia's Marine Extension Center, and the largest coastal residential development in the Savannah area called The Landings. Though extensively developed by the Union Camp Corporation, the island today has one of the best state parks in Georgia, with two breathtakingly beautiful nature trails and a full complement of facilities. The Marine Extension Center has the best aquariums in the Savannah area and an excellent nature trail that follows Skidaway Narrows.

The 6,300-acre Pleistocene island is defined by the Wilmington River to the north, Skidaway Narrows to the west, the Vernon River to the south, and Romerly Marsh and Wassaw Island to the east. High ground on the island is roughly 8 miles long by 3 miles wide. Skidaway has had many different spellings throughout history. Some believe Oglethorpe named Skidaway in honor of his Indian friend Tomochichi's wife, who was called Scenawki.

Older than Wassaw, Skidaway is one link in Georgia's Pleistocene barrier island chain that would have been oceanfront property at some stage approximately 40,000 years ago during the last Ice Age. With the melting of the glacial ice and the rise in sea level, Skidaway's younger sister Wassaw came into being approximately 5,000 years ago. The older, Pleistocene islands like Skidaway tend to be flatter with well-developed soils, whereas the younger, Holocene islands like Wassaw have many dune ridges and poor soils.

Skidaway, with its rich marsh filled with oysters, mussels, clams, and whelks, had long been a hunting and ceremonial ground for Timucua Indians that lived in the area. Archaeologists have found 56 sites on the island with evidence that Indians used the island at least 4,000 years before General Oglethorpe sailed up the Savannah River. Three ceremonial shell rings, dating back to 1750 B.C., have been found on the island. These rings are a type of New World pyramid and fewer than 20 of them have been discovered, all in the southeastern United States except for one in Ecuador. The shell rings are perfectly symmetrical and uniform in height and thickness of wall. The interior centers of the rings were kept very clean and any debris found in them were left behind by later groups. The Timucua were targets of mission activities by the Spanish in the 1630s, and became extinct by the 1760s from European plagues and English-sponsored slaving. Paleontologists have also found on the island the fossils of Georgia's megafauna, such as mastodons, mammoths, giant sloths, and native horses, which became extinct five to ten thousand years ago for reasons unclear today.

Oglethorpe assigned five families and six single men to Skidaway Island, and they built a small fort at the northern end of the island (later a fort would be built at the southern end of the island as well). The fort commanded the river, with one carriage gun and four swivel guns. Methodist founder John Wesley visited the area in 1736. Despite attempts to gain a foothold, by 1740, the island was abandoned when the pioneers were unsuccessful in farming the infertile soil. The next period of settlement was from 1754 to 1771, when 29 grants of land on Skidaway were issued to settlers who were to be more successful. An early grantee was John Milledge, who established the plantation Modena, which is believed to be named for the Italian town that was the seat of the silk culture, an early industry on the Georgia coast. His son, John Jr., became a U.S. representative and senator, governor of Georgia, and founder of the University of Georgia, then called Franklin College. Modena Plantation survived until the mid-1800s, and today is the site of the Skidaway Institute of Oceanography and University of Georgia's Marine Extension Center. The Roebling family, whose great great grandfather engineered and built the Brooklyn Bridge, was one of the last owners of property. Locals still call the area Modena.

During the Revolutionary War, Skidaway saw a small skirmish when Patriots attacked and drove off a forage party of British Marines. Between the War for Independence and the Civil War, the area saw relative prosperity, with approximately 2,000 inhabitants and plantations producing cotton, indigo, corn, cattle, and hogs. During the Civil War, earthen batteries were established on the island to defend the southerners from northern attacks and the 4th Georgia Battery was posted here. (A battery can be toured on the Big Ferry Interpretive Trail at Skidaway Island State Park). With the success of the Union blockade in 1862, Skidaway was abandoned, and when the South lost the war and slavery was abolished, the plantations fell into ruin.

Black freedmen were the next to try their luck on Skidaway. These former slaves were assisted by the Freedman's Bureau and Benedictine monks, the latter who established a monastery and school for black children near Priest's Landing on the eastern side of the island. (Priest's Landing is located at the end of Osca Road off of McWhorter Road.) A tidal wave in 1889 ruined the freshwater supply and farming failed from infertile soil and Skidaway was abandoned again. During Prohibition of the early 1900s, Skidaway became a prime bootlegging site because of its isolation. An abandoned still from this era is founded at Skidaway State Park on the Big Ferry Interpretive Trail.

In the war-torn, defeated rebel states, southerners had only their property and natural resources to climb out of poverty. The industrialized North had the financial and political advantage over its impoverished southern neighbors and used it across the South. Skidaway was no exception, and various northern interests gained control of the island in the late nineteenth and early twentieth centuries. The largest of these, Union Camp (then called Union Bag and Paper Corporation) consolidated its holdings and used Skidaway for pulpwood production in the 1940s. By 1964, Union Camp had designs to develop residential property on the island, but Skidaway lacked a bridge that would provide easy access for cars. Union Camp offered to donate 500 acres to the state if Georgia would build a bridge to the island. Nothing came of this offer until 1967, when Union Camp donated 500 acres that became the site of the University of Georgia's Marine Extension Center and the Skidaway Institute of Oceanography. The bridge was built in 1971, and Union Camp subsequently developed the gated, residential golf community called The Landings, which today features six 18-hole golf courses.

SKIDAWAY ISLAND STATE PARK

[Fig. 6(5)] This state park has it all, including a swimming pool. But more important are the natural communities that grace the 533-acre tract, best viewed by hiking or biking the 1-mile Sandpiper Nature Trail or the 3-mile Big Ferry Interpretive Trail. The park, along with the 500 acres that the University of Georgia's Marine Institute of Oceanography sits on, was given to the state by Union Camp Corporation, which owned much of the island and wanted a bridge built to the island so it could develop The Landings. The property was transferred in 1967, the bridge was built in 1971, and Skidaway Island State Park was officially opened in 1975. Today, it is one of the finest parks in the state system. The park is on the Colonial Coast Birding Trail established by the Georgia Department of Natural Resources.

Herons frequent the marshes of Skidaway Island State Park.

The park borders Skidaway Narrows, which once was a narrow, shallow tidal creek. In 1905, the U.S. Army Corps of Engineers first dredged the channel and eventually made it part of the Atlantic Intracoastal Waterway. The park consists of maritime forests, tidal creeks, freshwater sloughs, and salt marsh. Trees you will find here are old live oaks with tremendous growths of Spanish moss, cabbage palms, longleaf pines, magnolias, red bays, and other species. The salt marshes consist of *Spartina* species and needlerush, with fiddler crabs and marsh snails in abundance.

The park has 88 pull-through campsites with water and electrical hookups. Elevated tent pads with grills and tables are also provided. Picnickers have the choice of five covered shelters on 10 acres. Two restrooms are located here along with playgrounds for children. A group shelter is available for rent, with a capacity of 150 people. It comes with a range, refrigerator, bathrooms, grill, and tables and chairs. An outside oyster-cooking shed is available to rent. A public boat ramp is found on the south side of the Diamond Causeway bridge where it crosses Skidaway Narrows before you reach the park.

Directions: Located 6 miles southeast of Savannah on the Diamond Causeway on Skidaway Island. Exit from I-95 at Exit 16/94. Drive 12 miles toward Savannah. Turn right onto Montgomery Cross Road and proceed 1.4 miles to Whitfield Avenue. Turn right onto Whitfield Avenue. This becomes Diamond Causeway. Proceed 5 miles to entrance of the park.

Activities: Nature hiking, biking, camping (primitive, intermediate, recreational vehicle), interpretive programs, swimming, picnicking, historic touring.

Facilities: Museum, bookstore, bathrooms, hiking trails, handicapped-accessible facilities, boat ramp, picnic area.

Dates: Open 7 days a week 7–10.

Fees: $2 parking fee. Additional fees for camping.

Closest town: Savannah.

For more information: Skidaway Island State Park, 52 Diamond Causeway, Savannah, GA 31411-1102. Phone 598-2300. Reservations phone (800) 864-7275.

HIKING TRAILS AT SKIDAWAY STATE PARK

Two trails are featured at Skidaway: the 1-mile Sandpiper Nature Trail and the 3-mile Big Ferry Nature Trail. The Sandpiper Nature Trail is for hiking and viewing the marsh ecosystem; the Big Ferry Nature Trail is for learning about maritime forest and Skidaway's human history.

THE SANDPIPER NATURE TRAIL

The Sandpiper Nature Trail is easily hiked, with a boardwalk that extends out into the marsh. Here during low tide you will see countless fiddler crabs, looking from above like a miniature herd of wildebeests, stampeding through the marsh and salt pan. At least four kinds of small land-preferring crabs are easily found in marsh: sand fiddlers or red-backed crabs (*Uca pugilator*), mud fiddlers or blue fiddlers (*Uca pugnax*), brown square-backed crabs (*Sesarma cinereum*), and purple square-backed crabs (*Sesarma reticulatum*). Square-backed crabs are also known as wharf crabs.

Fiddler crabs are recognized by their one large claw. This claw is used by the male in defense and attracting a mate. Females lack the large claw. The sand fiddler, as its name suggests, prefers sandy habitat or flats near the marsh where it can strain out bits of food from the detritus. The sand fiddler is identified by its whiter carapace (the mud fiddler carapace is brown) with conspicuous pink and purple patches. Mud fiddlers prefer muddy marshy habitat. Neither lives in the tall streamside marsh grass area: This is the preferred habitat of the square-backed crabs.

These crabs are perhaps the most numerous creatures in the marsh and are an important link in the coastal food chain, consuming diatoms, algae, and decaying *Spartina* and becoming themselves food for higher level animals such as birds, fish, and mammals.

The Sandpiper Nature Trail is a good place to see wading birds in the marsh, such as herons and egrets. The shy clapper rail or marsh hen is also found here. Osprey, or "fish hawks," are often seen cruising the waterway looking for prey. Confederate earthwork fortifications are a feature of the trail.

Trail: The 1-mile trail begins and ends near the swimming pool and Visitor Center Park Office.

BIG FERRY NATURE TRAIL

This is one of the best trails on the Georgia coast. A 3-mile loop takes hikers through beautiful pine and maritime forest, across freshwater sloughs, past Prohibition-era liquor stills, and to a Civil War mortar battery before looping back past an observation tower to the original Skidaway causeway. You can bike the trail, but only skilled cyclists equipped with a mountain bike should attempt it. Insect repellant is very recommended. The trailhead is marked by a sign located near a gate on the left past the picnic area. Although the natural communities are second growth, the area is well worth your time

The first part of the trail is the Big Ferry Causeway, which once served as the main road on the island. Where the road terminates at the northern end of the island was the location of a ferry that carried passengers across Skidaway Narrows to Savannah. Man-made freshwater ditches or sloughs on both sides of the road support freshwater vegetation and are an important fresh water source for wildlife on the island. Alligators are frequently found in the slough.

The trail leaves the causeway and crosses a natural freshwater slough. Here you may witness wading birds or hear the splash of shy frogs. As you hike on, notice how the forest changes from older pine to live oak and red cedar. Woodpeckers are found in the pine forest, utilizing the old snags that park managers have left to succumb to natural causes. These old, decaying trees are important feeding and nesting sites for a variety of woodpeckers and other birds, and as the tree dies and falls to the ground, it helps enrich the soil. Found near the trail is the state flower, the Cherokee rose (*Rosa laevigata*), which is not a native species but nonetheless has managed to become established here. Magnolia and sweetgum are also found in the forest, adding to its diversity. Growing out of the sandy soil is a live oak forest with many stately, beautiful trees draped with Spanish moss. The emerald green resurrection fern (*Polypodium polypodioides*) grows on the trunks and branches of live oaks as well. When the weather is extremely dry, the fern's leaves dry and curl up. After a rain, the ferns earn their name by coming alive with color. The understory is classic maritime forest, with saw palmettos indicating high and dry ground. The saw palmetto (*Serenoa repens*) gets its name from its toothed stem. White-tailed deer are a frequent sight on the trail.

Farther along the trail, hikers come to the remains of a liquor still. Moonshining was a popular and lucrative activity on the island in the 1910s and 1920s. Operators could easily hide their activities and transport their product to boats hidden in the marsh. Moonshiners would take corn or grain, ferment it, and then heat it up in a boiler, causing alcohol to be vaporized out and into the coils of the receiver. According to park records, moonshining continued in the area up until the 1970s and approximately 30 former still sites are known in the park.

A short distance from the still hikers find shell middens—or deposits—left by Indians who hunted and lived on the island. Harvested with relative ease, the oysters, mussels, crabs, and fish of the marsh provided important sustenance to the Indians. The middens are frequently recognized by the cedar trees found growing on top of them. Cedars like the limey soil created by decaying oyster shells.

At the farthest point on the trail are the earthworks of a Civil War fort believed to be built by slaves. To the right is a mortar battery. The fort was abandoned in March 1862 when officers determined that it was too isolated and incapable of resisting a Union assault.

Returning, hikers are refreshed by views of the salt flats, salt marsh, and Skidaway Narrows. An observation platform gives hikers views of the entire area. Hikers return to the trailhead by the old causeway.

UNIVERSITY OF GEORGIA MARINE EXTENSION CENTER AND SKIDAWAY INSTITUTE OF OCEANOGRAPHY

[Fig. 6(6)] This site on Skidaway consists of two parts: the open-to-the-public University of Georgia Marine Extension Center and the open-to-the-public-with-reservations Skidaway Institute of Oceanography, both of which share a 691-acre campus dedicated to providing an understanding of Georgia's ecologically valuable coast.

The Marine Extension Center, located on a bluff overlooking Skidaway Narrows, is open to the public and well worth your time. The best public saltwater aquarium in the state is housed in the center, along with educational exhibits, an educational sales shop, and public restrooms. Outside the building is a nature trail that winds through a maritime forest that overlooks the water. Picnic tables are found here and the public is allowed to stop, eat a lunch, and take in the marsh views.

Inside the red brick building, 14 aquariums holding almost 10,000 gallons of brackish water feature species native to the Georgia coast and are a good starting place to learn some of the creatures one may encounter in nearby waters. In fact, most of the fish have been caught in local waterways, many aboard the University of Georgia trawler *Bull Dog*. Some of the more popular species are a loggerhead turtle, longnose gar, nurse shark, lookdown fish, and spiny lobster. Also on display are many impressive fossils, including mammoths and extinct whales. Shark teeth fascinate impressionable youngsters.

The Jay Wolf Nature Trail is approximately 1 mile long if one hikes the long loop and half that length if one takes the short trail. It begins behind the aquarium and follows along the Skidaway River before turning back and finishing at the parking lot. The forest is not a true climax maritime forest, due to the disturbance the land experienced when the area consisted of plantations. Notice barbwire used to fence in cattle and hogs that were raised in the area. However, the trail is marked well and helps the novice learn major floral species, including laurel cherry (*Prunus caroliniana*), sugarberry (*Celtis laevigata*), live oak (*Quercus virginiana*), cabbage palm (*Sabal palmetto*), laurel oak (*Quercus laurifolia*), and sweetgum (*Liquidambar styraciflua*). Other species noted are Spanish bayonet or yucca, red mulberry, beautyberry, muscadine, and saw palmetto. Oyster middens, deposited by Indians who hunted and fished on Skidaway, are also evident. More modern structures built by early colonists are also found on the property.

Southern red cedar is an alkaline-loving coastal relative of the Eastern red cedar, so it is found growing where oyster middens are part of the soil. When oyster shells break down, they release lime into the normally acid soil, lowering the pH and creating the necessary chemistry for the red cedar.

The Skidaway Institute of Oceanography came into existence in the late 1960s due to a donation of land from Union Camp Corporation and the strong interest from scientists at the University of Georgia in creating an educational arm to study the natural processes of the coast and ocean. The University of Georgia's Marine Sciences Program was established in 1976 and designated a school in 1992. The Marine Sciences Program is responsible for the coordination and management of the Marine Institute, the Marine Extension Service, the Georgia Sea Grant College Program, and the Department of Marine Sciences. The Marine Institute, located on Sapelo Island, was established in 1953 at the invitation of R.J. Reynolds, the multimillionaire owner of Reynolds Tobacco Company, who owned Sapelo Island from 1933 until his death in 1965. Research on Sapelo has centered mainly on basic marsh ecology, examining the factors regulating the metabolism of the salt marsh ecosystem and providing an understanding of energy flow and cycling of minerals and nutrients though the marshes and nearby ocean.

The Marine Extension Service helps to solve problems related to the state's marine resources. The Marine Resources Center on Skidaway is the major marine education facility for schools and colleges in the state. The educational center's facilities include laboratories, touch tanks, a teaching aquarium, a museum, a dormitory, a cafeteria, a library, an audio-visual room, and a distance-learning classroom. The educational staff provides programs for school groups from elementary to college level, as well as adults, teachers, and other groups that have an interest in learning about the coast. Scheduled groups can use one of the University of Georgia's research vessels to tour the marsh, or study on the grounds that serve as an outdoor classroom or laboratory with nearly 700 acres of coastal forest, along with 1,000 acres of salt marsh and 18 acres of freshwater ponds. Visits range from an hour or two to a full-week program for a complete unit on marine science. Programs range from historical studies to trips to Wassaw Island. The programs are popular so reservations must be made well in advance.

An additional extension station is found in Brunswick, where specialists monitor and support commercial fishing and seafood processing industries.

The Georgia Sea Grant College Program, established in 1971, is part of the National Sea Grant College Program. Sea Grant promotes the wise use of marine resources through a coordinated program of research, education, and advisory services. Because of excellence in these areas, the University of Georgia earned Sea Grant College status in 1980, becoming only the 15th educational institution in the country to attain that rank.

Trail: Jay Wolf Nature Trail, 1-mile loop.

Directions: Located 6 miles southeast of Savannah on the Diamond Causeway on Skidaway Island. Exit from I-95 at Exit 16/94. Drive 12 miles toward Savannah. Turn right onto Montgomery Cross Road and proceed 1.4 miles to Whitfield Avenue. Turn right onto Whitfield Avenue. This becomes Diamond Causeway. Look for signs to the Skidaway Marine Extension Center. Proceed to McWhorter Drive. Follow McWhorter to the left to the entrance to the aquarium.

Activities: Aquarium, exhibits, nature hiking, picnicking, field trips. Special events and programs are scheduled at the Marine Extension Service. Call ahead for details.

Facilities: Aquarium, bookstore, bathrooms, hiking trail, handicapped accessible facilities, picnic area.

Dates: Open Monday through Friday from 9–4, Saturday noon–5. Closed on major holidays.

Fees: There is a small fee to tour the aquarium or attend special educational programs. Nature trail is free.

Closest town: Savannah.

For more information: The University of Georgia, Marine Extension Service, 30 Ocean Science Circle, Savannah, GA 31411. Phone 598-2496.

CABBAGE PALM
(Sabal palmetto)
Young trees of this southeastern palm tree have a thatched skirt of crisscrossing dead leaf stalks.

Savannah River and Tributaries

The Savannah River is an alluvial stream, which means its headwaters originate in the Georgia mountains and Piedmont. (The only other alluvial river on the Georgia coast is the Altamaha. The rest are essentially blackwater rivers or tidewater rivers.) The river is famous for its fossil oysterbeds located upstream. Technically, the Savannah River is a 300-mile-long river originating near Hartwell, Georgia at the confluence of the Tugaloo and Seneca rivers in the Piedmont. But the headwaters of these streams are in the Blue Ridge Mountains of Georgia, North Carolina, and South Carolina. The Savannah River drains a surface area of more than 10,500 square miles, of which approximately 5,800 are in Georgia, 4,500 are in South Carolina, and 175 are in North Carolina.

The Savannah River has two characters: the impounded alluvial Piedmont stream north of Augusta, and the natural flowing Coastal Plain river south of Augusta. The character of the mountain stream north of Augusta is forever obliterated by many hydroelectric dams, which creates a river that's more like a lake in most stretches. Eight miles below Augusta, the river meets its final dam before being left to its own devices in the Coastal Plain of Georgia. This lower portion to Interstate 95 near the City of Savannah is deeper and calmer, and canoeists are treated to a more pristine environment, with oxbow lakes, river swamps, and bottomland forests.

Here nature lovers will find typical river swamp species including canopy trees such as baldcypress, swamp blackgum, tupelo, overcup oak, water hickory, and green ash, and understory flora such as swamp dogwood, swamp privet, and swamp palm. Fauna found along the Savannah River include muskrat, otter, beaver, mink, opossum, raccoon, fox, skunks, and white-tailed deer. A diversity of reptiles and amphibians is encountered including poisonous snakes such as eastern cottonmouths, southern copperheads, and rattlesnakes.

Legions of anglers were once attracted by the abundant populations of striped bass that were found in the Savannah River, the best such fishery in Georgia and South Carolina. But intrusions of salt water from dredging to increase the river's depth, along with the Back River tide gate, increased salinity levels that wiped out 95 percent of the fish's eggs. Officials stopped using the tide gate, and striped bass populations are in recovery.

As colonists spread out in America, they frequently sailed upriver to the interior looking for a high (and thus dry) bluff to build a settlement. Georgia was no exception. In 1733, Gen. James Edward Oglethorpe first established Savannah on Yamacraw Bluff on the Savannah River. The river is known as having the highest bluffs of any Georgia river. One year later, German Lutherans seeking religious freedom sailed 30 miles up the river to establish the town of Ebenezer. In 1736, a fort was established farther up the river at Augusta, which later developed into one of Georgia's major cities. The first eight counties established in the original Georgia Constitution of 1777 reflect this pattern of development, with four on the coast (Chatham, Liberty, Glynn, and Camden) and four upriver from Savannah along the river (Effingham, Burke, Richmond, and Wilkes). The river also became important as a source of cheap energy, and cities were established on rivers along Georgia's fall line (Columbus, Macon, and Augusta) to harness their power for emerging industries.

TUCKASSEE KING LANDING

[Fig. 3(1)] Tuckassee King Landing, in Effingham County 3 miles east of Clyo on 119, is a popular access site to the Savannah River, and features an unusual natural area. Tuckassee King was named for a Yuchi Indian chief from a nearby village and was the first county seat of Effingham County. Here the early Baptists in coastal Georgia first organized, and a short distance away is an exact replica of the first Baptist church in Georgia. The boat ramp is located on a creek 200 yards from the Savannah River beside a picturesque mesic (moist) bluff approximately 75 to 100 feet high. A mesic bluff is a flat-top geological feature formed by river erosion over many years. Due to the elevation, moisture content of the soil, and northern (cooler) orientation, a forest may develop with herbs, shrubs, and trees that are more characteristic of the mountainous region of Georgia. Near Tuckassee King Landing, an unusual variety of plants are found including liverworts, mosses, and wild ginger. Legendary naturalist William Bartram traveled through the region in 1775-1776 and noted the strange assemblage of plants.

EBENEZER CREEK

[Fig. 3] In Effingham County near the historic community of New Ebenezer is Ebenezer Creek, a tributary of the Savannah River. Ebenezer Creek, a backwater stream, is one of only three of Georgia's designated Wild and Scenic Rivers, and the only one on the coast, and is certainly a natural treasure. Also designated a National Natural Landmark by the National Park Service, the river swamp consists of unusual virgin dwarfed baldcypress, with huge swollen buttresses from 8 to 12 feet wide, supporting unusually small diameter tree trunks. Some of these trees are estimated to be more than 1,000 years old. The tupelo gum exhibit unusual counterclockwise twisting, which remains a scientific mystery as to the cause. Eight miles of the tributary creek, according to Dr. Charles Wharton, are a type of elongate lake, created by the damming effect of natural levees and water levels of the Savannah River.

When the Savannah River rises to a particular height during seasonal floods and heavy rains, it backs up water in the Ebenezer tributary, not unlike the hydrologic system in coastal marsh areas when tides back water up the channels of tidal creeks and rivers. This elongate lake rarely goes dry, but water levels may fluctuate as much as 8 feet and can remain high for long periods of time, Wharton writes. Low nutrient input, unusually long periods of high water levels, and a lack of floodplain to provide nutrients may cause dwarfing, and long periods of deep inundation with low oxygen levels may be responsible for the enormous buttresses. Scientists believe the swollen buttresses are an adaptation that provides inundated trees with increased surface area for oxygen intake.

Savannah's Harbor and Cargo Ships

The Port of Savannah is the nation's 10th busiest container ship port, and is directly or indirectly responsible for about 70,000 jobs, according to the Ports Authority. In 1998, approximately 1,500 container ships moved close to 9 million tons of goods and materials through the port.

The Savannah River, which normally is 24 feet deep, has experienced three major dredgings with a fourth proposed for the future. Each dredging has affected the fresh water-salt water composition of the river, impacting the flora and fauna of surrounding marshes. In 1896, the 24-foot-deep river channel was dredged and most obstructions were removed, including Civil War wrecks and blockade structures. In 1945, the Georgia Ports Authority was formed and the river was dredged to 38 feet. In 1994, the channel was deepened to 42 feet. Now plans are in the works to deepen it even more to 48 feet, or twice its normal depth.

Container ships became prevalent in the 1960s, and since then they have grown in size. In essence, the cargo ships stack the trailer part or "container" of a semitrailer truck that one sees on the highway. A 20-foot container unit, or TEU, is the industry term that refers to a standard 20-foot-long container. In the 1960s, the ships were smaller, with TEUs of 600 to 1,000, and could easily navigate the current depths of the Savannah River. But as worldwide trade has grown, so has the size of container ships, with current behemoths carrying 6,000 TEUs, or the equivalent of 6,000 semitrailers. These huge ships, longer than a 100-story building and as wide as a 14-story building, require a deeper harbor to land their cargo.

Impoundments upstream from the Savannah River have altered and interrupted the natural hydrologic patterns of Ebenezer, causing concern for the health of the backwater stream. The U.S. Army Corps of Engineers has experimented with altering water release patterns from J. Strom Thurmond Dam near Augusta to see if high-flow releases could help the swamp. The unusual swamp has a low-nutrient natural system that makes it more sensitive to nuisance aquatic plant growth, which negatively affects water quality. Florida exotic plants—alligator weed and water hyacinth—have recently invaded the swamp and become a nuisance to the native species.

The creek is traditionally an excellent spot for fishing for striped bass, which spawn here, and canoeists will witness turtles, snakes, alligators, and many species of birds including woodpeckers, wading birds, and vultures. Insects abound here as well, so bring your repellant. Botanically, the creek supports many aquatic species including pennywort, parrot feather, carnivorous bladderwort, floating mosquito fern, and duckweed. The mosquito fern forms large floating mats and during the winter, its leaves turn bright red. The baldcypress and water tupelo host epiphytes such as Spanish moss, resurrection fern, greenfly orchid, and the parasitic mistletoe, which is much more obvious in wintertime.

The ruins of ancient railroad bridge pilings near the southern end stand in pairs as testament to the water-resistant qualities of cypress. Water tupelo near this section stand over 100 feet tall, making a hardwood cathedral.

Huge cargo ships are frequent sights on the lower Savannah River.

Canoeists who don't mind paddling upstream can access the backwater stream at Ebenezer Landing, at the end of GA 275 near New Ebenezer. Paddle upstream in the Savannah River, navigating into the first tributary on the left to access Ebenezer Creek. Suggested downstream day trips on Ebenezer include the following: GA 119 to Logs Landing (off GA 21, 0.5 mile on a dirt road at the Georgia historical marker of Old Ebenezer Town), 5 miles, preferable in times of high water during winter and early spring. Logs Landing to Long Bridge (GA 953, 1.2 miles northwest of GA 275), 4 miles, preferable during high water but also navigable in moderate water. Long Bridge to Ebenezer Landing at the Savannah River at the end of GA 275 near New Ebenezer, 5.5 miles. Paddle upstream for about 0.5 mile to view virgin cypress swamp before heading downstream to Savannah River.

In 1734, Lutherans escaping religious persecution in Salzburg, Austria arrived in the 1-year-old town of Savannah looking for a new home. Gen. James Edward Oglethorpe directed the group approximately 30 miles up the Savannah River to Ebenezer Creek. The Germans traveled another 6 miles up the creek where they established the town of Ebenezer. After two years of struggle at this location, they relocated back downstream to the Savannah River, where they established the settlement of New Ebenezer (*see* New Ebenezer, page 70).

Ebenezer was the historic setting of an infamous Civil War incident. During Sherman's March to the Sea campaign for Savannah, Federal troops under Union Gen. Jefferson C. Davis filed across Ebenezer Creek on December 8, 1864, destroying their pontoon bridge behind them. This action stranded on the other side of the river more than 600 slaves that have been following the army column. With Confederate cavalry under Wheeler approaching, many slaves panicked and drowned as they tried to flee by attempting to cross the creek.

Just past Interstate 95, the canoeist encounters the Savannah National Wildlife Refuge. The river cuts several channels to the east, working its way through freshwater marsh that historically served as rice plantations in antebellum Georgia. Nearby on the western bank of the river north of the Highway 17 bridge is the old plantation site of Mulberry Grove, granted to Nathanael Greene in appreciation for his service during the Revolutionary War. Eli Whitney, who was tutor of the Greene children, invented the cotton gin here in 1793.

The wildlife refuge serves as a vital haven for many species of waterfowl during the winter. Alligators, snakes, and turtles are very common in the refuge, and during spring and early summer, the bellows of many large alligators can be heard as they perform their ancient mating rituals. The wildlife refuge has many meanders, cuts, and canals and can be fruitfully explored for days (see Savannah Wildlife Refuge, page 73).

Below Savannah, the river picks up more of the characteristics of a tidal river, with more treacherous currents, brackish water, and coastal marsh surroundings. Canoeists will encounter heavy commercial maritime traffic, with huge ocean barges carrying their cargo up to the Port of Savannah. Canoeists need to think and prepare carefully before paddling this stretch to the ocean.

The best resource for canoeing and appreciating Georgia's coastal rivers is *A Paddler's Guide to Southern Georgia*, by Bob Sehlinger and Don Otey. This book lists access points, rates the quality of the canoeing, and describes natural features found on Georgia's rivers.

Suggested canoe trips on the Savannah River: Tuckassee King Landing (3 miles northeast of Clyo) to Ebenezer Landing (north end of Highway 275), 22 miles. Ebenezer Landing (north end of Highway 275) to Purysburg Landing, South Carolina, 13 miles. Purysburg Landing, South Carolina to US 17 bridge,16.5 miles.

▨ NEW EBENEZER

[Fig. 3(2)] The historic community of New Ebenezer, founded in 1736 on the high bluff overlooking the Savannah River 30 miles upstream from Savannah, features the oldest public building in Georgia in a beautifully serene coastal setting of old cypress, oaks, and flame azalea. Today, those appreciating American, Georgian, Lutheran, and German history can tour Jerusalem Lutheran Church, the old cemetery, and the Georgia Salzburger Society Museum, and learn more about the failures and successes of this colonial town near the wilderness of the Georgia coast. The church is the oldest facility in America with an active congregation. New Ebenezer started Georgia's first public school in 1734 and the first orphanage in 1737.

The industrious Protestant Germans fled Salzburg, Austria in 1734 in search of religious freedom. After consulting with Gen. James Edward Oglethorpe in Savannah, they decided to establish their colony of Ebenezer approximately six miles up Ebenezer creek. Disease and other hardships at that site caused them to relocate to New Ebenezer. Laid out by Noble Jones of Wormslow Plantation in a manner similar to Savannah, this community was much more successful, growing to more than 1,600 residents. Each Salzburger family was given a white mulberry tree from the Trustees' Garden in Savannah, an essential plant in the production of silk. Silk is a naturally produced thread that was a much-valued commodity in colonial times. Many had high hopes for establishing a lucrative silk industry in the New World. However, many difficulties squashed these hopes, except at New Ebenezer, where the silk culture thrived, becoming a good source of income for the Lutherans and earning the town the appellation of "Silk Capital."

All that remains from the original community is the Jerusalem Lutheran Church, the cemetery, and one home. The Jerusalem Lutheran Church, built in 1769, is the second church built on the spot. The 21-inch thick walls consist of handmade brick created from Georgia clay fired in a nearby kiln and carried by women and children to the church site. Some bricks on the front of the building reportedly bear the fingerprints of the Salzburger children. Notice the swan on the steeple, Martin Luther's religious symbol. The Salzburgers of Bavaria who founded the community adopted this symbol. The swan comes from a legend. John Huss, an early reformer of the church, was about to be burned at the stake when he made this statement: "You may burn this goose but out of these ashes will be a swan."

During the Revolutionary War, the British under Col. Archibald Campbell captured the town, set fire to many of the buildings, seized the Salzburgers' possessions, and ruined their gardens. They used Ebenezer as a holding center for prisoners, and the church as a hospital, a storehouse, and then a horse stable. In 1782, the Patriots under Gen. Anthony Wayne drove the British out and in July 1782, the Georgia Legislature met in the church. After the Revolutionary War, with the town in ruins, most of the Salzburger families stayed away.

Today, much of the grounds and buildings have been restored and are in use as an active museum, church, and cemetery. The two-story brick museum, built in 1971, is modeled after the first orphanage and sits on the original site. Inside are many relics from the colonial period. Nearby, the 1755 Salzburger house depicts the type of structure built by early settlers. The cemetery across the street contains a monument to Israel Christian Gronau and John Martin Bolzius, the ministers who led the first Lutherans to Ebenezer. Their actual burial site remains a mystery. A monument near the church is to John Adam Treutlen, an original Salzburger colonist and American patriot who became the first governor of Georgia, only to be murdered in 1782 by Tories near Orangeburg district, South Carolina.

Salzburger descendants return every year on the anniversary of their ancestors' arrival in Georgia on March 12 for a big family reunion that features a religious service and presentations on the history of the colonists. A Family Retreat and Conference Center has been built to reflect the environment of the eighteenth century and is available to church groups, family reunions, school groups, and Scouts. A nature trail connects to the retreat center and British fortifications are found on the grounds.

Directions: From Savannah, exit I-95 at Exit 19/109. Take GA 21 north to GA 275 between Rincon and Springfield. Turn right on GA 275 and proceed approximately 6 miles. New Ebenezer is on the Savannah River at the dead end of GA 275.

Activities: Historic touring, nature hiking, religious services. Special events occur every year on the anniversary of Salzburgers' arrival. Interpretive programs, lodging, and tours available by prior arrangement. Call ahead for details.

Facilities: Georgia Salzburger Society Museum, Jerusalem Lutheran Church, family retreat center, bathrooms, hiking trail, handicapped-accessible facilities, nearby boat ramp.

Savannah National Wildlife Refuge

The Savannah National Wildlife Refuge, the largest federally protected tract of land on the Georgia coast, stretches approximately 20 miles along the Savannah River and consists of 26,349 acres of freshwater marshes, tidal rivers and creeks, and bottomland hardwoods.

Legend:
- Forest
- Impoundments
- Marsh
- Dike
- Diversion Canal
- Laurel Hill Wildlife Drive

Entire Savannah National Wildlife Refuge Area

Ref: Department of the Interior

Dates: Museum open Wednesday, Saturday, and Sunday 3–5. Church service 11 a.m. Sunday. Reservations needed for Family Retreat and Conference Center.

Fees: Museum: donations appreciated. Contact center for rental rates.

Closest town: Rincon.

For more information: 2887 Ebenezer Road, Rincon, GA 31326. Email: retreat@newebenezer.org Phone 754-9242.

Savannah National Wildlife Refuge

[Fig. 8, Fig. 5(1)] The Savannah National Wildlife Refuge, one of the best bird-watching spots in Georgia, is the single largest federally protected tract of land on the Georgia coast, stretching 20 miles along the Savannah River and consisting of 26,349 acres of freshwater marshes, tidal rivers and creeks, and bottomland habitat. (Cumberland Island is second with approximately 23,000 acres.) The refuge is one of the most important wildlife preserves on the East Coast, and during migratory periods is visited by 21 species of warblers and thousands of ducks of more than 13 species, including the rarely seen cinnamon teal, Eurasian widgeon, and fulvous whistling duck.

Located north of Savannah, the refuge straddles the Georgia-South Carolina state line where the Savannah River splits into separate channels and is fed by freshwater tributaries. As it flows south, the Savannah River splits into three forks below Interstate 95: the easternmost Back River, the centrally flowing Middle River, and the western Front River. The refuge includes the Middle and Back rivers, and the eastern bank of the Front River, which is maintained by Army Corps of Engineers dredging and used as a deep shipping channel for the Port of Savannah. Major travel arteries I-95 and GA 25/SC 170 cross the Savannah National Wildlife Refuge, which is also located across from a large industrial area on the western shore of the Front River.

Easily accessed by the outdoor enthusiast is the 6,000-acre southern portion located near US 17 in South Carolina. Here you find a 4-mile wildlife drive, nature trails, fishing, information, and bathrooms. Approximately 40 miles of intersecting dikes are open to hikers during daylight hours. (Automobiles are allowed only on the wildlife drive.) Biking on the dikes is permitted, but can be difficult if not impossible where the soil is very soft and sandy.

The northern portion of the refuge, known as Argent Swamp, makes up almost half of the refuge and is accessible only by boat. The 12,493-acre hardwood freshwater swamp tract was added in 1976, when The Nature Conservancy acquired a purchase option from Union Camp Corporation, then transferred it to the U.S. Fish and Wildlife Service which bought the land and added it to the Savannah National Wildlife Refuge. Argent Swamp straddles Georgia and South Carolina, and contains baldcypress and tupelo in wet areas and water oak, blackgum, red maple, sycamore, and sweetgum on drier, higher land. The freshwater impoundments attract over 13 species of waterfowl in winter while a variety of wading birds use this area throughout the year. During winter months, thousands of wood ducks are known to roost and forage in the bottomlands and bald eagles are frequently seen cruising over the swamp.

In Georgia, Native Americans built their settlements near rivers, a reliable source of food and water and important for transportation and trade. The area of the wildlife refuge, with navigable waters and abundant game, was no exception, and archeologists have found evidence of Paleo-Indian activity going back 7,000 years. Shell mounds provide evidence that the area was inhabited to various degrees between 5,000 and 1,000 years ago. Other clues reveal that Indians grew maize (or corn) 1,000 years ago in the Savannah National Wildlife Refuge. Unfortunately, like most parts of Georgia, extensive archeology work has yet to be conducted and probably won't be for a long, long time as experts believe most of the evidence is located under the rich muck of the freshwater pools and marsh that serve as sanctuary for many bird species.

In the late 1700s and early 1800s, American colonists believed the area was ideal for growing rice. Slaves and Irishmen cleared the mostly cypress and gum swamps that buffered the river during flooding. At least 13 rice plantations were constructed within the current boundary of the wildlife refuge. Colonists converted bottomland habitat into marshland by constructing impoundments, dikes, and trunks (water-control structures) to control the natural flow of fresh water from the river and tributaries. Across the river from the refuge was Nathanael Greene's Mulberry Grove plantation, where Eli Whitney invented the cotton gin and forever changed the history of the South. Trunks, or rectangular, wooden culverts with flap gates at both ends, were built from naturally decay-resistant cypress and installed under the dikes to control the flow of fresh water between the tidal river and the rice field impoundments. Rice plantations like these, dependent on back-breaking labor from slaves, flourished along freshwater tidal rivers from Georgetown, South Carolina to Brunswick, Georgia. The Civil War effectively ended Southern plantation culture, which struggled to survive after the war but collapsed without the benefit of slaves and with few economic resources to fall back on. The property was eventually purchased in 1927 and made into the Savannah National Wildlife Refuge, the oldest on the Georgia coast.

The well-engineered dikes, built by slaves and Irishmen, remain in place and today are used by U.S. Fish and Wildlife Service managers to benefit wildlife. Approximately 6,000 acres of former fields are maintained in 20 water-controlled impoundments to provide food and safe havens for wading birds during the year as well as migratory waterfowl that arrive during the winter. Because of the abundant avifauna, the refuge is popular with bird watchers, who have recorded 260 species at the refuge. The refuge is an example of man's interference with nature to benefit wildlife. If left alone, the former rice fields would convert to natural freshwater marsh and support smaller numbers of waterfowl and wading birds. Four major kinds of habitat make up the refuge: tidal freshwater marsh, freshwater pools and marsh; hardwood hammocks consisting of oaks and other species; and bottomland consisting of cypress and tupelo gum. Each has its natural complement of flora and fauna. Alligators are plentiful in the freshwater pools, including one whopper well over 12 feet long. More than 100 alligators have been counted in the diversion canal alone. In the spring, the bellowing of males will stop hikers in their tracks. The dike trails are great places to find signs of alligator crossings, with matted down marsh grass on either side and a connecting groove in the sand created by the crawling alligator's tail. It looks like he drew a line in front of your path daring you to cross it. During cooler months, the cold-blooded reptiles are seen on the banks of the canals bordered by dikes warming themselves in the sun. During summer months, they spend most of their time in the water, with just their eyes and noses protruding above the surface.

Also in the pools are abundant frogs and turtles, and snakes. Abundant but not commonly seen are the cottonmouth, brown water snake, banded water snake, mud snake, and rainbow snake. Frogs include the bullfrog, the bronze frog, and the green treefrog. Fish found here include bream, largemouth bass, crappie, gars, and bowfin. The refuge is an excellent place to look for butterflies and wildflowers.

If you love birds you will consider the wildlife refuge to be a natural treasure. Take a pair of binoculars and a bird book. The Savannah Coastal Refuges office has a free brochure that lists bird species found at the national wildlife refuges under its management. The brochure specifies the bird species that are found in the refuges, how common they are, what season they are usually seen, and whether or not they nest there.

Freshwater impoundments contain many plants such as millet, smartweed, and redroot, which are excellent foods for migratory waterfowl that visit the refuge during the winter months. Native plants include cattails, arrow-arum (*Peltandra virginica*), giant cutgrass (*Zizaniopsis milacea*), and golden club (*Orontium aquaticum*). A large, diverse group of bird species can be found nesting here. (A checklist is available from Refuge headquarters.)

Bird-watching is good all year but is best from October through April when temperatures are milder and a greater variety and abundance of waterfowl and other wintering birds are present. Be aware that from December 1 to February 28, entry into the impoundment areas Nos. 1 through 9 north of SC 170 is prohibited to reduce disturbance to wintering waterfowl.

The serenity of the natural scenery is visually disturbed by the ominous look of smokestacks rising from the nearby plants of Savannah's industrial sector. The implied threat has been realized on two fronts: first, unfortunate releases of toxic pollutants into the refuge and second, encroaching salt water from the dredging of the Front River for cargo ships.

Historically, intended and unintended releases of toxins into the Savannah River from nearby industries have polluted the refuge. Eight major industries are located directly opposite the refuge. Before the harmful effects were clearly understood, DDT and other chlorinated hydrocarbons and toxic chemicals worked their way into the food chain, interfering with the success rate of nesting birds. Local industries have periodically footed the bill for cleanups of asphalt and oil spills and other mishaps. Today, with stricter water quality standards, local industry is much more careful with its wastes, and the refuge's water quality is carefully monitored.

The refuge's natural communities are dependent on clean, fresh water. Left alone, the Savannah River is naturally 24 feet deep. But to create a more commercially competitive harbor that can allow new classes of even larger cargo ships to navigate the river, over the years the U.S. Army Corps of Engineers has had to dredge the river to even greater depths. Each year, the U.S. Army Corps of Engineers dredges out 7 million cubic yards of sediment. As this book goes to press, plans were being drawn up to increase the depth from 42 feet to 48 along 26 miles of the Savannah River. This will allow more seawater to back up the river, raising the salinity of the river water. If it gets too salty, fresh water-dependent aquatic flora and fauna of the refuge will die or move away.

To create a kind of "natural" dredge, the U.S. Army Corps of Engineers built a tidal gate to control the Savannah River. The tidal gate was installed on the Back River to block one channel of the Savannah River. This, in turn, was designed to force the river's flow to accelerate through the remaining open channel, which would naturally flush river sediment and thus reduce the expensive need to dredge. As part of the $2.5 million project, the U.S. Army Corps of Engineers decided to build a freshwater diversion canal to insure that the refuge was supplied enough fresh water. Unfortunately, salt water backed up farther than engineers thought it would, to where the southern intake point couldn't be used. The gate was abandoned in 1990, after almost completely wiping out the striped bass fishery of the Savannah River. With the tide gate now inactive, the refuge uses the diversion canal to distribute fresh water to its impoundment system and neighboring private plantations. This helps support the freshwater marsh and pools that the migratory waterfowl are so dependent on every winter.

Directions: From Savannah take US 17A across the Talmadge Bridge. Drive approximately 8 miles until 17A intersects US 17. Turn left and follow US 17 west toward the Savannah Airport. The refuge entrance (Laurel Hill Wildlife Drive) is about 2 miles on the left.

Activities: Bird-watching, wildlife drive, historic touring, nature hiking, biking, fishing, hunting.

Facilities: Hiking trails, bathrooms, exhibit shelter, marked and unmarked trails, wildlife drive.

Dates: Open 7 days a week sunrise to sunset. Closed 2 weeks annually for managed hunts in fall and winter. Portions of refuge close annually to prevent disturbance to nesting, wintering, or migrating birds. The wildlife drive is closed when wheelchair-dependent hunters are permitted on the refuge to hunt deer.

Fees: None.

Closest town: Savannah.

For more information: U.S. Fish and Wildlife Service, Savannah Coastal Refuges, Parkway Business Center, Suite 10, 1000 Business Center Drive, Savannah, GA 31405. Phone 652-4415.

LAUREL HILL WILDLIFE DRIVE

[Fig. 8] This is the most popular and used portion of the Savannah Wildlife Refuge. Here you will see alligators sunning themselves on the banks, long-legged wading birds, deer, turtles, and possibly an otter or other shy creature. Aside from the brick cistern located on the cistern trail, visitors will see few historic artifacts from the area's plantation era. The drive follows a 4-mile route on top of dikes constructed in the late 1700s and early 1800s through four of the rice plantations that were located in the area. The Wildlife Drive has an appropriate surface for a mountain bike. Hikers may want to drive this route and hike on the quieter portions of the refuge.

The drive begins at the entrance to the refuge on the southern side of SC 170 east of the Savannah River. Here you find an exhibit shelter with a map and brochures detailing the drive, parking, and bathrooms. Near the entrance you will notice some beautiful, large live oaks that bordered the Laurel Hill Plantation home. The 400-acre rice plantation was purchased in 1813 by James Hasell Ancrum, who had 150 slaves quartered at a site now occupied by the refuge boathouse across the highway. The only structural remains of the plantation are a few bricks from the foundation of a steam-powered mill located near the site of the main house.

As you proceed on the drive, you will see the reclaimed rice fields and dikes that are now managed for wildlife and waterfowl. Worth examining are the rice field trunks that control the flow of water between the Little Back River and the 2,800-acre impoundment system. These simple mechanisms were vital to the economy of Georgia's coastal plantations. Traditionally, they were made of rot-resistant cypress, but today they are made of cheaper pressure-treated pine. As one brochure states, "in a tidal situation, a more efficient, economical water control device has not been found."

To flood the pools, the gate on the river side is raised while the inner gate remains down. As the tide rises, water flows through the culvert or "trunk" beneath the dike pushing open the inner gate. To maintain a constant water level in the freshwater pools, both gates are lowered and water cannot enter or escape. To drain the pools, the poolside gate is raised while the outer gate remains down. As the tide falls, water from the pool flows into the river, pushing open the outer gate. Flooding or draining cannot be completed during one high or low tide. But during the process, water flow is controlled because one gate remains down and closed by the pressure of water either in the pool or the river.

As the wildlife drive enters the historic property of the former Recess Plantation, you will encounter the cistern trail. Recess Plantation was bounded by Laurel Hill to the north and Moreland Plantation on the south. The cistern, a 7-foot-deep brick structure that collects rainwater, is the only remaining relic from the refuge's plantation past. A 300-foot-long trail leading from the cistern goes through a hardwood hammock, a good place to encounter migratory songbirds such as hermit thrushes, and white-throated and fox sparrows (winter). Not only do you find the usual hardwood hammock flora, but also found here are exotic Chinese parasol trees.

The drive goes by the 5.5-mile-long freshwater diversion canal, a popular site for fishing. Common catches include bream, crappie, and largemouth bass. Wading birds also join in the hunt for food.

As the wildlife drive turns back to SC 170, visitors will see many freshwater pools where alligators make their homes. Some of the pools are maintained at a depth to suit water birds such as wood ducks that nest in boxes supplied by the refuge managers. A lack of suitable nesting cavity sites in older trees (due to logging) in traditional wood duck habitat has spurred many waterfowl refuges to build and install these structures to help prop up populations of the beautiful wood ducks.

Trail: 4-mile wildlife drive.

HIKING AND BIKING TRAILS

Because the northern end of the refuge is swamp, accessible only by boat, the best place for hiking or biking is a 3,000-acre section of the wildlife management area on the southern end of the refuge. Here, hikers can use 40 miles of dikes as a trail system. This is not one big looping trail, but a network of intersecting trails located just north and south of SC 170. The best approach is to use a map and select a section of dikes and head out early in the morning, when birds and wildlife are more active. Motorized traffic is prohibited on all these roadways except for the Laurel Hill Wildlife Drive. For a more peaceful, less crowded hike, choose impoundments Nos. 1 through 9 on the northern side of SC 170. Because these trails follow along freshwater pools, insects can be a tremendous nuisance if you are not protected. Binoculars and a bird identification book are highly recommended.

One route you may want to consider starts near the exit of Laurel Hill Wildlife Drive on the north side of SC 170. From here, walk 2 miles on the eastern side of the freshwater diversion canal. This will take you to the Tupelo Swamp Trail, which is the only opportunity in the refuge for hiking into swamp habitat. Prothonotary warblers nest near this trail. Vernezobre Creek acts as the northern boundary of this area and provides excellent habitat for wildlife.

Biking on the dike trails is a dicier affair. In some places, the path is too sandy for a mountain bike, and depending on the weather, the trail may be too soft and muddy. Where the trail is hard-packed enough, biking can be a great way to view the marsh. Scout the trail before committing to your plans.

Trail: About 40 miles of marked and unmarked hiking trails on the dike system.

FISHING AND HUNTING

Fishing is popular at the refuge. Fishermen catch everything from largemouth bass and bream to more primitive eels and gar. All refuge canals and pools are open to fishing from March 1 to November 30 and tidal creeks are open year round. Bank fishing from the wildlife drive is permitted all year. Kingfisher Pond, located off SC 170 one mile north of the junction of SC 170 and US 17 is also open to fishing year round. The refuge administers deer, feral hog, turkey, and squirrel hunts during the fall and winter. Since the refuge is divided by the states of Georgia and South Carolina, those wishing to hunt in the refuge should familiarize themselves with the area in which they wish to hunt and obtain the appropriate state licenses. Also, as in all wildlife refuges, permits are necessary and are obtained from the Savannah Coastal Refuges Office in Savannah.

BOAT ACCESS

A public boat ramp is found off GA 25 on the Savannah River adjacent to the Houlihan Bridge in Port Wentworth, Georgia. A historical marker across GA 25 from the ramp signifies the importance of GA 25, the oldest road in Georgia, which linked Savannah to Darien. It dates back to 1736 and was laid out with the assistance of General Oglethorpe's Indian friend Tomochichi, the mico of the Yamacraws.

Islands Near Tybee

OATLAND, WHITEMARSH, WILMINGTON AND TALAHI ISLANDS

[Fig. 6, 9] As travelers head east to Tybee Island on US 80 from Thunderbolt or the Island Expressway from downtown Savannah, visitors will cross the Wilmington River, Turner's Creek, and Bull River. On the right and left are the residential communities of Oatland, Whitemarsh, Wilmington, and Talahi islands, built on high ground in the salt marsh. Approximately 16,000 residents call these islands home. Residential construction continues on the islands and gated communities are found along various tidal creeks. As a major residential area, the islands have all the usual commercial businesses that you find anywhere else. If you are on Tybee and need a specific bank, pharmacy, or Happy Meal, Wilmington Island is probably the place to find it.

Located on Wilmington Island is the Savannah Inn and Country Club, built in the 1920s in the Spanish style. A private golf course is located here. A small shrimp fleet docks at Turners Creek Bridge. Wilmington Island Seafood Co-op, a popular fresh seafood market, is found on a short dirt road on the right on the western side of Turner Creek on Johnny Mercer Boulevard after you cross over the bridge. This is a good place to pick up fresh fish, crabs, and other tasty low country edibles.

RESTAURANTS ON WILMINGTON ISLAND

Williams Seafood Restaurant. 8010 E. US 80. In the Savannah area, this is one of the most famous restaurants, which started as a roadside stand selling live and cooked blue crabs in the 1930s. Today, it is popular for fried seafood meals and family friendliness. Lunch and dinner. *Moderate. 897-2219.*

OATLAND ISLAND EDUCATION CENTER

[Fig. 6(2)] Nestled into a mixed maritime forest only 10 minutes from downtown Savannah is an environmental education center that serves as a valuable resource to the state. With 175 acres of pine and maritime forest, salt marsh, freshwater pond, and a dock to the Richardson River, Oatland Island Education Center provides an excellent outdoor classroom where students can learn about the natural communities and processes so important to the Georgia coast. The general public is also welcome to walk the hiking trails that wind through woodland and marsh, leading to exhibits of live animals that are or were native to the area including alligator, fox, bison, black bear, wolf, panther, bobcat, birds of prey, and wading birds. The trail also features a heritage homesite and a barnyard with sheep, cows, chickens, goats, and turkeys.

The center is owned and operated by the Savannah-Chatham County Public School System, and is open to local and out-of-county schools. Some 20,000 public and private schoolchildren use it every year, making the signs along the entrance drive charmingly appropriate: "Slow—Children and Animals in the Road." More than 40 programs are available, including marine and estuarine ecology, invertebrate and botanical studies, freshwater pond study, endangered species, and astronomy. Kindergarten children can learn from an hour-long barn animal program, and more advanced students can use one of the two observatories that house 10- and 16-inch reflector telescopes.

A cabbage palm-lined drive leads to the impressive white-columned, brick main building that serves as headquarters, indoor laboratory, gift shop, and exhibit hall. It was built in 1927 as a retirement home for the Brotherhood of Railroad Conductors, then used as a Public Health Service hospital during World War II. The U.S. Centers for Disease Control and Prevention then used it as a technical development laboratory, and when it was declared surplus in 1973, it was given to the Chatham Board of Education. The picturesque building was used in the movie *The General's Daughter,* starring John Travolta.

An unusual set of whale bones is on display inside the building. They are the skeletal remains of a 50-foot-long fin whale, an endangered species that washed ashore on some rock jetties on Tybee Island in 1989. Hans Neuhauser, a primary investigator of whale strandings at the time, obtained the bones for the education center.

The forests that seem such a permanent part of Oatland Island are actually second growth. In the eighteenth and nineteenth centuries, the area was cleared for a cotton plantation belonging to the McQueen family. The McQueens were made famous in Eugenia Price's novel, *Don Juan McQueen,* and have another island named for them near Fort Pulaski (*see* McQueens Island Nature Trail, page 90). Fortunately, the forests have grown back, and feature natural communities worth examining. Oak, pine, and magnolia are some of the trees you will see, along with cedar, sweetgum, bay, and crape myrtle with Spanish moss. Sawtooth palmetto, yaupon holly, and winged or shining sumac are common plants. One section of forest is carpeted with green ferns, and muscadine grape vines hang in the midstory. The marsh consists of *Spartina* species and the more high-ground-preferring needlerush.

No school system funds are used for animal food, veterinary care, or construction of the habitats. These activities are supported by grants, gifts, and donations. Students volunteering in programs such as the Youth Conservation Corps and Young Adult Conservation Corps built most of the original habitats boardwalks, trails, docks, and observatories.

Directions: Exit I-95 at Exit 17A/99A and proceed to Savannah on I-16. I-16 ends at

Montgomery Street. Go straight to Bay Street where you turn right. Proceed on Bay Street to the President Street Extension. This becomes Island Expressway. Approximately 1 mile after crossing the Wilmington River Bridge, look for signs to Oatland Island Education Center on right. Turn right onto Barley Drive and proceed to the main gate on left.

Activities: Nature hiking, bird-watching, educational exhibits, interpretive programs by prior arrangement, special events called Second Saturdays at Oatland are planned every year. Contact Oatland Island Education Center for changing list of events.

Facilities: Hiking trails, exhibits, study sites, visitor contact station, gift shop, bathrooms.

Dates: Open Monday through Friday 8:30–5, Saturday 10–5.

Fees: Admission is $2 per person.

Closest town: Savannah.

For more information: Oatland Island Education Center, 711 Sandtown Road, Savannah, GA 31410. Phone 897-3773.

OATLAND ISLAND DISCOVERY TRAIL

An hour and a half, comfortable walking shoes, and insect repellant are recommended for fully appreciating this nature walk. This is a chance to not only observe some common native species still found in the wild but also learn about animal species that used to roam the Southeast until they were pushed out by man. It will surprise some people to learn that bison, wolves, and panthers used to be found in Georgia.

Observing the shy animals in their enclosures requires sharp eyes, a quiet approach, and a bit of luck. Beginning at the main building, pick up a trail guide and follow the dirt path to the bird aviary. From there, the trail goes by an alligator exhibit and a panther exhibit before crossing over the marsh on an excellent boardwalk. The 500-foot wooden walkway allows nature lovers a close view of the marsh rarely afforded by boat or road. Look for marsh snails and periwinkles climbing the green stems of *Spartina* grass. Just past the 0.5-mile mark is the bobcat exhibit. After viewing the bobcats, the hiker goes past a fox pen before crossing the main entrance road to the aviaries where southern bald eagles and other birds are on display. These birds were crippled and brought to the center for rehabilitation. Their handicaps prevent them from surviving on their own and they remain in captivity. At the 1-mile mark, hikers will see a 2-acre compound that holds large white-tailed deer. A quarter mile from here is the heritage homesite. These traditional settler cabins of the coastal area, built circa 1837, were moved here from Wayne County (Tilman cabin) and Gumbranch, Liberty County (David Delk). Not far from here is the 6-acre Ledbetter pond, which is used for studying freshwater environments. Frogs and turtles are common here. Finishing up the trail are three large mammal exhibits. First is a black bear enclosure, then an easy walk to some majestic wolves that have been extirpated from the Southeast. Notice their dens dug into the earth. The final treat is a small herd of bison.

Trail: 1.75-mile wildlife trail.

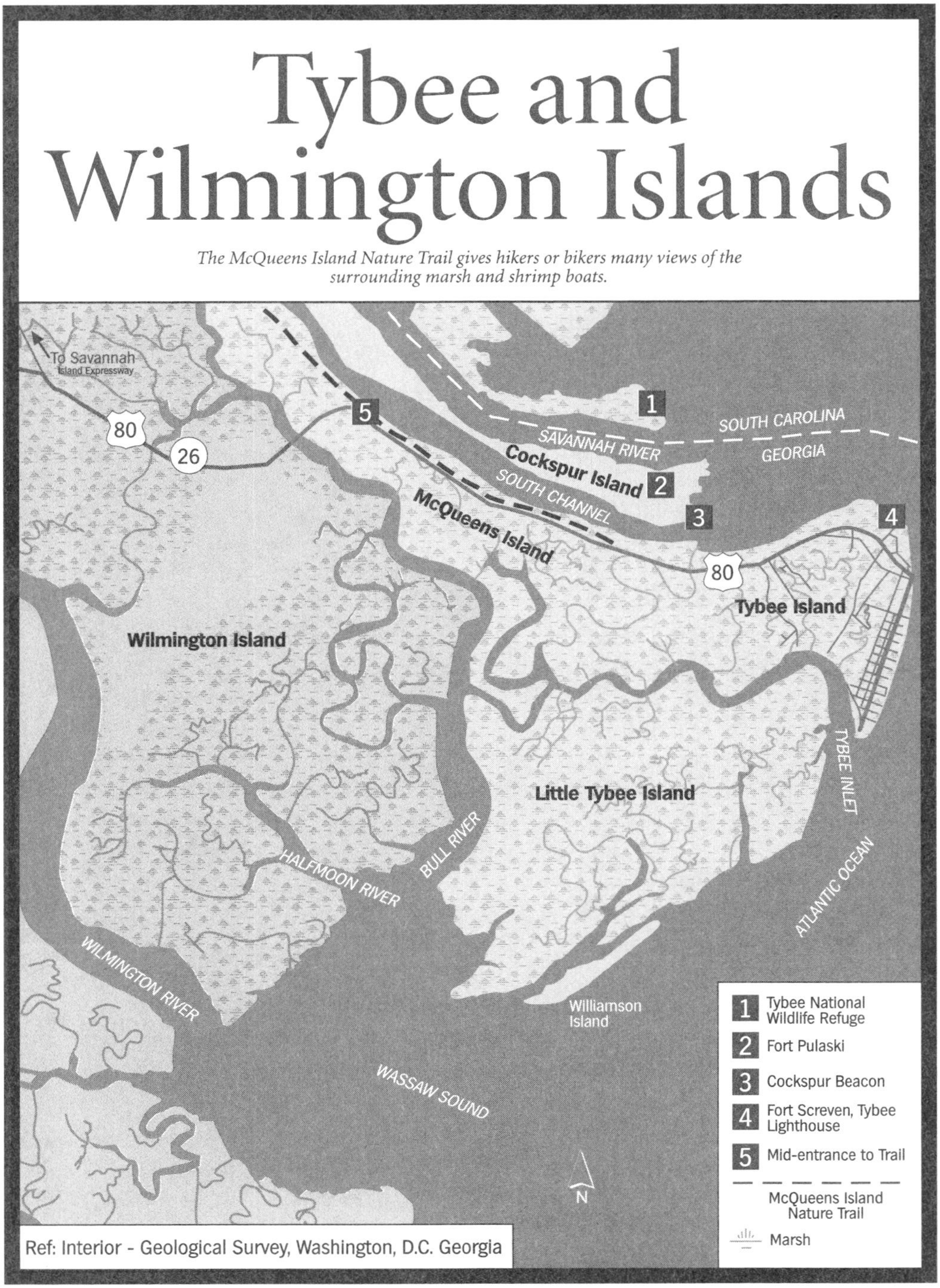

Tybee and Wilmington Islands

The McQueens Island Nature Trail gives hikers or bikers many views of the surrounding marsh and shrimp boats.

To Savannah
Island Expressway

80

26

5

SAVANNAH RIVER

1

Cockspur Island

2

SOUTH CHANNEL

McQueens Island

SOUTH CAROLINA

GEORGIA

3

4

80

Tybee Island

Wilmington Island

TYBEE INLET

Little Tybee Island

HALFMOON RIVER

BULL RIVER

WILMINGTON RIVER

ATLANTIC OCEAN

Williamson
Island

WASSAW SOUND

N

1	Tybee National Wildlife Refuge
2	Fort Pulaski
3	Cockspur Beacon
4	Fort Screven, Tybee Lighthouse
5	Mid-entrance to Trail

McQueens Island Nature Trail

Marsh

Ref: Interior - Geological Survey, Washington, D.C. Georgia

Cockspur and McQueens Islands

⬚ FORT PULASKI NATIONAL MONUMENT

[Fig. 9(2)] Fort Pulaski National Monument, located on Cockspur Island in the Savannah River before you reach Tybee Island, is one of the finest national parks in the U.S. Whether you are interested in Civil War history or want to walk the island's nature trails, Fort Pulaski is great for families and exciting to visit. While its historic value is evident, its natural communities are also worth the visitor's attention. The park is a stop on the Colonial Coast Birding Trail established by the Georgia Department of Natural Resources.

President James Madison commissioned the huge brick fort in 1816 as a reaction to the War of 1812 as one of the Third System of coastal fortifications, created when the U.S. Congress decided that the new nation needed a better system of forts to protect its harbors and cities. The British during the War of 1812 successfully attacked Washington, D.C. and burned the White House.

Pulaski was not the first fort to be built on Cockspur Island. Fort George, a palisaded blockhouse, was constructed on Cockspur Island in 1761 by John G.W. DeBrahm. Its

Fort Pulaski National Monument still bears scars from shelling by Union guns.

primary purpose was to defend Savannah from the Spanish in St. Augustine. When hostilities with the Spanish died down, it remained in service as a quarantine and customs house. When the Revolutionary War broke out in 1776, Patriots abandoned and dismantled the fort. Its exact location remains a mystery. British warships seized the island and it became a refuge for Royalists who supported the British cause. One refugee was Sir James Wright, the popular royal governor of Georgia, who escaped from house arrest on February 11, 1776 in Savannah and resided here and on British man-of-wars until he fled to Nova Scotia for three-and-a-half years. After the war, Wright returned to Tybee to sail with Tories back to England.

Fort Greene was built on Cockspur Island from 1794–1795 to provide defense for the new republic. In September 1804, the island was pounded by one of the most powerful hurricanes in history, obliterating all traces of the fort. According to a Charleston newspaper, the hurricane moved a 4,000-pound cannon 40 feet. The site of Fort Greene is believed to be a hammock southeast of Fort Pulaski.

Construction on Fort Pulaski began in earnest in 1829 on Cockspur Island, a marshy delta island that was chosen for its strategic location at the opening of the Savannah River. The island's name is derived from the spur-shaped reef that juts out into the northern channel of the sound. The marshy island is also known as Long Island. The island's first recorded name was Peeper Island, given to it by Gen. James Edward Oglethorpe in 1733, because as ships sailed around Tybee Island's northern shoulder, they saw the island "peeping" at them.

The fort is named for Count Casimir Pulaski, the Polish hero of the American Revolution who lost his life in the unsuccessful siege of Savannah in 1779. He died leading the French and American attack on the British who had possession of Savannah.

Designed by Gen. Simon Bernard, the structure was built by Army Corps of Engineers Captain J.F.K. Mansfield with 25 million bricks in 18 years at a cost of $1 million. A series of dikes, worked on by recent West Point graduate and Second Lieutenant Robert E. Lee from 1829–1831, was constructed to produce a protective moat and keep the fort and island dry. By the end of 1860, as southern secessionist and northern abolitionist emotions were reaching the boiling point, the fort had yet to be garrisoned or outfitted with a full complement of artillery.

On January 3, 1861, two weeks after South Carolina had seceded from the Union and one week after U.S. troops had occupied Fort Sumter in Charleston Harbor, Georgia militiamen seized the Federal fort. They were under orders from Governor Joseph E. Brown, even though Georgia had not yet seceded from the Union. Brown was acting to protect Savannah, a city of 20,000 that at this time was one of the most prosperous seaports in America, trading cotton, timber, and naval stores.

After the famous Georgia Secession Convention at the state capital in Milledgeville on January 19, 1861, the fort transferred to Confederate control. By the end of April, 11 southern states had left the Union and were at war with the northern states. President Abraham Lincoln ordered the naval blockade of the South as a part of his master strategy to starve and strangle the South. On November 7, 1861, U.S. forces struck Port Royal Sound, and seized Hilton Head. From here, Federal forces established a headquarters where they planned actions against Fort Pulaski and the rest of the South Atlantic coast. On November 10, 1861, intimidated Confederate

*Robert E. Lee, who helped engineer the construction of Fort Pulaski, drew this diamondback terrapin (*Malaclemys terrapin*) on Cockspur Island in 1831.*

forces abandoned Tybee Island, and U.S. troops under Engineer Capt. Quincy A. Gillmore established a base of operations on the island.

What happened next changed the history of modern warfare. Gillmore believed he could bombard the fort from the island with the new experimental "rifled" cannon. He and his 1,100 men spent two months dragging 36 mortars and smoothbore and rifled cannon across the marsh to establish 11 Union batteries from which to fire on the fort. Much of the backbreaking work occurred at night to hide their plans.

Fort Pulaski was commanded by Col. Charles H. Olmstead. Aware of the Federal presence on the island 1 mile away, the young commander believed the distance from Tybee to the fort protected it from serious harm. Most heavy ordnance of the day was effective at half that distance. In fact, Gen. Robert E. Lee, who had more than a passing acquaintance with the fort, told him the Federal gunners could "make it pretty warm for you here with shells, but they cannot breach your walls at that distance."

Lee was wrong. On April 10, 1862, Gillmore asked for the Confederates to surrender the fort. When Olmstead refused, the Federals opened fire. The rifled cannon were devastatingly accurate, destructive, and effective, breaching the 7.5-foot-thick walls of the southeast angle of the fort and threatening the main powder magazine. Five of the 10 rifled guns used by Federal troops were 30-pound Parrott guns, which had an effective range of 8,453 yards—much longer than conventional smooth-bore artillery. The technical innovation that made the difference were spiraled or rifled grooves on the inside of the cannon barrel and an expansion skirt or ring around the end of the projectile that gave the bullet-shaped shell a spin when fired. The spin gave the projectile increased range, accuracy, and penetrating power that doomed the Confederates inside Fort Pulaski. Olmstead surrendered the fort and his 384 men only 30 hours after the bombardment began, writing, "Guns, such as have never before been brought to bear against any fortification, have overpowered me." Gillmore was a northern hero and was breveted a brigadier general. The rifled cannons on Tybee Island ended the age of masonry forts across the globe. Once thought to be nearly invincible, brick and masonry forts were now obsolete, and rifled cannons became a technical innovation that continues to be used today by the big guns on battleships.

Fort Pulaski remained under Federal control until the end of the Civil War. On April 29, 1865, upon receiving the news that Confederate Gen. Robert E. Lee had surrendered, Union troops fired 200 guns from the ramparts, symbolically marking the end of Lee's 35-year military career that had begun on Cockspur Island. A few weeks later, Confederate President Jefferson Davis was captured in Irwinville, Georgia, as he tried to flee from Union cavalry. He spent the night as a prisoner aboard a ship in the lee of Cockspur Island as he was being transported to Fortress Monroe.

By 1880, only a caretaker and lighthouse keeper remained at the fort. Eventually, the fort was completely abandoned until October 13, 1924, when the 537-acre site was made a national monument by presidential proclamation. In 1933, serious restoration began on the fort. Today, it is in excellent condition, still bearing the marks of the Federal bombardment almost 140 years ago.

The fort is fascinating to tour. A short movie at the visitor center explains what visitors are about to see. Beautiful views of the marsh from the fort's walls belie the buggy boredom, disease, and general misery troops endured while serving at the fort. Try to imagine the strenuous work involved in firing one of the heavy guns—or the dread in waiting for a responding, incoming shell. The entire perimeter of the fort offers much to see, including the damaged wall still pocked with craters and holding shot from Union artillery, to the cistern system that trapped more than 200,000 gallons of fresh water for the fort's thirsty troops. Other highlights include the surrender room and the northwest magazine that held 40,000 pounds of gunpowder, and the earthen demilune system constructed from 1872–1875 based on concepts learned right here during the Civil War.

Perhaps the most impressive engineering feat of the fort is largely unseen. Building an enormously heavy masonry fort on unstable marsh required elaborate underpinnings. At the southwest bastion, an area has been left in original condition to display various construction details of the fort. Brick arches under the terreplein carry weight to counter arches in the floor that are supported by pilings that are driven 70 feet into the mud of the island. The quality of the engineering is obvious by the still-straight lines of bricks at the water edge of the fort's moat.

Other features worth noting at Fort Pulaski National Monument include nature trails, Battery Hambright, and the John Wesley Memorial.

Directions: From Savannah, go approximately 13 miles east on US 80. Look for signs after leaving Wilmington Island. The park's entrance station is on McQueens Island on the left before you reach Lazaretto Creek.

Activities: Historic touring, nature hiking, biking, picnicking. Special events occur every year on the anniversary of the siege of Fort Pulaski. Call ahead for details.

Facilities: Museum, bookstore, bathrooms, hiking trails, handicapped accessible facilities, boat ramp, picnic area.

Dates: Open every day except Christmas, 8:30–5:30, with extended hours during summer.

Fees: $2 per person or $4 per family.

Closest town: Tybee Island.

For more information: Superintendent, Fort Pulaski National Monument, PO Box 30757, Savannah, GA 31410-0757. Phone 786-5787.

HIKING AND BIKING TRAILS AT FORT PULASKI NATIONAL MONUMENT

The wildlife found on Cockspur fascinated even Second Lieutenant Robert E. Lee, who made drawings of flora and fauna he found here while constructing the dike system. While the island's uplands are mostly man-made from dredge material from the Savannah River and kept artificially dry by the dike system, a mix of plant communities provide proof that in the coastal environment, given a chance, vegetation will start to take hold on any piece of high ground.

Cockspur historically was a low-lying coastal island with a few high spots that was frequently washed over by storm tides, killing plants that had little tolerance to salt water before they had a chance to become established. The draining of the island and the addition of soil has added more high ground, leading to a more ecologically diverse island. Today, along with the southern red cedar (*Juniperus virginiana*) hammocks, *Spartina*, and salt flats that would have been found in Robert E. Lee's day, you also find new species such as sugarberry trees, recognized by their warty bark; shining or winged sumac, identified by the narrow leaves that grow along the step; and yaupon holly (*Ilex vomitoria*). The island is covered with climbing vines, including muscadine (*Vitis rotundifolia*), which produces an edible grape-like purple fruit that is made into jellies and wine. Several species of *Smilax* and Virginia creeper (*Parthenocissus quinquefolia*) also grow here.

The high ground has stimulated the growth of a variety of plants that produce fruit and other food for wildlife. Many birds depend on the high-energy content of the berries, which ripen in time for the fall flight of migrants. Look for painted buntings, white-eyed vireos, and yellow-billed cuckoos. Common mammals found on the island include marsh rabbits, gray squirrels; rice, cotton and black rats; raccoons, minks, and white-tailed deer.

The dikes on the island trap fresh water important

YAUPON HOLLY
(*Ilex vomitoria*)
This species name recognizes the effect of drinking a tea made from the plant's berries.

Muscadine Wine

According to nineteenth century naturalist Francis Porcher, the following recipe will produce muscadine wine: "Muscadine wine: two pecks of the mashed grapes are added to one gallon of boiling water. Allow it to ferment 36 hours, add a little sugar to each gallon and lay it aside. It must not be sealed closely at first…"

to wildlife, and frogs and the occasional alligator are seen and heard in the long canals. Frogs and toads found on the island include the southern toad, Eastern narrow-mouthed toad, green treefrog, squirrel treefrog, southern cricket frog, and southern leopard frog. Snakes include the Eastern cottonmouth, Eastern diamond-back rattlesnake, rough green snake, corn snake, yellow rat snake, Eastern kingsnake, and southern black racer. Look for lizards sunning themselves such as the green anole, ground skink, southern five-lined skink and Eastern glass lizard.

Fish living in the canals include gray mullet, ladyfish, Atlantic mummichog, sheepshead minnows, sailfin molly, mosquitofish, and black seabass larvae.

The three interconnecting trails, which total three miles, are worth doing. All are nature trails, but not all are called nature trails. The longest, the 1.8-mile dike system trail, is great to experience on a bike, with many views of the surrounding marsh and glimpses of shrimp boats in Tybee Roads. Riding along the top of the dike system is a great way to appreciate the engineering efforts needed to build Fort Pulaski. Located halfway out into the marsh between the fort and Cockspur Beacon was Fort George. Today you may see a great blue heron, marsh rabbit, raccoon, or an Eastern diamondback snake. All are seen on Cockspur Island.

The 0.5-mile picnic trail (one-way), beginning across from the visitor center at the northern end of the parking lot and ending at the picnic area, takes the hiker through a maturing maritime forest consisting of alkaline-loving southern red cedar and cabbage palms.

The 0.75-mile nature trail, a loop that connects up with the picnic trail, takes the hiker through yaupon shrub and mixed shrub-juniper plant communities. Interesting plaques, placed by a local Boy Scout troop, highlight natural and human history of the area. A particular emphasis is on the medicinal qualities of the plants, with notes and recipes from Francis Porcher, who wrote *The Medical Botany of the Southern States* in 1889. Yaupon holly was used by Native Americans as an emetic, creating what they called the "black drink," which according to Porcher was "like opium, it excites the torpid and languid, while it calms the restless and introduces sleep."

Part of the nature trail features a religious site important to Methodists and a Spanish-American War era battery. The Wesley Memorial is where the founder of Methodism, John Wesley, preached his first sermon in the New World on February 6, 1736. Wesley, 1703–1791, spent 21 months spreading the gospel in scattered settlements in Georgia before returning to England in 1737 after a falling out with his parishioners.

Battery Hambright, located near the memorial, was part of the Fort Screven coastal fortification system intended to protect Savannah shipping lanes in anticipation of hostilities from Spain, which had a stronghold in its colony of Cuba. The battery, located inside a large protective mound of dirt, is one of six built for Fort Screven, and the only one on Cockspur Island. The battery is named for Horace George Hambright, a young officer who died in 1896 on the North Dakota frontier during the Indian wars. Construc-

*Gulls congregate and feed
in the intertidal areas of the beach.*

tion started in June of 1899 after the Spanish-American War had ended, and the battery consisted of two 3-inch rapid-fire gun placements.

Stretching across the Savannah River from the battery was a submarine minefield. It was electronically controlled by a mining casemate built in 1895 and located under a mound of earth near Fort Pulaski. The mines were anchored to the bottom of the river, but floating above them was a buoy. When passing ships struck the buoy, an electronic signal was sent to the casemate. The two or three men working in the casemate would determine if the ship was friend or foe. If the ship was an enemy, more than 500 pounds of explosives could be detonated.

At the end of a side trail is the North Pier, where supplies and men were brought in to build Fort Pulaski. Here the visitor is treated to an excellent view of the Savannah River and surrounding marsh.

Trail: Dike system trail, 1.8-mile circuit grass trail; nature trail, 0.75-mile asphalt loop; picnic trail, 0.5-mile one-way dirt trail. Suitable for hiking or cycling on a mountain bike.

COCKSPUR BEACON

[Fig. 9(3)] Cockspur Beacon, also known as Little Tybee Light and South Channel Light, is one of Georgia's five remaining lighthouses. The Savannah River has two entrances or two channels, the north and the south. Cockspur Island Beacon marked the southern entrance and a twin lighthouse on Oyster Bed Island, no longer in existence, marked the northern entrance. First erected in 1849, and then rebuilt with Savannah grey brick on the original foundation in 1857, Cockspur Beacon lost importance in 1879 when many ships started using the northern channel and was deactivated in 1909 when all ships switched to using the northern channel of the Savannah River. Today, the southern channel is much more silted in than the northern channel, which is dredged. Standing 46 feet tall, with a 16-feet base, the lighthouse is situated on an oyster shell bed off the southeastern end of Cockspur Island, where it continues to be used as a daymark.

For such a small structure, the lighthouse has seen a lot of action. During the 1857 reconstruction, a keeper's house and dock facilities were added, but lightning struck the house in 1880 and in 1881 a hurricane blew it away. The lighthouse was in the line of fire when Union batteries fired upon Fort Pulaski on April 10, 1862, but luckily was not hit. Tragedy struck the second lighthouse keeper, Cornelius Maher, who drowned at the lighthouse when his boat capsized in 1853. The fourth keeper, Thomas Quinfiven, died of yellow fever after only four months of service. In 1881, George Washington Martus became the lighthouse keeper. His sister, Florence, known as the "Waving Girl," was born on Cockspur Island and became famous for greeting every ship that passed by her home on Elba Island. She is immortalized in bronze with a statue of her on River Street on the waterfront in Savannah.

In its heyday, the beacon used a sixth order Fresnel lens, which was illuminated by an oil lamp that burned 90 gallons of sperm oil a year. Sixth order Fresnel lenses are the smallest, and mark rivers or channels. Abandoned by the U.S. Coast Guard in 1949, the beacon fell under the control of the National Park Service and today is the responsibility of Fort Pulaski National Monument. Open to the public, the lighthouse is generally surrounded by water and not accessible from Fort Pulaski. Caution: Be very careful about visiting this lighthouse. Approached at low tide by boat, adventurous souls can brave the slippery and sharp oyster shells at the base to see the beacon up-close. A slippery and crumbling internal staircase can be climbed at your own risk to the top of the lighthouse.

The old beacon is in need of restoration work and perhaps someday in the future preservation funds can be allocated to preserve this historic structure.

▓ OLD SAVANNAH-TYBEE RAILROAD (MCQUEENS ISLAND NATURE TRAIL)

[Fig. 9] This is one of the best biking trails on the coast. A rails-to-trails conversion, the 5.8-mile trail follows the length of McQueens Island toward Savannah, following the Savannah-Tybee railroad bed. Accessed at the entrance of Fort Pulaski or at the trail's halfway point 3 miles west of the entrance on US 80, the trail consists of crushed oyster shell and limestone, which makes a nice surface for a mountain or beach bike. In 1887, Daniel G. Purse and John J. McDonough of the Savannah and Atlantic Railroad built the Savannah-Tybee Railroad, an important part of the area's history, which linked Savannah with downtown Tybrisa Pavilion. The Central of Georgia Railway purchased the railroad in 1890 and operated it until 1933, when it was put out of business by the automobile highway that linked the island with the coast.

In history books, the hour-long rail trip is recounted with no small amount of nostalgia, telling how vacation-bound travelers, excited to get to Tybee, were kept cool even in the middle of summer with fresh marsh breezes blowing in through the windows of the train. Train tickets cost 18 cents for adults, 10 cents for children.

Today, abandoned railroad ties, pushed off the banks into the adjacent marsh, lie ignored and forgotten. But hikers and bikers can't help but be impressed with the strenuous efforts that got them here in the first place or the beautiful railroad journey railroad passengers must have enjoyed in the Roaring Twenties.

McQueens Island is defined by the south channel of the Savannah River to the north, and tidal rivers Lazaretto Creek, Oyster Creek, Bull River, and St. Augustine Creek to the south. Lined with cabbage palm trees, southern red cedar, and live oaks, a hiker or biker will be treated to views of salt marsh on one side and the Savannah River on the other. Plant communities include salt marsh, high marsh, salt pan, and mixed shrub and juniper. The dominant plant in the lower elevations of the Holocene marsh, much of it growing to 6 feet in height, is *Spartina alterniflora.*

The great egret (Casmerodius albus) *is recognized by its yellow bill and black legs.*

Wildlife is plentiful. As fiddler crabs scurry out of your way, look farther down the path and you may see the shy and elusive willet (*Catoptrophorous semipalmatus*) crossing the road into the marsh. Hundreds of willets nest in the area. Redwing blackbirds, great egrets, and great blue herons are commonly seen along the trail, as are Carolina diamondback terrapins, raccoons, bobcats, and an occasional Eastern diamondback rattlesnake.

Wide enough for two bikes to pass each other comfortably, the well-maintained pathway has exercise stations for joggers, picnic tables for families, and wooden platform overlooks for classes or photographers. Plaques along the way give distances and illustrate fauna commonly found in the salt marsh. At the western end of the trail, you find a beautiful live oak festooned with Spanish moss and more portable toilets. The halfway access point also has portable toilets and a paved path to a wooden deck that overlooks the marsh. Motorized vehicles are prohibited on the trail.

Trail: The trail is 5.8 miles one-way. Access is gained at one end at the Fort Pulaski National Monument entrance, or the halfway point 3 miles west of the entrance on US 80 just past Bull River. Suitable for mountain bikes.

Directions: From Savannah, go approximately 13 miles east on US 80. Look for signs to Fort Pulaski after leaving Wilmington Island. The park's entrance station is on McQueens Island on the left before you reach Lazaretto Creek. The trail's entrance is on your left marked by a large sign. The halfway entrance is 3 miles west of here on US 80 past Bull River.

Activities: Nature hiking, biking, picnic areas.

Facilities: Bathrooms, hiking trails, picnic areas, exercise stations, handicapped accessible minitrail to overlook at midpoint, viewing platforms, educational signs, parking.

Dates: Open every day.

Fees: None.

Closest town: Tybee Island.

Tybee Island

Tybee is Georgia's northernmost barrier island and it measures approximately 2.5 miles long by 0.75-mile wide.

River's End Campground & RV Park

North Beach

Van Horn St.

Byers Bay

1

2

3

P

80

Campbell Ave.

South Campbell Ave.

Sixth Ave.

First St.

Lewis Ave.

Seven Ave.

Second Ave.

Second St.

Lovell Ave.

Butler Ave.

Third St.

Fourth St.

Memorial Park

Fifth St.

Sixth St.

Center St.

Center Ter.

Center Pl.

CHIMNEY CREEK

Eleventh St.

N

Eighth St.

Ninth St.

Tenth St.

CHIMNEY CREEK

HORSE PEN CREEK

Tybee Island

Venetian Drive

Terrace Drive

Twelfth St.

Jones Ave.

Eleventh St.

Second Ave.

Eighth Pl.

Shady Rd.

Tenth Ter.

Tenth Pl.

ATLANTIC OCEAN

2nd Ave.

6th Ave.

5th Ave.

4th Ave.

Thirteenth St.

Fourteenth St.

Lovell Ave.

Butler Ave.

Little Tybee Island

Fifteenth St.

BACK RIVER

Back River Pier

Chatham Ave.

Miranda St.

Tybee Dr.

P

5

4

Ider Dr.

16th Pl.

16th St.

6

Inlet Ave.

17th St.

17th Ter.

18th St.

18th Pl.

P

1	Fort Screven Historic District
2	Tybee Lighthouse
3	Tybee Museum
4	The Pier and Pavillion
5	Tybee Island Marine Science Center
6	Tybee South Beach Area

Tybee Island

[Fig. 10] Tybee Island, the most densely developed barrier island on the Georgia coast, consequently lacks most of the natural communities found on Georgia's other barrier islands because of past use and poorly planned development. Here you have renourished beach on the eastern side, dunes with sea oats and pioneer plants at the northern and middle beach areas, and salt marsh on the Back River.

That's not to say Tybee Island doesn't have its own unique appeal. The island is a good place to stay to walk the beach, bird watch, go fishing, ride a bike, and take easy day trips to nearby attractions, including the city of Savannah. Tybee is also loaded with fascinating characters, excellent fishing, gorgeous views, and cold mixed drinks. If Ernest Hemingway were alive today, he might be living and writing books on Tybee.

One reason Tybee Island is significant is that it is one of only four of Georgia's 15 major barrier islands that can reached by car, which has been true since 1923. DOT plans call for making four lanes of US 80, the transportation artery linking Tybee and Savannah, which means even more cars, visitors, and development are in the future of this small island.

Tybee is Georgia's northernmost and 11th-largest barrier island, measuring approximately 2.5 miles long by 0.75 mile wide. The Holocene island consists of 3,100 acres, of which 1,500 acres are uplands. Nearly 3.5 miles of beach runs roughly north and south before curving toward Savannah at the north end, where it reaches the Savannah River. Across the river and Tybee Roads (the busy shipping mouth of the river) lies South Carolina and Daufuskie and Hilton Head islands. Tybee Island has a permanent resident population of 3,000, which swells on summer weekends to 30,000.

Early in Georgia's history, Tybee Island was recognized as a strategic piece of land to protect the port of Savannah. At different periods of Georgia and U.S. history, lighthouses were erected on the northern end to guide ships and coastal forts were built and manned to protect the coast (*see* Tybee Lighthouse, page 103 and Fort Screven, page 101). The last lighthouse is still in use, and the last military installation called Fort Screven—an active base from 1897 to 1945—is now a national historic district, with some of the fort's emplacements and structures used as homes, garages, apartments, and a museum.

It is hard to walk far on Tybee Island without making a friend of a local, who will regale you with what I call "True Tybee Tales." Some locals relish calling their town the "Redneck Riviera" or "Truckstop by the Sea," but Tybee's local color is actually more diverse than these monikers suggest. Very rich and very poor families, surfers and soldiers, old timers and babies, straights and gays, Yankees and rednecks, environmentalists and litterbugs, blacks and whites, the beautiful and not-so-beautiful, all democratically share Tybee's beaches in close quarters without seeming to notice one another. You quickly realize that you are not strolling the exclusive beach at Sea Island. This is not to say that there's perfect harmony among the locals. Islanders pack the seats at city council meetings, which are considered "must-see" entertainment. Epic political battles are

Tybrisa Pavilion and Pier—Where to Meet on Tybee

Built in the early 1900s, Tybrisa Pavilion once defined the heart of Tybee culture. Located near the south end, the Pavilion was located near many hotels and beach clubs on or near the Strand (Strand Avenue), including the famous Tybee Hotel. The pavilion, the largest and most popular on the island, connected to a bathhouse and restaurant and eventually to a bowling alley, skating rink, arcade, and lounge. A pier jutted out from the pavilion into the Atlantic.

In the first half of the twentieth century, Tybrisa's large dance floor hosted the country's best bands, such as those of Benny Goodman, Tommy Dorsey, Cab Callaway, and Guy Lombardo, and many young couples sparked their first romance here. Families and friends used the pavilion as a meeting spot, for picnics, or for other social outings. The pavilion, featured in postcards of Tybee, was first owned and operated by the Central of Georgia Railway and purchased in 1924 by the Tybrisa Company. A long boardwalk was connected to the Pavilion, the scene of much social activity, to judge by photographs of the era. In 1967, Tybrisa Pavilion was burned down by an arsonist. Plans to rebuild the pavilion finally came to fruition when the 1996 Olympic Games came to Georgia. In 1996, the new pavilion opened at 16th Street and Strand Avenue, featuring a long fishing pier and a new pavilion, where bands play and young couples dance again.

waged over stop signs, barking dogs, and other matters of national significance.

Those looking for controlled-access communities, plush golf courses, and color-coordinated housing and residents need to look elsewhere because Tybee proudly embraces what locals call "Tybee Tacky." Take a stroll through the local legend department store bouillabaisse that is T.S. Chu's and I guarantee you won't be confused that you are in Neiman Marcus. One popular establishment, Earl's, remains prepared for any holiday by leaving all its decorations—Halloween, Thanksgiving, and Christmas—on display just in case. Status on Tybee goes to the person who has the most rustproof rims on his or her beach bicycle. Not that there isn't money on the island. You just can't tell by the locals' footwear, which is more frequently bare feet than Bruno Maglis.

No one's absolutely certain where the name "Tybee" originated. In the Yuchi Indian language, *tybee* means "salt." Some believe the name came from a Choctaw chief named *Iti ubi*, which means "wood killer." Some believe the name came from the corruption of the word "tabby," a oystershell-limestone mix that was used as a construction material by early colonists on the Georgia coast. Tybee, sometimes spelled Tiby on early maps, was first incorporated in 1887 as the town of Ocean City, and was known as Savannah Beach during its heyday as a resort for the city of Savannah. Today, it is incorporated as the town of Tybee.

Tybee has been the playground of Savannah's wealthier citizens for more than a century, and today the island's many beautiful homes with docks leading out to expensive watercraft testify to the fact that its popularity endures.

When the island became more accessible in the mid-1800s with the development of the steamboat, the general public started coming more often. Resort hotels, such as the Bolton Hotel and Ocean House, were established, and lots were sold for $200, plus $150–$200 for a frame house. Tybee's development as a resort picked up more steam after the Civil

The Tybee Island pier and beach were popular destinations in the 1930s.

War, when public transportation to the island improved with the establishment of a rail link with Savannah in 1887. The three-hour steamboat journey was reduced to an hour train ride, if the train didn't break down. By the Roaring Twenties, more people called Tybee home, and thousands of visitors would come to the island in the summer.

Photos reveal that beach outings were quite a different sartorial event in the early 1900s. Men wore suit coats and long pants with ties and bowler hats while women wore fancy hats, fine long dresses, and high-heeled shoes—as dressed up as any Sunday church gathering today—as they walked on the beach.

Tybee was dominated by a cottage culture, with more than 400 summer residences built on the island. A photograph hanging in City Hall (a duplicate is also in the Tybee Museum) shows a row of cottages facing the beach behind a set of dunes from 11th Street to 5th Street, or the mid-beach area. These family cottages had wrap-around sleeping porches to take full advantage of cooling ocean breezes at night. The builders of these cottages wisely set them back behind the second dunes, looking for protection from storms. A sidewalk ran in front of these cottages, some of which featured grand wooden staircases centrally located and oriented toward the beach.

The fact that these early homeowners built back from the beach affected development patterns to come because the property in front of their houses became valuable. Since the 1960s and 1970s, ownership of many of these cottages has turned over from one generation to the next, with second generation family or developers developing four or five homes directly in front of these charming cottages.

As it usually happens with historic properties, some have fallen into neglect, others have been remodeled, obliterating their historic character with stucco and frosted windows, and others have been torn down to make way for half-a-million dollar homes. But some cottages retain their elegant beach character and a few of the residents have successfully resisted upgrading their free, natural cooling systems for air conditioning.

The main hub of social activity on Tybee Island was the Tybrisa Pavilion and the old and new Tybee Hotels (the first one burned), popular gathering sites at the south end of the beach. When the palm-lined Tybee highway was opened on June 21, 1923, linking Tybee with Thunderbolt, a new era was ushered in. In the 1920s and 1930s, Tybee Island was one of the busiest seaside resorts in the Southeast.

Butler Avenue at one time had a train running down the middle of it, with a turntable rail yard at the end near 17th Street. The steam engine would drop its passenger cars, be turned around, then push the passengers back to Savannah. The Tybee Highway replaced the train tracks, and Butler became a wide, palm-lined, divided road. But the palms were cut down to make way for parking spaces on either side of the street, which added to municipal coffers but took away from the attractiveness of the avenue.

With the boom in population and recreation coming to all of America's shorelines, prosperity in the form of real estate development has had its effect on working class residents. Locals will quickly tell you a story of how a house and lot purchased for $15,000 only 20 years ago sold last week for over $300,000. One island native, Michael Bart, says Tybee Island has changed more in the last 10 years than the previous 50, with property taxes on a steady march upward. Because of the desirability of the beach, developers are staying busy with redevelopment on the island, tearing down older structures and filling in with new. Today, the sound of hammers and saws competes with the cries of seagulls as Tybee Island continues to change.

The **Tybee Visitor Center and TAG Shop** is found at US 80 and Campbell Avenue on the right as you approach Tybee's beaches. This is a good place to stop and inquire about lodging and events on the island, shop in the knick-knacky TAG Shop (Tybee Antiques and Gifts) that features local arts and antiques, buy some ice cream or baked goods, or purchase some fresh vegetables at a small farmers' market. It is open 7 days a week, 9–5. Phone (800) 868-2322 or 786-5444.

TYBEE ISLAND'S NATURAL FEATURES

Ecologically, Tybee Island would be a great place to earn a Ph. D. on the effects of development to a barrier island. Barrier islands are very impermanent geological entities. The sand is always on the move, leaving to go somewhere else or arriving from somewhere else. Tybee Island is no different and the struggles the island has gone through to literally hold its ground are instructive for all barrier island communities.

Despite its small size and overdevelopment, Tybee Island surprisingly still has threatened loggerhead sea turtles nesting on its beaches—as many or more than St. Simons Island, another developed island. In 1998, three brave turtles nested on Tybee Island compared with a solitary individual on St. Simons Island. Not that this is anything to brag about, when considering historic numbers that probably reached the several hundreds before Europeans came to the coast. (Cumberland and Little Cumberland islands lead the Georgia coast with a combined 10-year average of 242 nests a year.)

Tybee Island's natural beach sand is not as fine and white as that of the beaches of the Gulf of Mexico because of Tybee Island's high organic mix and the quantity of rough dark granite in its sand. Beach sand on the Atlantic and Gulf coasts generally consists of three components: fine minerals, crushed seashells (calcium carbonate), and detritus from other dead organisms, including marine plants and animals. Low wave energy on the Georgia coast prevents heavy deposits of calcium carbonate and the sand grains found on the beach are rougher, due to a lack of rounding from wave energy.

The higher the quartz content, the finer and whiter the beach sand, such as you find near Grayton Beach, Florida. When you hear the sand squeak under your feet, that's the angular, translucent crystal of quartz rubbing together. This quartz has been brought down to the beach from the Appalachians. In essence, you are walking on the Blue Ridge Mountains when you are walking on a southeastern Atlantic or Gulf of Mexico beach. Some beaches, such as ones near St. Augustine and in the Bahamas, have a high calcium carbonate component and when viewed with a hand lens will be revealed as crushed sea shells.

Sand on a barrier island beach does not stay in one place for long. Wind, rivers, tides, and currents all play a role in growing, shaping, and destroying barrier islands. Tybee's mineral components have, over the millennia, come from the Appalachian Mountains via the Savannah River drainage. A mix of quartz and granite gives the beach a gray color. The black streaks are pulverized granite, washed down from the mountains.

The Savannah River has historically been a contributor to Tybee's beaches. But at least three major impoundments or dams trap sediments upstream from Tybee Island, keeping natural sediments from adding to the shoreline. Also, a deep channel cut, or trench, is maintained by the U.S. Army Corps of Engineers for the Savannah River Harbor, allowing large commercial freighters access to the Port of Savannah. This 42-foot-deep trench, which left to natural forces is 24 feet deep, traps southward-moving sands from South Carolina, preventing the natural renourishment that sustains and helps create the beaches. As the trench fills, dredging operations collect the sediments and move them to official Savannah Harbor Ocean Dredge Material Disposal Sites (ODMDS). The sediments, totaling 7 million cubic yards a year, are not all beach compatible. Some of them are, however, which leads some people to argue that the sandy component should be deposited on Tybee.

The bottom line is that Tybee Island, like many barrier islands in the U.S., has been losing beach, especially at the northeast end, as prevailing currents, tides, and winds have moved sand southward from the island. Take a walk north on the beach at high tide from the Tybee Pier and you will run into trouble as you pass Third Street on your left: you run out of beach. Over the years, officials have built more than 100 beach-trapping structures of different degrees of effectiveness in an ongoing effort to stop the island from losing its beach. In 1941, a sea wall was constructed along the length of Tybee on the eastern side from the north to the south end.

To help the situation, the U.S. Army Corps of Engineers periodically pumps sand from offshore "borrow" sites and transports it to eroding areas, a stopgap measure that costs usually a million dollars a square mile. Local governments pay approximately 5 percent, state and county taxpayers pitch in about 30 percent, and the federal government pays the rest. The Tybee beaches have been renourished several times. In 1975–1976, with the northeastern end in trouble from erosion not unlike it is today, a major renourishment project was launched to build up 3 miles of beach with sand from nearby shoals. Today, another round of renourishment is in the works, possibly from materials dredged from the Savannah River as it is deepened.

Beach renourishment changes the mix and look of the beach. Occasionally, beachcombers can find hardened clay balls washed up on the beach. These were created when renourishment operations pumped clay up on the beach, and waves rolled it into small, rounded, bricklike aggregate stones. Beach renourishment has a negative effect on burrowing sea life in the littoral zone, which in effect is buried alive when sand is pumped up on the beach.

Older strategies that employed sea jetties or groins to hold sand in place prove eventually to be disastrous. These structures, which run perpendicular to the shore, interrupt the normal littoral drift of sand and sediments, essentially robbing Peter to pay Paul, depriving down-coast areas of natural replenishment and causing erosion. This damming of the natural flow of the river of sand eventually causes severe erosion either in front or behind the jetty. Sea walls, which run parallel to the shore, protect structures directly behind them, but deflect and increase wave energy that eventually undercuts the structures and causes erosion. On the southern end of Tybee, beyond the seawall, there used to be 15-foot high dunes. After the renourishment project, the dunes washed away for 30 feet behind the seawall. Controlling barrier islands is unpredictable and some beaches grow despite of these structures.

As the sand builds up, pioneering plants that can tolerate salt spray, exposure to the sun, and tenuous soil conditions start to colonize an area. They trap blowing sand and eventually create a dune. As the dune stabilizes, a greater diversity of plants develops, with some plants on the exposed top of the dune (sea oats) and others in the more protected, moister bottom. On Tybee Island, a young Holocene island (4,000–5,000 years old) the best natural dunes are found on the North Beach area and in the Mid-Beach area around 10th Street.

In the long run, barrier island beach-holding strategies can only have a temporary effect. Statistically, the Georgia coast should experience six major hurricanes a century. In the 1900s, Georgia has been lucky and not experienced even one, making homeowners and developers somewhat overconfident about their real estate investments. In the nineteenth century, the Georgia coast was hit by six major hurricanes. The most destructive was the hurricane of Aug. 27, 1881, which completely submerged Tybee Island under a 20-foot storm surge, destroying most of the island. Ominously, most experts believe it is only a matter of time before another one lands on the coast.

🐦 BIRD-WATCHING ON TYBEE ISLAND

The North Beach area has traditionally seen the greatest variety of species, but new development has decreased sightings of shy species. Regardless, the north end is a stop on the Colonial Coast Birding Trail established by the Georgia Department of Natural Resources.

Seen at the north end, as well as on the rest of Tybee's beaches, have been Wilson's plovers in the summer, and during winter red knots, pectoral sandpipers; royal, sooty, Caspian, Sandwich, and gull-billed terns; black skimmers, dunlins, and piping and semipalmated plovers. Occasionally seen in summer flitting through tree canopies on the northern end are painted buntings and yellow-billed cuckoos, and in winter various warblers are uncommon visitors, including the orange-crowned. Common on the beach are ring-billed gulls, brown pelicans, black skimmers, and boat-tailed grackles. During the winter, migrating species are seen in the air heading south in their V-shaped formations. Rock jetties attract ruddy turnstones and purple sandpipers. The interior creeks on the western side are home to the American oystercatcher, which feasts on the exposed oyster beds at low tide. Dunlins and black-bellied plovers are seen here as well.

Tybee Island: Fort Screven, North, and Mid-Beach Areas

[Fig. 9(4)] The Fort Screven and North Beach area offers fascinating military history, beautiful dunes, long beaches, a nice park, and an eclectic community of homes that is fun to observe on foot or bike. The natural dunes, with sea oats and other dune plants and animals, along with a view of Tybee Roads and Daufuskie and Hilton Head islands, make for a beautiful natural setting worth visiting. Also attracting attention are the mammoth container cargo ships, some almost as long as a 75-story building, plowing the waters of Savannah harbor. The Fort Screven installation gave Tybee a military character for more than 50 years, when 30 percent of Tybee Island's population consisted of military personnel. Today, the abandoned base is a National Historic District.

The north end of Tybee Island has been considered strategically important for hundreds of years. The first Europeans to visit the area were the Spanish, who explored the area 212 years before Gen. James Edward Oglethorpe established the town of Savannah in 1733. The Spanish claimed the area from Port Royal, South Carolina to St. Augustine, Florida, as Spanish territory, naming it *La Florida* or *Bimini*. In 1526, only 34 years after Columbus, a lawyer named Lúcas Vázques de Ayllón sailed along the Georgia coast from the Antilles, looking to establish the first colony in the New World. The location of the first Spanish mission, San Miguel de Gualdape, is still unknown, but some archaeologists believe it was somewhere in McIntosh County near Sapelo, St. Catherines, or Blackbeard islands. Disease destroyed the mission, which was abandoned after only two

Fresnel Lenses

Fresnel lenses were used in orders or strengths depending on the intensity needed for a particular location. First order lights are for primary landfall coastal lighthouses and second order lights are considered seacoast or landfall lights. Third and fourth order lights (such as St. Simons Lighthouse) mark harbor entrances, and fifth to sixth order lights, like the one used by Cockspur Island Beacon, are used for rivers and channels. Tybee Lighthouse's first order lens, valued at $3 million, is 9 feet tall and can shine a light that can be seen 18 miles away. The Fresnel lens was invented by French physicist Augustin Fresnel in 1827, who used prisms to capture and concentrate 90 percent of a lamp's light and focalizing it into an intense horizontal beam. The precise manufacturing needed produce the lens—hand-ground from perfectly molded lead crystal—required the skill of an artisan. His invention improved lighthouses' range from a few miles to almost 20. Some other first order lighthouses include the ones in St. Augustine and Pensacola, Florida, and Block Island Southeast.

months, leaving behind the bodies of Ayllón and 200 colonists. When Hernado DeSoto visited Tybee in 1540, he found a rosary and knife he believed belonged to the Ayllón explorers.

The first written description of Tybee was by another Spaniard, Captain Francis de Ecija, who described Tybee Roads at the mouth of the Savannah River as "The Bay of Shoals." When Oglethorpe began the colony of Savannah, he established the first "permanent" structure on the island, a 90-foot lighthouse designed by Noble Jones of Wormsloe (*see* Tybee Lighthouse, page 103, and Wormsloe, page 55) and built in the Fort Screven area north of Brumby Battery, it is believed. A stronghold named Fort Tybee was established near the lighthouse. During this period, the island was used as a hiding place for pirates such as Blackbeard, and today beachcombers patiently scan the beaches with metal detectors for buried treasure.

During the Revolutionary War, the French Fleet, the greatest gathering of foreign ships ever assembled in American waters, anchored off Tybee in support of American Patriots in their losing effort to take Savannah back from the British.

In 1808, recognizing its strategic value, the Federal government acquired jurisdiction in the Fort Screven area. Between 1812 and 1815, a lookout tower and fort known as a Martello tower was constructed by Isaiah Davenport of Savannah. Today, nothing is visible of the round structure, except what remains for archeologists to find. (In 1794, the British attacked a round stone tower at Martello Point, Corsica, and were greatly impressed with its defensive qualities. The British built more than 100 Martello towers on the south and east coasts of England between 1805 and 1812.) At various times in its history, the tower served as headquarters for the Georgia Telephone and Telegraph Company and was a post office. During the antebellum plantation era, the tower was a popular site for duels between South Carolina "Southern gentlemen" who used pistols to decide an issue. It also housed Union troops during their occupation of Tybee Island during the Civil War. It was serving as the Fort Screven post office when it burned in 1913. In 1914, the tower was blown up to clear the field of fire for Fort Screven's guns.

In 1819, President James Monroe traveled from Savannah to Tybee on the steamboat *Savannah*, which later became the first steamship to cross the Atlantic.

The Fort Screven Historic District was home to a military base that was active from the Spanish-American War of 1898 through the end of World War II. Initially a fort for the Coastal Artillery, in 1929 it was taken over by the famous 8th Infantry. During the Great Depression in 1932, Fort Screven was commanded by Lieutenant Colonel George Catlett Marshall, who went on to command the entire U.S. military during World War II and author the Marshall Plan, which rebuilt war-torn Europe after the war and earned him the Nobel Peace Prize in 1953. In 1940, the Coastal Artillery Corps took over again. During the years of World War II, a diving school was established to train engineers for underwater salvage operations and the repair of bomb-damaged ports. The United States Army Engineer Diving and Salvage School became the only school of its type operated by the Army in the United States. At the end of World War II the fort was declared surplus and sold to the City of Savannah Beach (now Tybee Island) for $200,000, which in turn auctioned it off to the public.

Today, Fort Screven is an unusual hodgepodge of historic military quarters, huge concrete military batteries, charming summer cottages, new condos, winding roads with live oaks, and beach and dunes. Less than 1 square mile, the area is fun to tour on a bike.

TOURING FORT SCREVEN NATIONAL HISTORIC DISTRICT

[Fig. 10(1)] Located at the north end of the island facing the mouth of the Savannah River, the Fort Screven coastal defense combined the strength of poured concrete and granite with the defensive and camouflage qualities of earthen fortifications. The U.S. Army Corps of Engineers drew up plans for a fort on the northern end of Tybee in 1872, acquiring the land in 1875. Ten years later, President Grover Cleveland commissioned Secretary of War William C. Endicott to study U.S. coastal defenses. Endicott submitted a 400-page report that made recommendations for the Atlantic, Pacific, and Great Lakes coasts, and requested $97 million. But appropriations for construction were slow in coming, and it wasn't until 1896 that contracts were made for construction. At first the new fort was to be called Fort Tybee, then Camp Graham, but finally it was named Fort Screven in honor of Revolutionary War hero General James Screven, who was killed in Liberty County in action near Midway, Georgia in 1778.

Eventually in the Fort Screven area six batteries were built. Only one, Battery Garland, is open to tour. The others are on private property and must be viewed from the street. Some of these old concrete structures have been incorporated into private homes. Originally, they all would have been covered and camouflaged with sand and dune plants. Much of the sand was removed to help build US 80 connecting Tybee with the mainland.

Our Rocky Coast

The rock jetties are an interesting marine community to examine. The rocky shore ecosystem is a natural phenomenon in New England that has been intensely studied. Here in the Southeast, a "mini" rocky shore is found at these artificially placed rock walls. Man builds a rock sea wall in a sandy beach and tidal mud flat area, and quickly life starts to occupy it—life of the rocky coast, not the beach and mud flat.

Rocky shore communities consist of three main zones: the splash zone, above the high tide line; the intertidal zone, between the high and low tide lines; and the subtidal zone, located beneath the low tide line. Flora and fauna have different survival strategies in each of these zones. Lichen and algae will thrive in the splash zone. Periwinkle (*Littorina* sp.), oysters, and barnacles will be found in the intertidal areas, whereas crabs may be hiding below the rocks in the subtidal zone. Scrambling over and around the rocks you may notice inch-long cockroach-looking arthropods called sea roaches. They consume rotting flotsam that gets trapped in the rocks.

When a hard-surfaced object is placed in sea water, plants and animals almost immediately start colonizing it, called "fouling succession." First, bacterial slime settles on the surface, and diatoms and protozoa follow within the first day. Then hydroids and bryozoa start to colonize the area on the second to third day, followed by barnacles and algae. Depending on environmental conditions and the swimming larvae that are present, you may then get a colony of oysters, or other sea life such as mussels.

The batteries were executed along Endicott's design: many batteries, with few guns at each, spaced well apart and hidden from the enemy. The batteries were protected by 20-foot-thick walls and surrounded by 30 feet of earth.

Battery Garland, located across from Tybee Lighthouse, was built in 1899 and armed with 12-inch rifled guns (Tybee Museum is located inside). Battery Brumby, located next to Battery Garland, was built in 1898 and armed with four 8-inch guns on disappearing carriages, and was the only fortification finished in time for the Spanish-American War. These guns could fire 200-pound projectiles over 8 miles. Battery Fenwick, located next to Brumby on Taylor Street, was armed with two 12-inch guns. Battery Backus, located on Pulaski Street, was built in 1898 and had a 6-inch rapid-fire gun, then later was enlarged and equipped with 4.7-inch guns that originally were used at a fort on Wassaw Island. Battery Gantt, also on Pulaski Street, was completed in 1900, and was armed with two 3-inch rapid-fire guns in 1903, and is considered to be the most intact of the six batteries at Fort Screven. Battery Habersham, at Pulaski Street and Van Horn Drive, was armed in 1900 with eight 12-inch steel rifled mortars, the most devastating artillery at Fort Screven. These guns would fire 700-pound shells in a high arc from four or eight guns at a time, with the intention of landing shells on the deck of an enemy ship at once. One of these mortars is part of the Fort Screven logo at the Second Avenue Gate No. 2

entrance. (Another Fort Screven battery, Battery Hambright, is located at Fort Pulaski and open to the public. See Fort Pulaski, page 83).

There are many other structures in the historic district that are still in existence from the Fort Screven era. Some are private residences and apartments, and at least one is a bed and breakfast, the Fort Screven Inn. A large, long brick structure on Van Horn Street near Gate No. 2 Sentry Booth served as the base movie theater. Officer's Row houses on Officer's Row Street—many of which have been cut into smaller apartments—rest on top of an artificial berm, looking out to the Savannah River and Atlantic Ocean over a new development of luxury beach homes designed in a style to match. The impressive officer's homes were constructed of cypress and pine and raised above ground level on brick and granite piers.

Behind the Officer's Row houses is the former parade ground. Today is it Jaycee Park. This is the best park on the island, equipped with a jogging path, exercise stations, and a baseball field. Lieutenant Colonel George Catlett Marshall during his command here planted the moss-bearded crape myrtles. A small creek winds through the park, adding to its attractiveness, as do the live oaks, cedars, bayberries, and wax myrtles. Connecting the park with US 80 is palm-lined Campbell Street, which served as the main entrance to Fort Screven. The large building where Campbell Street meets the park was Gate No. 1 Sentry Booth for the fort.

TYBEE LIGHTHOUSE AND TYBEE ISLAND MUSEUM

[Fig. 10(2)] Tybee Lighthouse is a national treasure that is a must-see for anyone visiting the island. The view from the observation deck—145 feet above the ground—is one of the best on the Georgia coast. To enjoy the view requires paying a modest admission to the Tybee Historical Society and climbing 178 black stairs. The admission fee also gets you into the Tybee Island Museum, located across the street from the lighthouse in Battery Garland at Fort Screven (see Fort Screven, page 101). More than 70,000 people visit the lighthouse each year, a testament to the romantic lure these old structures have on the public. The Tybee Historical Society recently received funding to launch long-needed restoration work on the lighthouse and cottages.

Originally used to guide British ships into Savannah, the lighthouse was also helpful to pirates. Blackbeard, who headquartered his crew in the Tybee area, is believed to have buried his treasure in the sands of Tybee Island. During the Civil War, the lighthouse was an important observation post. Today, it continues to guide ships from around the world safely into Savannah Harbor.

Tybee Lighthouse is the tallest (154 feet) and oldest (the lower portion is 225 years old) in Georgia and one of only 20 of the 850 lighthouses in the U.S. that still has its original support buildings. Tybee Light is one of the 450 still active lighthouses, and one of 122 that are open to the public. Most—339—use modern lighting devices. Tybee Lighthouse is one of only 13 that still uses its first order Fresnel (pronounced fre-nel) lens. Tybee Lighthouse was the second established in the colonies and is the second oldest in the U.S. using its original tower. The Tybee Island Light Station is nominated for National Landmark Status.

What you see today is actually two lighthouses: the third lighthouse (the bottom 60 feet completed in 1773) and the fourth lighthouse (the top 94 feet added to the original foundation in 1867). The octagonal structure is made of brick, with 12-foot-thick walls at the base tapering to 18 inches at the top.

Tybee's first lighthouse was a daymark—a lighthouse without a light—designed and constructed by Noble Jones of Wormsloe Plantation for Gen. James Edward Oglethorpe three years after Oglethorpe had founded the English colony of Savannah. This first structure, said to be the tallest structure in America at that time, was a 90-foot octagon made of brick and cedar piles. Storms and beach erosion (nothing new on Tybee) first threatened then carried away this first effort in August of 1741, forcing the commission of a second lighthouse.

The second lighthouse, finished in March of 1742, was a 90-foot stone and wood tower, with a 30-foot flagpole, used to communicate with passing ships. Oglethorpe said this structure was "much the best building of its kind in America." However, it too was built too close to the Atlantic Ocean and was threatened by forces of the sea.

In 1768, the third lighthouse was authorized to be built on the current site, much farther inland than the original two. Finished in 1773, it was built of Savannah grey brick, with interior wooden stairs, and stood 100 feet tall. It was also a daymark. When Georgia ratified the U.S. Constitution in 1790, the lighthouse and property came under the ownership and management of the United States Lighthouse Service, and lights were installed, using large candles and a large metal disc as an illuminate. Later, 16 whale-oil burning lamps were installed. George Washington personally reviewed the rebuilding of the woodwork of Tybee Lighthouse. When given the choice of "a hanging staircase for the sum of 160 pounds" or "a plain staircase for 110 pounds," the frugal and laconic Washington wrote the following: "Approved with the plain staircase. G. Washington."

In the 1800s, the lighthouse survived several powerful hurricanes, damage by Confederate soldiers, and even an earthquake.

In 1857, the lighthouse was improved by installing an 8-foot-tall, second order Fresnel lens, meaning the keeper had only to keep one lamp lit, making trips up the stairs with heavy oil a much easier task. During the Civil War, with Federal troops using Tybee Island, Confederate volunteers at Fort Pulaski grew concerned that the lighthouse would be an aid to Union gunboats. So one night a raiding party, under the command of Captain James B. Read, removed the lens, exploded a keg of gunpowder, and burned the stairs. Union troops quickly repaired the stairs, and used the lighthouse as an observation tower to plan and watch the successful bombardment of Fort Pulaski on Cockspur Island in spring of 1862.

In 1866, the fourth lighthouse was approved for Tybee made of brick and cast iron. Engineers used the lower 1773 portion as the foundation, added 94 feet to the top, and installed a first order Fresnel lens. The new light shone for the first time on October 1,

The Smaller Creatures of the Beach

To the untrained eye, the beach looks like an impoverished environment, devoid of life. But actually, the hard-packed beach is literally crawling with creatures, so many that if people really knew what they were sitting on, they might think twice about where they put their blankets and umbrellas. The firm beach gives these animals a stable habitat that protects them, where they can burrow and use siphons, tubes, or tunnels to hide and feed.

Under the pier at the base of the supports where it is washed by waves is a good place to collect sand for seining to learn about smaller burrowing coastal organisms, such as coquina clams, sand fleas, mole crabs, and other species. You can use a vegetable strainer with a fine mesh or some of the children's toys sold at Christy's or T.S. Chu's. A magnifying glass helps observe the fauna you are about to collect. Put the sand in the strainer and flush it out with sea water and look very closely at what's caught at the bottom. The whitish, transparent, wiggling creatures may be sand fleas or mole crabs. Sometimes you will catch worms, juvenile crabs, or other creatures. The small, colorful clams are coquina. Place them in a bucket with an inch of sand and wait. In a short time, the clams will probe their siphons outside their shell, turn upright, and burrow quickly into the sand. You can fish them out and watch them do it again. Children can be entertained with this for quite some time.

These burrowing creatures feed on plankton that washes over and down into the sand. These burrowers, in turn, are eaten by ghost crabs, birds, fish, and other animals.

1867. The lighthouse required three keepers to maintain the light, each taking a three-hour shift and responsible for carrying 5 gallons of fuel to the top. In 1871, the lighthouse was damaged by a storm that pounded the coast, and in 1886 was cracked in several places by an earthquake that centered on Charleston, South Carolina.

Since the late 1800s, the lighthouse has seen relatively few changes. The 1867 lens rests in its original supports and visitors ascend the same cast iron staircase to marvel at the view. In 1933, electricity powering a 1,000-watt bulb replaced kerosene as the energy source for the light, and only one lightkeeper was needed. George Jackson, the last keeper, served in that capacity until he died in 1948 and the U.S. Coast Guard took over the operation and maintenance of the lighthouse. In 1987, the Coast Guard relocated to Cockspur Island and formed a joint partnership with the City of Tybee Island and Tybee Historical Society, which is responsible for maintenance and restoration of the six historical buildings on the 5-acre site delineated by a neat, white picket fence.

A $400,000 restoration of the lighthouse was undertaken in 1998 and 1999, changing the daymark to the 1916 to 1964 version of black, white, and black (the longest running version—the lighthouse has had five daymark changes), and completing other long-needed repairs. Tybee Island Historical Society Director Cullen Chambers, who previously restored lighthouses in Key West and St. Augustine, Forida, directed the work. The society was helped by the donation of $63,000 by Bill Younger of Younger & Associates and the Harbor Lights Collectors Society—the company that makes lighthouse collectibles. The Georgia Department of Transportation provided a $250,000 reimbursement grant through a federal I.S.T.E.A. program. The Tybee Island Historical Society also plans to restore three of the cottages to their circa-1900 appearance.

A 1939 garage building has been transformed into an excellent gift shop and admission building. Nearby, there is a large bell stamped with U.S.L.H.S., which stands for United States Lighthouse Society. The bell is stamped with the year 1938, which is the year before the Society was reorganized into the U.S. Coast Guard. The bell was used to call volunteers during emergencies, such as when a ship ran aground or was stuck on a sand bar.

TYBEE ISLAND MUSEUM

[Fig. 10(3)] The eclectic Tybee Island Museum has the advantage of being in a historic structure of Battery Garland. You can tour the museum and view its Indian, gun, doll, Civil War, Johnny Mercer, and Fort Screven exhibits. A bell is on display that once was used on a Georgia Railroad steam locomotive and later summoned schoolchildren to Tybee Elementary. For the naturalist, there are collections of shells and bones of marine animals. The museum itself is interesting to walk through and imagine what military duty was like inside these concrete batteries. Walking through the museum requires the ability to climb stairs so is inappropriate for strollers or wheelchairs. An observation deck on top of the battery offers a good view of Tybee Roads and South Carolina's barrier islands. A submarine periscope is fun for children. The museum has a gift shop.

Outside in the parking lot is an unusual monument to Second Lieutenant Henry Sims Morgan, who died in an act of heroism. On August 31, 1898, during a terrible hurricane, the Italian Bark *Noe* wrecked in Tybee Roads, putting the crew in jeopardy. The 24-year-old Morgan, who was in charge of the fortification work at Fort Screven, and a crew of five volunteers attempted to rescue the imperiled crew. Morgan and one volunteer lost their lives in the attempt. In 1903, classmates dedicated a plaque to Morgan's memory at West Point. In 1923 at Fort Screven, a duplicate was mounted on a large granite stone, which was moved to Fort Pulaski when Fort Screven was decommissioned but later returned to this spot in 1994.

Directions: From Savannah, go approximately 18 miles east on US 80 to Tybee Island. At Tybee Island, look for a small sign to lighthouse on left before US 80 curves and becomes Butler Avenue. Go left at traffic light at Campbell Street, left on Van Horne, then immediately right on Meddin. Lighthouse is on left, museum is on the right.

Activities: Historic touring.

Facilities: Museum, bookstore, gift shop, bathrooms.

Dates: Open every day except Tuesdays, Thanksgiving, Christmas, and New Year's Day. Special extended hours during summer.

Fees: Admission is charged.

Closest town: Tybee Island.

For more information: Director, Tybee Island Lighthouse, PO Box 366, Tybee Island, GA 31328. Phone 786-5801. Museum: Phone 786-4077

░ RECREATION ON TYBEE ISLAND'S FORT SCREVEN, NORTH AND MID-BEACH AREAS

On the northern side of the Battery Garland and Brumby is a large parking lot and boardwalk access over the dunes to the North Beach area of Tybee Island. For the naturalist, this is a good area to examine dune formation processes. Gulls and pelicans are common out on the flats. Some locals say the North Beach area has the best shelling, but this could be because it is not as heavily used. Fishermen try their skill casting off into the river currents of the sound. Bikers can enjoy a relaxing trip through Fort Screven's funky neighborhoods, as they ride along narrow roads lined with wax myrtle, palms, and live oaks and view the former military base's hulking concrete batteries, eclectic homes, and converted military buildings.

░ LODGING ON TYBEE ISLAND'S FORT SCREVEN, NORTH, AND MID-BEACH AREAS

Fort Screven Inn. 24 Van Horne, Fort Screven Historic District. If you want a more peaceful stay on Tybee, consider the Fort Screven Inn, a circa-1900 house that housed military officers serving Fort Screven. This is an excellent location for exploring the historic Fort Screven and North Beach area and innkeeper Tess Jones knows how to make her guests feel at home. Air-conditioned suites with private baths. *Moderate. 786-9255.*

The Marsh Hen B&B. 702 Butler Avenue, Tybee Island. This small B&B is located on 7th Street in the residential Mid-Beach area. Two bedrooms with private baths are available and the B&B is located near the beach. *Moderate. 786-0378.*

Econo Lodge Beachside. 404 Butler Avenue, Tybee Island. One of the first motels you see when you reach the Tybee beaches after a big right turn on US 80 is the Econo Lodge, which is located on beach. The 1970 motel has been remodeled to gear it more for families as opposed to the one-night party crowd. Rooms have porches and the second-floor balconies have ocean views. Owners have added an excellent restaurant, The **Grill Beachside**, plus a bar and grill overlooking the beach. A great place to drink a margarita while listening to a local Jimmy Buffett. With 60 remodeled rooms, a swimming pool, beach volleyball, and a playground for children, there's plenty for the family to explore. It's located across the street from Tybee's public park where tennis and basketball courts, along with picnic shelters and grills can be found. Econo Lodge also rents five nice beachfront condos, with elevators for the handicapped, just steps away. *Moderate. (800) 786-0770. Restaurant: 786-4745.*

Condo and Home Rentals. Contact the Tybee Island Visitors Center for Tybee Island rentals. (800) 868-2322. Other management companies offering rentals across the island include **Tybee Island Rentals**, (800) 476-0807; **Tybee Beach Rentals**, (800) 755-8562; and **Beachside Realty**, (800) 786-0770.

▒ RESTAURANTS ON TYBEE ISLAND'S FORT SCREVEN, NORTH AND MID-BEACH, CHIMNEY CREEK, AND LAZARETTO CREEK AREAS

North Beach Grill. 41A Meddin Drive, Fort Screven Historic District. Wedged between batteries Brumby and Garland at Fort Screven, is a popular restaurant with a coastal flair. Here you find a slightly more upscale crowd drinking wine and eating jerk chicken with plastic forks out of wax-paper lined baskets. The food is Caribbean-coastal, sometimes spicy, and usually very good. The asparagus-blue crab appetizer is delicious. Fresh fish dishes are worth your money. Indoor and outdoor seating. Open for lunch and dinner, daily except Tuesday. *Moderate. 786-9003.*

Lazaretto Creek

Georgia's original charter had an antislavery provision, based on founder Gen. James Edward Oglethorpe's opposition to the "peculiar" institution. But Georgia's planters, seeing the profits made from the use of slave labor by their South Carolina plantation neighbors, overruled Oglethorpe's wishes and in 1749 repealed this provision and passed an act permitting the establishment of slavery in the young colony. This act ordered the erection of a lazaretto, or quarantine station, on Tybee Island. In 1767, approximately 100 acres on Tybee's extreme western tip at the mouth of what became Lazaretto Creek were purchased from Josiah Tattnall to build the quarantine station. The next year, several hospital buildings were completed. Here, voyagers who arrived ill were treated and those who died were buried in unmarked graves. The lazaretto was in continuous use until 1785, when the buildings were in disrepair and a new station was built on Cockspur Island.

MacElwee's Seafood Restaurant. 101 Lovell Avenue, Tybee Island. Tybee's oldest seafood restaurant (more than 15 years) is a cut above the usual family seafood places you find at the beach. Very good service. Besides fresh fish dinners, the stuffed oysters are very good as well as the hand-cut black angus steaks. Takeout is available. Open for dinner Monday through Saturday. *Moderate. 786-4259.*

The Crab Shack. 40 Estill Hammock, Chimney Creek. In the 1930s it was a fish camp, then it was a marina, then a bar, then a seafood restaurant, then a larger seafood restaurant. If you want to go "low country," this is the best place to do it. Crack blue crabs or slurp raw oysters under live oaks while watching someone slide their boat into the marsh or a manatee swim by. Or observe a great blue heron hunting for food in the salt marsh so close you can spit on it. This is the kind of restaurant that you could only find on the Georgia coast. The owner, Jack Flanigan, lives on the property in a trailer near the parking lot. To reach the restaurant, go west on US 80 off of Tybee Island, turn left at Chimney Creek (before Lazaretto Creek), and follow the signs. Indoor and outdoor seating. Bar. Open for lunch and dinner. *Moderate. 786-9857.*

Bubba Gumbo's and Cafe Loco. 1 Old Tybee Road. These two restaurants are located roughly next to one another in the salt marsh facing west on Lazaretto Creek. This is a good place to watch the sun go down while you eat some of freshest shrimp you've ever tasted. Bubba Gumbo's, a Yankee's idea of a good name for a seafood restaurant, serves only shrimp recently brought from the docks located nearby. Believe it or not, eating fresh Georgia shrimp at a Georgia coastal restaurant is rarer than you might think. It's cheaper to sell imported shrimp than Georgia shrimp, and many Fried Captain Platter Restaurants do just that. The Bubba's Platter, consisting of fresh shrimp, oysters, and catfish dipped in beer batter, is excellent. Cafe Loco, with more of a night life, is much the same in the food department. Flip a coin. Indoor and outdoor seating. Lunch and dinner. *Moderate. Bubba Gumbo's: 786-9500. Café Loco: 786-7810.*

Tybee Island: South Beach Area

[Fig. 10(6)] South Beach is where the action and crowds are. Here you find the Tybee Pavilion and Pier, Tybee Island Marine Science Center, public beach parking, surfing, restaurants, motels and condos, and honky-tonks. The central commercial strip is Tybrisa Street, formerly 16th Street, where bars, ice cream parlors, and beach shops compete for your attention.

South Beach is probably the best easily accessible public beach in Georgia. As sand has drifted southward on the island, it was trapped here by now-buried jetties and groins. Notice how the beach is working its way up the steps of the boardwalks over the dunes. The snow fences were established a few years ago, and now the dunes are forming around them. Pioneer dune plants are starting to take hold, including morning glory, recognized by the yellow and white flower. Sea oats, important for their beach-holding character with their 30-foot-long roots, have not yet colonized these new dunes, so the dunes' futures are uncertain.

The beach is broad and flat, so tides move quickly up and down the beach. Twice a day, the water moves 6 to 9 feet vertically, and up to 300 feet horizontally. Tybee Island rookies set up their umbrellas and chairs, only to move them back in five minutes, then move them again five minutes later with irritation.

At low tide, where South Beach wraps around to the Back River area, sand bars or shoals become exposed, stretching southward toward Little Tybee. From the far end, it looks like an easy swim to Little Tybee, but don't try it. Every year someone drowns in the attempt, underestimating the outgoing tides and currents. Where longshore currents meet outgoing and incoming tides in the sounds, tremendous turbulence is created, making for dangerous conditions.

These sand bars are the best places to go beachcombing in the South Beach area, especially at low tide. Here you will find Van Hyning's cockle, a large, pretty shell that resembles a heart when two halves are closed together. Other sea life you will find here are pen and scallop shells; sand dollars; hermit, blue, and spider crabs; starfish; knobbed whelks; and oyster drills. Shorebirds prowl the rills and sloughs looking for trapped fish and other meals. Keep a watchful eye on incoming tides so you don't become trapped on a quickly disappearing sand bar.

[Fig. 10(4)] **The Pier and Pavilion** is a great place to drink a coffee and watch the sun come up—or wet a line with local fishermen when the sun goes down. Built in 1996 in time for the Olympics, the pier juts 700 feet out into the ocean. The 20,000-square-foot Pavilion can be rented for private parties. Many fish the pier at night, and a fish-cleaning sink is located here. On weekend nights, walking the pier is such a popular pastime that you are transported into a different, simpler era—before Nintendo and cable and VCRs—when you knew your neighbor. Bands play in the sheltered pavilion during the summer.

Below the pier, the pilings located in the intertidal zone are a good place to examine what quickly happens in a marine environment when a hard surface is introduced to the sea. Here you will find oysters, mussels, barnacles, and other marine life clinging to the concrete supports.

The pier south to the main jetty is officially approved for surfing. On days with good wave action, you will see quite a few trying their luck. Surfers also try the waves on the north side of the pier, but officially are not supposed to.

Other wildlife you will see on the beach, not including *homo sapiens*, includes sea birds begging for handouts. One gull can quickly become a scene from Alfred Hitchcock's *The Birds* if you give in to the temptation to feed it. You will see menhaden and other fish stirring in the water plus a full complement of sand-dwelling fauna responding to the tides such as sand dollars, mole crabs, cochina, and ghost shrimp. Insects may bite in the summer during sunset if the usual sea breeze is absent, but usually they are not a problem.

TYBEE ISLAND MARINE SCIENCE CENTER

[Fig. 10(5)] Located at the base of the Tybee Pavilion and Pier, the Tybee Island Marine Science Center is perfectly located to educate the general public on Georgia's valuable natural resources found at the shoreline. A beach walk with one of the center's educators is a great start to a vacation at the beach and helps the curious of all ages understand the natural processes and flora and fauna that share the beach with man. Volunteers pull a seine net through the surf and analyze the contents. The center, open free to the public, has a museum with many exhibits and aquariums featuring native species found along Georgia's shore. More than 30,000 people visited the center in 1997.

For more than 10 years, the center has been conducting seinings and beach walks guided by volunteers. The doors of the center opened in 1988, with the City of Tybee and the University of Georgia Marine Extension Service as initial sponsors. In 1990, these two groups were joined by the Gray's Reef National Marine Sanctuary office of the NOAA. The City of Tybee Island provides the building, which currently is shared with Tybee's lifeguards, and Gray's Reef funds the aquarium and educational supplies. The Tybee Island Marine Science Foundation was formed in 1990 to give the center more stability and allow for donations from major sponsors and individuals.

The museum holds nine aquariums and a touch tank featuring native species, many of which are brought to the center by Tybee's fishermen. Excellent exhibits will educate both children and adults about sharks, fossils, marine mammals, shells, marine pollution, and sea turtles.

The museum has a homemade look to it, but in many ways it is superior to the sleek, expensive aquariums found around the U.S. because it offers hands-on educational activities in the natural setting that is its focus. In other words, you can apply what you learn just steps away from the center, something you can't do at Chicago's Shedd Aquarium exhibit on whales.

The center sees a lot of traffic from school groups, and conducts popular summer programs including Sea Camp, a summer camp for children ages 3–12; Tuesdays at Tybee, a free guest lecture series held at the pavilion; and beach walks. The center also conducts teacher workshops and group programs for organizations such as the Girl Scouts.

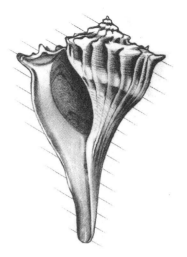

KNOBBED WHELK
(Busycon carica)
This common mollusk is the official state seashell and is caught by commercial fishermen and sold as conch meat.

Due to the success of the center, there are plans to expand, according to Director Susan Brockway. Grants have been secured and the center hopes to renovate and use more of the building to make its educational message even more effective. Center officials want to add an additional classroom, and build a third-floor auditorium and a fourth-flour observation deck. Fund-raisers have been held by Sea Kayak, Inc., raising more than $2,500 to help the Tybee Island Marine Science Center.

Directions: From Tybee, drive south from the big anchor on Butler Avenue. Turn left onto 14th Street. Enter the 14th Street parking lot and drive straight ahead. The center is located directly behind the Tybee Pier and Pavilion.

Activities: Beach walks, seining, touch tank, lectures, sea camps, field trips.

Facilities: Museum, aquarium, exhibits, gift shop, bathrooms.

Dates: Summer hours: Monday through Saturday 9–4, Sunday 1–4; Winter hours: (Thanksgiving–St. Patrick's Day) Monday through Friday 9–4.

Fees: Museum and aquarium free, but donations welcome.

Closest town: Tybee Island.

For more information: Director, Tybee Island Marine Science Center, PO Box 1879, Tybee Island, GA 31328. Phone 786-5917.

LODGING ON TYBEE ISLAND'S SOUTH BEACH

The South Beach area of Tybee Island has the greatest selection of motels, B&Bs, and condos for rent.

Motels: Ocean Plaza Beach Resort. 15th Street and Strand Avenue. Owned and operated by local developer Harry Spirides, it is the largest (240 rooms) family-oriented motel on the island, offering some rooms with ocean views that are steps away from the beach, kitchenettes, a pool, and suites. The Ocean Plaza is built on the location of the famous Tybee Hotel, the north wing of which is still standing and in use as a conference center located near the pool. The current motel is built on the old front lawn of the Tybee Hotel. Notice the palm-lined road, the historic center walkway to the beach. Spirides plans to build a $2 million glass-fronted beach view restaurant that will be the largest restaurant on the island and one of its tallest commercial structures. *Moderate. 786-7777.*
Days Inn. 1402 Butler Avenue. This is the first ever in the popular chain of inexpensive motels. Recently renovated and not far from the beach. *Moderate. (800) 325-2525.*
Best Western Dunes Inn. 1409 Butler Avenue. A family-oriented motel, with private balconies, beach access, kitchenettes and jacuzzi rooms. *Moderate. 786-4591.*

B&Bs: *See* Hunter House, page 113.

Rental Properties: South Beach Ocean Condos. Strand Avenue and 17th Street. New condos with porches, some overlooking the beach, others just a few steps away, are available by the week or month. Units have 1, 2 and 3 bedrooms and 2 bathrooms. Well equipped and well located in the South Beach area. *Moderate. (800) 565-0107.* Other options in area are available by calling the **Tybee Island Visitors Center**. *(800) 868-2322.*

RESTAURANTS ON TYBEE ISLAND'S SOUTH BEACH

There aren't a lot of choices, but the offerings run the gamut from hamburger grills to chicken-finger honky-tonks to fine dining. (*See* also Night Life on Tybee's South Beach, page 113.)

Earl's. 16th Street (Tybrisa Street). A great place for a sloppy burger, Earl's is a locals' hangout that serves food with extra condiments and atmosphere. Earl Hoggard opened his grill in 1982, and his legendary hamburgers have since fed happy thousands. The décor is genuine eclectic (as opposed to fake eclectic—what TGI Friday's does), with Christmas lights, photos of customers' children, newspaper clippings with personal commentary scrawled in the margins, and a stained glass Martin Luther keeping watch on the proceedings. Gyros, subs, sandwiches, and Earl's famous olive burger are popular here. Beer is sold as well. Wednesday to Sunday from 11 a.m. to 8:45. Takeout. *Inexpensive. 786-5695.*

Breakfast Club. 1500 Butler Avenue. A Tybee legend, the "World Famous" Breakfast Club is the best place for breakfast on Tybee, if not the entire southeastern coast. Owned by chef Jodee Sadowsky, locals and tourists alike frequent the popular restaurant at the corner of 15th Street and Butler Avenue. Famous for its omelets, waffles, Polish sausage, and hot coffee, the Breakfast Club features excellent service and a restaurant policy that calls for your order to be served as soon as it's ready. No cold eggs here. Sadowsky was hired to cook for the John F. Kennedy Jr. wedding on Cumberland Island. The decor is *trés* Chicago, with signed photos of former Cubs manager Don Zimmer and shortstop Ernie Banks. Try the Grill Cleaner's Special, a yummy concoction of diced potatoes, Polish sausage, peppers and onions, two scrambled eggs, and jack and American cheese. Open 7 days a week, 6 a.m.–1 p.m. *Inexpensive. 786-5984.*

The Hunter House. 1701 Butler Avenue. Fine dining in a 1910 summer cottage. A 10-year-old B&B with four rooms and more planned for the back, the Hunter House is more famous for its dinner specials than its lodging. John Hunter prepares a short list of specials each night, but whatever you choose, it promises to be very good. Reservations recommended. *Moderate. 786-7515.*

Marlin Marina Bar and Grille. 1315 Chatham Avenue. This Back River marina and restaurant is a great place to look at some boats, eat some shrimp, nurse a cold drink, and watch the sun set. Occasionally live music is featured. *Moderate. 786-7508.*

NIGHT LIFE ON TYBEE'S SOUTH BEACH

Some of South Beach's eating establishments double as nightspots, sometimes with live music. You have several honky-tonks to choose from:

Doc's. 16th Street (Tybrisa Street). The longest continually operating bar on the island, Doc's has been serving drinks since 1948. Doc's is to Tybee what the original Sloppy Joe's was to Key West. Here you will hear many "True Tybee Tales" and meet many of the people who make Tybee an interesting community. A centrally placed bumper pool table has witnessed many an epic battle. *786-5268.* **Spanky's**. Strand Avenue. Spanky's moved from its rowdy DeSoto Motel location to near the pier, where it offers bar food staples such as chicken fingers and nachos. A deck overlooks the ocean. *786-5520.* **Fanny's**. 1613 Strand Avenue. A new deck on top of Fanny's gives the margarita and beer crowd a beautiful view of the beach and Atlantic Ocean. Known for its 15 kinds of gourmet pizza. *786-6109.*

CAMPING ON TYBEE ISLAND

River's End Campground & RV Park. 915 Polk Street. River's End is the only campground on the island, located at the north end of the island only "3 blocks to the Atlantic Ocean." Whether you are carrying a tent or driving an RV, River's End has the full range of amenities you would expect, with 130 campsites, full hookups, pull throughs, water and electricity, fuel, ice, dump station, pool and bathhouse, laundry, store, exercise equipment, picnic tables, and primitive tent sites. *(800) 786-1016.*

BIKING AND KAYAKING ON TYBEE ISLAND

Because the island is small, biking is a favorite way to get to know the town. And the beach is hard-packed enough to accommodate a beach or mountain bike cruise down the length of it. Traffic hasn't increased on the island to where you feel unsafe. Bike rentals are available at **Pack Rat Bicycle Shop**, 1405 Butler Avenue. *786-4013.*

An excellent method of experiencing the Georgia coast is under your own steam in a sea kayak. **Sea Kayak Georgia** is based on Tybee and offers instruction in surfing, navigation, open water rescue, and eskimo rolls. They also offer guided tours with ACA-certified coastal kayak instructors and naturalists. For more information, contact Sea Kayak Georgia at *786-8732.*

FISHING, MARINAS, AND CHARTERS ON TYBEE ISLAND

Sport fishermen use the Tybee and Back River piers, surf cast from the north and south ends, and book charter boats for deep-sea and inshore fishing trips. Sport crabbers use piers, docks, and bridges. Deep-sea fishing of the Gulf Stream and snapper banks is a longer and more expensive commitment, and focuses on catching snapper, grouper, sea bass, triggerfish, shark, king and Spanish mackerel, barracuda, amberjack, dolphin, wahoo, sailfish, tuna, and marlin. Inshore fishing is less time consuming and expensive, with trout, bass, flounder, sheepshead, tarpon, whiting, and shark as the fisherman's game. Nature tours feature trips to Little Tybee and Wassaw islands and dolphin cruises. These playful, intelligent marine mammals are common in the tidal rivers around Tybee.

Marlin Marina is the only marina located on the island. This is the closest marina to the ocean in Chatham County, found in the Back River area at 1315 Chatham Ave. It has a ramp, dock, hoist, fuel, bait and tackle, and a restaurant. You can book fishing trips and nature cruises to Little Tybee and Wassaw islands and dolphin and bird cruises from here. *786-7508.*

Other Tybee Island charter activities occur just off the western side of the island at Chimney and Lazaretto creeks. At **Chimney Creek Fish Camp** you will find a ramp, dock, hoist, fuel, bait and tackle. *786-9857.* A shrimp fleet docks at **Lazaretto Creek Marina** located on Tybee Island before crossing the Lazaretto Creek Bridge toward Wilmington Island. Several fishing charters leave from here. Fishing trips and nature cruises can be booked by calling Lazaretto Creek Marina & Dolphin Tours, *(800) 242-0166;* **Palmetto Coast Charters**, *786-5403;* and Tybee Island Charters, Inc., *786-4801.*

TYBEE NATIONAL WILDLIFE REFUGE

[Fig. 9(1)] This 400-acre wildlife refuge was established on May 9, 1938 as a protected breeding area for migratory birds. Located in South Carolina north of the Savannah River shipping channel, above the Georgia state line, the majority of the island is covered with sand deposits from U.S. Army Corps of Engineers dredging activities. Historically known as Oyster Bed Island, a beacon similar to Cockspur Island Beacon used to be located here to mark the north channel of the river until a storm destroyed it. Today only wild animals use the island, and the public is prohibited from landing on the island or disturbing it in any way.

Salt marsh borders certain areas of the island. Higher and drier portions of the island are densely covered with typical hammock species such as red cedar, wax myrtle, and groundsel. At low tide, the shoreline provides a resting and feeding site for many species of migratory birds, and pelicans, egrets, herons, and gulls are commonly seen here. Willets are recorded as nesting and raising their young here as do American oystercatchers, killdeer, clapper rails, and red-tailed hawks. Some winter visitors include whimbrels, purple and pectoral sandpipers, dunlin, redknots, and northern gannets. Permanent residents include clapper rails, fish crows, and boat-tailed grackles.

Bird watchers should probably pilot their boats toward a different wildlife refuge than Tybee, with this one located so close to heavy shipping traffic and the strong currents of Tybee Roads. Some bird watchers view the island with a telescope from the northern side of Fort Pulaski National Monument.

For more information: U.S. Fish and Wildlife Service, Savannah Coastal Refuges, Parkway Business Center, Suite 10, 1000 Business Center Drive, Savannah, GA 31405. Phone 652-4415.

Little Tybee, Williamson, and Cabbage Islands

[Fig. 9, Fig. 11] Little Tybee, Williamson, and Cabbage islands are sparkling young jewels on Georgia's coast, reachable only by boat and open to outdoor recreation. If you can reach these islands, you will be treated to a barrier island in its unspoiled state. On Little Tybee and Williamson islands, shelling, picnicking, nature hiking, bird-watching, and fishing are first-class experiences. Little Tybee, with 6,780 total acres including marsh, is actually more than twice the size of Tybee Island to the north. Its beach is as long as Tybee's, but its upland is half the size of Tybee's with only 600 acres. Williamson is a recently emerging island that has evolved from a sand bar. Cabbage Island, located south of Wilmington Island and west of Little Tybee, is mainly marsh with some beachfront.

Visitors must be careful not to disturb sensitive species that depend on this island complex. Found on these islands are declining species of rare sea and shorebird species. Least terns, Wilson's plovers, and American oystercatchers use sand scrapes right on the beach sand as nests. Their eggs and young are vulnerable to mammalian predators such as raccoons and hogs as well as thoughtless humans who interfere and destroy the nests or bring destructive dogs to the island. Many sea and shorebirds use these beaches as migratory stopovers or wintering habitat and arrive at Georgia's coast with depleted energy reserves so even minor disturbances can negatively impact them by interrupting their feeding and resting habits. Threatened loggerhead sea turtles nest on the islands.

Little Tybee is visible from the south end of Tybee Island. Between the islands is Tybee Creek and Inlet. Williamson is at the southern end of this island complex, and its southern end looks over to Wassaw Sound and Wassaw Island about 4 miles away. Little Tybee is a young, Holocene island that has developed in the last 4,000 years.

RED CEDAR
(Juniperus virginiana)
Cedars are found growing in the
alkaline soils of ancient shell mounds
left behind by coastal Indians.

Little Tybee and Cabbage islands, purchased in 1968 by the Kerr-McGee Corporation, were to be mined for their rich phosphorites then filled for development. Then Georgia Governor Lester Maddox assembled an advisory team from the University of Georgia to assess the environmental impact of the mining activities. The committee reported that the operation had the potential of breaking through the layer of clay that protects coastal Georgia's freshwater aquifer, contaminating it with salt water. Also, the oxygen demand created by the mining operation could have depleted oxygen levels, threatening the entire estuary by suffocating the shrimp, crabs, fishes, and other creatures that depend on the inshore nurseries.

Public outrage at the plan eventually resulted in the passage of the Coastal Marshlands Protection Act of 1970, which effectively prohibited Kerr-McGee from developing the islands' mineral assets. In 1990, the Kerr-McGee Corporation donated the islands to The Nature Conservancy of Georgia, which in turn sold them to the state for $1.5 million. The state was helped by a generous $1 million donation from a private donor. Today, The Nature Conservancy retains a conservation easement over the islands, which are managed by the Georgia Department of Natural Resources.

Geologists believe Little Tybee and Williamson islands have been created from southward migrating sands from Tybee Island and shoals located offshore. They both have the traditional look of a recurved spit, which is the geological result of twice-daily tides and longshore currents.

Natural communities on the islands include tidal creeks, salt marsh, hammock, and beach. *Spartina* is found in the marshes, while maritime forests of live oaks, cabbage palms, and saw palmetto are found on the upland sand ridges. Pines, cedars, and wax myrtles colonize the high ground, and dune plants and sea oats are found trapping blowing sands and growing the dunes.

Williamson Island is the newest kid on the block on Georgia's coast. Before 1957, the island didn't exist in aerial photographs. In the 1960s, it started developing as a peninsula attached to Little Tybee. In the early 1970s, a tidal creek had effectively cut the peninsula off from Little Tybee, creating a "new" island from migrating sands. By 1976, the island consisted of 250 acres with 2 miles of beach, and it was large enough to acquire the name of Williamson Island, in honor of the then recently deceased former mayor of Darien, who served on the Georgia Board of Natural Resources. The state claimed ownership of the new island, and by the mid-1980s, this ephemeral piece of land appeared to be shrinking and migrating westward toward the privately owned Little Tybee Island. Today, the small sand bar island continues to be important and protected nesting habitat for rare species of birds, such as the least tern.

Shaped like a quarter moon, Williamson is fascinating to scientists who study the still-mysterious development of barrier islands. Forty years ago, Williamson was merely shoals under the water threatening watercraft. Today, pioneer plants struggle to develop and gain a foothold, ghost and hermit crabs scuttle across the sandy beaches, and migrating shorebirds depend on its remote and undisturbed habitat. The island is like a living laboratory, where scientists can observe the natural succession of plants and animals to learn how natural communities evolve.

In July 1997, public concern over threats to critical shorebird nesting sites led to the formation of a state committee to study the problem. In April of 1998, the Board of Natural Resources approved the Bird Island Advisory Committee's recommendation to make the interior of Williamson Island off limits. The north and south ends of the island and the entire beach along the front are open to recreational use, but dogs are strictly prohibited. Visitors to Williamson Island should be particularly careful not to disturb nesting sea or shorebirds in the Williamson Island Bird Conservation Area. Pamphlets with additional information on the restricted conservation area (located in the center of the island) may be found at local marinas.

Little Tybee Island was very busy in the summer of 1996 as the site of Olympic yachting events. A temporary marina was built just off Little Tybee Island in Wassaw Sound to accommodate the competitors.

Beach recreational activities are permitted on these islands, such as picnicking, shelling, and fishing. Shelling is frequently excellent as visitation is light.

Approaching these islands, which must be done in a boat, can be very tricky even for experts. Be very aware of the tides. Many have gotten their boats stuck on shoals and had to wait 12 hours for a rising tide to carry them out. The water is shallow and the currents can be treacherous and deadly if you try to swim to the islands. Some get as close as they can, anchor their boat, and wade ashore. If you do this, you may want to consider leaving someone in the boat who can keep an eye on the tides.

Directions: All three islands are south of Tybee Island. There are no roads to these islands, so a boat must be used to reach them. Novice boaters may want to charter a nature cruise from a charter service out of the marinas listed here. It can be confusing trying to understand where one island begins and another one ends, so a nautical chart is necessary. The islands can be approached from the north end from Marlin Marina on Tybee Island, phone 786-7508; the southern end from the Bull River Marina, phone 897-7300; or Hogan's Marina on Wilmington Island, phone 897-3474.

Activities: Beachcombing, fishing, picnicking, bird watching, nature hiking, kayaking, camping. No pets.

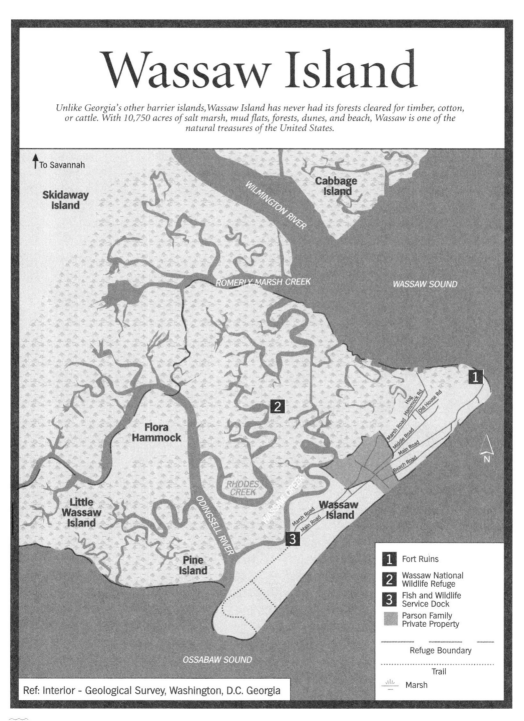

Wassaw Island

Unlike Georgia's other barrier islands, Wassaw Island has never had its forests cleared for timber, cotton, or cattle. With 10,750 acres of salt marsh, mud flats, forests, dunes, and beach, Wassaw is one of the natural treasures of the United States.

To Savannah

Skidaway Island

Cabbage Island

WILMINGTON RIVER

ROMERLY MARSH CREEK

WASSAW SOUND

Flora Hammock

2

1

Hog Hammock Rd

Old House Rd

Marsh Road

Middle Road

Main Road

Beach Road

N

RHODES CREEK

Little Wassaw Island

ODINGSELL RIVER

Pine Island

Marsh Road

Main Road

Wassaw Island

3

1	Fort Ruins
2	Wassaw National Wildlife Refuge
3	Fish and Wildlife Service Dock
	Parson Family Private Property
	Refuge Boundary
	Trail
	Marsh

OSSABAW SOUND

Ref: Interior - Geological Survey, Washington, D.C. Georgia

Facilities: None.

Dates: Open 7 days a week. Some areas posted off limits.

Fees: No fee charged.

Closest town: Tybee Island.

For more information: Georgia Department of Natural Resources, Nongame/ Heritage Section, 116 Rum Creek Drive, Forsyth, Georgia 31029. Phone (770) 761-3035.

Wassaw Island

WASSAW NATIONAL WILDLIFE REFUGE

[Fig. 11] If you are looking for an unspoiled barrier island, it does not get any better than Wassaw. Unlike Georgia's other barrier islands, Wassaw Island has never had its forests cleared for timber, cotton, or cattle. Today part of the National Wildlife Refuge system, this migratory bird refuge is considered the most primitive island on the Georgia coast and is the best representation of what the barrier islands looked like before Europeans arrived. Hiking, shelling, bird-watching, nature study, and fishing are excellent activities here. Facilities are sparse, so if you intend to stay for more than 5 minutes, come prepared with bug repellant, water and food, and toilet paper.

With 10,070 acres of salt marsh, mud flats, forests, dunes, and beach, Wassaw National Wildlife Refuge is one of the natural treasures of the United States. Located southeast of the Pleistocene, older Skidaway Island, the Holocene, younger Wassaw Island has roughly 7 miles of deserted beach and 2,500 acres of beach dune and upland forest communities, roads, trails, and administrative land. The woodlands consist of lush virgin stands of oak, pine, and cedar along with magnolia, cabbage palm, and holly. Virgin forests are extremely rare not only on the coast but anywhere in Georgia. The remainder of the refuge is tidal saltwater marsh, which is excellent for fishing and where one can quickly become engulfed in its natural beauty.

As one approaches the island, it is obvious from the height and size of the pines and oaks that it is a precious reserve of wilderness on America's rapidly developing coastlines. The lack of disturbance has allowed natural climax plant communities to flourish, which in turn support a natural diversity of animal species. More than 204 bird species have been identified on Wassaw. The island is home to rookeries for egrets, herons, and other wading birds, which are abundant in the summer months. Bird watchers will appreciate the thousands of migrating songbirds that visit Wassaw in spring and fall to feast on insects, seeds, and fruits during their long journeys to and from breeding grounds. Migrant songbirds include worm-eating, black-throated blue, chestnut-sided, Cape May, Nashville, Blackburnian, and black-throated-green warblers. Waterfowl such as widgeons, mallards, and mergansers use the small freshwater ponds during fall and winter. Painted buntings (summer residents), rufous-sided towhees, and cardinals are common in the interior forests. A large variety of migratory birds use Wassaw as a sanctuary, and some unusual species have been reported, including roseate spoonbills, magnificent frigatebird, parasitic jaegers, peregrine falcons, and piping plovers. Southern bald eagles and osprey nest here, as do American oyster-catchers, terns, and plovers.

Rainwater is trapped between dunes, creating freshwater pools and sloughs that support a population of 200 alligators, along with other reptiles and amphibians. In the tidal rivers behind the island, bottle-nosed dolphins are a common sight, observed gliding through the estuary as they hunt unlucky menhaden. Manatees have been tracked near Wassaw in the spring. Tracks on Wassaw's beach attest to nighttime visits by threatened loggerhead sea turtles that come ashore for egg laying then return secretively to the sea before the sun rises. Two months later, the eggs hatch and the tiny turtles scurry to the ocean. Approximately 80 loggerheads nest a year on Wassaw.

Wassaw is a very young island geologically, having formed in 400 A.D. Because of its youth, it hasn't had the time to develop the richer soils found on its older neighbor to the west, Skidaway Island. The island displays its ocean-related origin in a series of parallel dune ridges that mark the position of former shorelines. The main topographic feature of the island is a centrally located dune ridge that extends the length of the island, reaching elevations of 45 feet above sea level at the south end. The sea continues to influence the island, by eroding the north end and creating a boneyard beach of live oaks, and by accreting new land at the southern end.

Historically, the near-pristine Wassaw has experienced some minor impacts from human activities. Like all of Georgia's barrier islands, Native Americans used the island as a reliable hunting ground for shellfish, fish, fowl, and reptiles. The name of the island is derived from the Creek word *wiso*, pronounced wee´-so, meaning sassafras, a plant found on the island. Indian artifacts have been found dating back to 500-600 A.D.

The island's recorded history began in the early 1800s with Anthony Odingsell, a black planter who owned 11 slaves and Little Wassaw Island. In 1846, in an attempt to escape a cholera epidemic, 300 slaves from Liberty County were brought to Wassaw. According to records, they died and were buried on Wassaw Island, but the location of their graves is unknown. During the Civil War, the island was successively occupied by Confederate and Union troops. George Parsons, a wealthy New England businessman who wanted Wassaw as a holiday retreat for family and friends, purchased Wassaw Island in 1866. His attempts to establish quail, turkey, pheasant, and hog populations for hunting failed, but introduced populations of deer and gray squirrel thrive. (Deer hunting is allowed during periods in October and November by permit from the U.S. Wildlife Service.) Parsons built a home in the center of the island, along with 20 miles of interior roads.

During the 1960s when nearby Skidaway was undergoing development, Parsons family descendants became concerned about the future of their wild island. This started efforts to protect the island for future generations, and in 1969, The Nature Conservancy of Georgia purchased the island for $1 million from the Wassaw Island Trust, the legal entity set up by Parsons's descendants. On the open market, Wassaw Island could have sold for many millions more. The $1 million came from a private donation to The Nature Conservancy. The Parsons family retained 180 acres in the center of the island for their personal use. The Nature Conservancy, in turn, sold the island for $1 to the Federal government, which incorporated it into the Savannah Coastal Refuges system on October 20, 1969. Today, it is a national wildlife refuge [Fig. 11(2), Fig. 11(3)] managed by the U.S. Fish and Wildlife Service, which maintains a dock and small headquarters on Wassaw Creek on the southwestern side of the island. The entire Wassaw National Wildlife Refuge consists of Wassaw Island, Little Wassaw Island (Pine Island and Flora Hammock), and 20 acres of leased land on the mainland (Priest Landing). Little Wassaw has 384 acres of upland, with the remaining acreage consisting of salt marsh, marsh hammocks, and tidal creeks.

A special activity on Wassaw Island is a loggerhead sea turtle research program run by volunteers. Almost 10 percent of Georgia's nesting sea turtles crawl across the sands of Wassaw and Pine Island to lay their eggs. Endangered loggerhead sea turtles are dependent on undeveloped beach to nest and continue their species. In the last 50 years, loggerhead turtles have been sliding toward man-caused extinction due to the loss of suitable nesting habitat, among other factors. The Caretta Research Project, initiated in 1973, is aimed at learning more about the population levels and habits of loggerhead sea turtles and improving survival rates of their eggs and hatchlings.

The program is a cooperative effort between the Savannah Science Museum, the Wassaw Island Trust, and the U.S. Fish and Wildlife Service. Project volunteers, who volunteer for one week between mid-May to mid-September, are charged with observing, tagging, and recording nesting females, then relocating nests to protected hatchery sites. When the eggs hatch two months later, volunteers record the success of the baby turtles. Major predators of loggerhead nests are raccoons, ghost crabs, and feral pigs. Hatchlings fall prey to raccoons, ghost crabs, gulls and other birds, and fish. Adult turtles are killed by sharks, motor boats, and shrimp nets. If you are interested in volunteering, see page 123.

Other than the Parsons family homestead and the National Wildlife Refuge headquarters, the only other major development on the island was the construction of a Spanish-American War fort. Built in 1898 into the dunes on the north end of Wassaw, it was part of the Endicott system of coastal forts. Today, erosion has removed the dunes, and high tides now are working against the remains of the fort—a huge, slumping block of poured concrete, oyster tabby, and North Georgia granite—which probably won't see a second 100 years. Constructed by civilians supervised by U.S. Army Corps of Engineers under 24-year-old Second Lieutenant Henry Sims Morgan, this fort was part of the military buildup that produced Fort Screven on the north end of Tybee. Armed with two 4.7-inch rapid-fire guns, it was the largest single fortification built in Georgia specifically for the Spanish-American War, and it was designed to protect the southern approach to Savannah by way of the Wilmington River. Lieutenant Morgan was later assigned to help build

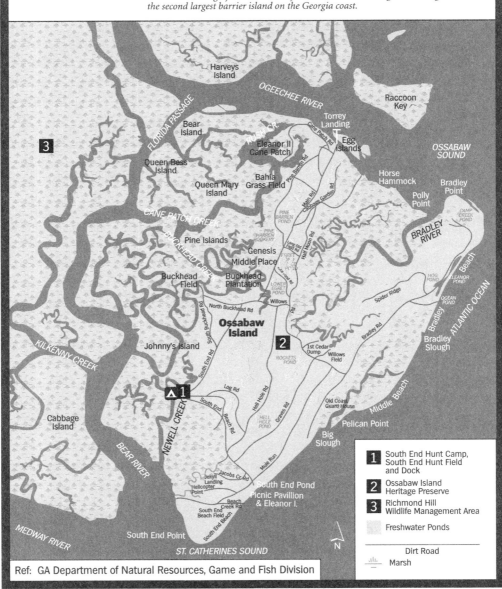

Ossabaw Island

Shaped like a wishbone with marsh filling the middle, Ossabaw consists of 25,000 acres, of which 11,800 are upland and almost 10 miles are beach. It is roughly twice the size of Bermuda and, counting total acreage, the second largest barrier island on the Georgia coast.

1 South End Hunt Camp, South End Hunt Field and Dock

2 Ossabaw Island Heritage Preserve

3 Richmond Hill Wildlife Management Area

Freshwater Ponds

Dirt Road

Marsh

Ref: GA Department of Natural Resources, Game and Fish Division the batteries on the north end of Tybee, where he lost his life attempting to rescue shipwrecked sailors in Tybee Roads during the hurricane of 1898. Some historians have suggested the battery be named Fort Morgan [Fig. 11(1)] in his honor. A monument dedicated to him is found in the parking lot of the Tybee Island Museum.

Directions: Wassaw National Wildlife Refuge is reachable only by boat. Novice boaters may want to charter a nature cruise from a charter service out of the marinas listed here. It can be confusing trying to navigate the various tidal rivers, so a nautical chart is a must. The closest marina to Wassaw Island is **Delegal Creek Marina**, phone *598-0023* or **Salt Water Charter**, phone *598-1814*. Many visiting Wassaw launch from the Isle of Hope and unload at the U.S. Fish and Wildlife Service dock on Wassaw Creek on the interior of the island, then anchor in the creek. **Isle of Hope Marina**, 50 Bluff Drive, phone *354-8187*. Wassaw Island can also be approached at the northern end by boating up the Wilmington River from **Hogan's Marina** on Wilmington Island, phone *897-3474*. Or by the **Wassaw Water Taxi**, 112 Palmetto Drive, Wilmington Island, phone *897-2277*.

Activities: Hiking, bird-watching, shelling, fishing, picnicking, nature studies, biking, kayaking. Strictly prohibited are camping, fires, pets, firearms, and collecting of plants, animals, and artifacts. Deer hunting is allowed by special permit during two periods in October and November. The island is closed on hunt days and the day before and after each hunt period. Dates and bag limits change each year. For information, contact the Savannah Coastal Refuges office at 652-4415. Volunteers for the loggerhead research project should write or call Caretta Research Project, Savannah Science Museum, Inc., 4405 Paulsen Street, Savannah, GA 31405. Phone 355-6705.

Facilities: Federal dock, exhibit shelter with island map.

Dates: Open sunrise to sunset. Closed annually for deer hunts in fall and winter. Portions of beach may be closed to prevent disturbance to nesting, wintering, or migrating birds.

Fees: None.

Closest town: Skidaway Island.

For more information: U.S. Fish and Wildlife Service, Savannah Coastal Refuges, Parkway Business Center, Suite 10, 1000 Business Center Drive, Savannah, GA 31405. Phone 652-4415.

Ossabaw Island

▨ OSSABAW ISLAND HERITAGE PRESERVE

[Fig. 12] Ossabaw, the northernmost member of the historically defined Golden Isles, has a fascinating natural and human history to share. Humans have lived on Ossabaw Island for more than 4,000 years, enjoying and putting to use its rich salt marshes, freshwater ponds, ancient maritime forest, wind-swept dunes, and deserted white beaches. Shaped like a wishbone with marsh filling the middle, the island consists of

A feral hog on Ossabaw Island.

25,000 acres, of which 11,800 are upland and almost 10 miles are beach, making it roughly twice the size of Bermuda and counting total acreage the second largest barrier island on the Georgia coast. The island was the first acquisition of the Heritage Trust Act of 1975, which protects the island from overuse and development, but makes public access difficult and rare.

By state law, all of Georgia's barrier island beaches are open to the public, and Ossabaw is no exception. During daylight hours, the public is allowed to use the beach for hiking, picnicking, or shelling. However, the interior of the island is off limits to the public without permission. The management of the island is the responsibility of the Georgia Department of Natural Resources. As a heritage preserve, the island is open to individuals or groups for "natural, scientific, and cultural purposes based on environmentally sound practices."

Geologically, Ossabaw's two pieces of the wishbone consist of the Pleistocene western part fronting the interior marsh and the Holocene, eastern part facing the sea. The western piece is around 35,000 to 40,000 years old and the eastern piece is roughly 5,000 years old. The older the island, the more time it has had to develop richer soils to support a greater diversity of flora species, and the more likely it is to have developed new species.

Atlantic barrier islands tend to migrate westward toward the mainland. Rivers carry sediment to the ocean. When the river currents meet the tides and the south-moving longshore current, the sediment is pushed to the south, growing islands on their northern ends, giving them a turkey-leg shape.

Geologists believe the two parts of Ossabaw are fused at the southern end, as opposed to the northern end, because of copious outflows of sediment from the Ogeechee River, which has slowed the northern end's westward migration. This effect from rivers is also seen among the islands north of Ossabaw and the St. Simons Island group.

Located 20 miles south of Savannah, the island fronts the salt marshes of Bryan and Liberty counties, but surprisingly is in Chatham County due to a wayward county line. Its northern, wide end looks over Ossabaw Sound (the largest sound on the Georgia coast, which is created by the Ogeechee River) to Wassaw Island, and Ossabaw's narrow, southern end looks over the St. Catherines Sound (created by the Jerico and Medway rivers) to St. Catherines Island. The island's relationship to the Ogeechee River is obvious in the fact that Ossabaw's first European name was *Ogeche*. Today's name of Ossabaw is considered one of the oldest place names in Georgia. The island's name is the anglicized spelling of the Guale village of *Asapo* found on the southern end of the island, believed to mean "yaupon holly bushes place."

Yaupon (*Ilex vomitoria*) is a common shrublike plant with red berries found on Ossabaw and all the other Georgia barrier islands. For ceremonies, Indians used yaupon berries to make a "black drink" that caused vomiting and visions. (CAUTION: Don't experiment with this plant. The leaves and berries are poisonous to humans and should not be eaten.) The island can't claim to be in the pristine natural condition of its neighbor to the north of Wassaw. Ossabaw's development history is typical of most Georgia coastal islands. Over its history of human occupation and use, virgin forests of live oak, water oak, laurel oak, and pine were cleared for timber and for growing sea island cotton, rice, and indigo and raising free-range livestock such as cattle, horses, hogs, and donkeys.

The island's natural communities have been allowed to recover from its 1700s–1800s plantation era under management by the Georgia Department of Natural Resources and the Ossabaw Island Foundation. Today, whatever barrier island natural communities you are looking for, they are represented on the island in abundance. Productive salt marshes and tidal creeks dominate the western side of the island, providing nursery grounds for a wide variety of fish and shellfish, such as trout, bass, oysters, crabs, and shrimp. Egrets and herons are frequently seen wading in the marsh, and vultures glide in their familiar circles overhead. Queen Bess Island, a marsh hammock, supports many nesting bird species, including the endangered bald eagle. Low-lying areas support red bay, American holly, and southern magnolia. The maritime forest consists mainly of live, water, and laurel oaks, and slash and loblolly pines. Eastern red cedar and cabbage palm are found in the upper marsh border and transition zone between marsh and maritime forest. The understory is dominated with abundant saw palmetto and wax myrtle, along with less frequent wild azalea, sparkleberry, beautyberry, sassafras, and yaupon. Catbrier, peppervine, and muscadine vines climb on branches of woody vegetation, bearing their fruit that provides important food energy to migrating songbirds.

Interior freshwater marshes, with cattails (*Typha* sp.) and bulltongue (*Sagittaria* sp.), are home to alligators, frogs, and small fish. Wading birds are common, and migrating waterfowl are also seen using the habitat. The island has noisy bird rookeries, where herons roost and raise their young. Freshwater ponds provide refuge to migrating waterfowl using the Atlantic flyway.

The sandy, dense interdune communities support a healthy population of lizards and snakes, including the Eastern diamondback rattlesnake, which grows to its maximum size due to the protected status of Ossabaw. Wax myrtle (*Myrica cerifera*) is common vegetation. Yucca earns its common name of Spanish bayonet with its succulent leaves with very sharp points. Other prickly plants worth avoiding are the spurge-nettle (*Cnidoscolus stimulosus*), and devil-joint (*Opuntia pusilla*), a small pricky pear cactus with barbed spines.

Primary dunes support flora communities consisting of beach panic grass (*Panicum amarum*), salt meadow cordgrass (*Spartina patens*), beach elder (*Iva imbricata*), sandspur (*Cenchrus tribuloides*), and the dune pioneering sea oats (*Uniola paniculata*), Russian thistle (*Salsola kali*), and morning glory (*Ipomoea* sp.).

Each summer Ossabaw's dunes attract approximately 160 nesting loggerhead turtles, which are drawn by primordial urges to its dark, sandy shoreline. The threatened piping plover winters on the shores of Ossabaw.

If you don't see deer or wild hogs as you travel the island, you aren't on Ossabaw. The island is home to an overpopulation of both, and they are frequently sighted crossing roads. One official estimates that 2,000 hogs and 1,000 deer roam the island. The hogs eat turtle eggs, which is a problem for the threatened loggerhead sea turtle. The first written record of deer hunting on the island was made in 1687, and hunting continues today. So popular is hunting on Ossabaw Island, the Georgia Department of Natural Resources is forced to hold a lottery each year, with lucky applicants receiving the right to shoot a prescribed limit of deer or hogs as well as spend the night on the island.

Ossabaw has a rich human history, with tales of Indian hunting parties, Spanish missionaries, rich plantations, African slaves, millionaire owners, and artist communes.

The first property transfer in the new colony of Georgia involved Ossabaw. Gen. James Edward Oglethorpe made a land deal with Tomochichi, the mico of the Yamacraws, receiving the tidewater region between Savannah and the Altamaha in exchange for granting Ossabaw, St. Catherines, and Sapelo islands to the Indians in perpetuity. The Indians made a subsequent deal, granting the hunting islands to Mary Musgrove, an interpreter of mixed Indian and European parentage, who was considered princess of the tribe. Musgrove, and her second husband Thomas Bosomworth, were granted the Indian hunting islands "as long as the sun shall shine or the waters run in the rivers, forever." Not much happened with the islands until Georgia lifted its ban in 1749 on slavery, which was necessary to operate profitable plantations in the south. Musgrove moved to establish plantations on her three islands, but the Royal Trustees protested the legality of her title to the islands. Despite the dispute, the Bosomworths built a home and planted fields on St. Catherines, and raised cattle on Ossabaw. After 11 years, the case was settled by granting them St. Catherines, and Sapelo and Ossabaw were put up for public auction with the proceeds going to the Bosomworths.

The island passed through several hands until John Morel, who became the first owner to clear and cultivate the property, bought it in the 1760s. Morel was from a successful family of South Carolina planters. He built a home on the north end and planted an avenue of live oaks that remains today and is considered to be the longest, oldest dirt road still in use in America. The Morels planted indigo, cotton, and rice on the island. Indigo production was especially labor intensive, requiring hundreds of slaves to settle on the island. Morel divided the island into three parts for management purposes. When John Morel died, his three sons each received a different part: Bryan Morel inherited North End Place, Peter Henry received Middle Place, and John II was deeded the South End. The names of the three parts are still used today.

After the War of 1812, sea island cotton was the dominant crop and led to great prosperity among plantation owners. The island was abandoned by the Morels during the Civil War, and the Union blockaded the sound, built batteries on the north end of the island, and stationed a small number of troops here. After the Civil War, the property transferred hands until it was almost entirely owned by the Wanamakers of Philadelphia, who used the island as a hunting club.

In the early twentieth century, Ossabaw passed through different owners until Dr. H.N. Torrey of Grosse Point, Michigan, purchased it in 1923 for a winter residence. It took two years to build the family's vacation home at the North End, which became a massive, two-story stucco residence in a Spanish style, with Bermuda pink walls and a Castilian tile roof, harkening back to the days of the Spanish empire on the Georgia coast. In the two-story, chapel-like wood beam living room is a large, centrally located fireplace built of ballast stone. Near the mansion, several other support buildings were constructed, and beautiful gardens were maintained on the grounds. The island again saw its share of parties and famous visitors. Henry Ford is the first signature in the mansion's guest book.

Ownership of the island eventually passed down to Dr. H.N. Torrey's daughter, Eleanor Torrey (Sandy) West and some nieces and nephews. In 1961, Sandy West created The Ossabaw Foundation, which launched many unique programs on the island, such as the Ossabaw Island Project. This interdisciplinary program supported recommended individuals "of creative thought and purpose in the arts, sciences, industry, education, and religion" to come to the island to share their ideas with other creatives and pursue their work without interruption. West herself is a creative artist who has produced children's books, exhibited watercolors, and made documentary films.

Renowned creatives from architect Robert Venturi to writer Annie Dillard stayed at the mansion during the program's run from 1961–1982. Another program launched in 1970, called the Genesis Project, was a rustic experiment in cooperative living at Middle Place, replete with a tree house with a marsh view and solar-powered sauna, among other buildings. Here around 10 students from colleges around the country shared community tasks such as gardening, milking their cow, and maintaining the buildings while they studied the island's environment and history and pursued personal artistic projects, such as making pottery from the island clay.

In the late 1970s, West and her relatives sold the island to the state to keep it from developers. The Nature Conservancy of Georgia purchased an option in 1977, and transferred it to the state in 1978. Valued at $15 million, the island sold for $8 million, with the remaining amount being a charitable gift from West and her family. The State of Georgia provided $4 million, and the remaining half of the purchase price was a donation from The Coca-Cola Company President Robert W. Woodruff, which was the largest private grant for conservation at that time. The island became the first heritage preserve in Georgia [Fig. 12(2)] that allows the conservation of land for specifically stated purposes, and in this case it is to be used in an ecologically sound way for scientific and cultural purposes. West retains a life estate, including the Torrey mansion and 24 acres.

The island has more than 100 miles of dirt roads and trails. At or near the North End of the island is a dock, the Torrey mansion, tabby slave quarters, the island manager's quarters, and one of the first pre-fabricated houses ever built. Brought from Philadelphia where it was

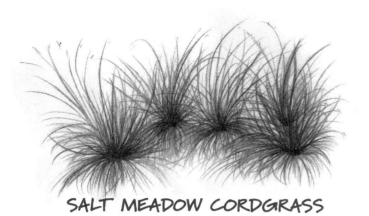

SALT MEADOW CORDGRASS
(Spartina patens)
Smaller than alterniflora, this grass grows in drier areas of the marsh and on primary dunes.

exhibited at the Philadelphia Exposition of 1898, the state plans to rehabilitate the historic two-story wooden structure with grants through the Georgia Heritage 2000 program. Feral horses and Sicilian donkeys roam the area. Cotton was grown at the North End.

Tabby ruins of indigo plantations are found at Middle Place, along with several buildings from the Genesis Project period of the island. A huge, ancient live oak, perhaps 600 years old, is found near here. The South End is home to Department of Natural Resources hunting quarters and a dock for arriving sportsmen. A causeway leads across the interior marshes to the Holocene dune ridges of the eastern half of the island. The beach is wild and deserted, and features some of the best shelling found off the Georgia coast. Like the rest of the island, the beach continues to change and be shaped by natural forces. In the 1970s, island officials could drive the entire length of the beach, but today, a tidal creek has divided the beach at Bradley Slough.

Directions: South End: Kilkenny Fish Camp, a full-service marina, provides closest access to South End Dock by Kilkenny Creek and the Bear River to Newell Creek. South End Dock is used mainly by hunters with permits. If traveling to the North End, many use Fort McAllister, Coffee Bluff, and Isle of Hope marines (*see* Appendix A, Fish Camps and Marinas). Those traveling with the Georgia Department of Natural Resources on cultural visits leave from Vernon View Dock on Shipyard Road on Burnside Island.

Activities: During daylight hours, only the following activities are allowed on the beach: hiking, bird-watching, shelling, fishing, picnicking, nature studies. The island's interior is not open to the public without permission. Hunting is allowed on the island by special permit only. Hunting on Ossabaw Island for deer and feral hogs is probably the state's most popular hunting activity, with thousands of sportsmen applying for the limited number of permits that are issued each year. Those who are chosen are governed by special regulations that apply to the island. Call 262-3173 for details.

Facilities: Two docks used only with permission, hunting camp.

Dates: Beach open sunrise to sunset. Interior closed unless permission is granted by the Georgia Department of Natural Resources on cultural mission or by special hunting permit, or the Ossabaw Island Foundation.

Closest town: Richmond Hill.

For more information: Wildlife Resources Division, Georgia Department of Natural Resources, Brunswick, GA 31520. Phone 262-3173. Ossabaw Island Foundation, Public Use and Education, Ossabaw Island, PO Box 13397, Savannah, GA 31416. Phone 233-5104.

Bryan County

Bryan County features an excellent state park, Fort McAllister State Historic Park; the scenic and wild Ogeechee and Canoochee rivers; and the Richmond Hill Fish Hatchery. Bryan has become a fast-growing bedroom community of Savannah, a fact recognized by its inclusion into the statistical metropolitan area of Savannah, and is predicted to double its 1980 population of 10,000 residents to 20,000 by the year 2000. Ossabaw Island protects Bryan County's marshes, but the officials who drew the Chatham County line made a southern detour with their pens, placing the island under Chatham County jurisdiction.

RICHMOND HILL FISH HATCHERY

[Fig. 5(4)] Established by the automobile magnate Henry Ford and the state of Georgia in 1938, this facility raises more than 30 million fish of all species and sizes each year. Open to tour, children are often fascinated by the hatchery's operations, which have a tremendous impact on the state's native fisheries. Fish produced here are stocked in reservoirs, lakes, and streams all around the state. The hatchery is also working on saving the rare robust redhorse, a sucker that was believed to be extinct only to be found a few years ago in the Oconee River.

With 41 ponds (21 acres of water on 87 acres), the hatchery annually produces approximately 1.2 million bluegill and 250,000 redear sunfish, 100,000 largemouth bass, and 120,000 channel catfish fingerlings for stocking private ponds and public lakes. More than 20 million striped and hybrid bass fry are artificially propagated each spring from wild broodstock collected from inland reservoir populations. Roughly 1.4 million striped and hybrid bass fingerlings are reared for inland reservoir stockings, and 50,000 intermediate size striped bass—8 to 10 inches long—are produced for restoration of the Savannah River population. Popular fishing rodeos, called Kids Fishing Events, are held each year at three ponds that hold channel catfish.

Henry Ford built a manufacturing plant in Atlanta in 1915. Like Thomas Edison before him, Ford became interested in the area around the Ogeechee River known then known as Ways Station. He purchased an 85,000-acre tract next to the river, and named it Richmond Plantation. When Henry McAlpin's Savannah plantation of Hermitage was dissolved, Ford purchased the huge mansion and used it to construct his winter home. Part of his property included Fort McAllister, a famous Civil War fort, which Ford worked to restore in the 1930s (see Fort McAllister State Park, page 131). After Ford's death, the home fell into private hands and is not open to the public.

Ford donated the original land for the Richmond Hill Fish Hatchery to the State of

Georgia in 1936 with the express purpose of establishing a fish hatchery. The first fish spawned in the hatchery were American shad, which were to be used to stock the Ogeechee River.

Civilian Conservation Corps workers performed initial construction under the direction of J.O. Bacon, and in 1938, the hatchery was opened and operated by the Georgia Game and Fish Division. The hatchery has been renovated and expanded several times since then.

Hatcheries around Georgia perform important restoration work for fish species threatened with extinction. The Richmond Hill Hatchery perhaps represents the last, best hope for a very rare species of fish, the robust redhorse (*Moxostoma robustum*). This large fish, growing to 30 inches long and 17 pounds, was a plentiful and easily captured source of food for Indians in Georgia and the Carolinas, according to archeologists. With a delicious, white flesh and a predictable migratory behavior, the robust redhorse was to southeastern Indians what salmon was to Indians of the Pacific coast: a dependable food source. Plentiful in Piedmont and Upper Coastal Plain rivers of Georgia and the Carolinas, vast numbers of large fish would migrate in April and May to shallow gravel bars to reproduce—so shallow that their backs would be exposed and easy for Indians to spear.

In 1870, the great naturalist Edward Drinker Cope captured a robust redhorse and wrote a brief, two-paragraph description of the fish. He sent it to be held in a natural history collection but the specimen was lost. More than 122 years would go by before anyone was to again capture the fish, realize what it was, and describe it for science. Since Cope's time, the Piedmont and Upper Coastal Plain rivers have gone through tremendous changes from damming, siltation, and pollution. Robust redhorses suffered as a result, along with the effects of loss of suitable nesting habitat, the extirpation and extinction of their favorite food (mussels), and predation by introduced species such as flathead catfish. How much Georgia's rivers have changed is not widely understood by the public. When geologist Sir Charles Lyell wrote about the Altamaha River in 1845, he emphasized how clear it was, which is hard to believe today if one has spent any time on that magnificent, muddy river.

In 1991, five large robust redhorses were collected from the Oconee River by fishery biologist Jimmy Evans and technician Wayne Clark of the Georgia Department of Natural Resources. The fish were unlike any species known to occur in that river and they were shipped to fisheries experts for further study. Dr. Byron Freeman of the University of Georgia eventually recognized that this fish was the same described by Cope many years ago. Some of these reproducing fish have been captured, and thanks to fishery science and a grant from Georgia Power, propagation techniques were developed which eventually produced 8- to 10-inch juveniles. These fish were released into the Broad River to see if they could survive. Only time will tell if the robust redhorse will recover, or be lost again, this time forever.

Directions: I-95 south from Savannah to Exit 15/90. Go east on GA 144 approximately 1 mile. Hatchery is on left.

Activities: Nature study, touring, Kids Fishing Events. Call for scheduled events.
Facilities: 87-acre fish hatchery with 41 ponds.
Dates: Open 7 days a week.
Fees: None.
Closest town: Richmond Hill.
For more information: Georgia Department of Natural Resources Fisheries, 22814 Highway 144, Richmond Hill, GA 31324. Phone 727-2112

RICHMOND HILL HISTORIC SOCIETY AND MUSEUM, RICHMOND HILL CITY RECREATION AREA

[Fig. 5(5)] This museum is dedicated to the history of the Richmond Hill and south Bryan County area. Exhibits cover the plantation, Revolutionary War, Civil War, and Henry Ford eras. Georgia's first royal governor, John Reynolds, tried to move the state capital from Savannah to a nearby site on the Ogeechee River, which he wanted to name Hardwicke. He preferred the Ogeechee River because compared with Savannah, the river at that time had a deeper channel, had a less lofty bluff, was more centrally located on the coast of Georgia, and was located farther away from the rival port of Charleston. He wrote that Hardwicke "has a charming situation, the winding of the river making it a peninsula; and it the only fit place for the capital." His plan was thwarted due to a lack of funds.

Having more influence on the area was Henry Ford, who found refuge in the area from the pressures of his automobile enterprise. Ford purchased 85,000 acres and built 292 residential and commercial buildings, including churches, schools, commissary, medical facilities, Richmond Hill Fish Hatchery, and his winter home, Richmond Plantation.

Located on GA 144 behind the Richmond Hill City Hall is the Richmond Hill City Recreation Area, a new 335-acre park that is a charter member of the Colonial Coast Birding Trail. Opened in the summer of 1999, the park borders Gill's Canal and features 300 acres of wetlands, a 5-acre lake, and 35 acres of park uplands. A network of trails are found at the park, including the 3-mile birding trail that borders the wetlands.

Directions: I-95 south from Savannah to Exit 15/90. Go east on GA 144 approximately 1 mile. Museum is on right.
Dates: Open Monday, Thursday, Friday from 9–3, and Saturday and Sunday from 10–4.
For more information: Richmond Hill Historic Society and Museum, 4164 US 17, Richmond Hill, GA. Phone 756-2676. Richmond Hill City Recreation Area: 756-3345.

FORT MCALLISTER STATE HISTORIC PARK

[Fig. 5(6)] With this 1,700-acre park you get a great two-for-one deal: first, a park featuring a fascinating Civil War fort on the southern bank of the Ogeechee River, and second, a park that offers camping and boating in the beauty of Georgia's maritime forests and salt marsh—all just 30 minutes from Savannah.

The park is named after Fort McAllister, a Civil War fort that guarded the back entrance to Savannah. The other part of the park was called Richmond Hill State Park before it was folded into Fort McAllister in 1980. It is one of only four recreational state parks on Georgia's coast. The park is a stop on the Colonial Coast Birding Trail established by the Georgia Department of Natural Resources.

Fort McAllister is located at Genesis Point, the first high ground found upstream from the mouth of the Great Ogeechee River. Genesis Point is actually the northern end of an ancient barrier island of the Pamlico series of sand ridges formed during the Pleistocene era. The high ground was popular with Indians and was the site of the Guale Indian village of *Satuache* and a Spanish mission *San Diego de Satuache* from 1610–1663.

A cannon at Fort McAllister State Historic Park.

Whoever served at Fort McAllister was treated to one of the prettiest views on the Georgia coast. Today, visitors are captivated by views of the sumptuous salt marsh, along with high and low tides that expose productive oyster beds. Solitary wading birds fish in shallower areas and osprey hunt from the sky for finned prey. Lucky observers may see bottle-nosed dolphins playing in the river. Busy woodpeckers and shy songbirds enliven the canopies of the live oaks, magnolias, bays, and pines that thrive on the high bank.

Considered today to be the best preserved earthwork fortification of the Confederacy, Fort McAllister was the southern anchor in a chain of Confederate defenses of Savannah built to prevent attack by sea from Union naval forces. It denied the use of the river to Union vessels, protected King's Bridge (2.5 miles north) and the Savannah and Gulf Railroad Bridge, and preserved river plantations from Union raids. At the time, there were three transportation links between the City of Savannah and the Ogeechee River: a road, a railroad, and a canal that connected the Savannah River with the Ogeechee river, allowing the shipment of goods to and from Savannah (*see* Savannah-Ogeechee Canal, page 50).

The fort is historically important and has been placed on the National Register of Historic Places. The success of Fort McAllister, an inexpensive earthwork fort, stands in sharp contrast to the strategic failure of the expensive brick Fort Pulaski, proving dirt is much more resilient to rifled cannon fire than masonry. Fort McAllister survived seven Federal naval attacks, including bombardment from an ironclad that fired the largest shells yet fired by a naval vessel at a shore work in the Civil War.

Named for a local family that had a nearby plantation and built by Confederate Capt. John McCrady, the engineer who designed the defenses of Savannah, Fort McAllister was a massive fort that was described by a Union officer as "a truly formidable work." It featured seven gun emplacements separated by large traverses;

10 other cannon; a 10-inch mortar located outside the fort; a center bombproof used as hospital, supply area, and bomb shelter when the fort was shelled; a barracks and officers quarters; and several powder magazines.

When Fort Pulaski on the Savannah River was lost to the Union guns on Tybee Island, effectively closing the "front door" to Savannah, the "back door"—the Ogeechee River—increased in strategic importance. Confederates obstructed the river, allowing only friendly vessels to navigate the river. One vessel was the Confederate blockade runner *Nashville* (later called *Rattlesnake*), which had escaped into the Ogeechee River after being chased from Charleston where the vessel had been unable to penetrate the Union blockade. The Union Navy pursued the faster side-wheeled steamer to the Ogeechee, but was turned back by Fort McAllister after four attacks on the fort and *Nashville*.

On January 27, 1863, the *Montauk*, the second monitor-class ironclad constructed by the Union, led a five-ship armada up the Ogeechee to within 1,500 yards of the fort, and opened fire with its big guns. Captain John Worden, who captained the original *Monitor* against the C.S.S. *Virginia* (or *Merrimack*) in the classic battle at Hampton Roads, Virginia, shot 61, 15-inch shells at the fort for five hours. They created huge craters in the ramparts but caused no damage of consequence and no casualties. Confederate guns scored 15 direct hits on the ironclad but did little more than make slight dents in her armor. That night at the fort, the Confederates sneaked out of their bombproof and filled the huge holes with sand, making it as good as new.

Frustrated, Worden and his men returned on February 1, 1863 to make another effort to destroy the fort. Their 48 strikes on the fort did little damage to the Confederate battery, but the commandant of the garrison, Major John B. Gallie, was killed while directing part of the defense. Located upstream was the *Nashville*, which had been converted into a raider and renamed *Rattlesnake*. On February 27, the ship came downriver to attempt to escape, but was forced to retire by the blockading Federal Navy. At Seven Mile Bend on the Ogeechee, she ran aground and could not be freed. The next morning, the *Montauk* navigated up the river and fired on the *Rattlesnake*, while two other Union vessels fired on Fort McAllister, which fired on the *Montauk*. The *Rattlesnake* caught fire and exploded, which shook windows 12 miles away in Savannah. Returning downstream later that day, the *Montauk* struck a mine, causing another explosion and damage to the Union gunboat. Several days later, the ironclad was unable to join the Federal squadron of nine vessels—three ironclads, three wooden gunboats, and three mortar schooners—that fired on the fort for seven hours in the heaviest bombardment the fort was ever to experience. At the conclusion, the commanding officer, Captain Percival Drayton, decided that no damage had been done that "a good night's work could not repair." The Union Navy retired, to leave the fort unmolested for 21 months.

Fort McAllister was to fall, however, to Union Gen. William T. Sherman's men, who attacked the fort from the mainland on December 13, 1864. Sherman, frustrated at the defenses of Savannah, was desperate to open up a supply line from the Ogeechee River for his hungry troops, but Fort McAllister was protecting the entrance to the river. The fort, garrisoned by little more than 200 men, was stormed by 4,000 Union troops, which simply overran the fort's defenses and fought the Confederates hand to hand in 15 minutes of action. "The fort was never surrendered," reported Confederate Maj. George W. Anderson, "It was captured by overwhelming numbers." When Confederate Capt. Nicholas Clinch was told to surrender, he responded with a blow from his sword, and hand-to-hand combat ensued, with Clinch going down only after three saber, six bayonet, and two gunshot wounds. The Confederate losses were 48 killed and 54 wounded and the Union losses were 134 killed and 110 wounded. Capture of the fort sealed the doom of Savannah, which was evacuated the night of December 19, 1864.

In the late 1930s, automobile industrialist Henry Ford purchased the fort site and spent $200,000 restoring the fort, a kingly sum in the 1930s. In 1958, International Paper Company, which had purchased the property from Henry Ford's estate, deeded the property to the state for a historic park. The Georgia Historic Commission continued Ford's work and renovated the fort to its 1863 appearance. In a large land preservation deal with International Paper Company in the late 1970s, The Nature Conservancy added 1,503 acres to the park.

Today, you can tour the fort and learn its fascinating history in the picturesque setting of the Ogeechee River. A museum is located at the site, and has books and a video related to the history of the area. Beside the parking area are large pieces of machinery salvaged from the wreck of the *Rattlesnake*.

Near the fort is an extensive picnicking area sheltered under giant oak, pine, palm, and bay trees with a refreshing view of the Ogeechee River and coastal marshlands. Wading birds, warblers, squirrels, and an occasional snake are the most common wildlife. Biting insects can be fierce in the warmer months and insect repellant is highly recommended.

The recreational part of the park is located down a gated road near the park's visitor center. A mile-long causeway crosses a tributary of Redbird Creek and salt marsh leading to Savage Island, where camp facilities, a boat ramp and dock, and the Magnolia Nature Trail are located. From here, visitors can fish, crab or shrimp for their evening meal, or enjoy the scenery over a campfire.

The natural communities and wildlife associated with salt marsh, mature second-growth maritime forest, and freshwater sloughs are featured on the 1.3-mile Magnolia Nature Trail. Brochures are found at the beginning of the trail, which loops from the campground going out to the tidal creek and affords two marsh views before working its way back. Live oaks with Spanish moss, magnolias, pines, and hickories are the dominant tree species found in this forest, and in the canopy one may see shy migratory songbirds or a great horned owl or tiny screech owl. Sweetgum, wild cherries, and American hollies are also found producing food for wildlife along with red bay, bayberry, sparkleberry, and the climbing muscadine vine with its grapelike fruit.

Mammals commonly seen are raccoons, marsh rabbits, gray squirrels, deer, and deer mice. Reptiles and amphibians one might encounter are yellow rat snakes, diamondback rattlesnakes, green treefrogs, and other species. Fiddler and square-backed crabs populate the salt marsh dominated by smooth cordgrass (*Spartina alterniflora*). Wading birds such as great blue herons and great egrets fish in the knee-deep portions, and green-backed herons patiently work shallower areas from mud banks. Flying above the marsh may be osprey and red-tailed hawks. The freshwater sloughs, with waterlilies, arrowheads, cattails, and pickerelweeds, are important shelter, reproduction, and food habitats for amphibians, fish, and insects.

The boat ramp and dock give access to Redbird Creek, which leads to the Bear River and access to the Ogeechee River. Canoes can be rented for an adventure in the tidal creeks. Savage Island has all the "conveniences" of home with 65 campsites with water and electrical hookups, two comfort stations with hot showers, washer/dryer, dumpster, and phone.

Scouts and volunteers are constructing a second nature trail adjacent to the picnic area. The 3-mile Red Bird Creek Nature Trail will give hikers more easier access to the 1,700 acres that make up the park. The park is good for light biking over the causeway and on US 144.

Trails: 1.3-mile Magnolia Trail and 3-mile Red Bird Creek Nature Trail.

Directions: I-95 south from Savannah to Exit 15/90. Go east on GA 144 approximately 6 miles. Turn left on Spur 144 and continue 4.5 miles to the park and museum.

SMOOTH CORDGRASS
(*Spartina alterniflora*)
Roughly 70 percent of Georgia's salt marsh consists of smooth cordgrass.

Activities: Historical touring, camping (primitive, intermediate, recreational vehicle), picnicking, museum touring, hiking, biking, fishing, shrimping, crabbing, boating, canoeing, guided tours by prior arrangement, nature study. Call for special scheduled events, such as Fourth of July BBQ and re-enactment events.

Facilities: Museum, AV theater, bookstore, fort, 50 picnic sites, grills, 2 shelters, restrooms, swings and playground. Savage Island Campground: 65 tent and trailer sites with water and electric hookups, grills, and tables. Canoe rental, 2 nature trails, 2 comfort stations with heated showers, flush toilets, washer/dryer, telephone. Pioneer campground for organized groups and Scouts. Boat ramp: In the Savage Island Campground a dock and boat ramp are available to registered campers only. Public boats are permitted to launch at the Ogeechee River boat ramp and courtesy dock located at the park's entrance. Marina: Fort McAllister Supply Company: gas and oil, bait and tackle, ice and refreshments. Phone 727-2632.

Dates: Closed Mondays except for federal holidays. Call ahead for fort, museum, and campground hours, which operate independently and change seasonally. 727-2339.

Fees: Separate fees are charged for museum, fort, park, and camping. Call for fees: 727-2339.

Closest town: Richmond Hill.

For more information: Fort McAllister State Park, 3894 Fort McAllister Road, Richmond Hill, GA 31324. Phone 727-2339. Reservations: (800) 864-7275.

▓ RICHMOND HILL WILDLIFE MANAGEMENT AREA

[Fig. 5(7), Fig. 12(3)] Approximately 3,720 acres in Bryan County are open to hunting for deer, turkey, small game, foxes, bobcats, raccoons, opossums, and doves. The property is west of Kilkenny Creek and east of GA 144, located west of Ossabaw Island.

Directions: From the town of Richmond Hill, go southeast on GA 144 to Oak Level Road and follow the signs to the check station.

For more information: Wildlife Resources Division, Georgia Department of Natural Resources, Brunswick, GA 31520. Phone 262-3173.

Ogeechee River

[Fig. 12] This 245-mile blackwater river has many devotees who love its primitive qualities. Canoeists glide through the reflective water, exploring the meandering river swamps. Anglers set out trotlines at night, hoping for catfish but watchful of cottonmouths and alligators. Ministers wade down the river's sandy banks and baptize believers in the clean, cold waters. And yelping children swing on a tree rope, dropping into the Ogeechee's tea-stained waters on the Fourth of July.

The Ogeechee is one of the few untamed major rivers in America. Originating at 650 feet above sea level with small spring-fed creeks near Interstate 20 in Greene County, the river picks up volume as it flows south to the fall line. Leaving the Georgia Piedmont, it enters the Upper and then Lower Coastal Plain, where it picks up volume, depth, and width, with miles of adjoining river swamps buffering the river, holding back civilization and adding to its mystery. Just north of Interstate 95, it enters the tidal zone and is joined by its main tributary, the Canoochee River, where it meanders through tidal marsh until it meets the ocean at Ossabaw Sound at the coast.

The Ogeechee River basin totals 5,535 square miles and its drainage to the coast plays a significant role in forming Wassaw, Ossabaw, St. Catherines, Blackbeard, and Sapelo islands. Most rivers flow into other rivers or impoundment lakes and lose their name, or join other rivers and adopt a different name. For example, the Chattahoochee becomes the Appalachicola at the Florida border below Lake Seminole and the Altamaha is formed by the Oconee and Ocmulgee. But the Ogeechee is the Ogeechee from beginning to end, the longest river in Georgia to keep its name throughout its course.

With intimate swamps and bottomland hardwoods adjoining the river, it retains a

Ogeechee River Shad

Shad is one of Georgia's "salmon" species: It begins life in freshwater rivers, leaves to grow into an adult in the ocean, then returns several years later to its natal stream to reproduce.

Georgia has at least six anadromous fish species: the American shad, hickory shad, blueback herring, Atlantic sturgeon, mullet, and striped bass. Anadromous species are those species that for a part of their life cycle live in a saltwater habitat but use the freshwater river systems for spawning and nursery purposes.

Traditionally, shad has been prized for its rich, delicate flesh and delectable roe, and landings of shad have traditionally led other fish species in commercial value. But overfishing has depleted their numbers on the Georgia coast from a high of 618,000 pounds in 1969 to 125,872 pounds worth $93,540 in 1997. The Ogeechee variety of shad is especially well known and sought after. During the early part of the year, it can be found on some local menus.

For thousands of years, fishermen have depended on the regular shad runs up southeastern Atlantic rivers during the first four months of the year. Females swim up the river from the Atlantic Ocean to lay their eggs, which hatch and develop as they float downstream. The juveniles leave the rivers in October for the Atlantic Ocean, and travel as far away as Canada and develop into adults. Four or five years later, when it is time to reproduce, they return to the streams of their birth.

Shad are caught in nets and have had their numbers depleted over the years. Regulation of shad fishing has helped stabilize declines and there is hope that shad may be allowed to survive into the twenty-first century without going the way of the dodo bird.

pristine quality and provides food, water, and shelter for large numbers of raccoon, deer, otter, beaver, and mink. Trees found in the wetter areas include tupelo and cypress, and the bottomlands support water oak, laurel oak, red maple, swamp blackgum, and sweet gum. The river has a namesake tree, the Ogeechee lime (*Nyssa ogeche*), whose bright red fruits are found floating in quiet eddies of the river during the fall. Several rare plants are also found near the river, including pitcher plants, witch-alder, needle palm, spider lily, and others. Blooming in the spring is wild azalea. The secluded river swamps are a haven to a wide variety of birds that use the river as a protected greenway, including woodpeckers, ducks, songbirds, and wading birds. Osprey and Mississippi and swallowtail kites are seen cruising the river, and a variety of owls and hawks feeds on the small mammals found in the bottomland forests. Water snakes and alligators are common in the Ogeechee River. In the lower reaches, wood storks and southern bald eagles use the river as a feeding ground, and West Indian manatees occasionally visit the river near the coast. The fish fauna of the Ogeechee, much sought after by fishermen, includes American shad, redbreast, crappie, striped bass, shellcracker, and catfish. The endangered shortnose sturgeon (*Acipenser brevirostrum*) breeds here. Where the river becomes salt marsh, commercial fishermen catch blue crab, and small operators throw cast nets for shrimp and baitfish.

It is believed the name Ogeechee comes from the Muskogean word meaning "River of the Yuchis," which was an Indian tribe that lived near the river.

CANOEING THE OGEECHEE RIVER

There are two threats to the canoeist on the Ogeechee: first, getting trapped and swamped by deadfall, and second, getting lost in the extensive river swamps. It is advisable to check with local marinas or fish camps concerning river running conditions, and use maps and a compass for longer trips. During colder, wetter months, be prepared to get soaked as one is forced to portage around fallen trees. During high water periods, additional channels open up, misleading even the experts into dead ends. Despite these hazards, the Ogeechee is one of the best natural canoeing experiences in Georgia and worth the trouble.

Only one impoundment is found on the Ogeechee, at Ogeechee River Mill not far from the headwaters. Below this still-operating gristmill, it is a wild and untamed natural treasure. Shoally in parts of its upper reaches as it flows through the Fall Line hills in Hancock County, the river is choked with deadfall, and the river runner wishes for a chainsaw to make quick work of the frequent limbs and tree trunks. As it reaches Louisville, the state capital of Georgia from 1794–1807, it becomes friendlier to canoers, widening to 35 to 50 feet and leveling out into the serpentine, winding conditions that are more characteristic of the Ogeechee River.

RIVER OTTER
(Lutra canadensis)
A shy, water-loving mammal seen in coastal rivers and occasionally in marsh areas.

Many visitors fall under the river's enchanting spell as they navigate past a lush landscape of bottomland forests of sycamore, oaks, and willow, and moss-draped swamps of sweet gum, tupelo, and cypress. Decaying vegetation and tannic acid from tree roots and bark of the adjoining swamps make the water a burgundy color and give it a highly reflective quality.

Below Millen, the river cuts through sand and clay bluffs that make popular high-and-dry campsites for boaters. The natural communities found on these sand hills are fascinating in their own right, and if one chooses to camp here, one must tread lightly. Farther downstream, the sand hills fall away, the terrain flattens, and the river widens. The woodland corridor expands, with large primeval bottomland forests and freshwater sloughs buffering the river's flow.

Below GA 24, the river continues to widen and the channel becomes better defined. North of its intersection with the Canoochee, the river becomes tidal and gradually takes on the aspects of Georgia's marshlands. Near where the Canoochee and Ogeechee meet was the site of Fort Argyle, erected on the west bank of the Ogeechee in 1733 by Gen. James Edward Oglethorpe. He garrisoned a detachment of rangers here to command one of the main passes by which enemy Indians had recently invaded South Carolina, and to give protection to the settlers of Savannah from anticipated raids by Spaniards from Florida. This area is recommended by the Georgia Ornithological Society for bird-watching (*see* Bird-Watching at Fort Argyle, page 141).

The best resource for canoeing and appreciating Georgia's coastal rivers is *A Paddler's Guide to Southern Georgia*, by Bob Sehlinger and Don Otey. This book lists access points, rates the quality of the canoeing, and describes natural features found on Georgia's rivers.

Suggested canoe trips on the Ogeechee: GA 56 at Midville to County Road 191 near Herndon, 9.1 miles. County Road 191 to US 25 at Millen, 15.7 miles. US 25 to County Road 190 near Scarboro, 11 miles. County Road 190 to County Road 57A near Rocky Ford, 6.5 miles. County Road 57A to County Road 581 near Ogeechee, 7 miles. County Road 581 to US 301 near Dover, 6.2 miles. US 301 to GA 24 near Oliver, 15.2 miles. GA 24 to GA 119 near Guyton, 23.2 miles. GA 119 to US 80 near Blitchton, 12 miles. US 80 to GA 204 (Morgan's Bridge), 11.8 miles. GA 204 to Bellaire Woods Campground, GA 204, 9.8 miles. Bellaire Woods Campground to US 17 at Kings Ferry, 5.4 miles. US 17 to GA 144 near Rabbit Hill, 7 miles. GA 144 to Spur 144 at Fort McAllister, 11.8 miles.

FISHING ON THE OGEECHEE RIVER

Fishing on the Ogeechee River is more than just a hobby; it's a way of life. Many freshwater fishing activities are popular on the river, from setting nets for migrating American shad to simple cane pole fishing for red breast. They occur at different times throughout the year, so it's best to study regulations regarding seasons and check with fish camps and marinas to find out what's biting. High water periods are generally less favorable for fishing because freshwater species retreat to flooded swamplands to feed.

CAMPING AND PARKS NEAR THE OGEECHEE RIVER

Two major campgrounds are located near I-95 and the Ogeechee River. **Waterway RV Campground** is situated right on the Ogeechee River, with 32 RV sites, each with cement patios and picnic tables, and a full complement of amenities. A river dock and boat ramp can be used to enjoy the river, and the campground can furnish bait, tackle, and advice for upstream fishing—blue gill, red breast, bass—or downstream fishing for striped bass and other saltwater fish species. Waterway is located across from Kings Ferry Park [Fig. 5(3)] and Loves Seafood, on US 17 and the Ogeechee River on the southern bank of the river. Phone 756-2296. **Bellaire Woods Campground** is another good choice for camping on the Ogeechee. Situated on 24 acres on the Ogeechee River, the campground has RV sites, boat ramp, showers, boat and tackle rental, canoe rental, and a full list of other amenities. Located on GA 204, 2.5 miles west off Exit 16/94 on Interstate 95. Phone 748-4000.

Kings Ferry Park. This is a popular county park located on the northern side of the Ogeechee River where US 17 crosses. Visitors can picnic, swim, fish from a dock, or launch a boat at the park. Restrooms are available. Located here was King's Bridge, an important crossing point on the Ogeechee River. During the Civil War, this bridge was crossed by Union forces to attack Fort McAllister from the rear, which was located downstream. After capturing the fort, Gen. William T. Sherman's Federal forces built a wharf and depot here to resupply his 60,000 men from the sea for his siege of Savannah.

Canoochee River

[Fig. 5] The Canoochee River is one of the most enchanting rivers in Georgia to canoe, with its tea-colored swamp water contrasting with white, sandy banks of the Coastal Plain. Beginning near Swainsboro in Emanuel County, the river flows 85 miles past extensive river swamps until it meets the Ogeechee River just north of Interstate 95 near Kings Ferry. Abundant wildlife species are found in the protective swamps, including many species of warblers, woodpeckers, owls, and occasional wading birds in the lower reaches. Turtles, snakes, and frogs thrive in the wet habitat, and alligators are seen peeking out of the water. The river's floodplain provides an important nursery for fish and in the main channel red breast, blue gill, crappie, sunfish, and channel catfish are common catches. The habitat provides refuge to many mammals such as raccoons, opossums, deer, and bobcats. The Canoochee has the reputation of supporting the most numerous and largest water snakes in Georgia. Wasp nests and spider webs hang from vegetation that borders the river. Ogeechee lime, cypress, black and sweet gum, willow, and swamp white oak grow along the banks.

The Canoochee in its upper reaches north of the Evans County line is difficult if not impossible to run most of the year without encountering many deadfalls and requiring countless portages. Some put in at a park northwest of Claxton where GA 169 crosses the Canoochee for a run to US 301, the location of a small public park and a sandstone outcrop known as The Rocks. The next run is from this park to Rogers Bridge where Nevils-Daisy Road crosses. Some choose to continue on to US 280. At US 280, Lotts Creek adds its flow to the Canoochee, creating a much more canoeable stream, and a small park provides easy access. However, 4 miles south from 280, the river enters Fort Stewart Military Reservation and continuing on requires advance permission, or you risk having your canoe confiscated by military authorities. The total run from US 280 to Kings Ferry is 54 river miles, with four access points between for shorter trips. The base provost marshal's office has details of river access on the base.

For more information: Fort Stewart Military Reservation, Phone 767-4794.

BIRD-WATCHING AT FORT ARGYLE

[Fig. 3(3)] Bird-watching is a recommended activity near the historic site of Fort Argyle. In 1733, Gen. James Edward Oglethorpe erected Fort Argyle near where the Canoochee and Ogeechee meet on the west bank of the Ogeechee. In 1734, it was the only important military outpost against the Spaniards, who occupied Florida. Oglethorpe garrisoned a detachment of rangers here to command one of the main passes by which enemy Indians had recently invaded South Carolina.

Fort Argyle is now contained by Fort Stewart Military Reservation, but approaches to the colonial fort site are good for bird-watching, especially resident and migratory songbirds such as prothonotary warblers, and great horned, barred, and Eastern screech owls. With permission, birding is allowed at Fort Stewart where bird watchers and can see colonies of Bachman's sparrows and red-cockaded woodpeckers.

Directions: South from Savannah on I-95, take Exit 15/90, and go west on Old Clyde Road for 3 miles. Go right and drive to first crossroad to historic markers for Old Fort Argyle. From here, birding is straight ahead over several bridges that span a creek and the river. The bridges are good areas to look for birds. The third bridge is off limits without permission.

For more information: Fort Stewart Military Reservation, Phone 767-4794.

PILEATED WOODPECKER
(Dryocopus pileatus)
This large, red-crested bird prefers mature forests.

RESTAURANTS IN THE RICHMOND HILL/OGEECHEE RIVER AREA

Love's Seafood Restaurant. US 17, Richmond Hill. Obadiah Love opened his fish camp/restaurant in 1949 on the banks of the Ogeechee River. Love's has the kind of history that makes a great fish restaurant. At first it was a fish camp. Mrs. Love accommodated local fishermen by frying their catch for 50 cents—if they cleaned it first. This evolved to selling catfish and shad dinners, then shrimp, oysters, scallops, and other local seafood delicacies. Today, it is a full-service restaurant operated by son Obadiah Love Jr. that offers steaks as well, but catfish remains the most popular dish, with approximately 800 pounds sold a week. Not only is the food good, but the view of the Ogeechee River is hard to beat. Producers of the movie *Forrest Gump* thought so, and selected it as a filming location. **Directions:** From I-95, take Exit 16/94, go left 2.5 miles to US 17. Go right and go 2.5 miles. Love's is on the right hand side before the bridge. Open Tuesday through Saturday, dinner. Sunday, lunch and dinner. *Moderate. 925-3616.* **River Oaks Seafood**, 2943 Kilkenny Road, Richmond Hill. Another Richmond Hill option is this seafood and steak restaurant with a magnificent view. Open for dinner Wednesday through Sunday. *Moderate. 727-3633.*

Liberty & McIntosh Counties

Liberty and McIntosh counties experience the least tourist traffic of the six Georgia coastal counties.

Savannah

25 250 129
Midway

67

63

204

17

Exit 17A-B
99A-B

16

Exit 16/94

144

Exit
15/90

Exit
14/87

Vernonburg

Vernon View

95

Fleming

196

144

Gum
Branch

67

Flemington

Hinesville

23

Belfast Keller

Midway

Ossabaw
Island

Dorchester

Sunbury

ST. CATHERINES
SOUND

301

Allenhurst
Walthourville

Exit
13/76

38

MEDWAY RIVER

25 82

38

Riceboro

Ludowici

17

Halfmoon
Landing

St.
Catherines
Island

Exit
12/67

Jones

57

131

2

South
Newport

131

1

Jesup

301

Shellman
Bluff

25

3

23 25

Townsend

Exit
11/58

Pine
Harbor

Eulonia

99

Cresent

Valona

SAPELO SOUND

4

Pine
Harbor

Sapelo
Island

Cox

95

Meridian

Carnigan

ATLANTIC OCEAN

Everett

Exit
10/49

Ridgeville

Ashintilly

ALTAMAHA SOUND

Darien

25

341

Exit
9/42

17

1	Harris Neck National Wildlife Refuge
2	The Smallest Church in America
3	Shellman Bluff
4	Blackbeard Island National Wildlife Refuge
	Liberty County
	McIntosh County

Ref: Interior - Geological Survey, Wash., D.C. Georgia

The Central Coast:
Liberty & McIntosh Counties

O f the six counties on the Georgia coast, Liberty and McIntosh experience the least tourist traffic. If you want to get off the beaten path, these counties offer many interesting excursions, with tours through traditional fishing villages, colonial fortifications, antebellum rice plantations, and rarely visited barrier islands. Travelers here will find distinctive pineywood settlements, marsh views, and local seafood restaurants that are some of the best on the Georgia coast.

The major attractions here are the LeConte-Woodmanston Plantation National Historic Site, Melon Bluff Nature and Heritage Preserve, Fort Morris State Historic Site, Harris Neck National Wildlife Refuge, Blackbeard Island National Wildlife Refuge, the town of Darien, Fort King George State Historic Site; Sapelo Island and the Sapelo Island National Estuarine Research Reserve; Gray's Reef National Marine Sanctuary, and the Altamaha River Bioreserve.

[*Above:* Shrimp boats work the offshore waters of the Georgia coast]

Liberty County

Liberty County features the historic sites of Midway National Historic District, Fort Morris Historic Site, and LeConte-Woodmanston Plantation National Historic Site.

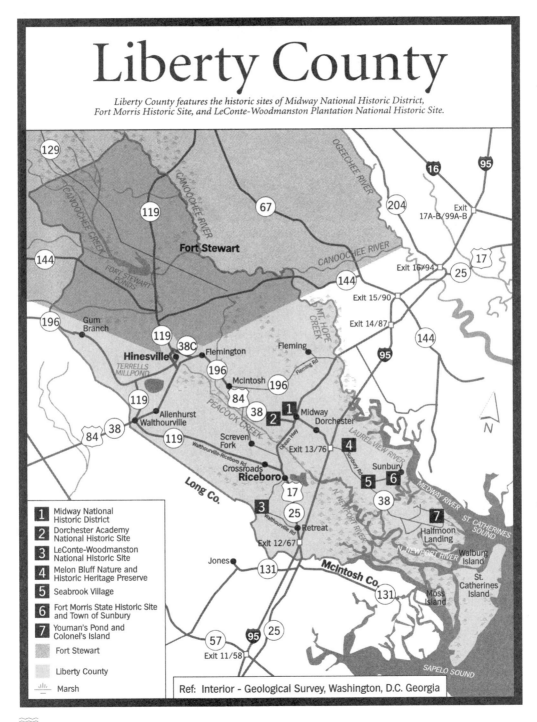

1. Midway National Historic District
2. Dorchester Academy National Historic Site
3. LeConte-Woodmanston National Historic Site
4. Melon Bluff Nature and Historic Heritage Preserve
5. Seabrook Village
6. Fort Morris State Historic Site and Town of Sunbury
7. Youman's Pond and Colonel's Island

Fort Stewart

Liberty County

Marsh

Ref: Interior - Geological Survey, Washington, D.C. Georgia

Liberty County

[Fig. 14] Liberty County features the Midway National Historic District, Fort Morris Historic Site, and LeConte-Woodmanston Plantation National Historic Site. Also in Liberty County is St. Catherines Island, a magnificent barrier island owned by a private foundation and closed to the general public. Liberty County is greatly influenced by the military activities of Fort Stewart, located near Hinesville. This military base, the largest east of the Mississippi River, controls one third of the property of the county, with most of the rest in the hands of pulp and paper companies who manage their acreage for slash pine production. Hinesville is by far the county's largest town, with a population of 22,000, and Midway is the next largest town with 900 residents. The total population of the county is 55,000.

MIDWAY NATIONAL HISTORIC DISTRICT

[Fig. 14(1)] Visitors to Midway can tour this pretty, live-oak shaded national historic district, soak up the colonial history of the coast, and learn about the liberty-loving Puritans of St. Johns Parish. Home to the second oldest church in Georgia, many of America's more illustrious citizens have their roots in this charming small town.

In 1630, a group of Puritans from Dorchester, England, fled that country and landed in Massachusetts, where they established a settlement called Dorchester. Years later, some of these colonists moved to South Carolina and established another town called Dorchester. After several years, they became dissatisfied with conditions there, and the entire community of 38 families moved again, this time to St. Johns Parish (Liberty County), and founded yet another town called Dorchester. What the Puritans lacked in imagination they made up in industriousness, and quickly St. Johns Parish became a prosperous community.

The small congregation of Midway Church had a tremendous impact on Georgia and American history and played a major role in representing the Georgia colony when America moved for independence from England. Two of the three Georgia signers of the Declaration of Independence, Dr. Lyman Hall and Button Gwinnett, were from St. Johns Parish. Midway's character was acknowledged in 1777, when the first Georgia Constitution reformed the English parishes of St. Johns, St. Andrews, and St. James into Liberty County, the only original Georgia county not named for a person but an ideal. The small settlement is considered "the cradle of Revolutionary spirit in Georgia" and today is a national historic district.

The settlers first arrived on May 16, 1752. They surveyed the area around Midway, liked what they saw, and petitioned the Council of Georgia for 31,950 acres of land. They were granted their request, and the hard-working Puritans quickly developed successful indigo and rice plantations. The first permanent Meeting House was erected in 1756, and the first service was held January 2, 1758. Midway, also spelled Medway in early documents, is named after the Medway River, believed named for its location "midway" between the Ogeechee and Altamaha rivers or the Medway River in England.

The first dramatic events of the American Revolution occurred in Massachusetts: the Boston Tea Party of December 17, 1773, then the closing of Boston Harbor by the British in June 1774. When independence fever subsequently swept the colonies, all but Georgia sent representatives to the First Continental Congress held in Philadelphia in September 1774. Feelings were mixed in the young colony concerning opposition to English rule. Georgia's royal governor, Sir James Wright, was a popular and influential leader and many of Georgia's citizens were Tories or Loyalists with business ties to England and did not want autonomy. Georgia's lack of participation at the First Continental Congress earned it resentment from the other colonies, especially South Carolina. The Continental Congress put Georgia under an embargo. South Carolina, furious with its southern neighbor, passed a law decreeing death to anyone who traded with Georgia.

The citizens of St. Johns Parish still had strong ties to Massachusetts, and were frustrated with Georgia's lack of support for their New England friends. So they decided to act independently of the colony. The colonists, called "those meddlesome Puritans at Midway" by Governor James Wright, decided to curtail trade with the rest of Georgia and asked to be annexed by South Carolina and be represented at the Second Continental Congress. When South Carolina denied its request, the parish sent its own delegate, Dr. Lyman Hall, with 60 barrels of rice and 50 pounds of sterling to help the suffering Boston people. He arrived three days after the Second Continental Congress opened, and sat in on deliberations but did not vote.

Hall was still representing Georgia when the revolution became a shooting war on April 19, 1775 at Lexington, Massachusetts. The start of war enflamed the passions of Georgians who supported independence, prompting Georgia's Second Provincial Congress meeting at Tondee's Tavern, located in Savannah at the corner of Broughton and Whitaker streets. Unlike the First Provincial Congress, when only three parishes bothered to attend, all 12 parishes were represented with more than 100 delegates. Four additional representatives were elected to join Hall in Philadelphia: Archibald Bulloch, John Houstoun, Noble Wymberly Jones, and the Reverand Joachim Zubly. Bulloch was elected governor of Georgia, and was too busy to go to Philadelphia. Houston and Jones went but had to return to Georgia. Zubly was discovered to have Loyalist feelings and was ousted from the group. Button Gwinnett and George Walton took their places, and were present with Hall when the Declaration of Independence was ready to sign. Thus they became immortalized on one of the most important documents in the history of mankind.

Midway's participation in the American Revolution was not limited to politics; the area also witnessed a battle and devastation during British occupation. Toward the end of 1778, the theater of war was transferred to the Southern Provinces. The British planned an invasion of Georgia from Florida. Approximately 700 British forces under Lt. Col. Mark Prevost were to attack Midway by land, then meet up with British naval forces numbering 500 under the command of Lt. Col. L.V. Fuser at Fort Morris and Sunbury on the Medway River (see Fort Morris, page 154). From there, they would move on Savannah.

Prevost set out for Midway, destroying plantations in his path, including historic LeConte-Woodmanston Plantation, owned by the famous LeConte family (*see* LeConte-Woodmanston Plantation National Historic Site, page 149). Continental Col. John White posted 100 Continentals with two pieces of light artillery at Midway Church and constructed a breastwork just south of it. General James Screven with 20 mounted militiamen arrived and repositioned the forces 1.5 miles south of the

Midway Church was built by Puritans in 1792.

church near Spencer Hill. On November 24, 1778, British forces overwhelmed the outnumbered Americans. Screven was wounded and captured and died of his wounds in the hands of the enemy. (Later, Screven County, the town of Screven in Wayne County, and Fort Screven on Tybee Island were named for him.) White retreated to Midway Church, but in doing so he left behind a fictitious letter intended to deceive the English. The letter said that the Americans were going to be receiving additional troops and making a vigorous stand at Ogeechee Ferry. Prevost, not knowing what to do, burned Midway Church and homes, slave quarters, and crops in the area, then returned to Florida without meeting up with Fuser at Sunbury. (Fuser, unable to meet up with Prevost's land forces, decided to not attack the town or Fort Morris.)

After the war, the Midway Society rebuilt the town. The current church, open to tour, was built in 1792 in a New England style and is the second oldest in Georgia. The area experienced prosperity until the Civil War, when cavalry forces with Union Gen. William T. Sherman invaded the area during his famous March to the Sea. Gen. Judson Kilpatrick occupied Midway and Sunbury for six weeks, destroying plantations, crops, and the railroad. Kilpatrick used the church as a slaughterhouse and the churchyard as a corral. The church's prized melodeon was used as a meat block. (It has been preserved and today is used as a communion table.) Midway was abandoned after the Civil War and the church stopped holding services. Today, the church is used for special events such as weddings.

The area has produced many famous people who have left their stamp on America, including several Midway ministers: the Reverand Abiel Holmes, father of Dr. Oliver Wendell Holmes, the author, and grandfather of Supreme Court Justice Oliver Wendell Holmes; the Reverand Jedidiah Morse, father of S.F.B. Morse, inventor of the telegraph; and Dr. I.S.K. Axson, grandfather of the first Mrs. Woodrow Wilson. General Daniel Steward, a member of the congregation, was the great grandfather of President Theodore Roosevelt. Five Georgia counties were named for Midway citizens: Baker, Gwinnett, Hall, Screven, and Stewart.

Midway Museum was built in 1957 in a raised-cottage style typical of those built on the coast in the eighteenth century. It houses many exhibits and materials about Midway's history, including exhibits and information on its Revolutionary War and Civil War periods. The museum's library can be used with permission for researching genealogy.

The beautiful, historic cemetery across the street contains huge live oaks that shade roughly 1,200 graves. Many burials are the final resting grounds of Midway's most distinguished persons, including General James Screven, General Daniel Stewart, and Louis LeConte of Woodmanston Plantation. The 6-foot-high, 18-inch-thick wall encircling the roughly 2-acre cemetery was built in 1813 of English brick, and was used as a corral by Union troops under Sherman. The monument in the center memorializes generals Stewart and Screven.

Directions: I-95 south from Savannah to Exit 13/76. Go west on GA 38/US 84 approximately 2.2 miles. Turn right on Martin Road. Drive 1.3 miles to Midway National Historic District. Cemetery is directly ahead across US 17 and museum and church are on right.

Activities: Historical touring, museum. Call for special scheduled events, such as Fourth of July BBQ and re-enactment events.

Facilities: Museum, bookstore, restrooms.

Dates: Closed Mondays. Call ahead for museum hours, which change seasonally. Phone 884-5837.

Fees: A small fee is charged for the museum.

Closest town: Midway.

For more information: Midway Museum, PO Box 195, Midway, GA 31320. Phone 884-5837.

DORCHESTER ACADEMY NATIONAL HISTORIC SITE

[Fig. 14(2)] Dorchester Academy, an example of Georgian Revival style architecture built in 1934, is most famous as being the site of Citizen Training by Dr. Martin Luther King Jr. during the Civil Rights movement. The Southern Christian Leadership Conference sponsored workshops here from 1962 to 1964, training more than 1,000 teachers and leaders. King prepared here in 1962 for the 1963 Birmingham campaign, one of the first major victories of the Civil Rights movement. King was the youngest winner of the Nobel Peace Prize.

In 1870, the American Missionary Association founded the academy with 1 acre and 77 students as a school for freed slaves. In 1890, named Dorchester Academy in honor of the area's Puritan roots, the school started boarding students. By 1917, the fully accredited high school had eight frame buildings and 300 students. In the 1940s, its academic program ended when a consolidated school for black youth was built in Riceboro.

The academy has historic markers, a heritage room, a pavilion and barbecue pit, and restrooms.

Directions: I-95 south from Savannah to Exit 13/76. Go west on GA 38/US 84 approximately 6 miles. Dorchester Academy National Historic Site is on the left.

Activities: Historical touring. Call for special scheduled events.
Facilities: Heritage room, pavilion with barbecue pit, restrooms.
Dates: Open by arrangement. Phone 884-2347.
Fees: None.
Closest town: Midway.
For more information: Dorchester Academy National Historic Site, phone 884-2347.

LECONTE-WOODMANSTON PLANTATION NATIONAL HISTORIC SITE

[Fig. 14(3)] The former plantation site of the famous LeConte family offers a variety of experiences for naturalists, including exploring the restored rice fields and gardens that belonged to the family and looking for wildlife that frequent the second-growth cypress swamps. Botanists with an interest in historic gardens will enjoy their time here.

Woodmanston, a 3,354-acre rice plantation, was established in 1760 in St. Johns Parish by John Eatton LeConte. It was one of the largest in the South. The 63.8-acre historic site, surrounded by pine plantations and Bulltown Swamp, protects the heart of the plantation where the main house and gardens were located. A nature trail leads from here over a trunk canal to former rice fields and a cypress swamp. With restored trunks in the dikes, the former fields can still be flooded using gravity flow, just as they were 240 years ago. LeConte-Woodmanston Plantation was unlike most coastal plantations that used tidal waters to flood their fields. The swamp water is dammed, then drained into the rice fields. Managers of the site plan to grow rice again as an educational tool. Hikers can explore the old fields and Bulltown Swamp blackwater ecosystem and cypress forest along the top of the centuries-old dikes, which were constructed by slaves from clays found in the swamp.

Bulltown Swamp is the headwaters of the South Newport River, which flows into Sapelo Sound. Vegetation at the site is the result of wild regeneration of land that has experienced farming and logging. More than 25 varieties of tree can be found on the property, including pond and baldcypress; overcup, live, laurel, water, and cherrybark oak; sweet and blackgum; and Ogeechee lime. The understory consists of red titi, wax myrtle, holly, and plum, and vines include Cherokee rose, smilax, trumpet creeper, and jessamine. Wet areas support swamp lily, iris, ferns, primrose-willow and pickerelweed.

Wildlife is plentiful, and it is common to observe deer, raccoons, opossums, armadillos, wild hogs, pileated woodpeckers, ibis, vultures, and kingsnakes. Waterfowl is abundant in the swamps during migratory seasons, as are otters during the entire year. Alligators are surprisingly absent.

Three generations of LeContes lived at Woodmanston, along with at least 200 slaves. John Eatton LeConte was the grandson of Guillaume LeConte, a French Huguenot who migrated to

CHRISTMAS FERN
(*Polystichum acrostichoides*)

New York in the 1690s to avoid religious persecution, and the nephew of Thomas Eatton, a prominent Savannah merchant who may have influenced LeConte to invest in Georgia. John Eatton LeConte had a brother, William, who founded Sans Souci Plantation in Bryan County. Naturalist William Bartram traveled through the property in 1773.

John Eatton LeConte was an early supporter of the American Revolution, and was entrusted with delivering rice and sterling to Boston patriots who were suffering from the British embargo of Boston Harbor. During the Revolutionary War, the original plantation house was burned by British troops in November of 1778 as they advanced on Midway down the Fort Barrington Road. Sometime before 1789, another house was built at the plantation. It was fortified and featured a palisade stockade. In 1789, this "fort" was attacked by Indians and was successfully defended by LeConte and his slaves. LeConte later had two sons, Louis, born 1782, and John Eatton LeConte Jr., born 1784.

Around 1812, Louis married Ann Quarterman of Midway and acquired Woodmanston. Louis, a graduate of Columbia College in New York, planted and nurtured the 1-acre floral and botanical garden of international repute at Woodmanston, and fathered two sons, John and Joseph, who were to go on to international fame as educators and scientists. His family is considered to be Georgia's most distinguished family of scientists. Both sons graduated from Franklin College, which was to become the University of Georgia. John was the first president of the University of California, and received national acclaim for his work in the field of physics. Joseph, an authority on ornithology and geology, achieved the greatest fame of all the LeContes, and published 200 scientific articles and seven books. He graduated from the first graduate course ever offered by Harvard University, studying under famed scientist Louis Agassiz.

Joseph became an expert on coral formation, which he studied with Agassiz in the Florida Keys. With his friend John Muir, Joseph co-founded the Sierra Club. Joseph's greatest expertise might have been as an ornithologist, and with his brother John, he published the first list of all bird species in the state of Georgia, a catalog of 273 species.

Louis LeConte not only ran a productive rice and cotton plantation, but he excelled in growing many unusual native and exotic plants, and was one of the first to cultivate *Camellia japonica* outdoors in the South. His garden was "the richest in bulbs I have ever seen," wrote Alexander Gordon in *Gardener's Magazine*. His son Joseph wrote in his *Autobiography of Joseph LeConte* that his father's "beautiful garden became celebrated all over the United States, and botanists from the North and from Europe came to visit it, always receiving welcome and entertainment, sometimes for weeks at his home." Joseph recalled that some of the camellias were "trees" that were 1 foot in diameter and 15 feet tall.

Louis LeConte's brother, Major John Eatton LeConte Jr., was at one time a co-owner of Woodmanston and considered the foremost authority on the natural history of Georgia at that time. John Eatton also was an accomplished artist—called "the Audubon of the turtles"—and collected many specimens of plants and animals that reside in the natural history collections of the Academy of Natural Sciences of Philadelphia. He was well known for his studies of American insects. Some of his paintings are in the collection of the University of Georgia. His son, John Lawrence LeConte, became a leading entomologist of the latter half of the nineteenth century. Two bird species are named for him: the LeConte thrasher (*Toxostoma lecontei*), and the LeConte sparrow (*Ammospiza leconteii*). The LeConte sparrow winters in south-eastern Georgia and was named for John Lawrence LeConte by John James Audubon. Not only do two birds carry the LeConte name, but so do two mountains (one in the Smokies and the other in the Sierras); many other landmarks in the Sierras including a lake, a falls, a divide, and a dome; a glacier in Alaska; three species of plants; three fossils; a pear tree (*Pyrus lecontei*); a mouse; a school; three university buildings; and three avenues (located in Athens, Atlanta, and Berkeley, California).

After Louis LeConte's death in 1838, the estate was divided into smaller tracts for his heirs and the gardens were soon neglected. After 1843, no member of the family resided in the old plantation house. During the Civil War, the plantation was raided and destroyed. Over time, the property was neglected, was farmed and logged, and became a pine plantation and reclaimed bottomland, and the plantation was lost.

Hard work and initiative rediscovered Woodmanston. An avid amateur horticulturist, Col. Claude A. Black, who learned about the plantation in 1971, began a dedicated search for the garden site. Finally, in 1973, he and a friend, William Fishback, found traces of the old garden: two sabal palm trees (one live, one dead), an ancient red seedling (Norman Red) camellia plant, and a few crape myrtles. Brunswick Pulp and Paper Company planned to log the site, but Black convinced the company to hold off. An organization was quickly formed to preserve the site, and it was placed on the National Register of Historic Sites. In 1977, the C.B. Jones family donated the tract to The Nature Conservancy and Brunswick Pulp and Paper donated the timber rights. The title was transferred to the Garden Club of Georgia, which transferred it to the LeConte-Woodmanston Foundation in 1993. The Foundation continues fundraising activities and restoration work at the historic property, and plans to build a visitors center.

Directions: I-95 north from Brunswick to Exit 12/67. Go north on US 17 for 3.7 miles. Turn left on Sandy Run Road. Drive 4.3 miles and turn left onto dirt road. Drive 1 mile south to historic marker. Follow signs to parking area for LeConte-Woodmanston.

Activities: Historical touring, botanical studies, hiking, nature study, bird-watching. Guided tours by prior arrangement. Call for special scheduled events.

Facilities: Botanical gardens, restrooms, 1-mile long nature trail.

Dates: Open year round. Phone 727-2339 for visitation hours.

Fees: Donations appreciated.

Closest town: Riceboro.

For more information: LeConte-Woodmanston Foundation, PO Box 179, Midway, GA 31320. Phone 884-6500.

MELON BLUFF NATURE AND HERITAGE PRESERVE

[Fig. 14(4)] Melon Bluff Nature and Heritage Preserve is one of the few privately owned nature preserves on the Georgia coast. The 3,000-acre preserve backs up to the North Newport River and offers more than 20 miles of trails through pinelands, coastal forest, and salt marshes that are open to hikers, bikers, kayakers, and horseback riders. History is also highlighted at Melon Bluff, with a former rice plantation on the property and a Civil War blockade-runner, *The Standard*, sunk at the bottom of the tidal river.

The preserve is a charter member of the Colonial Coast Birding Trail established by the Georgia Department of Natural Resources. Surrounded by coastal marsh, moss-draped oaks and pines, and freshwater ponds, it serves as sanctuary to resident and migratory bird species, including osprey, herons, egrets, wood storks, pelicans, spoonbills, wild turkeys, bluebirds, swallows, painted buntings, and purple martins. Bald eagles are occasionally identified. Commonly seen in the dense, mixed hardwood and pine forest are deer, opossums, raccoons, and squirrels.

Like most coastal property, Melon Bluff has not escaped human intervention. It has experienced timber operations and rice production. The preserve is named for the eighteenth century plantation that once existed on the property. More recently, the property had been managed for pine timber like much of coastal Georgia. Conservationists Laura, Don, and Meredith Devendorf have chosen to protect and allow the landscape to renew itself through the creation of a nature preserve from this land that has been in the family since the 1930s. The family was also instrumental in establishing Seabrook Village (*see* Seabrook Village, page 153).

An unusual feature of Melon Bluff is that it offers three historic B&B-style lodging options, Palmyra Barn (1930), Palmyra Plantation Guest House (1840), and The Ripley Farmhouse (1940). The three restored structures offer beautiful views of Dickinson Creek or the peacefulness of the coastal woodlands.

The Devendorfs keep a busy schedule of events year-round to interest visitors. The preserve participates in the national annual Audubon bird count and commemorates the anniversary of Prohibition with moonshine-making demonstrations and a kayak trip to an island where rum was stashed in the Roaring Twenties. Flatwater kayaking in the tidal rivers is featured, including sunrise excursions followed by a gourmet breakfast, heritage kayak tours, picnic paddles to a marsh island, and moonrise excursions followed by candlelit dinners. Another popular activity is a mule-drawn wagon tour of the preserve, where a guide describes the history of the area from Spanish times to plantation days.

The Melon Bluff Nature Center is where guests start their

OSPREY

(Pandion haliaetus)
Also known as the fish hawk, this large bird nests on dead trees, utility poles, and towers.

visit. Educational exhibits, a gift shop-bookstore, refreshments, and restrooms are available. Self-guiding nature and heritage tours are available. Bikes and binoculars can be rented, and on the weekend canoes and kayaks are supplied. Mule and wagon tours are scheduled at certain events or by special arrangement.

Directions: I-95 south from Savannah to Exit 13/76. Go east on GA 38 for 3 miles. Look for green Melon Bluff mailbox on right at 2999 Islands Highway. Nature Center and parking is on right.

Activities: Hiking, biking, kayaking, horseback riding, wagon tours, bird-watching, picnicking, nature study, historic touring. Call for special scheduled events and group educational programs.

Facilities: Nature Center with exhibits and educational programs, 20 miles of net-worked trails, gift shop-bookstore, refreshments, restrooms, maps, equipment rental, and parking. Primitive restrooms on trails. Stabling of horses is available. Lodging: Palmyra Barn, Palmyra Plantation Guest House, and The Ripley Farmhouse. Call number below for details. Moderate rates.

Dates: Closed Mondays. Open Tuesday to Sunday 9–4.

Fees: A variety of fees charged depending on use by visitor.

Closest town: Midway.

For more information: Melon Bluff, 2999 Islands Highway, Midway, GA 31320. www.melonbluff.com Phone (888) 246-8188.

SEABROOK VILLAGE

[Fig. 14(5)] This living history village features the rich African-American culture that developed when slaves were freed from coastal plantations. The focus is on the authentic portrayal of the struggles and successes of African-Americans from 1865 to 1930, with interactive demonstrations and programs on history, folklore, folklife, architecture, crafts, and found art. Here you can experience what it was like before modern conveniences by trying your hand at washing clothes on a scrub board or grinding corn into meal and grits. Exhibits display ingenious artifacts of the period, such as a peanut roaster made from sewing machine and bicycle parts, a photograph framed with matchsticks, twig furniture, and other items. Ongoing exhibits include the grave art of Cyrus Bowens, featured in *Drums and Shadows*. The 104-acre site has eight buildings built in the 1900s, including the one-room Seabrook School and various farm buildings.

A biracial local community group created Seabrook in 1990. One of the founders is Laura Devendorf, who also created the private nature preserve of Melon Bluff (*see* Melon Bluff, page 152). The best way to visit is by prearranging a group tour. Seabrook arranges for costumed interpreters who come from community families whose roots go back over 150 years. The tour lasts three hours, and full meal service, picnics, and entertainment are available. Special events include Old Timey Days, Country Christmas, storytelling, cane grinding, syrup making, rice planting, and clay chimney building. The site is open to self-guided walking tours as well.

Directions: I-95 south from Savannah to Exit 13/76. Go east on GA 38 for 4 miles to Trade Hill Road. Turn left and drive 0.6 mile. Seabrook Village office is on the left.

Activities: Historical touring, interactive tours for groups of 15 or more by prior arrangement. Special educational and Girl Scout programs available. Call for special scheduled events.

Facilities: Museum, restrooms.

Dates: Closed Mondays and Sundays. Open 10–4 Tuesday to Saturday.

Fees: A small fee is charged.

Closest town: Midway.

For more information: Seabrook Village, 660 Trade Hill Road, Midway, GA 31320. www.seabrookvillage.org Phone 884-7008.

FORT MORRIS STATE HISTORIC SITE AND TOWN OF SUNBURY

[Fig. 14(6)] Despite the sad fact that not one structure survives from the colonial town of Sunbury, once a busy seaport on the Medway River, there are nearby attractions that can invoke the ghosts of this early Georgia settlement. History buffs can enjoy the

Fort Morris was the site of a Revolutionary War battle.

beauty of the Georgia coast while touring the remains of a fort that protected the town during the Revolutionary War and War of 1812. Nearby, a historic cemetery contains the graves of some of Sunbury's prominent citizens. Fort Morris's natural charms are recognized by its selection as a site on the Colonial Coast Birding Trail established by the Georgia Department of Natural Resources.

The walking tour of the fort is a great way to learn Georgia's role in the Revolutionary War while enjoying beautiful views of golden marsh and shimmering tidal river.

From the bluff, one can look out on St. Catherines Sound and to barrier islands in the distance. Magnolia, live oak, southern red oak, water oak, sweetgum, cabbage palm, and slash pine grow on the 70 acres, providing sanctuary for many species of birds. Wax myrtle, yaupon holly, and assorted ferns thrive in the understory. The productive *Spartina* marshes absorb the tides, supporting many wading birds that can be seen year round, including snowy egrets, great blue and little green herons, wood storks, and anhingas. Yellow-crowned night herons nest here and are observed in spring and early summer. Bald eagles, Cooper's hawks, and red-tailed hawks are frequently seen in the fall and winter. Thriving in the woods are deer, raccoons, opossums, armadillos, and squirrels. Occasionally, snakes are spotted sunning themselves on the sandy banks.

The trees around the fort are second growth. The land was completely cutover when the fort was built, and the timber was used in building the fort and also to clear a field of fire. The fort you tour is actually the third or fourth built near this location. The earthworks seen today date back to at least the War of 1812, reshaped from the Revolutionary War fort, Fort Morris.

As the plantations of Midway and St. Johns Parish flourished, locals decided they needed a more convenient port than Savannah for shipping their exports of rice, indigo, skins, lumber, tar, and rosin. In 1758, Mark Carr chose 500 acres on a low bluff on the southern bank of the Medway River for a new settlement and port of entry called Sunbury. The river, with depths ranging up to more than 40 feet, provided safe passage and docking for large ships. (The Medway is believed to be one of the deepest natural rivers south of the Chesapeake.) The road from Midway to Sunbury followed one of the oldest Indian trails in the state, which linked Georgia's mountains to its coast with its southern terminus at Sunbury.

Town planners ambitiously laid out the village in a grid with 496 lots and three public squares—Kings, Church, and Meeting—and five wharves. It was named Sunbury, either for the English town on the Thames River or for its sunny location on the Medway River. The town prospered, and was said to rival Savannah in commercial importance, with Sunbury residents owning a third of all the wealth in Georgia by 1772. Records show that in 1773, Sunbury's port hosted 56 vessels compared with Savannah's 160 ships. At one point Sunbury consisted of 80 homes, a customs house, several businesses, and a naval office. Eighteenth century naturalist William Bartram visited the town several times during his travels in the 1760s, and described it as a town of two-story houses "with pleasant piazzas around them where the genteel, wealthy planters resorted to partake of the sea breeze, bathing, and sporting on the Sea Islands."

Forts protected Georgia's frontier towns from Spanish and Indian attacks, and Sunbury was no different. In 1755, a small battery was built just south of Sunbury on the first piece of high ground overlooking the Medway River. By 1760, a log fort had been added to protect Sunbury residents from Indian attacks. As the American Revolution approached, a new fort was constructed in 1776 to protect the town from British invasion. Constructed of earth and wood by slaves, this eventually was christened Fort Morris, named for Captain Thomas Morris, who commanded the company of artillery that first garrisoned the fort. The fort mounted 24 guns and housed 250 officers and men. A large, brick officers' barracks stood in the center.

In the fall of 1778, the British launched a two-prong invasion of Georgia. A land force under Lt. Col. Mark Prevost was to march from Fort Howe (Fort Barrington) on the Altamaha River to the Midway Meeting House, then turn and march east to Sunbury. A naval force under Lt. Col. L.V. Fuser was to attack Sunbury from the river, while the land force attacked from land. After the fall of Sunbury, they were to proceed to Savannah.

Several skirmishes were fought as the Americans attempted to delay or prevent Prevost from capturing Midway. Commanding the American patriots was Colonel John White. As he continued to fight Prevost, he sent Colonel John McIntosh and 127 men to reinforce Sunbury. When White realized he couldn't hold Midway, he abandoned the town and allowed a letter to fall into British hands that was intended to deceive them into thinking the Americans had reinforcements on the way. Prevost, who had learned that Fuser was delayed in his approach on Sunbury from the river, decided to burn Midway and retreat, burning and plundering on the way back to the British colony of East Florida.

Fuser, with a naval force of approximately 500 men, arrived at Sunbury in late November 1778 and put the fort and town under siege. He sent a message to the fort demanding its surrender. Colonel McIntosh, the ranking officer, answered the letter with the famous reply, "Come and take it." Fuser, learning that Prevost had retreated and unsure of the strength of the American troops at Fort Morris, decided to retreat as well. In December, a force of 3,000 British troops captured Savannah, thereby isolating Sunbury and Fort Morris. Again the British approached Sunbury and demanded Fort Morris to surrender. The fort's new commander, Major Joseph Lane, was under orders from his superiors to evacuate. But Lane decided to stay and fight. In the ensuing battle on January 9, 1779, the fort was lost to the British, with four Americans killed and seven wounded. The winners renamed the bastion Fort George in honor of King George III, and Sunbury became a military prison for patriot officers. Lane was later court-martialed for disobeying orders.

By the end of the war, the fort was dismantled and most of the town lay in ruins. In 1782, the British evacuated Georgia, and Sunbury attempted to rebuild. It was named county seat for the new county called Liberty, but never fully regained its prewar prominence. In 1793, Sunbury Academy was established. It became one of the finest schools in the South under the 30-year leadership of the Irish-born Rev. Dr. William McWhir, an outstanding Greek and Latin scholar who was a friend of George Washington. Located in King's Square, Sunbury Academy's students went on to become leaders in many fields.

At the turn of the century, much of Liberty County had recovered, but Sunbury was losing its importance as a seaport. New bridges and roads allowed easier access to Darien and Savannah ports, and Sunbury's population dwindled and the county seat was moved to Riceboro. The area was briefly revitalized in 1812 when Fort Morris was reconfigured into the smaller Fort Defiance that tourists see today. A body of students manned the fort in order to protect Liberty County from British invasion during the War of 1812 but no military assaults ever came. More destructive, however, were tremendous hurricanes and yellow fever epidemics that all but obliterated the town. During the Civil War, Union cavalry pillaged the county and burned a historic church in Sunbury as a signal to the Union Navy in St. Catherines Sound. After the Civil War, the few remaining buildings of any value were moved to Dorchester. The only building in the area still standing from the mid-1800s is Dorchester Presbyterian Church, built in 1854. The church's bell is originally from Sunbury. (Directions to Dorchester Presbyterian Church: From I-95, drive 2.2 miles to Dorchester historical marker on right. Turn right on dirt road and drive 0.2 mile to church on left.) The property was abandoned and left to relic hunters and the forces of nature for 100 years until the Georgia Historical Commission purchased the site in 1968.

The site was placed on the National Register of Historic Places in 1971, and in 1973, The Nature Conservancy helped the state acquire 3 more acres that contain the old earthworks.

Sunbury Cemetery is the only physical remains of the once thriving seaport. The cemetery is believed to have occupied the southeast corner of Church Square. Only 34 markers remain, with the earliest dated 1788 and the latest marked 1911. The most famous marker belongs to the Rev. Dr. William McWhir, the famous principal of Sunbury Academy, who died in 1851 at the age of 91.

Directions: Fort Morris: I-95 south from Savannah to Exit 13/76. Go east on GA 38, following signs to Fort Morris Historic Site, approximately 6 miles. Sunbury Cemetery: From park gate, go right on Fort Morris Road, and drive 0.5 mile to Old Sunbury Road on left. Turn left, go 0.1 mile to road on right. Turn right, go 0.2 mile to historical marker and cemetery.

Activities: Historical touring, picnicking, museum touring, hiking, guided tours by prior arrangement, nature study. Call for special scheduled events.

Facilities: Museum, nature trail, audiovisual theater, bookstore, fort, picnic sites.

Dates: Closed Mondays except for federal holidays. Open Tuesday to Saturday 9–5, Sunday 2–5:30.

Fees: A small admission fee is charged.

Closest town: Midway.

For more information: Fort Morris Historic Site, 2559 Fort Morris Road, Midway, GA 31320. Phone 884-5999.

YOUMAN'S POND AND COLONEL'S ISLAND

[Fig. 14(7)] This freshwater pond found on Colonel's Island is an excellent bird-watching site. It has supported an active rookery for many years, and many bird species have been identified here, including black-crowned and yellow-crowned night herons, blue herons, various egrets, wood storks, ibis, wood ducks, and common moorhens. Dabbling ducks are common during migratory seasons. Great horned and barred owls, osprey, and turkey vultures are frequently seen in the area.

The island is the easternmost piece of high ground in Liberty County before crossing the Newport rivers to St. Catherines Island. The southern half of the island is also known as Halfmoon Landing, named for the bend in the tidal river located here. Many bird species depend on a mix of habitats. They feed in the marsh and freshwater wetlands, then take refuge in nearby undisturbed maritime forest. Colonel's Island has a variety of natural habitats that support a diversity of avifauna.

In April 1773, the island was visited by famed naturalist William Bartram, who described the area in his famous book *Travels of William Bartram*. Bartram recorded "a great variety of trees, shrubs and herbaceous plants." He wrote that deer "… are numerous on this island; the tyger, wolf, and bear, hold yet some possession; as also raccoons, foxes, hares, squirrels, rats, and mice, but I think no moles … opossums are here in abundance, as also pole-cats, wild-cats, rattle-snakes, glass-snake, coach-whip-snake, and

St. Catherines Island

St. Catherines Island serves as an undisturbed habitat for osprey, and averages 119 sea turtle nests each year, trailing only Cumberland, Ossabaw, and Blackbeard islands.

Colonel's Island

Halfmoon Landing

Cedar Point

ST. CATHERINES SOUND

Walburg Island

2

WALBURG CREEK

North Beach

N. NEWPORT RIVER

N. NEWPORT RIVER

SEASIDE INLET

MOLLCLARK RIVER

Middle Beach

Persimmon Point

MCQUEENS INLET

1

Colonial Ruins

Middle Settlement

25 17

Moss Island

St. Catherines Island

Eagle Neck

JOHNSON CREEK

ATLANTIC OCEAN

Barbour Island

Wahoo Island

South End Tabby Ruins

Harris Neck Rd

JULIENTON RIVER

HARRIS NECK

L. MUD RIVER

South Beach

FLAG POND

N

Jullenton

S. NEWPORT RIVER

Fourmile Island

SAPELO SOUND

1 Harris Neck National Wildlife Refuge

2 Gwinnett Home, Cemetery, Cotton Gin, Tabby Ruins

St. Catherines Island

Marsh

Ref: Delorme Georgia Atlas and Gazetteer

a variety of other serpents." Deer are still common in the area, but tygers (panthers), wolves, and bears are long gone from Colonel's Island. One hopes the wildlife still living on Colonel's Island that depends on the sanctuary of Youman's Pond will not be driven away by further development.

Directions: I-95 south from Savannah to Exit 13/76. Go east on GA 38, continuing straight until GA 38 becomes a dirt road. Proceed through pastureland and stop at freshwater pond on right.

Activities: Bird-watching, nature study.

Facilities: None.

Dates: Open daily.

Fees: None.

Closest town: Midway.

For more information: Melon Bluff Preserve can provide information about Youman's Pond as well as other nearby birding sites. Phone 884-5779.

St. Catherines Island

[Fig. 15] While the interior of St. Catherines Island is not open to the general public, this important island needs to be described due to its ecological and historical significance. By state law, all of Georgia's barrier island beaches to the high tide line are open to the public, including St. Catherines. During daylight hours, the public is allowed to use the beach for hiking, picnicking, or shelling to the high-tide line. However, the interior of the island is off-limits to the public without permission.

The island is 10 miles long and ranges from 1 to 3 miles wide, with more than half of the island's 14,640 acres composed of tidal marsh and wetland meadows and ponds. The 6,780 acres of upland are densely forested, with pine and live oak being the predominant species. More than 11 miles of beautiful, white sandy beaches wrap around the eastern side of the island. Like most of the other islands on Georgia's coast, St. Catherines has Pleistocene and Holocene segments, with the older, landward part possessing richer soils that support lush subtropical vegetation and the younger, beach section fronting the sea. Where the two epochs meet at the northern end, a dramatic 25-foot bluff is formed, which was used by Guale Indians as an observation point and may be the most unusual geologic feature on any of the Georgia barrier islands. The island serves as an undisturbed habitat for osprey, and averages 119 sea turtle nests each year, trailing only Cumberland, Ossabaw, and Blackbeard islands in popularity with the endangered reptiles.

Owned by the St. Catherines Island Foundation, the island's interior is operated for charitable, scientific, literary, and educational purposes. The foundation aims to promote conservation of natural resources, the survival of endangered species, and the preservation of historic sites, and to expand human knowledge in the fields of ecology, botany, zoology, natural history, archaeology, and other scientific and educational disciplines.

In this capacity, the island serves as a refuge of last resort for endangered species from around the world. It also has been the scene of innovative archeological work that has revealed much information about the mysterious Spanish mission period on the Georgia coast. The island also hosts environmental research projects on a wide variety of subjects such as beach erosion, mating and flocking habits of certain birds, and behavior and population densities of native mammals, lizards, and insects.

The island has a variety of subtropical ecosystems that are naturally adapted to the management of endangered species from similar climates around the world, which has led to the establishment of the St. Catherines Island Wildlife Survival Center. Begun in 1974 by the New York Zoological Society with a pilot project of 10 gemsboks in a 5-acre pasture, the program has captively bred many exotic species of birds, mammals, and reptiles. The island serves as a type of Noah's Ark, where breeding colonies can be established to build up numbers of the rare animals, which are then returned to zoos or the wild. Some of the animals that have been raised and protected on the island include Grevy's zebras, ring-tailed lemurs, dama gazelles, St. Vincent parrots, rhinoceros hornbills, Aldabra tortoises (a very rare tortoise related to the Galapagos tortoise), Florida sandhill cranes, and Jackson's hartebeests. More than 14 zoos participate in the program.

Today the island is dedicated to scientific research, but in earlier times it was the busy center of political activity on the Georgia coast. Registered as a National Historic Landmark in 1970, St. Catherines was a favorite hunting ground of Indians, and a settlement called Guale in the center of the island served as headquarters for their chief, also named Guale. The Guale were the last in a long line of Indians stretching back 4,000 years that appreciated the island's natural resources. Here, the Spanish established a mission and garrison called Santa Catalina de Guale, from which the island takes its name. Button Gwinnett, a signer of the Declaration of Independence, established a plantation on the island. After the Civil War, the capital of a black separatist sea island kingdom was established here.

Most history books about Georgia begin the story with English Gen. James Edward Oglethorpe sailing up the Savannah River in 1733. This neglects the influence of the Spanish, who built missions on the Georgia coast 207 years before Oglethorpe ever sighted the barrier islands of Georgia. The first mission was established by Lúcas Vásquez de Ayllón in 1526, preceding St. Augustine by 39 years, Sir Walter Raleigh's "lost colony" by 60 years, the English at Jamestown, Virginia by 81 years, and the Pilgrims' landing on Plymouth Rock by 94 years. The Ayllón mission failed within a year, and its exact location remains a mystery, but historians studying maps believe the location of the site was somewhere near St. Catherines and Sapelo islands. Despite Ayllón's failure, the Spanish under Pedro Menendez tried again in 1565 from their base at St. Augustine and succeeded in establishing missions across the Southeast and Florida, and at one time they had approximately 70 Franciscan missionaries serving 25,000 Indians at 38 missions in the Southeast.

In 1566, Menendez explored the Georgia coast and met with an Indian chief named Guale (pronounced wally) on St. Catherines. During early European colonization, the Guale chiefdom extended from the mouth of the Ogeechee to the mouth of the Altamaha

River and included the islands of Ossabaw, St. Catherines, and Sapelo. The Guale spoke Muskogean. A different chiefdom, the Timucuan-speaking Mocama, extended south of the Altamaha to the St. Johns River and inhabited St. Simons, Jekyll, and Cumberland islands. For many years, writers have erroneously asserted that the Georgia coast was called Guale. In truth, the coast was divided by two Indian chiefdoms and there was no original Indian name for the Georgia coast.

On St. Catherines, the Spanish established a mission, Santa Catalina de Guale, which in 1587 was the northernmost outpost of the Spanish Empire in America. In the struggle for the New World, the English pushed south from Virginia and the Spanish pushed north from Florida, which made Georgia the frontline of the battle. The area between Charleston, South Carolina and St. Augustine, Florida, was called "the debatable land" for the territorial dispute. Georgia was not completely in English hands until Oglethorpe defeated Spanish troops on St. Simons Island at the Battle of Bloody Marsh in 1742 and a peace treaty was subsequently signed.

In 1597, a Guale Indian named Juanillo led an uprising against the Spanish, killing five Franciscan friars and destroying missions along the Georgia coast. On St. Catherines, two missionaries were killed and the settlement burned. Juanillo was captured and killed, and eventually the Spanish rebuilt. The next 80 years were known as the Golden Age of Spanish Missions, with at least 15 established in Georgia, some located farther inland. Spanish hegemony remained relatively unchallenged in the Southeast until 1670, when the British established Charles Town in South Carolina. This sparked almost a century of heated conflict over "the debatable land." In 1680, the English with Indian allies attacked the mission on St. Catherines. The Guale were successful in repelling their attackers, but abandoned the mission, which was left to the ravages of time and disappeared under shifting sands and dense vegetation. This marked the end of Spanish settlement on the Georgia coast as well as the end of the Guale Indians, who were to vanish without much known about them.

Despite the long period of Spanish habitation on the Georgia coast, previous to successful efforts on St. Catherines, not a single mission site in Georgia had been identified archeologically. Many believed that tabby ruins found on various islands belonged to the early Spanish missionaries, but it was later discovered that they all belonged to the plantation period. The Spanish missions were built of wattle and daub: Timbers were set vertically, and cane was woven horizontally between them. Then the wattlework was plastered (daubed) with a mixture of sand, mud, and plant fibers. The roofs were covered with palmetto leaves. This made the structures entirely biodegradable. When left to the elements, the structure would wash away, making archeology very difficult if not impossible. But luckily for archeologists searching for the St. Catherines mission, it was burned, which effectively hardens the wattlework the way a clay pot is baked in a kiln, leaving solid evidence. But how to find it under a foot of dirt and dense vegetation over an area equivalent to 30 football fields?

American Museum of Natural History archeologist Dr. David Hurst Thomas, exploring

Indians' Complaints

The Guale Indians that lived on the Georgia coast were generally described as peaceful and accommodating toward Spanish missionaries, who established missions to Christianize the Native Americans. However, not all the Indians appreciated the Spaniards' attempts to change their customs and periodically hostilities would flare up into rebellion. One Indian bitterly complained that the missionaries "take from us women, leaving us only one and that in perpetuity, prohibiting us from changing her; they obstruct our dances, banquets, feasts, fires and wars, so that by failing to use them we lose the ancient valor and dexterity inherited from our ancestors; they persecute our old people, calling them witches; even our labor disturbs them, since they want to command us to avoid it on some days, and be prepared to execute all that they say, although they are not satisfied; they always reprimand us, injure us, oppress us, call us bad Christians, and deprive us of all happiness, which our ancestors enjoyed."

the island on a foundation project since the mid-1970s, used remote sensing equipment to find the lost mission. When subjected to intense heat, iron particles will orient north. The settlement's marsh mud walls contained some microscopic iron particles that were thus altered when the mission burned. Using a sensitive magnetometer, Thomas was able to identify the mission site. There he found more than 400 graves of Christianized Indians, many artifacts, and other clues that have yielded much fresh information on the Guale Indians and the Spanish mission period.

St. Catherines, along with Ossabaw and Sapelo, was involved in the first property transfer in the new colony of Georgia. Gen. James Edward Oglethorpe granted Ossabaw, St. Catherines, and Sapelo islands to the Indians in perpetuity for property rights to the tidewater region between Savannah and the Altamaha River. The Indians made a subsequent deal, granting the hunting islands to Mary Musgrove, an interpreter of mixed Indian and European parentage who was niece of the Indian chiefs and considered princess of the tribe. When Georgia lifted its ban in 1749 on slavery, Musgrove and her second husband Thomas Bosomworth established plantations on her three islands. The legal status of her ownership of the islands was protested by the Royal Trustees, and remained in dispute for 11 years. Nonetheless, the Bosomworths built a home and planted fields on St. Catherines, and raised cattle on Ossabaw. In 1760, the case was settled by granting them St. Catherines, and Sapelo and Ossabaw were put up for public auction with the proceeds going to the Bosomworths.

Mary Musgrove died soon after the decision, and Thomas Bosomworth remarried and sold the island to Button Gwinnett in 1765. Gwinnett, a failed businessman who fled creditors in England for the New World, purchased the island entirely on credit. In Georgia, he earned the reputation as a hotheaded character who had trouble staying out of debt. As the colonists debated the push for independence, Gwinnett supported popular suffrage, unlike the power elite of Savannah, the Christ Church Whigs, who believed only the landed aristocracy should be allowed to vote. His opposition to Christ Church endeared him to the Puritans of St. Johns Parish who wanted to break their northern neighbor's hold on power in the colony. (Savannah's Christ Church was so important to the town that the parish was named Christ Church Parish.) He showed aptitude for politics, and served as speaker of the Commons House of Assembly, president of the Council of Safety, representative to the Second Continental Congress, and commander-in-chief of the armies of Georgia. He helped draw up Georgia's first constitution, redrawing the state's parishes into counties. A rivalry developed between Gwinnett and Gen. Lachlan McIntosh of the Georgia Army, who was a coastal planter and a member of Christ Church. Gwinnett said McIntosh's brother aided Loyalists and relieved McIntosh of his command. At a hearing to decide if Gwinnett's action was justified, McIntosh called Gwinnett a "scoundrel and lying rascal." Gwinnett challenged McIntosh to a duel, which was held on the outskirts of Savannah on May 16, 1777. Both were shot, but Gwinnett died of his wounds on May 19. McIntosh was reassigned to Valley Forge where he served with distinction under George Washington. Both Gwinnett and McIntosh eventually had counties named for them or their families. Gwinnett remains a mystery man, with no known reliable portrait of him in existence, and his rare signature fetches more than $100,000 from collectors. Gwinnett left a wife and child in debt, and the island was put on the auction block. Ownership returned to Thomas Bosomworth, who moved back to the island and lived there until he died and was buried on the island.

A house on the north end of the island, called the Old House, is believed to have belonged to Button Gwinnett. The house and tabby slave cabins from 1800 are used by the foundation.

After the Civil War, General Sherman created an independent state for freed slaves consisting of the sea islands from Charleston, South Carolina, to northern Florida. In 1865, establishing himself as virtual king of this state was Tunis Campbell, who reigned over a government with a legislature, a court, and a 275-man army from his capital at St. Catherines Island. Whites called Campbell "the most feared man in Georgia." Congress repealed Sherman's directive and Federal troops forced Campbell off the island in 1867 to McIntosh County, where he continued his "rule." (Today, he is remembered with a June festival in Darien every year. *See* Appendix D.)

The island changed hands over the years, with various families growing cotton and using the island as a private hunting preserve. Howard Coffin, who owned Sapelo Island and developed Sea Island, once owned St. Catherines and restored and enlarged Gwinnett's Old House.

Edward John Noble of New York purchased the island in 1943 and used it to raise purebred Angus cattle. He died in 1958, and in 1968 the island was transferred to the Edward J. Noble Foundation, which later conveyed the island to the St. Catherines Island Foundation.

Directions: The island can be reached by boat from Shellman Fish Camp, McIntosh County, phone 832-4331 or Halfmoon Marina, Colonel's Island, Liberty County, phone 884-5819.

Dates: Island interior is closed to visitation unless permission is granted by the St. Catherines Island Foundation.

Fees: None.

Closest town: Midway.

For more information: St. Catherines Island Foundation, Inc., Route 1, Box 207-Z, Midway, GA 31320.

▩ MARINAS AND FISH CAMPS IN LIBERTY COUNTY

The North and South Newport and Medway rivers that define Liberty County's boundaries and coastline are productive and popular fisheries. Common inshore catches include southern kingfish (also called whiting), spotted seatrout, sheepshead, striped bass, black and red drum, southern flounder, skate, and Atlantic croaker. Tarpon and shark are caught in St. Catherines Sound, where the large fish patrol the deep waters looking for prey.

Liberty County has two major marinas near the coast and both are located on Colonel's Island: Yellow Bluff Fishing Camp and Colonels Isle Marina. **Yellow Bluff Fishing Camp** provides access to the Medway River and St. Catherines Sound via Ashley Creek. It offers gas, hoist, bait and tackle, refreshments, and dry storage. *884-5448.* **Colonels Isle Marina** provides access to the North and South Newport Rivers, or downstream to St. Catherines Island and Sound. It offers gas and diesel, hoist, bait and tackle, camping, lodging, and dry and wet storage. A public boat ramp is found in Sunbury. *884-5819.*

RESTAURANTS IN LIBERTY COUNTY

Most restaurant options are located in Hinesville, but closer to the coast and I-95 is **Holton's Seafood Restaurant**, I-95 and US 84, which is known for its fried shrimp and other local delicacies. Open for lunch and dinner, 7 days a week. *Moderate. 884-9151.*

McIntosh County

With fewer than 10,000 residents, McIntosh County offers the greatest diversity of attractions and the least foot traffic of any county on the Georgia coast. The county features several commercial fishing villages, three wildlife refuges, one marine sanctuary, numerous coastal restaurants, two historic forts, several antebellum rice plantations, and the magnificent Altamaha River. Because it is a little off the beaten path, McIntosh County still retains the flavor of the "good old days" on the Georgia coast, but this may be changing as development comes to the county.

McIntosh County is fronted by three barrier islands to the east: Blackbeard, a national wildlife refuge; Sapelo, a wildlife refuge and research reserve; and Wolf, a national wildlife refuge that is predominately tidal marsh. To visit Blackbeard, one must charter or use one's own boat. Sapelo is reached by a ferry that carries tourists twice a week to the island. Wolf Island National Wildlife Refuge can be viewed from the water by private boat or charter, but the beach and all upland areas are closed to the public. Harris Neck National Wildlife Refuge, located on the mainland, is very accessible and is excellent for bird watchers and naturalists.

The most difficult wildlife habitat to see is Gray's Reef National Marine Sanctuary, located offshore 17.5 miles east of the McIntosh County, and 60 feet below the surface. The sanctuary attracts both fishermen and scuba divers that are interested in the live bottom's marine life.

McIntosh County is defined by the South Newport River to the north and the Altamaha River to the south. At the northern end of the county, Interstate 95 and US 17 enter at the middle of the county and cross the Altamaha River channels near Darien at the southern end. Most of the attractions described here are east of these highways. A great place to start is at the McIntosh County Welcome Center located in Darien next to the US 17 bridge, where excellent maps and tourist information are readily available. To visit attractions in the northern portion of McIntosh (north of the Sapelo River) such as Harris Neck National Wildlife Refuge and Shellman Bluff, use Interstate 95 Exits 12/67 and 11/58. For other attractions, use Exit 11/58 at Eulonia or 10/49 at Darien, and proceed on GA 99, which makes an arc from Darien to Eulonia along the eastern front of McIntosh County, past the historic marsh-front communities of Crescent, Cedar Point, Valona, Meridian, Ridgeville, and Ashantilly. (The best book about McIntosh County is the 858-page *Early Days on the Georgia Tidewater* by Buddy Sullivan, one of the finest county histories ever written.)

A navigational note: Many roads are poorly marked. Local restaurants and other attractions have responded by putting up numerous small signs to their establishments. Some citizens believe the signs are tacky road trash, other say they are part of McIntosh County's charm. As you leave Interstate 95 or US 17 looking for one of these attractions, you might want to look for signs that will lead you to your destination.

THE SMALLEST CHURCH IN AMERICA

[Fig. 13(2)] Near the community of South Newport is "The Smallest Church in America," a popular local landmark that is open to the traveling public 24 hours a day. Located near US 17, the church is situated in a pine grove called Memory Park that is deeded to Jesus Christ to prevent it from ever being sold. The diminutive Christ's Chapel has room for 12 worshipers, not including a priest, within its 10 feet by 15 feet dimensions. Weddings and special services are held at the church from time to time. It was built in 1950 by a rural grocer named Mrs. Agnes C. Harper. She wanted to provide travelers a quiet sanctuary for meditation and interdenominational worship. The church's interior features a high-pitched roof with exposed beams, along with stained glass windows. A glass star in the roof permits light and inspiration into the interior.

Directions: From I-95, take Exit 12/67 to US 17, go south 1.2 miles to church on left.

🖾 HARRIS NECK NATIONAL WILDLIFE REFUGE

[Fig. 13(1), Fig. 15(1)] During World War II, P-39 and P-40 fighter planes were common in the skies over Harris Neck when the refuge served as an U.S. Army Air Force base. Today, the airfield is a small but important national wildlife refuge where hawks, egrets, herons, and ducks cruise above abandoned runways.

With 2,765 acres, the Harris Neck National Wildlife Refuge is one of the smaller coastal refuges in Georgia, located on the northeastern end of McIntosh County on the South Newport River. Ten Harris Neck refuges could fit into the Savannah National Wildlife Refuge. Despite its modest size, the refuge's diversity of habitat and network of roads providing easy access make it popular with birders, and the refuge is a stop on the Colonial Coast Birding Trail. The freshwater pools, open fields, mixed hardwoods, and salt marsh support many species of wildlife. Besides the birdlife, a variety of flowering plants are found on the refuge. Prickly pear are abundant and can be seen blooming in the fields during May and June.

More than 15 miles of paved roads cross the old airfield, which make the refuge easily accessible to families, photographers, and the physically handicapped. Visitors will enjoy their experience more if they bring binoculars, a bird book, and bug spray. Most popular is the 4-mile wildlife drive, which meanders through the refuge. Near the GA 131 entrance are two fishing piers that are popular with crabbers and shrimpers and an adjacent ramp provides access for boaters into the nearby tidal rivers. Another public boat ramp is found at the southeastern end of the refuge at Barbour River Landing, which is used by boaters and fishermen. Managed hunts are scheduled each year that allow permit holders to hunt deer and hogs.

In the summer, freshwater ponds and flooded woodlands south of the airfield support large rookeries of tricolored, green-backed, and little blue herons; anhingas; white ibis; and wood storks. In spring and summer, many ducks use the ponds, including common moorhens, purple gallinules, and wood ducks. Large concentrations of ducks such as teal, mallards, and gadwalls gather in the freshwater pools and marshlands in the winter.

During spring and fall migrations, the woodlands attract many songbird species. Warblers, vireos, sparrows, and thrushes flit from branch to branch in the live and water oaks and pines as they sing their signature songs. Pileated woodpeckers make use of hardwoods for food and shelter. Year-round residents are deer, feral hogs, raccoons, rabbits, opossums, armadillos, snakes, and fox squirrels. Lucky visitors may see flocks of wild turkeys feasting on acorns or dusting themselves on the refuge's sandy fields. The open fields are hunting grounds for a variety of raptors, including red shouldered hawks, northern harriers, and American kestrels. Occasionally, the birder is treated to a southern bald eagle or

WOOD DUCK
(Aix sponsa)

peregrine falcon. Stalking fish in the tidal marsh are wading birds such as great blue herons and egrets. A checklist of bird species identified at the refuge is available by contacting the Savannah Coastal Refuges office.

The refuge is the northern end or "head" on top of the long, narrow isthmus that was named for Harris Plantation. Several plantations were located on the strip of high ground, which experienced cotton, livestock, timbering, and rice cultivation activities. The most famous of these was the antebellum Peru Plantation belonging to the Thomas family. After the Civil War, much of Harris Neck was sold in small plots to former slaves, who practiced subsistence farming and raised cattle and chickens. The most famous resident of Harris Neck was Pierre Lorillard, the tobacco magnate, who first spied the area from the deck of his yacht and decided to build a winter retreat here. In 1890 on Harris Neck near the South Newport River, he started on a home that included outdoor fountains and pools. He did not use the estate much because he died within a decade of building the home, which later became federal, then county, property.

BALD EAGLE
(Haliaeetus leucocephalus)
Bald eagles build huge nests that can weigh more than a thousand pounds.

In the mid-1930s, the Federal government established an emergency landing field at Harris Neck to serve airplanes using the Jacksonville-Richmond air route. After the attack on Pearl Harbor on December 7, 1941, the government moved to prepare for World War II in earnest. By July 6, 1942, the Federal authorities condemned 1,200 acres, most of it owned by black farmers, and built Harris Neck Air Base, which consisted of 11 prefabricated buildings and several concrete runways. The army installation was used as an integral part of submarine air reconnaissance. Planes watched for German U-boats that patrolled Georgia's shoreline during World War II. Fighter-bomber training operations were also conducted at Harris Neck.

Abandoned in 1944, the air base became property of McIntosh County. Controversy erupted when the airfield and nearby Lorillard estate were looted and stripped of anything of value while under the management of county authorities. Two county commissioners were charged with stealing, but a local judge dropped charges. The Federal government then took action, reclaiming the property and making it a national wildlife refuge in 1962.

The wildlife drive winds around the property, going past Bluebill and Woody ponds south of the runways. Then the route turns north before turning east right down the middle of a runway, traveling past Snipe, Goose, Teal, and Greenhead ponds. After passing Greenhead Pond, a spur on the left goes north to the South Newport River. Heading right, or south, the visitor passes Wigeon Pond and approaches Barbour River

Landing and historic Gould's Cemetery, used by the Gould family, who were coastal settlers, and later black families from Harris Neck.

Hunting: Managed hunts for deer and feral hogs are offered each year. Those wishing to hunt in the refuge must apply for a permit for the particular period when a hunt is scheduled. Bow hunting for deer and hogs is permitted during a period in in September and gun hunting for deer is permitted in a period in November. Contact the Savannah Coastal Refuges office for regulations and an application form.

Trails: 15 miles of networked trails and abandoned roadways. 4-mile auto tour. Biking is excellent on the trails.

Directions: I-95 south from Savannah to Exit 12/67. Go east on US 17 for 1 mile to GA 131. Go east on GA 131 for 7 miles to refuge gate.

Activities: Wildlife drive, bird-watching, hiking, biking, fishing, hunting, boating, canoeing, picnicking, nature study. Guided tours are occasionally available to conservation-oriented organizations through the Savannah Coastal Refuges office.

Facilities: Restrooms, exhibit shelter, boat launch, fishing piers, trails, auto tour. Boat ramps: Harris Neck Creek Recreation Area, located near the entrance of the wildlife refuge, has a boat ramp suitable for small motorized boats and canoes. Fishing piers are popular with anglers. Open sunrise to sunset 7 days a week. Barbour River Landing, located at the termination of GA 131 on the Barbour River, is open 4 a.m. to midnight. Jet Skis are prohibited.

Dates: Open sunrise to sunset 7 days a week. Closed two weeks annually for deer hunts in fall and winter. Portions of refuge may be closed seasonally to prevent disturbance to wood stork rookery.

Fees: No charge.

Closest town: Shellman Bluff.

For more information: U.S. Fish & Wildlife Service, Savannah Coastal Refuges, Parkway Business Center, Suite 10, 1000 Business Center Drive, Savannah, GA 31405. Phone 652-4415.

Shellman Bluff

[Fig. 13(3)] Shellman Bluff is a peaceful, picturesque fish camp village that retains the distinctive charm that once was common on the Georgia coast but has become harder to find. This is the real thing. Quaint, screened fishing cottages sit back among oaks festooned with Spanish moss. All the dirt roads of the quiet village seem to lead inevitably to the high bluff that overlooks the Broro and Julienton rivers. Winding along the edge of the high bluff is another sandy road that offers one of the best coastal views in Georgia. In the morning, the sun rises from behind Harris Neck, lighting the green marsh and dappling the tidal rivers. Birds roost in distant hammock islands, oblivious to the friendly conversation of anglers preparing to head out for another day of sport-fishing. Speed's

Kitchen, a local restaurant, describes the area for out-of-towners on its menu: "SHELL-MAN BLUFF. Not a place for Fast lane folks. Ain't got no red lights. No 4-lanes. We move slow here. Try it—good for your health."

Shellman Bluff and Sutherland Bluff, located on Broro Neck, were the locations of several large plantations. Shellman Bluff was the location of Shellman Plantation, operated by William Cooke until his death in 1861. South of Shellman Bluff is Sutherland Bluff, the scene of Revolutionary War shipbuilding activity and the antebellum Brailsford Plantation. Today, it is Sutherland Bluff Plantation, a community of homes that overlook the river and Sapelo Hammock Golf Club.

Today, Shellman and Sutherland Bluff have several excellent low-country seafood restaurants and is a great place to charter a boat for fishing, a nature outing, or a trip to Blackbeard Island National Wildlife Refuge.

MARINAS AT SHELLMAN BLUFF

Shellman Fish Camp, located in "Downtown Shellman Bluff" is a great place to pick up fishing supplies, use a boat lift, get advice on fishing conditions, arrange an inshore or offshore fishing trip, or plan an excursion to Blackbeard Island. Operated by the hospitable Iler family including Sands, Ron, Gary, and Dot. *832-4331*. **Kips Fish Camp** is a full-service marina as well, with hoist, bait and tackle, gas, charters, and camping. *832-5162*. Another option is **Fisherman's Lodge**, which has a full complement of marina services and supplies (but no lodging). *832-4671*.

RESTAURANTS AND NIGHT LIFE AT SHELLMAN BLUFF

Hunter's Café and The Mud Bar. Shellman Bluff. Locals and travelers enjoy the food and hospitality at Hunter's Café, operated by Bo and Byron Lewis. Located across from the marsh and boat docks on the Broro River, Hunter's serves up some delicious local seafood, including fish and shrimp dishes that are hard to beat anywhere on the coast. The mood and décor of the Café and Mud Bar are laid-back and rustic, where trophy fish, nautical charts, and photos of happy patrons fight for attention on the walls. The Mud Bar is a popular local nightspot featuring cold beers and mixed drinks and friendly locals who will regale you with the latest greatest fish tale. Its motto is "You're Never A Stick In The Mud At The Mud Bar." The restaurant is open Tuesday through Saturday for breakfast at 7 a.m., lunch from 11–2, and supper from 5 p.m. On Sundays, the restaurant is open from 7 a.m.–2 p.m. and closed for supper. The restaurant is closed on Mondays. The bar opens at 5 p.m. *Inexpensive. 832-5771*.

Speed's Kitchen. Shellman Bluff. Located on Speed's Kitchen Road, this pineywoods coastal restaurant is a McIntosh County fixture, despite the temporary look of the place: a couple of doublewides and trailers hooked together to make a fried seafood shrine. Crab stew, shrimp cocktails, and oyster stew are your appetizer options, and then it's on to belt-loosening entrées such as the monster seafood platter (fish, shrimp, oysters, scallops, crab, and cup of crab stew). Or try other delicious local fare such as crab au gratin or the stuffed flounder, which is stuffed with crab. Credit cards not accepted. Open Thursday to Saturday 5–10 p.m. Sunday noon–9:30 p.m. *Moderate. 832-4763.*

🟦 BLACKBEARD ISLAND NATIONAL WILDLIFE REFUGE

[Fig. 13(4), Fig. 17(1)] While there is no absolute proof that Blackbeard the Pirate visited or buried gold on this lush barrier island, it has carried his name for hundreds of years. Many have searched in vain for gold on the island, where legend has it that he and other pirates hid their plunder. The real treasure found here is the near pristine condition of this beautiful 5,618-acre national wildlife refuge, a jewel in the coastal refuge system. Large parts of the island contain mixed stands of live oak, slash pine, cabbage palmetto, magnolia, and holly. Wildlife enthusiasts will appreciate the excellent bird-watching opportunities, as well as the remote, natural experience of hiking its 9 miles of lonely beach and 15 miles of wilderness trails.

Like Blackbeard almost 300 years ago, visitors must use a boat to reach the isolated island, located approximately 50 miles south of Savannah. Blackbeard, at 6.4 miles long and approximately 2 miles wide, is the Holocene, or younger cousin of the Sapelo Island complex (less than 5,000 years old), separated from its larger cousin by Blackbeard Creek and coastal marsh to the west. Across from the island's northern end are Sapelo Sound and St. Catherines Island, and across from its southern end are Cabretta Inlet, created by Blackbeard Creek, and Cabretta Island, a small part of Sapelo Island. Blackbeard Island is roughly the size of Jekyll Island, with 3,900 acres of heavily forested uplands, freshwater and brackish ponds, grass plains, and parallel dune ridges offering many opportunities for exploration of native flora and fauna.

Blackbeard's 7 miles of dazzling beach are literally carpeted with shells, and offer two textbook examples of beach ecology. At the northern end, one finds a boneyard beach, where tidal currents and shifting sands are killing, stripping, and burying a forest of live oaks. At the southern end is a classic case of a recurved spit, where pioneer plants hug onto older, parallel dune ridges while meanders of Blackbeard Creek cut the ridges from behind, revealing layers of sand and clay from older geologic periods. Making regular use of the shoreline during summer are hundreds of birds including oystercatchers, willets, and Wilson's plovers. Royal terns, black skimmers, and least terns are also seen on the island. In September, large concentrations of blackbellied plovers, dowitchers, and dunlin are found. In December, bird watchers can see loons and large rafts of scaup resting in the tidal creeks, sound, and ocean.

The broad, white beach is important nesting habitat between May and September for threatened loggerhead turtles, which nest in proportionately large numbers on the island. Blackbeard averages 163 nests a year, second only to Cumberland Island, which has almost twice the beach. In fact, the second highest number of sea turtles nests ever recorded occurred on Blackbeard, with 265 nests in 1994. (Little Cumberland Island had 278 in 1972.)

At the northern end of the island are three ponds, North, Marsh, and Flag, providing approximately 700 acres of freshwater/ brackish habitat. The U.S. Fish and Wildlife Service created these impoundments to provide winter habitat for migrating waterfowl. In January, bird watchers will find peak numbers of gadwalls, canvasbacks, ring-necked ducks, widgeons, teal, and ruddy ducks. Wood duck nesting peaks in March. Blue-winged teal arrive in August.

The ponds are reached by a tributary of Blackbeard Creek, which is accessed at the north end of the island. A public dock at North Pond allows fishermen to tie up and

A boneyard beach on Blackbeard Island.

use the ponds for fishing. (Access can also be gained by wading ashore at the north end, but beware of rapidly changing tides and weather if you anchor your boat. You may return to find it sitting on the beach or in water too deep to wade.) With fresh water come insects, so come prepared with bug repellant and something to cover up with during the worst insect months on the coast.

Flag Pond supports a large population of alligators that become evident in summer when they emerge from their holes to soak up the sun. The ponds serve as sanctuary for frogs and snakes and are an important water source for deer, raccoons, and other mammals, which leave abundant signs of their visits. Blackbeard Island deer are a special subspecies, *Odocoileus virginianus nigribarbis*. Historically, the island has a reputation for large populations of big rattlesnakes, and many early diaries record killing multiple numbers of them, such as this journal entry of James Keen written on December 17, 1817: "This Day killed several Snakes. Adam Much killed a large Rattlesnake with 12 Rattles, on opening found it had swallowed a full grown Rabit..." Today, all wildlife, including rattlesnakes, are protected on the island refuge by federal law.

The grassy plains or toar savannas of the northern end are popular hunting grounds for marsh hawks and other raptors. Bald eagles and peregrine falcons are occasionally observed.

In spring and fall, the wooded acres abound with migrating songbirds. Summer tanagers and painted buntings are most common in summer. In May, herons and egrets begin nesting at Blackbeard Island, which has rookeries that have supported more than 1,000 pairs of birds including ibis, anhingas, and wood storks. A checklist of bird species identified at the refuge is available by contacting the Savannah Coastal Refuges Office.

With more than twice the acreage of Tybee Island, the island has 20 miles of roads and paths available to hikers. From the refuge headquarters, a path called South Beach Trail leads to the center of Blackbeard's beach. At the dock, visitors can be dropped off and boats can be tied up temporarily for loading and unloading purposes.

The southern end of Blackbeard is popular with naturalists, fishermen, and beach

Blackbeard and the Pirates of the Georgia Coast

Of all the pirates that roamed the Atlantic seas, perhaps the most notorious was Blackbeard. Much that has been written about Blackbeard blends fact with fiction, making the legendary pirate even more mysterious. In 1996, divers in Beaufort Inlet found a sunken ship that dates to Blackbeard's era and some believe to be his pirate ship the *Queen Anne's Revenge.* Efforts are ongoing to excavate and study the shipwreck and learn more about the age of piracy.

It is believed Edward Thatch (sometimes erroneously reported as Teach) was born in Bristol, England in the late 1600s. He had a commanding presence, standing 6 feet 4 inches and weighing 250 pounds, with long black hair and braided beard tied with ribbons. Blackbeard preyed on ships from New England to the Virgin Islands. On the stolen *Queen Anne's Revenge*, Blackbeard would attack ships that carried riches from the New World, pounding them into submission with his 40 cannon. Then looking like a brother of the Devil that he claimed to be, Blackbeard would storm aboard a captured vessel, with pistols and knives in his sash, cutlass in his hand, and dagger in his teeth. For additional effect, Blackbeard would light small pieces of slow-burning rope that were tied to his beard and hair, creating a smoldering hallucination of a beast from hell.

In the early 1700s, privateers were employed by England during the War of Spanish Succession to raid Spanish galleons that were returning from the New World with gold and silver stolen from Indian nations in the Americas. When the war ended in 1713, these buccaneers turned to freelancing, raiding any and all ships that might be carrying valuable cargo. Blackbeard seized a French ship in 1717 and began his reign of terror along the southeastern coast of the U.S. and Caribbean. His home base from 1716–1718 was in North Carolina, where he had an agreement with the royal governor.

It is widely believed that Blackbeard also used the Georgia coast, where its meandering tidal rivers, inlets, and barrier islands served as excellent hiding places. He and his crew would quickly strike at ships then retreat to hide. It is believed that somewhere on Georgia's barrier islands is buried treasure, and treasure hunters with metal detectors are a common sight on some of Georgia's developed islands.

Reportedly, Blackbeard bragged that no one but he and the Devil knew where he kept his treasure hidden, and the one who lived the longest could keep it. It appears that the Devil won that contest. Blackbeard met his match in June 1718, when he was killed off the coast of North Carolina in hand-to-hand combat with Lt. Robert Maynard of His Majesty's *Pearl*. Maynard decapitated the cruel pirate, displayed the head as a warning to other raiders, and cast the body into the sea. Legend has it that Blackbeard's skull was made into a macabre silver-plated cup, and Blackbeard's headless ghost guards his treasure somewhere on a remote, deserted isle—maybe Blackbeard Island.

lovers, who anchor off the western side and hike over a short path through two dune ridges to reach the beach on the eastern side. Sandspurs, Russian thistle, and sea oats are abundant. Nature lovers who cross the dunes in bare feet will regret it and perhaps find themselves cursing nature a little bit.

The dune ridges, like spines down the back, reveal the architecture of the island. The southern end is more dominated by pine forest. In 1975, 3,000 acres were set aside as a national wilderness, consisting of Blackbeard Creek tidal marsh to the west of the island and uplands south of the U.S. Fish and Wildlife Service headquarters.

Archery hunts are allowed periodically on Blackbeard Island by special permit. If hunters get a permit, they are treated not only to one of the peak archery hunts in Georgia, but also are allowed to camp on the island. Contact the Savannah Coastal Refuges Office for regulations.

Blackbeard has been the property of Indians, the French, and the Spanish. Before Oglethorpe arrived with his colonists in Savannah, pirates roamed the waters of the southern Atlantic and Caribbean, attacking Spanish and English ships and fleeing to hide in the tidal creeks and rivers of the Georgia coast. The most notorious of the pirates was Edward Thatch, also known as Blackbeard. He seized a French ship, changed the name to *Queen Anne's Revenge*, and wreaked havoc on ships off the Southeastern United States coast. In 1718, he was captured and beheaded by the English Royal Navy. Legends persist to this day that Blackbeard buried treasure on the island and marked it with a spike in an old tree, and it is said practiced other nasty pirate-like activities such as beheading his 16th wife and six crew members and burying them in a mass grave on the island. The myth of Blackbeard's treasure has been so persistent that in 1934 a group of explorers were allowed to search the island for 10 days, but were unsuccessful in finding the pirate's loot. Today, artifact and treasure hunting are strictly forbidden.

The U.S. Navy purchased Blackbeard in 1800 for $15,000 to use it as a naval timber reserve. The island's live oak was a superior material for the building of sturdy warships like the *Constitution*, nicknamed *Old Ironsides* for its resilient live oak planks that made enemy cannonballs bounce off its sides. The record is spotty, but some of Blackbeard's virgin live oaks were harvested from 1817 to 1818.

From 1880 to 1912, the U.S. Marine Hospital Service used the island as a quarantine station for yellow fever victims and for disinfecting incoming sea vessels with sulphur gas. The quarantine station had jurisdiction from St. Augustine to Savannah. All incoming ships had to first stop at Blackbeard before continuing on to their destinations. At the south end were a hospital and 12 other quarters, and at the north end were the wharf, cleaning station, crematorium, and other buildings. Not much remains visible from the quarantine station, which was destroyed by a hurricane and tidal wave in 1898 that put the island under several feet of water. However, at the north end of the island, boaters can see ballast stone islands that mark the end of the wharf where ballast stones were removed from ships undergoing disinfection. A brick structure located inland at the northwestern end is the crematorium built in 1904. In the early 1900s, the cause of yellow fever was conclusively identified and

CARDINAL
(Cardinalis cardinalis)
Males are bright red
and females are brownish
yellow with red on
wings and tail.

subsequent mosquito control measures virtually eradicated the outbreaks that had plagued the coastal colonies since the late seventeenth century and led to the closure of the station in 1912.

During the Spanish-American War from 1898 to 1901, a gun battery was built on the northern end to guard Sapelo Sound, as part of the fortifications ordered by U.S. Congress that produced Fort Screven on Tybee Island and Fort Morgan on Wassaw. A cast-iron carriage that remained on the island was donated to the National Park Service for display at Fort Pulaski National Monument near Savannah.

In October 1912, the U.S. Public Health and Marine Hospital Service leased Blackbeard Island to William Brinson of New York for $901.10 to use as a hunting preserve. In 1914, President Woodrow Wilson transferred the property to the Department of Agriculture for a "preserve and breeding ground for native birds" In 1915, Blackbeard Island was reverted back to the Treasury Department. From 1916 to 1922, the Georgia Fish and Game division used the island as a wildlife preserve.

Howard Coffin, the millionaire auto magnate who developed Sapelo and Sea islands, was given custody of the island in 1922. In 1924, Blackbeard Island was transferred back to the Department of Agriculture (Bureau of Biological Survey), as a bird refuge. In 1926, President Calvin Coolidge, by executive order, established Blackbeard Island "for use as a bird refuge and an experiment station for the acclimatization of certain foreign game birds." In 1940, Blackbeard Island was officially named a national wildlife refuge, and assigned to the Department of Agriculture, Bureau of Sport Fisheries and Wildlife, later to be known as the United States Fish and Wildlife Service, Department of the Interior. In 1972, President Richard Nixon designated 3,000-acres of Blackbeard Island as a wilderness area.

In the late 1940s, local and state officials pushed a plan to link Sapelo and Blackbeard islands by a causeway, and transform Blackbeard into a beach resort. Studies were done, but the plan was abandoned because of the $3 million price tag for the causeway was deemed too expensive and the Federal government was unwilling to turn over control of the island.

Directions: Blackbeard Island is reached only by charter boat. Charter a boat from Shellman Fish Camp at Shellman Bluff, phone 832-4331 or launch your own from Barbour River Landing at the termination of GA 131 at Harris Neck Wildlife Refuge.

Activities: Hiking, bird-watching, shelling, fishing, archery hunting, picnicking, nature studies, biking, kayaking. Strictly prohibited are camping, fires, pets, firearms, and collecting of plants, animals, and artifacts. Fishing is a popular activity at the northern ponds. Archery deer hunting is allowed one weekend each year by special permit. Dates and bag limits change each year. For information, contact the Savannah Coastal Refuges Office at 652-4415.

Facilities: Federal dock, exhibit shelter with island map.

Fees: None.

Dates: Open sunrise to sunset 7 days a week. Closed 2 weeks annually for deer hunts in fall and winter. Portions of beach may be closed to prevent disturbance to nesting, wintering, or migrating birds.

Closest town: Darien.

For more information: U.S. Fish & Wildlife Service, Savannah Coastal Refuges, Parkway Business Center, Suite 10, 1000 Business Center Drive, Savannah, GA 31405. Phone 652-4415.

HIKING BLACKBEARD ISLAND

The northern end features freshwater ponds and climax live oak and palmetto forest. North Trail goes between North Pond and Flag Pond, with a spur to the crematorium at the northern end. Middle Trail follows the eastern side of Flag Pond, and the East Trail follows the eastern edge of the grass savanna. A spur off East Trail leads to the beach. East and Middle Trails lead south to the wildlife refuge headquarters. From the headquarters, a short trail leads to the beach, and two trails, West Wilderness and East Wilderness, loop through the wilderness area of pine and mixed hardwood forest.

Trails: 15 miles of networked trails, 7 miles of beach.

RESTAURANTS IN CENTRAL MCINTOSH COUNTY

Pelican Point. Belleville. At this restaurant, it is difficult to decide which is more overwhelming: the gorgeous view of the golden *Spartina* marsh as the sun sets behind Sapelo sound and island, or the outrageous amounts of food that are offered at its buffet. One thing is for sure: you won't go away hungry. Pelican Point is located in Belleville, a traditional fishing village, and was the boyhood home of George M. Troup, who served as a governor and senator of Georgia in the 1820s. The family cemetery is within walking distance of the restaurant and might be a way to burn off some calories. Open for dinner Monday through Saturday at 5:30, Sundays at noon. Live entertainment Wednesdays through Saturdays. Alcohol is served and credit cards are accepted. Belleville is reached by taking Exit 11/58 on Interstate 95. Head east on GA 99 and follow the signs. *Moderate. 832-4295.*

Altman's Restaurant and Lounge. Eulonia. This is a full menu family restaurant serving breakfast, lunch, and dinner 7 days a week. Lunch specials feature meat and two vegetable options just like your momma used to make, along with many other choices in this friendly roadside restaurant popular with local working men and women. Located near Eulonia at the intersection of GA 99 and US 17 approximately 1 mile east of Exit 11/58 on Interstate 95. *Inexpensive. 832-6086.*

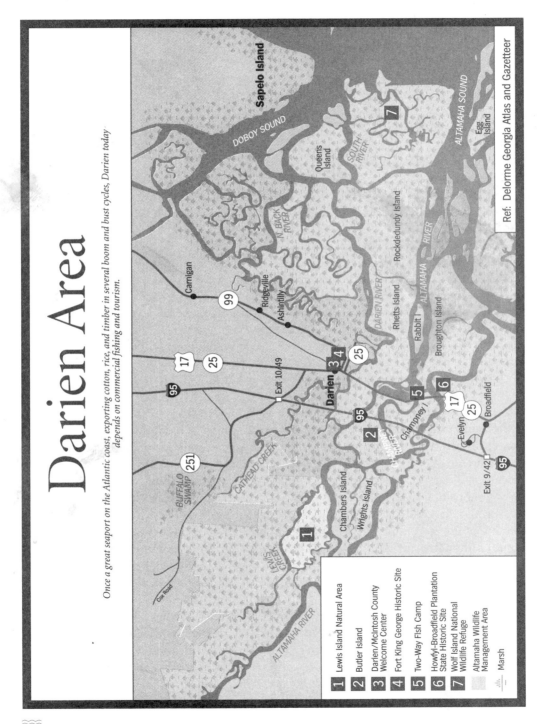

Darien Area

Once a great seaport on the Atlantic coast, exporting cotton, rice, and timber in several boom and bust cycles, Darien today depends on commercial fishing and tourism.

1 Lewis Island Natural Area
2 Butler Island
3 Darien/McIntosh County Welcome Center
4 Fort King George Historic Site
5 Two-Way Fish Camp
6 Howfyl-Broadfield Plantation State Historic Site
7 Wolf Island National Wildlife Refuge
Altamaha Wildlife Management Area
Marsh

Ref: Delorme Georgia Atlas and Gazetteer

Darien

[Fig. 16] This town of only 1,800 people has one of the most colorful histories of any town in Georgia, if not the United States. Once a great seaport on the Atlantic coast, exporting cotton, rice, and timber in several boom and bust cycles, Darien today depends on commercial fishing and tourism. The town's fortunes have always been linked to the propagation and harvesting of the extensive natural resources found in the county and upriver areas. More of Darien's interesting past would be evident if the town hadn't been burned during the Civil War. Despite that infamous event, there are plenty of fascinating sites and nearby excursions to appeal to the visitor. The town has a historic district, a commercial waterfront, nineteenth century churches, Victorian homes, tabby ruins, and Fort King George State Historic Site. A short distance from town are several places worth visiting, including Hofwyl-Broadfield Plantation, Sapelo Island, and the mighty Altamaha River. The Blessing of the Fleet festival, in honor of Darien's commercial fishermen, is a uniquely coastal tradition and the most important annual event held in McIntosh County (see Appendix D). Approximately 25 vessels participate in the old Portuguese custom, with festivities taking place on the banks of the Darien River.

Traveler are best served by starting their visit at the McIntosh County Welcome Center, located in downtown Darien near the foot of the US 17 bridge. Here, visitors can load up with brochures, maps, tickets, and advice and tailor an excursion that suits their needs.

Darien and McIntosh County have experienced significant changes to their natural ecosystems. Before the arrival of Europeans, the Coastal Plain uplands were composed of vast, fire-dependent longleaf pine forests towering over a grassy understory made up of many species of wildflowers and grasses. The swamps that adjoined the Altamaha River consisted of huge, ancient baldcypresses. Sand ridges, with nutrient-poor soils, supported unusual plant and animal communities found nowhere else. The Altamaha River ran clear and supported an abundance of fish, mussels, and other streamlife. Mud banks in the tidal marshes and estuaries were choked with oysters, and the surrounding waters were busy with birdlife, with huge rookeries of herons and egrets and colonies of alligators sharing freshwater wetlands. Thousands and thousands of sea turtles nested on the sandy beaches, while bear, wolves, and panthers stalked game in the maritime forests.

When we go to the shore today, we are much impressed with the natural beauty of the coast. But truthfully, we do not know, nor ever will know, what has been lost. The majestic longleaf forest and ancient cypress swamps located far upstream on the Altamaha, Ocmulgee, Oconee, and Ohoopee rivers were cut down by timber operations and floated down to Darien and exported to Europe. In their place today we have even-aged pine plantations growing slash pine for market. The grasses and wildflowers were lost when the natural forests did not regrow. Today's understory generally is hardwoods, controlled with chemicals. The unusual plant communities of the sand ridges were also replaced with yellow pine, making the chances of finding a healthy wild population of

The Burning of Darien

Union Col. Robert G. Shaw regretted the burning of Darien, which he later related in a letter home: "He (Montgomery) said to me, 'I shall burn this town.' He speaks always in a very low tone and has quite a sweet smile when addressing you. I told him, 'I did not want the responsibility of it,' and he was only too happy to take it all on his shoulders: so the pretty little place was burnt to the ground, and not a shed remains standing; Montgomery firing the last building with his own hand." In 1870, Shaw's mother sent $1,000 to the Darien Episcopal Church in the memory of her son, who died a month after the burning of Darien. She called the disaster an "unjustifiable and cruel deed."

Bartram's beautiful *Franklinia alatamaha* next to impossible (*see* William Bartram and *Franklinia alatamaha*, page 199). The lumber operations destroyed riverbanks and released millions of cubic feet of sediments into the river, changing its chemistry and killing many freshwater organisms that depend on clean, clear water. Introduced species of game fish and exotic plants have forced natives out. The populations of wild birds have decreased, as have sea turtles that require undisturbed beaches to reproduce. Sprawling maritime forests of live oak were cut for shipbuilding and other uses. Many wetlands were diked, drained, and used to grow cotton, rice, and indigo. The delicious oyster, its importance in the ancient diet evidenced by huge Indian shell mounds, has decreased in abundance from overharvesting, sewage, and other pollutants that have made many oyster beds off-limits to human consumption because oysters concentrate toxins in their flesh. Bears, wolves, and panthers are found only in zoos.

That's the bad news. The good news is that nature is resilient, and due to the efforts of conservation-minded citizens, there is much still to enjoy, preserve, study, and perhaps nurture back to health. Citizens are much more aware of the importance of a healthy environment and more likely to voice their opposition to unwise use of natural resources. However, these sentiments are running against the tide of population that is moving to American coastlines, and the challenge remains to protect the resource before it collapses beyond recovery.

Darien is positioned on a bluff overlooking the northern channel of the Altamaha River. South of Darien is the wide river delta with its many channels, coastal marsh, and cypress swamps. East of Darien are salt marshes and Sapelo Island, a barrier island that protects the mainland from the fury of the Atlantic. The high bluff, a Pleistocene sand ridge and former barrier island of the Princess Anne chain, has been popular for settlements going back thousands of years.

The human history of the area dates back 4,500 years, according to archeological remains found on Sapelo which confirm the area was settled by Indian tribes that used the coast as hunting and fishing grounds. From the 1560s to 1680s, Darien and the Georgia coast experienced Spanish expansion activities, led by Franciscan missionaries.

They recorded finding Guale Indian settlements named *Asao* and *Talaje* near current-day Darien, and between 1595–1661, the Spanish supported a mission called *Santo Domingo de Asao/Talaje.* This mission was relocated to the northern end of St. Simons Island in 1661 after English-allied slave raiders known as the Westo or Chichimeco Indians destroyed the mission. In the 1680s, the missionaries withdrew from the Georgia coast to focus their efforts on Florida, but into the 1700s, Georgia continued to be "the debatable land." England established Fort King George in 1721, with the military goal of defending the southern flank of the English colony against French expansion into the Altamaha region and Spanish conquest from Florida. While the fort was abandoned in 1727, England still had designs on Georgia, and Oglethorpe settled Savannah in 1733.

In 1736, Darien was founded by Scottish Highlanders who were lured to the Georgia coast by Gen. James Edward Oglethorpe. Oglethorpe wanted to establish towns and garrisons in the Altamaha region to protect the southern flank of the Georgia colony from Spanish expansion. English and Austrians from Salzburg were to settle St. Simons Island (Fort Frederica) and the Scots were to settle the abandoned site of Fort King George. The Highlanders named their village "Darien" in honor of the failed 1697 settlement of the same name in Panama.

Leading the Scots was John McIntosh Mohr (1698–1761), whose leadership of Darien and the heroic exploits of his famous offspring became illustrious chapters in Georgia and America's history. Their influence spread way beyond Darien, and when the coastal area was reconfigured from Liberty County, it was named for the celebrated clan. The Highlanders, who maintained their traditional dress and customs, were famous for their hospitality and excellent relations with Indians, as well as their bravery in war, and they became favorites of Oglethorpe. The Highlanders assisted Oglethorpe in an attack on the Spanish stronghold at St. Augustine in 1739, which was unsuccessful, and at the Battle of Bloody Marsh in 1742, which was successful. At Bloody Marsh, they defeated the Spanish who left Georgia, never to return. William McIntosh, son of John McIntosh Mohr, fought at that battle at the age of 16. William's son John was in charge of Fort Morris at Sunbury when he made his defiant reply to a British demand to surrender: "Come and take it!" William's brother, Lachlan, became commander of Georgia forces at the beginning of the American Revolution. He killed Button Gwinnett in a duel (*see* St. Catherines Island, page 159), and was transferred to George Washington's forces at Valley Forge. Later, he helped lead the unsuccessful Georgia and French attack on British forces entrenched in Savannah. Another McIntosh cousin, William, became chief of the Creek Indians. Creeks murdered him in 1825 for signing the unpopular Treaty of Indian Springs. John McIntosh Kell was one of the most distinguished officers of the Confederate Navy, second in command of the *Alabama*, the most successful Confederate raider in the Civil War.

The McIntosh name is associated with many firsts: They founded the first Presbyterian church in Georgia in Darien. When Georgia plantation owners moved to legalize slavery (which had been banned by Oglethorpe), the Scots opposed it in a 1739 petition believed to be the first recorded protest of slavery in America. The Highlanders built Fort Darien, which commanded the river with 10 cannon, and part of the Post Road, the first road in Georgia that connected Savannah with St. Marys. The Bank of Darien, with many Scots serving on the board, was established in 1818 and had many branches across the state. Half owned by the State of Georgia, it was reported to be the largest south of Philadelphia, according to historian Burnette Vanstory. Famed eighteenth century naturalist William Bartram wrote about various McIntoshes of the area and traveled with John McIntosh, whom Bartram described as "a sensible virtuous youth, and a very agreeable companion through a long and toilsome journey of near a thousand miles."

Darien has experienced many boom and bust cycles: booming when rice and cotton plantations were productive in the early 1800s, busting when fires, hurricanes, disease, and financial scandals devastated the town. From 1810 to 1845, the town grew as a seaport, leading the world in the export of cotton, which, along with timber, was grown inland and floated downriver on huge rafts called "Oconee boxes." Rice plantations were established in tidally influenced freshwater areas, and had a positive influence on Darien's economy. (For more about rice plantations, *see* Hofwyl-Broadfield Plantation, page XX.) During the Civil War, Darien was invaded, looted, and burned to the ground on June 11, 1863 by Union troops, which consisted mainly of black soldiers commanded by two white officers. Col. James Montgomery is blamed for the pointless destruction and was later relieved of his responsibilities. The other officer was 25-year-old Col. Robert G. Shaw, who died about a month later during a famous assault on Battery Wagner on Morris Island, which guarded the southern approaches to Charleston harbor. The movie *Glory* tells the story of Shaw and the burning of Darien. Because of this unnecessary conflagration, most of Darien's records were lost, and very little of the antebellum Darien exists. The Civil War devastated the South, and ended the plantation culture that depended on free labor from slaves and access to capital.

Slow to rebuild, Darien's next period was one of prosperity as it became the second leading timber exporting town in the South. Huge rafts—200 feet long by 100 feet wide—of southern yellow pine and cypress were cut in Georgia's interior, then floated down the Oconee, Ocmulgee, and Altamaha rivers to sawmills in Darien. After the raw wood was cut into lumber, it was loaded onto boats for export around the country and world. Most of the historic homes and structures in Darien and the rest of the county were built in this period, which lasted into the 1920s, when timber stocks were finally depleted and railroads became a more-favored method of transporting lumber.

Early in its history, Darien was dependent on natural productivity upstream; in the late 1880s, Darien shifted its dependence to natural productivity downstream: commercial fishing for oysters, shrimp, and crabs. Historically, commercial landings of shellfish and fish in McIntosh County are twice has high as in any other Georgia county.

From 1880 to 1910, McIntosh County oyster harvests were among the highest in the world—rivaling even the Chesapeake Bay—with a record harvest of 8 million pounds in 1908. Georgia oysters were plucked from beds by men using long-handled tongs. The oystermen would fill their small bateaux, then unload the oysters into 50-foot sloops. The sloops would transport the shells to canneries located in Valona, Cedar Point, and Darien, where workers would shuck and can the oysters. The oyster industry went into a long decline after the early 1900s, with only 38,000 pounds harvested in 1978. The decline is mostly blamed on overharvesting. Oyster young, or spat, require a hard surface on which to attach and develop. Early regulations that required oystermen to return shells to the harvest areas went unheeded and the extensive oyster banks are mainly a thing of the past. Oysters are very sensitive to changes in water quality and are considered a "canary in a coal mine." They suffer from sewage, toxins, and other pollutants in the water. Disease has also wiped out healthy oysterbeds.

Brown and White Shrimp

Shrimp are the most important commercial fishery in Georgia, since they are worth more per pound than any other seafood caught by U.S. fishermen. Shrimp, with their delicious cousins crabs and lobsters, are crustaceans from the order Decapoda, meaning "ten legs." The most common species of marine shrimp caught off the Georgia shore are brown shrimp (*Penaeus aztecus*) and white shrimp (*Penaeus setiferus*). The life cycles are relatively similar: Benthic (bottom dwelling) adults release their eggs freely into the offshore waters. Within a short time, the eggs hatch into planktonic larvae. After passing through several intermediate stages, the postlarval shrimp move into the estuary and adopt a benthic existence. They grow very rapidly, doubling or tripling their weight every month and assuming the adult form. As the water turns colder in October and November, they move through the sound to deeper waters offshore, where they migrate parallel to the shoreline. White shrimp account for two-thirds of the catch and brown shrimp make up most of the rest of the catch. Affecting the quantity and quality of shrimp is a complex interaction of factors, including temperature, salinity, circulation, and fertility of estuarine waters. Shrimp are caught by trawlers, which generally are regulated outside the sound limits but are free to drag their nets close to the shoreline.

As the oysterbeds were declining, a new commercial fishery developed: shrimping. In the early 1900s, Old World fishermen from Spain, Portugal, and Sicily were attracted to the southeastern coast for its abundant fisheries. With the advent of ice, refrigeration, and train transportation, the market for shrimp increased tenfold, and the Fernandina area became the shrimp capital of the Atlantic coast, with its influence spreading north to Georgia. With the invention of diesel engines, better nets, and boats custom designed for shrimping came increased harvests and profits. Larger McIntosh County shrimp boats starting traveling to the Gulf of Mexico in a wider search for shrimp.

Like any industry dependent on a commodity, shrimping has experienced ups and downs based on the supply and demand of shrimp, while costs associated with the industry such as diesel and loans on bigger, more expensive modern boats have gone up.

Today, Georgia's shrimpers struggle to survive against cheaper, imported shrimp from Ecuador and other countries. The shrimp served in Georgia coastal restaurants is generally imported from another country.

To supplement their incomes, commercial fishermen in McIntosh County started harvesting blue crabs and whelks. The market for live blue crabs, shipped to crack-and-eat restaurants on the East Coast, grew in the 1970s to 1990s, resulting in much more intense harvesting of this resource. Blue crabs can be harvested in Georgia and shipped to northern restaurants before northern crab fisheries are opened. Knobbed whelks, a gastropod that lives on the sandy ocean bottom, are harvested by shrimpers who market the meat as conch.

McIntosh County in the 1950s and 60s earned a reputation of being an outlaw county where prostitution and gambling were common practices along US 17 and were supported by local authorities in control of the county. US 17, called the Coastal Highway, was the main auto route used by tourists who were traveling to Florida. Crooked clipjoints would fleece travelers of their vacation funds in a variety of fixed gambling schemes. Attempts to shut down the illegal syndicates were unsuccessful, until the building of Interstate 95, which routed travelers and their money down a different route, putting the operations out of business. (Popular with critics but unpopular with many McIntosh citizens is the award-winning book about the era titled *Praying for Sheetrock*, by Melissa Fay Greene.)

Today, the county is experiencing development as it becomes more of a bedroom community for Brunswick and Savannah, and second homes and retirement homes are built by those who appreciate McIntosh County's natural beauty and outdoor recreation opportunities. Tourism in the area has increased as well.

TOURING MCINTOSH COUNTY
DARIEN/MCINTOSH COUNTY WELCOME CENTER

[Fig. 16(3)] From the Darien/McIntosh County Welcome Center, walkers can follow a path down to a large boardwalk that fronts the Darien River. From here, you can view part of Darien's active shrimp fleet. A paved trail follows the riverfront and leads you to tabby ruins that mark the location of Darien's old waterfront—so old that 100-year-old live oaks are grown on top of some of the ruins, which date back to 1815–1830. A picnic area shaded with cabbage palms and live oaks near the welcome center provides an elevated view of the river delta. Here one can contemplate what it must have been like when the river was jammed with logs, or when paddlewheel steamboats churned the waters of the Altamaha, or when Union soldiers ran from building to building, putting the torch to the town.

Across the US 17 bridge are several beautiful and significant sites, which are discussed elsewhere: the Altamaha Waterfowl Management Area (*see* page 203), Butler Island Rice Plantation (*see* page 205), and Hofwyl-Broadfield Plantation (*see* page 212).

Other highlights in the downtown area include the following:

First Presbyterian Church, at Bayard Square and Jackson Street, was rebuilt in 1900 after a fire the previous year. This was the home of the first Presbyterian congregation in Georgia, making Darien the cradle of Presbyterianism in Georgia.

Oglethorpe Oak and Highlander Monument. Located at US 17 and GA 99 (Adams Street). The old oak, which shaded units of Oglethorpe's men, survived hurricanes, fires, and other calamities until it finally expired in the 1960s, leaving just a stump. The Highlander Monument was dedicated in 1936.

Vernon Square. On Washington Street. In the 1800s this square was the business, cultural, social, and religious center of Darien. The Methodist Church was originally built in 1843, partially damaged during the Civil War, then rebuilt in 1884 with many of the materials of the first church. St. Andrews Episcopal Church was the site of the famous Bank of Darien. The church was built in 1878. Open Gates, a bed and breakfast, was built in 1878 by sawmill owner Isaac Aiken. Hilton House, on south Vernon Square, was built by timber baron Joseph Hilton in 1875.

Darien United Methodist Church.

First African Baptist Church. Located at Madison and Market streets, this church was erected in 1868 as a replica of the 1834 church that once stood on this site.

St. Cyprian's Episcopal Church. Located at Fort King George Drive and Boone Dock Road. A tabby church built in 1876 by former slaves and serving a black congregation, this church was named for a martyred African saint.

Ashantilly and St. Andrew's Cemetery. Only 1 mile northeast on GA 99 from the courthouse is the mainland home of Sapelo Island's Thomas Spalding, built in 1820. St. Andrews Cemetery was established in 1818 as the Spalding family cemetery.

The Ridge National Historic District. Approximately 3 miles north of Darien on GA 99 are Victorian homes from the late 1800s that were owned by prosperous timber barons and bar pilots.

Valona. Located 10 miles north of Darien on GA 99, and 1 mile down a county road to the right is a traditional commercial fishing community that grew up along Shellbluff Creek in the 1890s.

Pine Harbor. Travel 3 miles north of Eulonia on US 17, then turn left on Pine Harbor Road, and go 3 miles to Pine Harbor. This was the site of the McIntosh family's Mallow

Plantation. Today, historical markers and a family cemetery are found in the shade of live oak trees. The cemetery holds Captain William McIntosh, the father of the murdered Creek Indian chief.

For more information: Darien/McIntosh County Welcome Center, US 17, Darien, GA 31305. Phone 437-6684.

RESTAURANTS IN DARIEN

Archie's Restaurant. US 17, Darien. There should be a historical marker outside this restaurant, a longtime favorite of locals and tourists alike since 1938. Archie Davis Sr. started the restaurant (in a different location in Darien) and Archie Jr. runs it today. The restaurant's famous slogan remains as true today as it did 60 years ago: "Seafood Served in this Restaurant Slept in the River Last Night." Archie's World Famous Fried Shrimp features three dozen sweet Georgia shrimp that, unlike most shrimp served in coastal restaurants, have not been raised in Ecuador, frozen, and thawed, then fried. Some say Archie's Altamaha River Fresh Water Catfish is even better, featuring delectable river catfish Archie buys from local fishermen. You decide. Breakfast, lunch, and dinner served. Closed Sundays. *Moderate. 437-4363.*

LODGING IN DARIEN AND MCINTOSH COUNTY

Open Gates Bed and Breakfast. Vernon Square, Darien. This B&B is a great place to launch explorations of Darien and the rest of McIntosh County. Located on historic Vernon Square, Open Gates was built in 1876 by sawmill owner Isaac Means Aiken. Vernon Square was the heart of business, cultural, social, and religious activities in Darien. The square was laid out in 1806, then burned twice during the Civil War, and is today listed on the National Register of Historic Places. Open Gates is nestled in a beautiful setting of oaks and gardens, and has modern amenities, including air conditioning and a pool. Proprietor Carolyn Hodges is knowledgeable about the area's history and can arrange historic and nature tours. *Moderate. 437-6985.*

Motels in McIntosh County. Several reliable chain motels are found near Interstate 95. **Holiday Inn**. Darien. Five minutes from Darien and local attractions is a relatively new Holiday Inn. *Moderate. 437-5373.* **Days Inn**. Eulonia. Centrally located in McIntosh County just off the Interstate 95 at Exit 11/58, this motel offers a full-service restaurant and swimming pool. Children eat free. *Moderate. 832-4411.*

CAMPGROUNDS IN MCINTOSH COUNTY

Three privately run campgrounds are popular with travelers exploring the coast. Two are situated within 1 mile of Interstate 95: Lake Harmony RV Park and Darien Inland Harbor Campground. With their close proximity to the interstate, these are popular with travelers passing through the Georgia coast. A more low-country option, Belle Bluff Island Campground, is located on a tributary of the Sapelo River and is an excellent base for launching explorations of McIntosh County.

Belle Bluff Island Campground. Pine Harbor. Here you have access to a marina and charter fishing, along with RV and tent sites. The full-service marina has a boatlift, gas and oil, boat rentals, charters, bait and tackle, and a general store. A dock is used for crabbing and shrimping. The campground has tent sites and RV sites with full-hookups. Nature tours can be arranged through the office. **Directions:** from I-95, take Exit 11/58 and go 1 mile south to US 17, then turn left and go 2.25 miles to Pine Harbor Road. Turn right and go 2.5 miles to Belle Hammock Road, and turn left and go 1.25 miles to entrance of Belle Bluff Island. *832-5323.*

Lake Harmony RV Park. Townsend. Less than 1 mile west of I-95 off Exit 11/58, this campground offers a fishing lake along with 52 RV sites, full hookups, pull-through sites, tent sites, bait and tackle, laundry, swimming pool, and cable TV. *(888) 767-7864.*

Darien Inland Harbor Campground. Darien. Located east of I-95 off of Exit 10/49, Inland Harbor features RV sites, full hookups, pull-through sites, laundry, and bathhouse. *437-6172.*

▓ FORT KING GEORGE STATE HISTORIC SITE

[Fig. 16(4)] Twelve years before Oglethorpe founded Savannah, the British built a fort and cypress blockhouse on a bluff of the Altamaha River in Darien to counteract Spanish and French expansion. Fort King George, constructed in 1721, was the first British settlement in what would become Georgia and the southernmost military outpost of the English Empire in North America until 1736, when Oglethorpe built Fort Frederica on St. Simons Island. Fort King George was abandoned in 1727, but its historic importance is recognized at Fort King George State Historic Site, which features an excellent authentic replica of the fort, along with a museum dedicated to the period. From the blockhouse, which stands 40 feet above the ground, the visitor is treated to a scenic panoramic view of the river delta and marsh islands. The beautiful natural setting of the grounds offers wildlife viewing and nature observation, while it evokes feelings of isolation that surely were experienced by soldiers posted at this remote frontier fort. The historic site has exhibits on other settlements, including a Guale Indian village, a sixteenth century Spanish mission called *Santo Domingo de Talaje*, and nineteenth century sawmills. Be advised that due to the marsh and

Fort King George Historic Site.

freshwater pools on the site, insects can be bothersome without repellant.

English colonists from Charleston, South Carolina established the fort as a defensive measure. In 1720, John Barnwell, prominent planter in the Port Royal district, was sent to London to argue before the Board of Trade for funds and men to build a fort at the mouth of the Altamaha River. The French had control of Canada, the Gulf of Mexico, and the Mississippi River and were planning to colonize the Altamaha River, and the Spanish were well established in Florida. Barnwell's request was granted, and in 1721 he and Provincial Scouts built Fort King George, named for King George I. Situated on a peninsula below Altamaha Bluff called "low bluff," the fort was a triangular-shaped earthwork fortification, with the north branch of Altamaha River defending one side, and a palisaded moat on two other sides to defend against a landward attack. The fort's main structure was a 40-foot-high, 26-foot square blockhouse built from cypress cut from nearby wetlands. The gabled blockhouse had three stories: a powder, ammunition, and supply magazine on the first floor, a gun room with cannon ports for firing on the river on the second floor, and a lookout post on the third floor. Several other buildings, including a barracks, and officers' house, stood inside the earthworks. When the fort was originally built, it guarded the main channel of the Altamaha, but a navigational shortcut dug across a loop of the river in the mid-1800s caused the main currents to shift 1 mile from here, leaving behind the small tidal creek one sees today.

Life at the fort was a mixture of unrelieved boredom and suffering. Malnutrition and disease resulted in high mortality rates, with at least 140 British soldiers dying at the fort during its seven-year tenure. One year, more than two-thirds of the company died. Sixty-five British soldiers were buried in a nearby cemetery, which is believed to be one of the oldest British military cemeteries in the United States. The fort caught fire in 1725, damaging the blockhouse and destroying the barracks. The fort was partially rebuilt, but then in 1727, the fort was abandoned and the garrison moved to South Carolina. Two lookouts were left behind, possibly until Oglethorpe's arrival with a large group of Scottish Highlanders who were instructed to develop the settlement that came to be known as Darien.

Near the fort site was a Guale town called *Talaje* and later a Spanish mission settlement called *Santo Domingo de Talaje*, established in 1595. It was destroyed in the Guale Indian uprising of 1597. The Spanish returned and rebuilt, but the mission was destroyed and abandoned for good in 1661.

Fort King George was lost for some time until 1932, when it was rediscovered after searching colonial records. The Sea Island Company purchased the tract in 1926. In 1948, the property was deeded to the State of Georgia from Alfred W. (Bill) Jones Sr. of the Sea Island Company in order to build a state historic site. In 1967, a thorough archaeological investigation was undertaken. No trace of the blockhouse was found (many historians believe it was dismantled and shipped to another site), but the British cemetery and many other archeological findings convinced historians that this was the historic site, and it was placed on the National Register of Historic Places. In 1988, a joint venture between the Altamaha Historical Society and the Georgia Department of Natural Resources led to the faithful reconstruction of the fort, palisades, and breastworks based on old records and drawings found at the British Public Records Office. The new fort was built with the same materials and construction methods that were used in precolonial times. Ruins of three sawmills that operated on the site hark back to the nineteenth century, when Darien was a busy lumber exporting town and major seaport.

A short nature trail winds through brackish marsh and maritime forests composed of live oak, pine, red cedar, and baldcypress mixed with shrubs including groundsel, wax myrtle, and yaupon holly. Common wildlife seen in the marsh and freshwater ponds includes wading birds, clapper rails, snakes, and American alligators. Many songbirds have been identified at the site, such as prothonotary warblers, painted buntings, and Swainson's warbler in the summer, and yellow-throated and black-throated blue warblers in the winter.

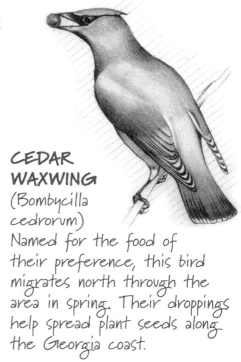

CEDAR WAXWING
(Bombycilla cedrorum)
Named for the food of their preference, this bird migrates north through the area in spring. Their droppings help spread plant seeds along the Georgia coast.

Living history demonstrations occur annually at the fort, and large groups can arrange for special interpretive programs. The museum features exhibits and a film that cover the various historic periods of the site. Picnicking is available on the grounds in a small grove of live oaks and cedars.

Directions: From I-95, take Exit 10/49 (Darien), turn east on GA 251 and go 1 mile to US 17. Follow signs to site.

Activities: Historic touring, nature observation, picnicking.

Facilities: Museum, historic cemetery, nature trail, film auditorium, bookstore, restrooms, picnic tables, observation platform, bus parking. Living history demonstrations occur every spring and fall, and candlelight tours are scheduled in October. Groups can arrange for special interpretive programs.

Fees: A small admission fee is charged.

Dates: Open Tuesday through Saturday 9–5, Sunday 2–5:30. Closed Mondays except on legal holidays. Closed Tuesday when open on Monday.

Closest town: Darien.

For more information: Fort King George State Historic Site, PO Box 711, Darien, GA. 31305. www.darientel.net/~ftkgeo Phone 437-4770.

Sapelo Island

Sapelo is Georgia's fourth largest island at 10 miles long and 4 miles wide. It retains many natural features despite its long history of human activities and its resident population.

INTERCOASTAL WATERWAY

SAPELO SOUND

Cedar
Point

Dog
Hammock

Valona

MUD RIVER

W. Perimeter

North Dike

Bay Hammock

Marsh Pond

North Trail

Flag Pond

Tout Savanna

Middle Trail

East Trail

2

3

1

Blackbeard **Island**

Northeast
Point

Middle
Beach
Rd

East Trail

South
Beach Trail

8

Bell Marsh Rd

Sapelo Island

West Wilderness Trail

East Wilderness Trail

Dogwatch Rd

Raccoon
Bluff

ATLANTIC OCEAN

N

INTERCOASTAL WATER WAY

Dixie Highway

East West Autobahn

East Perimeter Rd

Cabretta Rd

Marsh
Landing Dock

North South
Autobahn

DUPLIN RIVER

Hog
Hammock

BIG HOLE

Old Beach Rd

Cabretta

BLACKBEARD CREEK

Sapelo Island
National Estuarine
Research Reserve

4 **7** **5**

Beach Rd

DOBOY SOUND

Nannygoat
Beach

6 →

Gray's Reef National
Marine Sanctuary
(actual location 175 nautical miles from coast)

1	Blackbeard Island National Wildlife Refuge
2	Shell Ring
3	Chocolate Mansion
4	Sapelo Lighthouse
5	Main House
6	Gray's Reef National Marine Sanctuary
7	University of Georgia Marine Institute
8	Sapelo Island (R. J. Reynolds) Wildlife Management Area

Refuge Boundary

Trail

Dikes

High Ground

Marsh

Ref: Delorme Georgia Atlas and Gazetteer

Sapelo Island

THE UNIVERSITY OF GEORGIA'S MARINE INSTITUTE, THE SAPELO ISLAND NATIONAL ESTUARINE RESEARCH RESERVE, THE R.J. REYNOLDS WILDLIFE REFUGE, AND HOG HAMMOCK COMMUNITY

[Fig. 17] Going back at least 4,500 years, humans have prized Sapelo Island for its generous game, rich marshes, lush woodlands, and beautiful beaches. Man has used it for many things, including Indian hunting grounds, Spanish missions, French asylum, slave-supported cotton and sugar plantations, a navigational landmark, a millionaires' playground, and finally, a scientific research center and a state-owned wildlife preserve. These phases of Sapelo's history and the island's abundant natural resources are on display to travelers who buy a tour ticket and ride a ferry from the mainland, or have received an invitation from a resident on the island.

Larger than Bermuda, Sapelo is Georgia's fourth largest island at 10 miles long and 4 miles wide, and it retains many natural features despite its long history of human activities and its resident population. Doboy Sound is located off its southern tip, and the Duplin River separates it from the mainland to the west. Sapelo Sound is located off its northern end, and the tidal river Blackbeard Creek and Blackbeard Island protect the island's northeast flank. By state law, all of Georgia's barrier island beaches are state property and open to the public. The public is allowed to use Sapelo's beaches for hiking, picnicking, or shelling during daylight hours. However, the interior of the island is off-limits to the public without permission.

Located 60 miles south of Savannah opposite McIntosh County's mainland, Sapelo has four active components: the University of Georgia's Marine Institute, the Sapelo Island National Estuarine Research Reserve, the R.J. Reynolds (Sapelo Island) Wildlife Refuge, and the Hog Hammock Community. The four entities divide the 17,950-acre island (10,900 acres of uplands and 5.5 miles of beach) into different uses.

Headquartered at the southern end is the UGA Marine Institute [Fig. 17(7)], which conducts important research in marsh ecology and barrier island formation, established in 1953 through the invitation of R.J. Reynolds. (Reynolds was the multimillionaire owner of Reynolds Tobacco Company who owned Sapelo Island from 1934 until his death in 1964.) Most of the credit for the creation of the Marine Institute goes to Dr. Eugene P. Odum, acknowledged as the "father of ecology" and a personal friend of Reynolds. Dr. Odum led pioneering research into the mysterious relationship between the salt marsh and marine life (*see* University of Georgia's Skidaway Institute of Oceanography and Marine Extension Center, page 63).

In 1969, the widow of tobacco millionaire R.J. Reynolds, Annemarie Schmidt Reynolds, sold 8,240 acres of the island to the state, which became the R.J. Reynolds (Sapelo Island) Wildlife Refuge [Fig. 17(8)], managed by the state for deer and wild turkey as well as pine production.

In 1976, the southern portion of the island along with Little Sapelo Island and the tidal marsh around the Duplin River was acquired by the state and designated a National Estuarine Research Reserve by the National Oceanic and Atmospheric Administration (NOAA). The 7,400 acres became the second estuarine sanctuary established and today is one of 22 research reserves on the nation's coastlines. Its purpose is research and education about coastal resources.

The fourth part is 434-acre Hog Hammock, a privately owned community. Hog Hammock's 75 residents are descendants of the 400 slaves who lived on Thomas Spalding's Sapelo plantation in the early nineteenth century. The Gullah village, with its unique cultural, artistic, and linguistic traditions, is without a doubt the most unusual community in Georgia. Old timers speak geechee, a colorful creole that blends English with a number of African languages, primarily from the western coast. Hog Hammock was created in the early 1940s when R.J. Reynolds, who owned most of the island, consolidated the scattered black land holdings around the island. Blacks exchanged their holdings in Raccoon Bluff, Shell Hammock, and other communities for property and small houses with indoor plumbing in Hog Hammock.

Access to the island is controlled. Residents of Hog Hammock, state employees, and researchers with the Marine Institute are free to come and go as they please. The general public must buy a tour ticket that includes transportation to and from the island from the Visitors Interpretive Center (phone 912-437-3224) near Meridian, transportation on the island, and a guided tour of the island and historic mansions. Another option is to wrangle an invitation from residents, some of whom offer commercial lodging on the island.

The tour conducted by Sapelo Island NERR staff includes a marsh walk, a beach walk, and a tour of Hog Hammock, Reynolds Mansion, and other historic ruins on the island. The island's natural assets have been well documented by researchers, with the older Pleistocene uplands dating back 25,000 to 36,000 years, while the seaward portions date back 5,000 years. (Approximately 10 percent of Sapelo is Holocene.) The tour leads visitors past plants of the salt marsh, including *Spartina*, needlerush, sea oxeye, and glasswort. All of the lush marsh surrounding the Duplin River to the west of the island is protected by the Sapelo Island National Estuarine Sanctuary. Salt marsh on the island's northeastern shoulder surrounding Blackbeard Creek is protected as a national wilderness. Pioneering scientific research conducted here has revealed the critical importance of the salt marsh ecosystem as provider of basic nutrients to young marine creatures as the tides pulse and wash nutrients twice daily through the estuary and out into the sounds.

From the edge of the marsh to higher, drier ground, one will see red cedar, marsh elder, groundsel-tree, and yaupon. Maritime forests, identified by a distinct canopy, vary from live oak and palmetto communities, to American holly and laurel oak hardwoods, and pine forests consisting of longleaf, loblolly, slash, and pond pine. Neotropical migrants visit the dense forests, and found nesting here are yellow-throated warblers, parulas, and painted buntings that nest in the oak woodlands in summer. Some young cypresses are re-establishing themselves after significant drainage activities from nineteenth century owners of the island killed the water-loving older trees. Monoculture pine forests are found in some sections where the island is managed for timber production. An artificial freshwater pond on the north end of the island supports a noisy rookery of egrets and herons in spring and summer and waterfowl during winter migrations. Alligators are found in the pond, along with southern bullfrogs and leopard frogs and other freshwater-loving reptiles and amphibians. Bottomland hardwoods such as maples and sweetgum are found near freshwater drainage ditches and sloughs between dune ridges, which serve as breeding sites for frogs and toads, including the green, squirrel, and pine woods treefrogs, and southern and narrow-mouth toads. Eastern diamondback rattlesnakes are found on the island, as are cottonmouths, corn snakes, garter snakes, and kingsnakes. The most common lizard on the island is the green anole.

Interdune meadows of wax myrtle, Spanish bayonet, morning glory, butterfly pea, sea oats, *Andropogan* sp., dune meadow grass (*Spartina patens*), and camphorweed trap, hold, and use the drifting sands of Sapelo's beach. At the shore, many shells can be found such as the impressively large shed exoskeletons of horseshoe crabs, cockles, whelks, sand dollars, cochina, angel wings, and brown lumps called sea pork. Many species of birds

Tabby, the Coastal Concrete

Thomas Spalding was a big proponent of using tabby as a construction material. "I was born in the old town of Frederica in one of these Tabby house; I had seen time destroy everything but them," he wrote. "Tabby…a mixture of shells, lime and sand in equal proportions by measure and not weight, makes the best and cheapest buildings, where the materials are at hand, I have ever seen; and when rough cast, equals in beauty stone." In most places on the coast, there is no natural stone or soil appropriate for producing quality brick, and wooden structures were vulnerable to decay in the subtropical coastal environment. Tabby, called "coastal concrete," became a popular building material with settlers who wanted homes that could survive the rough coastal storms.

Tabby is created by mixing equal volumes of oyster shells, sand, lime, and water. Early builders would make ash-lime by digging a 4-foot hole in the ground, then setting afire a 10-foot-high kiln of oyster shells and heart pine logs in alternating tiers. The lime would be mixed with equal volumes of oyster shells, sand, and water, then poured in wooden forms 12 inches wide by 18 inches deep. After waiting a day or two, the process is repeated and the walls slowly grow one layer at a time. The exterior of finer homes were then covered with stucco, such as Savannah's Owens-Thomas House. Tabby ruins are found all along the Georgia coast, and historians once believed they dated back to the Spanish mission period, but archeologists have proven that the ruins date back to colonial and plantation periods.

feed and rest near the water's edge, such as gulls, terns, skimmers, and pipers. More than 225 bird species are known to visit or live on the island, which makes a bird handbook a useful companion to visitors. Sapelo is also an important nesting site for threatened loggerhead sea turtles. An average of 50 sea turtles a year crawl Nannygoat and Cabretta beaches during summer to lay their eggs.

Commonly seen on Sapelo are white-tailed deer and turkey, which have been managed to abundance for hunting. Of interest to hunters and birders alike is the chachalaca, an introduced Central American pheasant left over from hunting plantation days. The gamebird makes a loud racket during mating season with a high-pitched grating call. Though not as exciting as Cumberland Island's feral horses, Sapelo has feral cows that roam the island. (For those wanting to know more about the natural history of Sapelo, read *Portrait of an Island*, by Mildred and John Teal.)

Sapelo's history is as colorful as its wildlife. Hundreds of shell middens and a shell ring 12 feet high and 300 feet in diameter give silent testimony to the importance of the island to Paleo-Indians, who used it as a hunting and fishing ground [Fig. 17(2)]. Here archeologists have found pottery shards that date back 4,500 years, making them some of the oldest artifacts ever found in the New World. Later, the Guale Indians had several settlements located on the island, including a 158-acre village at Kenan Field. The island's modern name is derived from a Guale village named *Sapala* on the northern side of the island.

During the Spanish mission period on the Georgia coast from 1573 to 1684, missionaries were very active on and around the island, which supported a mission and garrison called *San Joseph de Sapala*, where a large plantation grew oranges, figs, peaches, artichokes, and onions. Some archeologists believe the lost mission of Ayllón of 1526 is located near Sapelo or on the mainland.

Sapelo was one of the three Hunting Islands reserved by the Indians when Oglethorpe settled Savannah, and it eventually passed into white hands. Plantations existed here leading up to the Revolutionary War, when British raiders seized slaves and valuables on the island. After the American Revolution, Sapelo was purchased by French Royalists who fled the French Revolution and landed here in 1789. They built a mansion called "Chocolate" [Fig. 17(3)] by their slaves, which today lies in ruins. One of the French noblemen was Christopher Poulain du Bignon, who later owned Jekyll Island. The noblemen planned on raising and selling slaves, but they quarreled among themselves and the scheme failed.

After the French, three wealthy businessmen owned and left their mark on the island. The first, the industrious Thomas Spalding, owned Sapelo from 1802–1851, and significantly changed the island with his various agricultural activities, including timbering and cultivation of sugar cane, rice, and sea island cotton. Spalding's slaves dug huge ditches and levees to drain the soil to make the island more suitable for agriculture. Spalding, a statesman and writer, was considered an agrarian genius. He practiced crop rotation, was one of the first to grow sea island cotton, and was considered the father of the Georgia sugar industry. He engineered a tide-powered mill and constructed a huge mansion at the south end of the island out of tabby. He was widely criticized for his benevolent treatment of his slaves. Each family had its own house built of tabby, and plots of land for gardens, and worked the fields much as tenant farmers. None were sold from the plantation during Spalding's lifetime. On the mainland, Spalding established the Bank of Darien and Ashantilly, his winter home where he was buried with his wife in 1851.

The plantation passed down to his grandson, but Spalding's descendants could not continue his success. Confederates troops were briefly stationed on the island, and during the Civil War and Reconstruction the island fell into ruin. The second millionaire to own the island was business visionary Howard Coffin, a Detroit automobile pioneer of Hudson Motors fame who purchased most of the island in 1912. He rebuilt the South End Mansion, building on top of the 100-year-old foundations an opulent mansion with

WHITE-TAILED DEER
(Odocoileus virginianus)
Now common throughout Georgia, the whitetail once was hunted to low numbers. The state was restocked by deer captured on Georgia's barrier islands and Michigan deer. Blackbeard and Sapelo islands have their own subspecies of deer, Odocoileus virginianus nigrisbarbaris.

indoor and outdoor swimming pools, Italian statuary, and a recreation room and lounge on the basement level. The mansion used Spalding's floorplan, but followed a Spanish-Mediterranean style, today seen at The Cloister on Sea Island, another Coffin development. Coffin was visited by President Calvin Coolidge, President Herbert Hoover, and aviator Charles A. Lindbergh, who landed his plane on the island.

Helping to manage the island was Coffin's young cousin Alfred W. (Bill) Jones Sr. Coffin and Jones drained and diked Sapelo's swamps, raised beef and dairy cattle, cut timber from the island's forests, and established an oyster and shrimp cannery on the island. Their influence in the area can't be understated, with projects affecting the marshes, Blackbeard, Wolf, St. Catherines, and St. Simons islands, and Darien and St. Marys. They managed a fleet of 27 boats and barges, including the luxury yacht *Zapala*. Coffin began scientific oyster farming, which produced prolific oyster beds but attracted poachers. He sponsored government research in Central America that brought to the island the Guatemalan chachalaca, and bred pheasants and wild turkeys.

In 1926, they also built a resort and real estate venture on Sea Island, northeast of

St. Simons Island. The stock market crash of 1929 and Great Depression resulted in the financial and emotional ruin of Coffin, who sold Sapelo to tobacco king R.J. Reynolds in 1934, in order to keep the Sea Island Company solvent. Coffin died from a self-inflicted gunshot wound in 1937.

R.J. Reynolds owned the island until his death of smoking-caused emphysema in 1964. During his tenure, he modernized the house and hired the well-known wildlife artist and muralist Athos Menaboni, who painted images of tropical birds, animals, and pirates on the walls of the solarium and other parts of the house. His most enduring legacy was the creation of the Sapelo Island Research Foundation in 1949, which led to the creation of the University of Georgia's Marine Institute in 1954, located in the south end dairy complex of buildings. Reynolds was a colorful character and popular with McIntosh county citizens, who benefited from his many charitable gifts to the community.

Directions: Sapelo Island is reached by a 30-minute ferry ride. The Sapelo ferry dock and Visitor Interpretive Center are located in Meridian, 8 miles northeast of Darien, off of GA 99. From Interstate 95 south to Exit 11/58, go left onto GA 99 and follow the road 9.1 miles to Landing Road. Turn left onto Landing Road (a church is on the corner) and follow the road to the visitor center.

Activities: Historic and nature touring, lighthouse touring, bird-watching, shelling, nature studies, pioneer camping, group tours, group lodging. Controlled hunting of deer, turkey, dove, raccoon, and small game is offered yearly. Contact the Wildlife Resources Division, Georgia Department of Natural Resources, 1 Conservation Way, Brunswick, GA 31520. Phone 262-3173.

Facilities: Dock, restrooms, historic mansion and ruins, meeting facilities. Reynolds Mansion Lodging: group accommodations for conferences, workshops and retreats for up to 29 people. Minimum 2 nights, 14 people. Rates include 3 meals per day, meeting facilities and transportation. Phone 485-2299. Pioneer Camping: Groups may camp near the beach on Sapelo's Cabretta Island. Minimum 2 nights for up to 25 persons. Comfort station with hot showers available. Phone 485-2299. Parties interested in group tours should phone 485-2251. Hog Hammock: The Weekender. Phone 485-2277.

Fees: Ferry tickets are $10 for adults and $6 for children ages 6–18, and free for anyone age 5 and younger.

Dates: Guided tours are offered Sept. through May: Wednesday 8:30 a.m.–12:30 p.m. and Saturday 9 a.m.–1 p.m. From June through August, an additional tour is offered Friday 8:30 a.m.–12:30 p.m. Extended tour: last Tuesday of each month, March through October, 8:30–3:00. Reservations are required. Phone 437-3224. Island is closed two weeks annually for deer hunts in fall and winter. Portions of beach may be closed to prevent disturbance to nesting, wintering, or migrating birds.

Closest town: Meridian.

For more information: Sapelo Island National Estuarine Research Reserve, PO Box 15, Sapelo Island, GA 31327. Phone 485-2251.

SAPELO LIGHTHOUSE

[Fig. 17(4)] Handsome Sapelo Lighthouse is one of Georgia's five lighthouses still in existence, and one of three open to the general public. The striking red and white stripes on the 170-year-old lighthouse make it a dramatic landmark on the southern end of Sapelo Island. Abandoned for 93 years, restoration of the lighthouse became a goal of the Department of Natural Resources, which eventually led an 8-month, $490,000 effort to repair and preserve the lighthouse. It was undertaken in 1998, resulting in a new spiral staircase, restoration of the brick and stucco exterior, a fresh coat of red and white paint, and a new electric beacon that will signal boaters 12 miles offshore. The lighthouse complex includes the remains of a brick oil house and a cistern. Roughly 600 feet east of the main tower is an iron range beacon built in 1877. Visitors interested in touring the lighthouse must book a ride on the Sapelo Island Ferry, which includes a guided tour.

The lighthouse's history began in 1808, when Thomas Spalding sold 5 acres of land on Sapelo's south end for $1 to the U.S. Government to build a lighthouse to help guide shipping into the growing port of Darien. An 80-foot tower was completed in 1820, built by Winslow Lewis of Boston, at a cost of $14,500. The 65-foot, round brick tower, with a 25-foot diameter base tapering to 12 feet, was topped by a 15-foot iron lantern containing reflectors lit with whale oil. Seventy-nine cypress steps spiraled the interior of the tower to the cupola.

Several keepers served at the lighthouse during the antebellum years. The lighthouse was ravaged by a hurricane in 1824, but was put back into operation until 1854, when it was upgraded with a fourth order Fresnel lens. When Confederate forces abandoned the island in 1862, they removed this lens as part of a strategy to hinder the Union blockade. From 1862–1865, Union forces used the lighthouse as an observation post during their blockade of Sapelo, Doboy, and Altamaha sounds.

After the Civil War, the lighthouse was repaired and reactivated by the U.S. Lighthouse Service in 1868, and the signature red and white daymark was painted on the exterior. In 1873, Irishman James Cromley was appointed head keeper of Sapelo Light, which started a 60-year tradition of Cromleys in charge of lighthouse operations on the island. The hurricane and "tidal wave" of 1898 put much of the island under water, and severely damaged the lighthouse's foundation. Cromley's son William was keeper of the lighthouse during the hurricane and was saved by "a colored man" who tied the unconscious keeper to a boat. (His brother, James, was keeper of Wolf Beacon Light. See Wolf Island National Wildlife Refuge, page 208.) A new lighthouse was ordered and in 1905, a 100-foot steel pyramid tower was built a few hundred feet north of the brick tower, taking over navigational responsibilities from the 1820 tower. The steel tower was deactivated in 1933 due to a decline of shipping in Darien, and the tower was dismantled and shipped to South Fox Island in Lake Michigan in 1934. The support buildings were also taken down. Located nearby, however, are the concrete foundations of a U.S. Army artillery emplacement constructed in 1898 as part of the coastal defense system during the Spanish-American War.

🦑 GRAY'S REEF NATIONAL MARINE SANCTUARY

[Fig. 17(6)] Undoubtedly, this is the hardest attraction to visit on the Georgia coast, because it is located 17.5 nautical miles east of Sapelo Island and 60 feet below the surface of the ocean. However, the 17-square mile sanctuary is very important to the understanding and health of the Georgia coast. Also called Sapelo Live Bottom, this natural reef formation provides an important home and feeding grounds for many marine species that would otherwise struggle in the barren, sandy bottom that makes up the majority of Georgia's coastal shelf. Gray's Reef is a popular site for fishing, scuba diving, scientific research, and marine education.

Sport fishermen are well aware of how beneficial underwater "structure" is to fish species, whether it is a submerged homesite at Lake Lanier or a rock outcropping off Georgia's coast. They know fish use these structures as shelter, feeding sites, and places to raise their young, and that is why fishermen use sonar devices to locate underwater "reefs," because that's where the fish are. Conservation organizations that support sport-fishing, such as Atlantic Coast Conservation Association, promote the creation of offshore artificial reefs that help saltwater species. Some activities include the sinking of old bridges, tug boats, liberty ships, and military equipment to create new fishing hot spots.

At Gray's Reef, the extruded limestone provides a base to which sponges, hard and soft corals, tunicates, hydroids, and other invertebrates can attach. These, in turn, support a myriad of more mobile creatures, such as sea cucumbers, urchins, sea stars, brittle stars, snails, crabs, snapping shrimp, squid, octopus, lobsters, and moray eels. Feeding on this "live bottom" are many fish species, including colorful tropical fish such as damsels, wrasses, butterflies, and angels, as well as popular game fish such as snappers, king mackerel, amberjacks, sharks, barracudas, and giant manta rays. Species counts during spring and fall have revealed that the reef is visited by more than 45 fish species, including the leopard toadfish, checkered blenny, red and longspine porgy, cowfish, gag grouper, red goatfish, spottail pinfish, belted sandfish, and black sea bass. Threatened loggerhead sea turtles forage and rest at the reef, and the waters are also used as winter calving grounds for the endangered right whale. Divers accustomed to the clear blue waters of tropical reefs may be disappointed by the lack of clarity of Gray's Reef, but the quantity and variety of marine life here rivals or surpasses that of coral reefs.

The reef was created from sandy, calcereous mud deposited during the Pliocene Epoch between 2 and 5 million years ago. In the following Pleistocene Epoch, sea levels rose and fell as a response to global changes in climate and the earth's ice sheet. At one time, the reef was an exposed, terrestrial environment subjected to processes of weathering, erosion, and lithification. It is now a submerged geologic feature, with ledges approximately 10 feet high (the highest is 22 feet) with caves and sandy troughs between.

The National Marine Sanctuary Program was created by congressional act in 1972, in order to promote comprehensive management of sensitive marine areas. Twelve sanctuaries have been established totaling 18,000 square miles, ranging from the 3,696 square miles of the Florida Keys National Marine Sanctuary to the less than 1-square-mile

Monitor National Marine Sanctuary. Gray's Reef was designated in 1981 and is one of the largest near-shore live bottoms off the southeastern United States. The reef was named in honor of the late Milton Gray, a pioneer in live bottom research at the University of Georgia's Sapelo Marine Institute. In 1986, UNESCO recognized the sanctuary as an international biosphere reserve. Gray's Reef is under the jurisdiction of the National Oceanic and Atmospheric Administration (NOAA). NOAA provides education and interpretive programs at the Marine Extension Center of the University of Georgia at Skidaway (*see* University of Georgia's Skidaway Institute of Oceanography and Marine Extension Center, page 63).

Regulations at the sanctuary prohibit the following activities: use of wire fish traps and poisons; setting electric charges, powerheads, or other explosives, or similar methods to take any marine animal or plant; using bottom trawls, specimen dredges, or similar vessel-towed bottom sampling devices; taking or damaging any bottom formation, marine invertebrate, marine plant, or tropical fish; depositing or discharging any polluting material, except fish or fish parts, baits, chumming materials, vessel cooling waters, and effluent from approved marine sanitation devices.

Directions: Gray's Reef is found on NOAA chart 11509. Buoy at 31 degrees 24.00′ N, 80 degrees 52.14′ W. Those wishing to fish at Gray's Reef must be aware of federal sanctuary regulations and use their private watercraft or an experienced charter service from a local marina. It is recommended that scuba divers travel with skilled dive charters who can provide experienced advice.

Activities: Fishing, scuba diving.

Facilities: None.

Fees: None.

Dates: Open year round.

Closest town: Darien.

For more information: Gray's Reef National Marine Sanctuary, 10 Ocean Science Circle, Savannah, GA 31411. Phone 598-2345.

The Altamaha River Bioreserve

This 137-mile alluvial river is one of the great natural treasures of the eastern United States, flowing undammed from its creation at the confluence of the Oconee and Ocmulgee rivers near Hazlehurst to the multichannel river delta near Darien. Crossed by roads only five times, the largely undisturbed river is believed to be more than 20 million years old, and pumps an average of 100,000 gallons of fresh water into the sea every second, making it Georgia's mightiest river. As impressive as the river's volume is—comparable to the Nile—even more significant are the 170,000 acres of magnificent river swamps that insulate the river almost the entire length of its course. The river, swamps, and sand ridges serve as refuge to at least 130 species of rare or endangered plants and animals, including seven species of freshwater mussels found nowhere else in the world; *Radford dicerandra*, a rare species of mint; and the only known Georgia population of Florida corkwood.

The Altamaha River is popular with naturalists and bird watchers for its flora and fauna, and with anglers who pursue its abundant game fish. A watercraft is necessary to experience the Altamaha at its greatest glory. The bird lover will find waterfowl, wading birds, owls, woodpeckers, raptors, and songbirds to be common residents and migrants of the river's swamps, bottomland hardwoods, oxbow lakes, and marshlands. Endangered species such as bald eagles and swallowtail kites soar above its banks. Reptiles such as alligators and a variety of snakes and turtles find refuge by the river, as do white-tailed deer, mink, otter, raccoons, rabbits, opossums, and armadillos. Endangered West Indian manatees have been seen swimming as far upsteam as Fort Barrington, and shortnosed sturgeon use the waters as nursery grounds. Botanical oddities attract naturalists, who know the legend of the *Franklinia alatamaha*, a flowering tree that was identified and collected near the river by eighteenth century naturalist William Bartram and never seen again (*see* Fort Barrington/Barrington Park, page 201). Some believe the tree may still survive somewhere in the wild near the river. Not only does the river possibly hide the world's rarest tree, it likely has the oldest trees this side of the Mississippi River. On Lewis Island, a 300-acre tract of virgin cypress contains ancient giants, including one that is believed to be 1,300 years old. Depending on their location on the river, fishermen try their skills for catfish, sunfish, crappie, bluegill, and bass upstream, and shad, mullet, striped bass, tarpon, and shark downstream (*see* Two-Way Fish Camp, page 214).

This river and its swamps are more important than just the variety of species found in them. They play a vital role in supporting the rich estuary located downstream. During times of low water, the river swamps accumulate organic matter in the form of leaves, twigs, and other detritus. During spring floods, high water picks up detritus and other small creatures in the woods and washes them into the main river, which carries this "natural fertilizer" downstream. The nutrients are trapped and used in the marsh, a belt of salt-tolerant grasses in a band 4 to 6 miles wide between Georgia's mainland and barrier islands. The marsh grasses incorporate the natural fertilizer into their stems and roots, and as the grass dies and disintegrates, it is consumed by decomposers of the estuary such as bacteria and fungi, which help phytoplankton and benthic algae. These are in turn eaten by primary consumers such copepods, mud worms and snails, shrimp, crabs, and oysters, which in turn support secondary and tertiary consumers including fish, birds, and mammals. The marshes release their nutrients gradually, creating one of the most productive ecosystems in the world. Without these marshes, the nutrients would be washed out to sea in one big pulse each year.

The big river also carries a tremendous sediment load, adding additional nutrients to the mix in river swamp and estuarine ecosystems and creating barrier islands. Without the river, it is believed, there would be no St. Simons Island. Little St. Simons Island continues to grow at a tremendous rate from sand washed down the Altamaha River.

The 14,500-square-mile Altamaha River basin is the second-largest watershed on the

William Bartram and *Franklinia alatamaha*

The beauty of the Altamaha River greatly impressed William Bartram, who wrote at length about his natural discoveries in the region. His descriptions of the Southeastern United States in *Bartram's Travels* became an instant classic and inspired writers and poets Carlyle, Emerson, and Coleridge, who used some of Bartram's imagery in his poems about Kubla Khan and the Ancient Mariner.

Bartram's most famous discovery was the "lost Gordonia," or *Franklinia alatamaha*: "I sat off early in the morning for the indian trading-house in the river St. Mary, and took the road up the N.E. side of the Alatamaha to Fort Barrington. I passed through a well-inhabited district, mostly rice plantations, on the waters of Cat-head creek, a branch of the Alatamaha. On drawing near the fort, I was greatly delighted at the appearance of two new beautiful shrubs, in all their blooming graces. One of them appeared to be a species of Gordonia, but the flowers are larger, and more fragrant than those of the Gordonia Lascanthus, and are sessile; the seed vessel is also very different." The plant has become so famous that the State of Georgia named a state park for one of its names, Gordonia Alatamaha State Park, near Reidsville (phone 557-6444). A Franklinia has never been found here, but a portion of the park consists of the sandhill environment believed favored by the tree, as well as its close relative, the flowering loblolly bay.

Eastern seaboard. The watershed drains more than a quarter of the state, with its northernmost headwaters in the Piedmont province 10 miles northeast of Gainesville in Hall County, Georgia. Small creeks run off the Chattahoochee Ridge, a spinelike geological feature that runs northeast to southwest and forces water westward and the Chattahoochee River and the Gulf of Mexico or to the east and the Oconee and Ocmulgee rivers, which meet near Hazlehurst to form the Altamaha. The river at Doctortown Landing near Jesup is a broad, meandering stream, surrounded by cypress, gum, and willow swamps. Set back up to 2 miles from the main channel are ancient bends of the river, isolated by time into curved, oxbow lakes with names like Whaley, Morgan, and Johnson, which serve as important spawning grounds for fish and freshwater sources for reptiles and birds. (The world's record largemouth bass was caught in an oxbow lake of the Ocmulgee River in Telfair County, part of the Altamaha River basin.) As the river's wanderings cut into the sand ridges that parallel the river, the higher and drier woodlands support bay trees and magnificent moss-draped oaks. Pine plantations, managed by pulp and paper companies, are planted adjacent to the river swamps.

Below Lewis Island, the river forks into different winding channels, and the river becomes affected by the twice-daily tides. The vegetation on the riverbanks changes into grasses and reeds, and behind these banks are the remnants of antebellum rice plantations, such as Butler and Hofwyl-Broadfield. Butler Island Plantation is where Fanny Kemble Butler wrote the powerful abolitionist book *Journal of a Residence on a Georgian Plantation* that was influential in keeping England from entering the Civil War in support of Confederates. Today, Butler Island is the Altamaha Waterfowl Management Area (*see* page 212) and Hofwyl-Broadfield is a state historic site (*see* page 212). The river meets the sea in four channels, from north to south: the Darien, Butler, Champney, and South Altamaha rivers.

The name Altamaha, pronounced All´-ta-mahaw´, is from an immigrant Yamassee Indian group descended from an interior chiefdom originally known as Altamaha or Tama, located on the Oconee River just below Milledgeville, visited by Hernando de Soto in 1540. The Altamaha chiefdom was forced into slavery, but rebelled and eventually settled in St. Augustine until it evacuated with the Spanish to Cuba in 1763. The Spanish referred to it during the 1600s as *Rio de Santa Isabel,* referring to an early mission called *Santa Isabel de Utinahica,* established in the Timucuan chiefdom of Utinahica located at the forks of the river near present-day Lumber City. The ruins of more than 1,000 Indian sites along the river are evidence of how important the river was to Indians, who relied on it for food and transportation.

The river has seen not only the dugout canoe, but also Spanish galleons, huge rafts of cotton and timber, and paddlewheel steamboats. Today, most watercraft are motor-powered bass boats that belong to sport fishermen. Hernando De Soto wrote about the river in 1539, and so did early naturalists who were fascinated by the New World flora and fauna found at "Georgia's Little Amazon." Fort Barrington witnessed military activity during the American Revolution, the War of 1812, and the Civil War. At Morgan's Lake, the Blue and the Gray faced off in a minor historic episode of Sherman's March to the Sea during the Civil War.

Protecting the river and its swamps, from The Forks to the place where the river meets the sea, has been a goal of many organizations since the late 1960s. Today most of the river is under some form of legal protection in a patchwork of various tracts. In 1969, Wolf and Egg islands at the mouth of the river became a national wildlife refuge. In 1972, the state acquired the 6,177-acre Big Hammock Natural Area and the 5,633-acre Lewis Island Natural Area. Big Hammock, located on the northern bank of the Altamaha near Glennville, consists mainly of bottomland hardwoods and sloughs, and an 800-acre sandhill community that supports the largest population of the Georgia plume (*Elliottia racemosa*). Lewis Island Natural Area contains virgin cypress tidewater forest, with Georgia's oldest trees. In 1974, the 1,268-acre tidewater rice plantation Hofwyl-Broadfield was preserved, and in 1978, the 1,331-acre Altamaha River Natural Area was created when ITT-Rayonier donated the tract to the State of Georgia, which includes a border of land extending 300 feet from the riverbanks in Long, Wayne, and McIntosh counties. Other protected tracts near Darien include the 752-acre Cathead Creek Preserve; the 6,259-acre Buffalo Swamp; and the 27,078-acre Altamaha Wildlife Management Area (or the Altamaha River Waterfowl Area), which includes Lewis, Cambers, Wrights, Butler, Champney, Broughton, Rhetts, Rockdedundy, and Dolbow islands; and the 15,526-acre Sansavilla Wildlife Management Area.

FORT BARRINGTON AND BARRINGTON COUNTY PARK

[Fig. 3(4)] Barrington County Park provides access to the river and a beautiful setting for picnicking, camping, or fishing on the Altamaha River near a historic colonial fort. Fort Barrington was built on a sand ridge in McIntosh County to control the best place to cross the broad Altamaha River in its southern section, a shallow ford north of where the river divides into four channels. In pre-Columbian times, Indians crossed the river here on their ancient overland trail between Savannah and St. Augustine, which in 1736 became Gen. James Oglethorpe's Post Road, traveled by Methodist minister John Wesley and Scottish Highlanders in their march on Fort Frederica.

The natural settings are a mix of sand ridges, river swamp, bay forest, and pine flatwoods. The sand hills are composed of nutrient- and moisture-poor soils, which support hardy flora such as turkey oak and longleaf pine, along with post and bluejack oaks and mockernut hickory. On lower areas southwest of the road are baldcypress and tupelo. On drier floodlands are bay forests consisting of sweetbay magnolia, loblolly bay, and red bay, and at higher elevations are pines such as slash and loblolly. Deer and feral hogs are common game animals seen near the property.

Near here on October 1, 1765, naturalists John and William Bartram found the legendary *Franklinia alatamaha,* a beautiful, 15-foot flowering tree that is a kind of holy grail for botanists. The Bartrams, thankfully, collected seeds from the unusual plant that was later successfully propagated. Today, all living *Franklinias* are descended from these seeds, and the plant is believed to be extinct in the wild. Eight years later, William Bartram returned without his father and rediscovered the plant, this time in bloom, and wrote about it in *The Travels of William Bartram.* In the Naturalist's Edition of *Bartram's Travels* (1958), Francis Harper writes that he believes the actual location of the tree to be on "a sand-hill bog on the north side of the (Fort Barrington) road at a point about 1.7 miles northwest of Cox."

The colonists of Darien worried about being attacked from the rear by the Spanish, French, and hostile Indians. In 1761, a square structure with 75-foot-long walls was built to stand guard at the river crossing. Called Fort Barrington in honor of a friend of Oglethorpe's, it was garrisoned by 25 rangers. During Revolutionary times, it was called Fort Howe. The fort was abandoned after being garrisoned during the Civil War. A ferry operated here from colonial times until the early 1900s, when railroads, roads, and bridges put it out of service.

Today, time has claimed the wooden fort, and the river has eroded half the earthworks. A hunting club owns the remaining earthworks, and unfortunately a private boat ramp runs down the middle of the fort. Nearby, Barrington County Park is open to the general public for boat launches, tent or RV camping, or a quiet picnic. Bathrooms and trash cans are found at the site.

Directions: From I-95, take Exit 10/49 (Darien). Turn right onto GA 251. Go 2.9 miles and turn left toward Cox at the fork, leaving GA 251. Proceed 5.7 miles, cross over former railroad tracks (sign on right) and turn left onto the first dirt road. Go 2.9 miles to fork in the road. Go left to Barrington County Park, or go right to former Fort Barrington site. **CAUTION:** The historic fort is on private property that is popular with hunters. Please respect their property rights and avoid the area during hunting season.

🦥 CANOEING THE ALTAMAHA RIVER

Canoeing the Altamaha River, in the main channel, is not the most intimate experience found on Georgia's smaller rivers, neither is it the most exciting whitewater trip. However, the Altamaha is the largest virtually unspoiled river in the Southeast, with beautiful river swamps bordering it along its entire length. In higher waters, canoeists can thread into river swamps for a true wilderness experience, and its upper reaches provide unforgettable canoe camping on its sandy banks.

Caution is urged. Access to the river is limited. If one got in trouble, it would be a difficult feat indeed to try to walk out through (for example) Penholoway Swamp with a broken arm. So the key here is planning. Visit your takeout site so you have a better chance of recognizing it from the water. The river swamps and multiple channels of the river can get confusing in a hurry so take good maps and know how to use your compass. Learn the landmarks or signs that mark your journey. In the lower reaches, the river widens to 1,200 feet in some places and the canoeist faces twice-daily tides and confusing marsh deltas. Strong currents and unexpected bad weather here can swamp your canoe in a hurry and wash you out to sea with the outgoing tides. Be very careful so your trip is a safe one.

LONG DAY TRIPS OR EASY OVERNIGHT TRIPS

Doctortown to Paradise Park, 19.6 miles. This trip takes the canoeist through The Narrows, perhaps the most scenic section of the entire river. Doctortown is located on the western bank of Wayne County near Jesup where US 301 crosses the river below river mile marker 65. Signs on US 301 direct you to the site. Paradise Park is accessed on the western side of the river, where Penholoway River enters the Altamaha after mile marker 46. The park is 1 mile upstream on the Penholoway, and is reached with care from Gardi by traveling east on River Road roughly 5 miles, then left for 1 mile to Paradise Park.

Paradise Park to Altamaha Park, 17.2 miles. This stretch of the trip takes the canoeist past Barrington Park on the eastern bank of the river (a good place to camp if you are looking for company) and into tidally influenced waters, finishing at Altamaha Park on the western bank. Altamaha Regional Park is located on Altamaha Park Road east of Everett on US 341 in Glynn County. Here, boats and campsites can be rented (*see* camping in Glynn County, page 221). 264-2342. Birders may want to turn right onto Pennick Road from Altamaha Park Road to visit the Atkinson Tract, which is a cut-over, swampy area that parallels the river. Here near Cowpen and Clayhole swamps, you may see nesting indigo and painted buntings, vireos, hooded warblers, summer tanagers, and yellow-breasted chats. See Fort Barrington/Barrington County Park, page 201, for directions to Barrington Park.

Altamaha Park to Darien City Dock, 13.7 miles. This last trip should be undertaken only with knowledge of current landmarks and daily tides. The canoeist travels 10.5 miles on the Altamaha River, taking the northern (left) channel, then negotiates narrow Rifle Cut 1.5 miles to Darien Creek for 1 mile. Then take the Darien River to the boat ramp for 0.7 mile. Lewis Island is a 2-mile detour on this trip by the way of Buzzard Creek. This adventure should not be undertaken without consulting local authorities concerning landmarks or blazes that mark the way to the ancient trees. Recall that the trees still remain because they were so hard to get to in the first place.

OTHER SUGGESTED DAY TRIPS

Paradise Park to Barrington Park, 11.8 miles; Paradise Park to Lower Sansavilla Landing, 9.5 miles (Lower Sansavilla Landing is found on Sansavilla Road east of Mt. Pleasant on US 341.); Lower Sansavilla to Altamaha Park, 7.7 miles.

ALTAMAHA WILDLIFE MANAGEMENT/ALTAMAHA RIVER WATERFOWL AREA

[Fig. 16] The 27,078-acre Altamaha Wildlife Management Area/Altamaha River Waterfowl Area (ARWA) is the second largest waterfowl area east of the Mississippi (the largest being the Chesapeake), and is visited by more than 30,000 ducks from mid-October through mid-April. A stop on the Colonial Coast Birding Trail, the area is equally popular with naturalists, bird watchers, duck hunters, and fishermen.

The ARWA consists of several "islands" that are created by the Altamaha's meandering channels: Lewis, Cambers, Wrights, Butler, Champney, Broughton, Rhetts, Rockdedundy, and Dolbow islands. Lewis Island is a naturalist's wonderland, containing virgin cypress stands over 1,000 years old. Most of the other islands are dominated by a variety of marsh grasses that have flourished since antebellum times, when hundreds of slaves cleared the land of timber, dug canals, and built water-control dikes that were used to establish successful rice plantations.

Some of these canal-crossed islands, such as Butler and Champney, are former sites of plantations that today are important nesting and refuge sites managed for migratory waterfowl. Freshwater plants such as giant cutgrass, pickerelweed, wild rice, cattails, widgeon grass, and wild millet help support the duck population. Many species use the freshwater sites, including mallards, scaup, ring-necks, black ducks, pintails, canvasbacks, buffleheads, gadwalls, scaup, widgeons, mergansers, shovelers, green-winged teals, and occasionally the fulvous tree duck. A large population of snipe is found in January and February, and rails are also common in the marshes.

Mammals observed in the wildlife management area include deer, red and gray foxes, beavers, cottontail and marsh rabbits, feral hogs, otters, bobcats, minks, opossums, armadillos, raccoons, bats, and mice. In the tidal waters are dolphin and an occasional manatee. More than 26 species of snake have been reported here, including coral snakes, cottonmouths, copperheads, and pigmy and diamondback rattlesnakes.

Directions: Part of the Altamaha Waterfowl Management Area is easily accessed by car on US 17 between Darien and Brunswick. The headquarters is located on Butler Island and is not open to the general public, but south of Butler Island is Champney

Island, site of the Ansley-Hodges Memorial Marsh Project, which has an observation tower and marked trail.

LEWIS ISLAND NATURAL AREA

[Fig. 16(1)] Without sandy beaches and high-rise condominiums, this is not what people generally imagine when you say "island." But Lewis Island, located five miles up the Altamaha River, is accessible only by boat and is a natural treasure that has fascinated scientists and naturalists alike. The 8-mile-long island contains a remnant of the great hardwood forests that bordered Georgia's Coastal Plain rivers, including the largest known grove of virgin tidewater cypress and tupelo gum trees in Georgia. One 300-acre stand of baldcypress has trees 6 to 7 feet in diameter, which are estimated to be 1,000 years old, with one tree believed to be over 1,300 years old.

The primitive island is defined on the west by the main channel of the Altamaha River and on the east by Lewis Creek and the broad, dense Buffalo Swamp. Loggers attempted to get to the trees, but thankfully logging cables were not long enough to reach them and today never will because the tract was purchased from the Georgia-Pacific Corporation by the State of Georgia in 1973 to be protected as part of the Altamaha State Wildlife Management Area.

The 5,633-acre natural area is home to deer, otters, raccoons, feral pigs, and gray squirrels. Swallow-tailed kites nest here, and also observed on the island are Mississippi kites, parula warblers, yellow-crowned night herons, green herons, Louisiana herons, pileated woodpeckers, egrets, ibis, and wrens. Snail-loving limkins have occasionally been seen near the island. Common reptiles are alligators, Florida cooters, yellow-bellied turtles, as well as rainbow, mud, cottonmouth, yellow rat, and red-bellied water snakes. Near the water's edge, streamside flowers such as the pink-flowered *Physostegia* are common, along with wild potato vine, spider lilies, and swamp mallow.

An interesting characteristic of Lewis Island is that it is a tidewater swamp, which means it has adapted to daily fluctuations in water levels and current flow, unlike river swamps that are affected mainly by seasonal fluctuations in water levels.

The island must be approached by boat. The floor of Lewis Island may be under water

BALDCYPRESS
(Taxodium distichum)
This characteristic species of Georgia's coastal rivers can survive in inundated soils.

from January to June, when the river leaves its banks, submerging a half-mile trail leading to the big trees. When the river is down the rest of the year, the trail reappears, but be sure to take shoes that can get wet and muddy. The trailhead is located approximately 0.25 mile southeast of the intersection of Studhorse Creek and Pico Creek. The Department of Natural Resources attempts to keep the trail marked, but floods may remove or hide the blazes, so its best to ask for directions and river conditions at the area's headquarters on Butler Island.

Directions: Access is difficult to Lewis Island, located 5 miles upstream from Darien. A boat is mandatory and an experienced guide is recommended for attempting the trip. Contact Two-Way Fish Camp for wildlife charters, phone 265-0410; or outfitters that offer guided wildlife tours, such as Southeast Adventure Outfitters, phone 638-6732, or Altamaha Wilderness Outfitter, phone 437-6010. For directions and local conditions, contact the area manager's office on Butler Island, phone 262-3173.

For more information: Altamaha River Waterfowl Area, Georgia Department of Natural Resources, One Conservation Way, Brunswick, GA 31523. Phone 262-3173.

BUTLER ISLAND AND CHAMPNEY ISLAND/ANSLEY-HODGES MEMORIAL MARSH PROJECT

[Fig. 16(2)] Butler Island and its southern neighbor Champney Island are readily accessible to the visitor without a boat and are good sites for bird-watching during waterfowl migrations. On Butler Island, the house and grounds are used as a private staff residence for the Altamaha Waterfowl Management Area and are not open for public tours. Tourists can view the property from US 17. An observation tower and marked trail on Champney Island provide easy access for wildlife viewing of the flat, marshy terrain. During the winter, the quiet observer may identify some of the refuge's known 18 species of ducks, including nesting wood ducks, and at other times discover numerous wading birds, including a variety of herons and egrets. Swallowtail kites and bald eagles are known to nest near the area, and alligators and a variety of snakes are common.

While migratory waterfowl benefit and depend on the flooded fields for food and rest, the islands did not always look like this. Butler Island was the site of one of the largest, most successful antebellum tidewater plantations in America. With the help of hundreds of slaves, Irish-born Major Pierce Butler created a grand rice and sugar plantation out of the cypress-and-marsh wilderness in the early 1800s.

The tidewater ecosystem was very suited to the production of rice. The high range of the twice-daily tides made it possible to flood the fields; the plantations' distance from the sea and volume of fresh water from the river protected crops from salt water; the rich alluvial soils deposited over thousands of years in the river delta were fertile for growing crops; and the availability of slave labor made the back-breaking work economical. The clay soils of the Altamaha delta are the richest in McIntosh County, according to soil surveys.

Today, the only signs of the enterprise are a 75-foot brick chimney that was a steam powered rice mill built in 1850 and the still-operational dike system, designed by engineers

Fanny Kemble On Slavery

"Scorn, derision, insult, menace—the handcuff, the lash—the tearing away of children from parents, of husbands from wives—the weary trudging in droves along the common highways, the labor of body, the despair of mind, the sickness of heart—these are the realities which belong to the system, and form the rule, rather than the exception, in the slave's experience."

from Holland. Located on the property is the two-story home of Col. T.L. Huston, a half-owner of the New York Yankees, who had a Guernsey dairy farm and a successful truck farming operation that shipped iceberg lettuce grown in the restored fields. The residence was built in 1927. In the 1920s, many baseball players visited Huston, including Babe Ruth.

Butler arrived in the American colonies in 1771 as an officer in the British Army. Excited by the opportunities in the New World, Butler resigned from the Army, married an American woman who was a daughter of a rich Charleston plantation family, and started a long, successful career as a planter and politician. Butler was an ardent pro-slavery advocate, defending the peculiar institution at the Constitutional Convention of 1787, and helping to draft the fugitive slave law and the Three-Fifths Rule whereby a black slave was considered to be only three-fifths a person. Butler was a friend of George Washington, Benjamin Franklin, Thomas Jefferson, James Madison, James Monroe, Alexander Hamilton, and Aaron Burr. (Burr sought asylum at Butler's plantations after he killed Alexander Hamilton in a duel in 1804.) Butler was chosen by the South Carolina legislature to be the state's first U.S. senator.

Eventually, Butler obtained the 1,500-acre tidewater island that he named for himself, as well as property on the northwest end of St. Simons. Butler Island became a rice plantation and Hampton Plantation grew sea island cotton. Butler was an absentee owner, spending most of his time away on business in Charleston or Philadelphia, so he depended on his plantation manager and slave overseer Roswell King Sr. to keep the plantations operating successfully. Friction between Butler and King resulted in King being relieved of his duties after 18 years working the plantations. Connecticut-born Roswell King Sr., who was known for his cruelty to slaves, moved to an area north of Atlanta in 1837 where he established Roswell Manufacturing Company. (King died in 1844, and the town was eventually incorporated as Roswell in 1854.) Butler died in 1822, and the property eventually passed down to his grandsons after they agreed to the will's stipulation that they use their grandfather's last name.

In 1834, Pierce Butler II married the celebrated English actress Frances (Fanny) Anne Kemble, and had two children, Sarah and Frances. In 1838–1839, he brought his wife to his grandfather's plantations. During this period, Fanny Kemble wrote letters to a friend about her shock and disgust at the treatment and conditions of the plantations' slaves, which by then were under the control of Roswell King Jr. She never sent the letters, and left Butler in 1845 and returned to England. In 1848, Butler filed for divorce and the following year, in a sensational court case, a Pennsylvania court awarded the divorce and custody of both girls to Butler.

Though pressured by abolitionist friends to publish her journal, Kemble held off until her children had grown up and the Civil War had started. Her writings were published in 1863 under the title of *Journal of a Residence on a Georgian Plantation in 1838-39* and have become one of the most famous antislavery treatises ever written. The descriptions of plantation life, slavery, Darien, and flora and fauna of the area make the well-written book fascinating reading. For example, we learn from Kemble that slaves were kept in four settlements on Butler Island, "consisting of from ten to twenty houses…[the slave] cabins consist of one room about 12 feet by 15…[where] two families (sometimes eight and ten in number) reside…"

During the Civil War, the property was abandoned. In 1866, Fanny's daughter Frances returned with her father in an attempt to restore the plantation's former glory. Frances, who adopted her father's proslavery views, also kept a diary, published in 1883, titled *Ten Years on a Georgia Plantation*, considered the best account of what it was like in Georgia during Reconstruction. Until the end, Frances remained loyal to her father, never doubting that blacks fared better under slavery than freedom, and she argues for the institution in her book. However, without slavery and in the postwar depression in the South, rice and cotton plantations were doomed, and the fifth generation of Butlers sold the remains of their lands in 1923.

Champney Island, also the site of a rice plantation, is today a 34-acre Ansley-Hodges Memorial MARSH Project built in 1989 and sponsored by Ducks Unlimited. An excellent observation tower a short walk away from the parking area gives bird watchers a perch to view waterfowl and wading birds in the freshwater marsh, including great and snowy egrets, least and American bitterns, and in the spring, black-necked stilts. Common migrating songbirds in the fall include the common yellowthroat, indigo bunting, and swamp sparrow. A 1-mile nature trail, with marked sites and brochures, explains the workings of the managed ecosystem. The road follows the perimeter of the island, looping up to Interstate 95 and back to US 17. Driving slowly on this road, or parking for short excursions, can be rewarding. Remember to bring your binoculars, bird book, and insect repellant for the most enjoyable visit.

Directions: The waterfowl area extends along US 17 from south of the Darien River Bridge to north of the South Altamaha River Bridge. Champney Island Interpretive Trail is on the right as you head south on US 17 after crossing the Champney River.

Activities: Bird-watching, nature hiking, historic touring, hunting, fishing.

Facilities: Observation tower, 1-mile loop interpretive trail.

Dates: Open year-round. Hikers and hunters should be aware that duck, deer, dove, and furbearers are hunted on the Altamaha Wildlife Management Area. The Waterfowl Management Area offers the best duck hunting in the state. Contact Wildlife Resources Division for more information about hunting seasons and regulations.

Fees: None.

Closest town: Darien.

For more information: Wildlife Resources Division, Georgia Department of Natural Resources, Brunswick, GA 31520. Phone 262-3173.

🌊 WOLF ISLAND NATIONAL WILDLIFE REFUGE

[Fig. 16(7)] This three-island wildlife refuge in the mouth of the Altamaha River consists mainly of salt marsh and provides critical sanctuary for rare migrating birds. Bird-watching from the water and saltwater activities (fishing, crabbing, and shrimping) are permitted within the boundaries of the refuge, but access to the beach and upland areas is strictly prohibited. Unlike many national wildlife refuges, no hunting is permitted on the island.

Wolf Island, the largest island in the refuge, is defined by South River to the north, Little Mud River to the west, Altamaha Sound to the south, and the Atlantic Ocean to the east. The island consists of 4,519 acres, with only 300 acres of dune and beach along its narrow, 4-mile-long eastern shoreline. The island fronts the sea in the Altamaha River delta, and is a physical barrier between Doboy Sound to the north and Altamaha Sound to the south. The interior of the Holocene island, which is 97 percent *Spartina alterniflora*, is divided by many tidal creeks, including Wolf, Beacon, and Beach, where fishing is reputably excellent. Needlegrass, sea oxeye, and glasswort are also found in higher places in the marsh along with some small shrub hammocks, and salt flats cover the central marsh. Sea oats, sand-spurs, smilax, and other beach-dune perennials flourish on Wolf Island's beach dunes, and higher ground supports scrub southern red cedar and wax myrtle.

The undisturbed island provides a haven for migratory birds. Thousands of birds use the island in fall and spring migrations, including royal, Caspian, and Forster's common terns; semi-palmated and black-bellied plovers; least sandpipers, dunlins, sanderlings, and ruddy turnstones; and a variety of gulls. Black skimmers, oystercatchers, great blue herons, brown pelicans, and common egrets use the island year-round, as do clapper rails that nest in the marsh. Waterfowl are less frequent, but mergansers, scaups, and buffle-heads are seen in the salt water bordering the island. The island also is an important nesting ground for endangered loggerhead sea turtles.

Tucked into the mouth of Altamaha Sound directly south of Wolf Island are Egg and Little Egg islands, the two other islands in the refuge. They comprise 593 and 14 acres, respectively, and support extensive salt marsh with only 70 acres of upland. Egg Island has some oak and pine trees and is used by migratory birds, and Little Egg Island has shielded colonies of royal terns, black skimmers, and laughing gulls. Nearby, Egg Island Bar, closed by the state to human use, supports the largest nesting colony of royal terns on the Atlantic coast, with more than 9,000 pairs. It serves as a rare nesting ground for black skimmers, gull-billed terns, and brown pelicans as well.

Wolf Island's recorded history is short compared with its larger island neighbors. The first owner was Christopher DeBrake, who was granted 150 acres of the island (the upland portion) on March 7, 1769 by King George III. Early diaries record that locals used the island for hunting, and as a temporary quarantine for sailors sick with yellow fever, as it was "a solitary spot washed by the waves of the Atlantic and miles from any human habitation."

Its strategic location at the mouth of the Altamaha Sound made the island an important feature in early navigational charts, and the U.S. Coast Guard erected a lighthouse at the northern end. In 1819, the Georgia Legislature ceded jurisdiction of Wolf Island to the United States for the purpose of building a 55-foot high beacon light to complement the lighthouse across Doboy Sound on Sapelo Island. The structure was built, along with a keeper's house, and was in operation by summer 1822. The beacon light was pounded by periodic hurricanes and blown up during the Civil War by Confederates who didn't want the light to aid the Union Navy. After the Civil War, a larger, grander structure was built on top of 11, 12-inch pilings driven to a depth of 28 feet. These pilings from 1868 can still be seen in the breakers near Wolf Island, evidence of how much the island has changed in the last 130 years. The beacon light was 38 feet tall, with a sixth order light that could be seen 11.5 miles away. The lighthouse had several keepers over the years, until the terrible hurricane of 1898, which destroyed the structure and killed several people on Wolf Island. A clubhouse built by hunters in 1891 on the southern end belonged to the Wolf Island Club. The 1898 hurricane swept the structure away and killed a female caretaker. An account of the storm in the *Darien Gazette* said the Wolf Island light keeper, Mr. James Cromley, "had a terrible time of it and says that in the future, the high land will be good enough for him." The light beacon was deactivated and remaining structures were moved to Sapelo lighthouse.

In 1930, the 538 acres under Federal control on Wolf Island were set aside as a sanctuary for migratory birds. In 1969, the protection of Wolf, Egg, and Little Egg islands became the goal of Jane Hurt Yarn, a prominent Atlanta environmentalist with The Nature Conservancy in the 1970s. She bought an option on Egg Island in 1969, guaranteeing full payment later. The money was eventually raised, and combined with other Conservancy property acquisitions on Wolf Island, lead to the creation of the 5,125-acre Wolf Island National Wildlife Refuge in 1972. Her purchase of Egg Island was one of the first actions taken by environmentalists to protect the coast.

Directions: Visitors must use a boat to reach the refuge, which is located 10 miles south of Darien between Doboy and Altamaha sounds. Marinas: Two-way Fish Camp has gas, hoist, bait and tackle, snacks, charters, and storage. Phone 264-9723.

Activities: Bird-watching, fishing.

Facilities: None.

Dates: All beach, marsh, and upland areas are closed to the public. Saltwater areas are open 7 days a week.

Fees: None.

Closest town: Darien.

For more information: U.S. Fish and Wildlife Service, Savannah Coastal Refuges, Parkway Business Center, Suite 10, 1000 Business Center Drive, Savannah, GA 31405. Phone 652-4415.

Glynn & Camden Counties

The southern coast of Glynn and Camden counties features five barrier islands in various states of development.

McKinnon

Mount Pleasant

251

99

Ridgeville

Sapelo Island

301

Everett

Exit 10/49

95

Ashintilly

23

2

25

Darien

Hortense

32

3

27

ALTAMAHA SOUND

Thalmann

341

Exit 9/42

99

17

Sterling

Exit 8/38

25

Little St. Simons Island

Nahunta

82

99

520

Exit 7A-B/ 36A-B

Sea Island

303

St. Simons Island

Hickox

Brunswick

St. Simons Island

259

110

17

25

Exit 6/29

82

ST. SIMONS SOUND

Waverly

95

520

Jekyll Island

Winokur

White Oak

JEKYLL SOUND

Tarboro

252

ST. ANDREW SOUND

SATILLA RIVER

301

252

Woodbine

Exit 4/14

23

110

17

ATLANTIC OCEAN

40

95

5

Folkston

Kingsland

Cumberland Island

Exit 2/3

40

40

N

1	Sansavilla Wildlife Management Area	5	Crooked River State Park
2	Rayonier Wildlife Management Area		Glynn County
3	Paulks Pasture Wildlife Management Area		Camden County
4	Earth Day Nature Trail		Marsh

St. Marys

ST. MARYS RIVER

CUMBERLAND SOUND

Ref: Interior - Geological Survey, Washington, D.C. Georgia

The Southern Coast:
Glynn and Camden Counties

T he southern coast of Glynn and Camden counties features five barrier islands in various states of development. Least developed are Little St. Simons Island and Cumberland Island National Seashore; moderately developed are Jekyll Island State Park and Little Cumberland; very developed are Sea Island and St. Simons Island. All have their charms. On the mainland are the towns of Brunswick and St. Marys, along with Crooked River State Park, several wildlife management areas, and two wild and beautiful blackwater rivers, the Satilla and St. Marys. Camden County and St. Marys are impacted by the Kings Bay Naval Submarine Base. The Okefenokee National Wildlife Refuge is covered in another chapter.

The southern coast is a fast-growing area. In 1990, Glynn County was the second most populated coastal county with 62,496 residents, with 14,000 on St. Simons and 16,433 in Brunswick. Glynn County is one of the eight original counties of Georgia, formed under

[*Above:* Magnificent live oaks add to the natural beauty of the Georgia coast]

Georgia's first Constitution in 1777. The county is named for John Glynn, a member of the British House of Commons who defended the cause of American colonies. Camden County had 30,167 residents, with 8,187 residents in St. Marys in the 1990 census.

Glynn County Area Attractions

HOWFYL-BROADFIELD PLANTATION STATE HISTORIC SITE

[Fig. 16(6)] Howfyl-Broadfield is like a time machine: Visitors to this historic site are transported back to the mid-1800s when rice plantations dominated tidewater Georgia. Maybe what's important here is what you *don't* see: Tara, the grand plantation indelibly etched in the popular mind from the movie *Gone With The Wind*. But it could be argued what you *do* see is very interesting: a historic working plantation with its original furnishings, complete with the freshwater marshes and dikes that supported five generations of owners.

Located in the Altamaha River delta, the plantation site measures 1,268 acres consisting of freshwater marsh, longleaf pine flatwoods, and farm pasture. The natural setting, with huge live oaks festooned with Spanish moss, provides a beautiful backdrop for a hike on a sunny day. Three trails should satiate nature lovers, and expose them to vegetation and wildlife typical of the Georgia coastal environment. The park is on the Colonial Coast Birding Trail for its abundant bird life and easy access.

Two champion trees are found on the property, including a national champion American holly (*Ilex opaca*) and state champion sweet-bay (*Magnolia virginiana*). Two live oaks found near the home are estimated to be over 300 years old and are as impressive as can be found, and two magnolias are believed to be over 100 years old. More than 144 birds have been identified on the property, and the pasture openings are good places to see deer, rabbits, and armadillos. Gray squirrels are the most common animal at the historic site, eating acorns from live oaks near the visitor center. Lucky observers may sight the endangered southern fox squirrel, a large squirrel with a black face and paws and a blond tail. Marsh rabbits and raccoons can be observed feeding in the marsh.

The plantation's beginnings trace back to 1807, when William Brailsford, a Charleston, South Carolina merchant of English descent, began carving a rice plantation out of the cypress swamps that bordered the Altamaha River. Brailsford's daughter, Camilla, married James M. Troup, brother of Georgia Governor George Troup. James Troup helped build the plantation into 7,300 acres of land, with 400 slaves and several homes. When he died, the plantation passed into the hands of his daughter Ophelia and her husband George Dent. In 1851, Dent built the plantation home that is open to tour at the historic site.

The rice plantation was successful until the outbreak of the Civil War. George Dent and his 15-year-old son James joined the Confederate Army, and Ophelia and the rest of the family moved to a refugee settlement called Tebeauville near the present city of Waycross. After the war, the Dents struggled to stay financially afloat, giving up significant portions of their property. In the 1880s, the property was taken over by James, their oldest son, who was married to Miriam Cohen. When James Dent died in 1913, the plantation was still in debt. Miriam, who was an astute businesswoman, took over the plantation and with her son Gratz converted it into a dairy farm around 1915. When she died, the plantation was inherited by her daughters Ophelia and Miriam, who took over the

Armadillos are exotic species that have invaded the Georgia coast from Florida.

duties of running the farm. The dairy served Glynn and McIntosh county homes, delivering 100–150 bottles of milk daily. It was closed in 1942, when the sisters had attained financial security, paying off the debt on the farm. Ophelia Troup Dent lived on the plantation until her death in 1973 at the age of 86. In her will, she left the farm to the State of Georgia to be preserved as a historic site.

Comfortable walking shoes and insect repellant are necessary at this site. The visitor center features a museum and a short slide show that explains the history and significance of rice plantations on the Georgia coast. From here, the 1-mile Plantation House Trail leads visitors through pasture to the plantation home and complex of support buildings, then loops through a maritime forest, with overlooks and observation decks, before returning to the visitor center. A tour of the plantation home, built in 1851, is highly recommended. Notice the pay shed, where farm workers were paid for their labors.

After leaving the house, the trail goes through forest adjacent to the rice marsh. Here one can find the state champion sweet-bay in a drainage ditch next to one of the footbridges on the trail, along with 100-year-old loblolly pines of great girth, and other oaks, sweetgum, and Eastern red cedar. Indian pipe (*Montropa uniflora*), a soprophyte that looks like a peace pipe, also grows in the forest. Wild rice, growing to 9 feet tall, is found in wet places in the marsh.

The second and third trails are located directly across from the historic site entrance on US 17. The first is the 2.5-mile Maritime-Pineland Woods Loop Trail. Looping off of it is the 0.5-mile Barrow-Pit Lake Loop Trail. The pinelands are especially interesting, featuring a climax stand of longleaf pine (*Pinus palustris*), which once dominated the Coastal Plain of the South. A fire-dependent ecosystem, the climax forest's ground cover has been described as the most diverse outside of the tropics. More than 90 species of plants have been identified in the pinelands' ground cover, including common St. John's wort (*Hypericum perforatum*), glaucous blueberry (*Vaccinium darrowi*), a variety of

WINGED SUMAC

(Rhus copallina)

This shrub, which grows in high dune areas, is identified by its "winged" leaf stems and red berries.

pawpaw species, persimmon, rattlebox, and witch hazel. The maritime forest contains loblolly pine, laurel oak, diamond-leaf oak (*Quercus laurifolia*), longleaf pine, and live oak. The understory supports bays and oaks, along with sassafras, yaupon, saw palmetto, and dwarf huckleberry. Muscadine grapevines are common, as well as greenbrier, catbrier, and yellow jessamine.

The Borrow-Pit Lake Trail circles a lake created when dirt was "borrowed" from the property to create a railroad bed. Vegetation around the lake consists of oaks, pines, bays, and maples, along with gallberry, wax myrtle, dog fennel, and dahoon. Several carnivorous plants, each with its own strategy for trapping and digesting small organisms, are found in the lake and canal including round-leaved sundew (*Drosera rotundifolia*), yellow butterwort (*Pinguicula lutea*), and floating bladderwort (*Utricularia inflata*).

Trails: 1-mile Plantation House Trail, 2.5-mile Maritime-Pineland Woods Trail, and 0.5-mile Barrow-Pit Lake Loop Trail.

Directions: I-95 south from Savannah to Exit 9/42. Go east on GA 99 approximately 1 mile to US 17. Turn left (north) on US 17 and drive 1 mile to park entrance on right.

Activities: Historical touring, picnicking, museum touring, hiking, nature study. Call for special scheduled events.

Facilities: Museum, AV theater, bookstore, picnic tables, restrooms, playground.

Dates: Closed Mondays except for federal holidays.

Fees: A small fee is charged for park admission.

Closest town: Darien.

For more information: Hofwyl-Broadfield Plantation, 5556 US 17 North, Brunswick, GA 31525. Phone 264-7333.

TWO-WAY FISH CAMP

[Fig. 16(5)] One of the more popular marinas on the coast is Two-Way Fish Camp, which allows boaters to go, ahem, two ways: either upstream in the South Altamaha River or downstream to Altamaha Sound and offshore waters. This is a great place to book a freshwater or saltwater fishing trip or nature excursion. The marina hosts an annual fishing rodeo in June and a trout-fishing event in the fall. Call for dates and details. Two-Way is a full-service marina, with gas and diesel, supply store, hoist, bait and tackle, guides and charters, dry and wet storage, and engine repair. Located on a short spur off of US 17 at the South Altamaha River. *265-0410.*

Mudcat Charlies at Two-Way Fish Camp. US 17 North at the South Altamaha River. This reasonably priced, relatively new seafood restaurant has the advantage of overlooking the glorious southern channel of the Altamaha River. Just steps away from the boats are offerings of shrimp, scallops, and oysters prepared fried, broiled, or buffaloed. Boiled blue crab and "mudcat wings" are other popular orders. And it's the only restaurant serving a Fanny Kemble After Dinner Drink. I wonder what she would have thought of the NASCAR decorations. Open for lunch and dinner, 7 days a week, 11 a.m.–10 p.m. *Moderate. 261-0055.*

GLYNN COUNTY WILDLIFE MANAGEMENT AREAS
PAULKS PASTURE WILDLIFE MANAGEMENT AREA

[Fig. 18(3)] With 17,000 acres of swamps and pine flatwoods in Glynn County, Paulks Pasture offers a large area to hunt and explore. Hunters stalk deer, turkey, dove, furbearers, and small game near Buffalo Swamp, which serves as headwaters to the Buffalo River, a tributary of the Turtle River. The swamp and river receive their name from the scarcely known fact that buffalo used to live in the southern river swamps in pre-Columbian times, and were hunted by Indians. Hikers should visit the area when it is not hunting season. Campers should check with the regional office concerning regulations.

Directions: From Brunswick, go north for 8 miles on US 341. Check station on left.

For more information: Wildlife Resources Division, Georgia Department of Natural Resources, Brunswick, GA 31520. Phone 262-3173.

RAYONIER WILDLIFE MANAGEMENT AREA

[Fig. 18(2)] Located across the Glynn County line in Wayne and Brantley counties is the 12,687-acre Rayonier Wildlife Management Area, used primarily by hunters during hunting season. Most of the tract consists of the Penholoway Bay Swamp, bottomland forest, and pine flatwoods, which serve as the headwaters of Penholoway Creek that flows north in an arc before turning south to the Altamaha River. Deer and turkey are the primary prey, along with furbearers and small game.

Directions: From Brunswick, go north on US 341 to Sterling. Turn left on GA 99 and go approximately 3 miles to GA 32. Turn right and go approximately 20 miles to Fendig and turn right on Fendig Road.

For more information: Wildlife Resources Division, Georgia Department of Natural Resources, Brunswick, GA 31520. Phone 262-3173.

SANSAVILLA WILDLIFE MANAGEMENT AREA

[Fig. 18(1)] Bordering the Altamaha River, this 17,814-acre wildlife management area straddling the Glynn-Wayne county line is popular for hunting deer, turkey, raccoon, and opossum, as well as launching boats into the Altamaha River from Lower Sansavilla Landing for fishing and wilderness excursions. Sansavilla derives its name from an Indian town, Santa Savilla, which existed on the 4-mile-long bluff overlooking the Altamaha

River at the mouth of Alex Creek. The southern end of the bluff, which looks across to Fort Barrington, was visited by naturalist William Bartram during his travels in Georgia in the eighteenth century. Those wishing to explore the area should visit when it is not hunting season. Camping is permitted, but check with regional office first.

Directions: From Brunswick, go north on US 341 toward Jesup for 20 miles to Mount Pleasant. Turn right and cross railroad tracks into area. Follow power lines to Lower Sansavilla Landing.

For more information: Wildlife Resources Division, Georgia Department of Natural Resources, Brunswick, GA 31520. Phone 262-3173.

EARTH DAY NATURE TRAIL, COASTAL RESOURCES DIVISION, GEORGIA DEPARTMENT OF NATURAL RESOURCES

[Fig. 18(4)] Glimmering in the marsh north of the Sidney Lanier Bridge is the Georgia Department of Natural Resources headquarters. Next to the building is an interpretive nature trail that provides a good basic introduction to the flora and fauna of Georgia's marsh ecosystem. Inside the building are aquariums with native marine fauna.

Called the Earth Day Nature Trail, it features two short looping trails that wind through maritime forest, complete with benches, boardwalks, interpretive signs, observation towers, and platforms. The trail provides an easy way to examine the plants and animals of the salt marsh, freshwater pond, and sandflat habitats.

On the trails, hikers will learn about sugarberry, mulberry, cabbage palm, and Eastern red cedar trees of the coast. An observation platform at the end of one spur provides access to an osprey nest. Sea oxeye, wax myrtle, and prickly pear cactus are three common plants one sees on the trail. Marsh rabbits are often glimpsed in the more wooded areas, and many wading birds are common residents such as egrets, herons, ibis, willets, and sometimes wood storks. Secretive clapper rails can be heard making their distinctive call. Periwinkles, mud snails, and ribbed mussels are very common mollusks seen slowly feeding in the *Spartina* marsh. Mud fiddlers and sand fiddler crabs are observed in habitats they're named after.

The Coastal Resources Division, Georgia Department of Natural Resources is the state agency charged with the responsibility of protecting the coast's natural resources, and it is appropriate that its headquarters is situated in the golden marsh. Inside the headquarters are restrooms and aquariums, and information on many coastal activities.

Trails: 0.5-mile Earth Day Nature Trail.

Directions: From Brunswick go south on US 17 past Brunswick city limits. North of the Sidney Lanier Bridge, turn left on Conservation Way. Follow sign to DNR Coastal Regional Headquarters. At northeast end of the parking lot is a sign and entrance to the trail.

Activities: Nature hiking and study, picnicking. Coastfest, the Department of Natural Resources' annual celebration of coastal natural resources, is held the first Saturday of October.

Facilities: Observation shelters, interpretive programs, aquarium display, orientation shelter, restrooms, drinking water, and binoculars available for checkout at headquarters.

Dates: Trail open daily. Headquarters open 8 a.m.–4:30 p.m., Monday through Friday.

Fees: None.

Closest town: Brunswick.

For more information: Coastal Resources Division, Georgia Department of Natural Resources, 1 Conservation Way, Brunswick, GA 31520. www.ganet.org/dnr/coastal Phone 264-7218.

Brunswick

Brunswick is a peaceful port city that has experienced many economic ups and downs since its founding in 1771. Brunswick's fortunes have always been linked to the sea, whether as a port of entry, a shipbuilding center, or a shrimping capital. Perhaps its most successful period was during World War II when Liberty Ships were built in local shipyards that employed 16,000 workers. Since 1960, the town has lost population from 21,000 to 16,500 as the county has grown, with residents relocating to St. Simons Island or unincorporated areas of the county. Today, the city is undergoing a quiet revitalization in its Old Town National Historic District and nearby Victorian residential area. At 14 feet above sea level, Brunswick has the lowest elevation of any city in Georgia, a fact made painfully clear when the hurricane of 1898 put the town under water. Shipping has a tremendous economic impact on Brunswick, which is Georgia's second leading port behind Savannah. The Port Authority plans to deepen the 30-foot harbor to 36 feet to allow for larger cargo ships.

The first European resident of Brunswick was Mark Carr, a Scottsman in Oglethorpe's regiment who was granted 500 acres in the area in the late 1730s. He established a plantation and built a military outpost 4.5 miles northwest of Brunswick on the north bank of the Turtle River known as Carr's Fort, which was attacked by Florida Indians in 1741. In 1771, the town of Brunswick was laid out on a tract of Carr's property.

Brunswick is proud of its English heritage. Named for Braunsweig, Germany, the ancestral home of King George II, the streets and parks still retain names honoring English royalty and geography, such as Halifax, Hanover, Gloucester, Norwich, Newcastle, and London, which gives the town a slightly English flavor. After the American Revolution, most colonial towns changed the names of their streets, parks, and landmarks to honor American heroes.

Before the formation of St. Simons Island to the east, Brunswick was oceanfront property. Geologically, the city of Brunswick rests on one of the ancient Princess Anne barrier islands, whose shorelines were washed by the Atlantic Ocean 60,000 to 80,000 years ago. During the Pleistocene Age 25,000 to 40,000 years ago, sea levels rose and fell several times, helping to create St. Simons Island. Marshes filled the lagoon between

Brunswick and St. Simons Island. The rivers feeding the Brunswick harbor are relatively short, low volume tidal rivers, which influenced the patterns of development. Unlike the Savannah, Ogeechee, Altamaha, Satilla, and St. Marys delta regions, river plantations never flourished in Brunswick's low country.

Visitors will want to begin their travels at the Brunswick and Golden Isles Visitors Bureau, located at the foot of the St. Simons Causeway and US 17. Here one can pick up brochures and other information about Brunswick and St. Simons and Jekyll islands. One can also examine a 23-foot replica of the Liberty Ships built in Brunswick and an iron pot where the first Brunswick stew was made.

Brunswick played an important role during World War II as the site of a blimp base known as Glynco Naval Air Station and the J.A. Jones Construction Company, which built 99 Liberty Ships in support of the Allied effort in the war. Early in the war, German U-boats patrolled off the Atlantic coastline with impunity, sinking ships with ease and sending their cargo into the depths of the Atlantic. By 1942, more than 500 million tons of ships and cargo had been lost to the German submarines, including several ships in waters near Brunswick. Military authorities decided to build a blimp base near Brunswick, which would perform submarine reconnaissance for coastal shipping. Six miles north of Brunswick, engineers built two blimp hangers. Because of the shortage of steel, the enormous structures were built completely out of wood. Each could hold six blimps simultaneously, and stood 1,000 feet long, 297 feet wide, and 150 feet high. They were destroyed by Hurricane Dora.

Brunswick's most impressive wartime effort was the construction of Liberty Ships. These were important all-purpose cargo vessels, 416 feet long and weighing 10,500 tons, that were needed to haul supplies to Europe in support of the Allied efforts. J.A. Jones Construction Company established a 435-acre shipyard, which at its peak employed 16,000 workers with a weekly payroll of over $1 million. The goal was to build the ships as fast as they could. The keel to the first ship was laid in early 1943, and by the end of the war in 1945, Brunswick had produced 99 ships.

A short distance south of the visitors bureau on US 17 on the left is Overlook Park and the Lanier Oak, where Georgia poet Sidney Lanier wrote his most famous poem, *Marshes of Glynn*. Overlook Park provides the breathtaking view of the expansive tidal marshlands that inspired the nineteenth century poet. Lanier, born in Macon in 1842, was a brilliant linguist, mathematician, musician, and lawyer. He fought on the Confederate side during the Civil War, and was captured while commanding a blockade runner and imprisoned in Point Lookout, Maryland. There he contracted tuberculosis. After the war, he stayed at his brother-in-law's house in Brunswick attempting to regain his health. It was during this period that he was inspired to write several poems, including *Marshes of Glynn*, considered a masterpiece of nineteenth-century American poetry. Lanier succumbed to his disease in 1881 at the age of 39. Lake Lanier in northeast Georgia is named for him.

From Overlook Park, take Gloucester Street west to Mary Ross Waterfront Park. This is where Brunswick's shrimp fleet is moored. Here one can photograph the boats as the sun goes down, buy fresh seafood, or relax and soak in the sights and sounds of a working commercial waterfront that has been called "The Shrimp Capital of the World." Harborfest and the Blessing of the Fleet Festival are uniquely coastal traditions that celebrate Brunswick's commercial fishermen. They are held annually on the second weekend in May (*see* Appendix D). The festival lasts three days and features parades, a road race, arts and crafts, and the "blessing" performed by a Catholic priest on roughly 50 vessels on the last day of the event. The blessing ceremony, an old Portuguese tradition, was initiated in Brunswick in 1938, when mariners of Portuguese descent dominated a much larger shrimp industry. The shrimping industry in Brunswick, like other commercial fishing towns in the U.S., has experienced declines due to tremendous competition from imported foreign shrimp. With more than 70 percent of the domestic market, imported shrimp

Georgia Shrimp

Available in coastal supermarkets and roadside fish markets, Georgia shrimp are appreciated by many seafood aficionados. Georgia's rich marshlands and estuaries are relatively unpolluted and so full of shrimp "food" that they produce more tender, sweeter, meaty shrimp, considered by many to be the best in the world. Gulf shrimp tend to have more iodine flavor compared with "sweet Georgia shrimp." Also, Georgia shrimpers fish close to the shore, so it is possible to buy shrimp in local stores that were caught 24 hours earlier and have not been frozen, unlike the vast majority of foreign shrimp sold in grocery stores around the state. Because they are fresh, they are more perishable and usually cost more per pound than the frozen shrimp found in stores.

dominates, as shrimpers from China, Indonesia, India, and Vietnam freeze their shrimp on huge trawlers, store it, and release it when market conditions are favorable. Also, 50 percent or so of foreign shrimp is raised in massive aquaculture operations in countries with low labor costs and few if any environmental regulations, an industry that is not likely to develop in America.

In 1989, the park was dedicated to Mary Ross, a member of one of Brunswick's shrimping families and a historian who coauthored an influential history of Georgia titled *The Debatable Land*. This book highlighted Georgia's Spanish history and unfortunately asserted that the tabby ruins were of Spanish origin. When this was proven to be wrong a decade later, Ross was devastated and vowed never to publish another word again. However, she did continue to research Georgia's Spanish heritage for the rest of her life, and many valuable documents were donated to the Georgia archives after she died.

Backtracking on Gloucester, the traveler enters Brunswick's Old Town National Historic District, which is bound by H Street, Newcastle Street, First Avenue, and Martin Luther King Jr. Boulevard. The following highlights are worth visiting:

Glynn County Courthouse, at Union Street and G Street, is an impressive building

Brunswick Stew

Brunswick claims to be the "official home" of Brunswick Stew. The following is the "official recipe" distributed by the visitors bureau. Start with the following ingredients: 1 3-lb. chicken, 1 lb. lean pork, 1 lb. lean beef, and 3 medium onions, chopped. Place meat in large, heavy pot. Season with salt, pepper. Add onions and cover with water. Cook slowly until meat falls from bones (several hours). Remove from heat and allow to cool. Tear meat into shreds and return to stock. Add: 4 cans (16 oz.) tomatoes, 5 T. Worcestershire sauce, 1½ bottles (14 oz.) catsup, 1 T. Tabasco sauce, 2 bay leaves, ½ bottle (12 oz.) chili sauce, ½ t. dry mustard, ½ stick butter. Cook 1 hour, occasionally stirring to prevent sticking. Add: 3 T. vinegar, 2 cans (16 oz.) small limas or butter beans, 2 cans (16 oz.) creamstyle corn, 1 can small English peas (3 small diced Irish potatoes and box of frozen, sliced okra—optional). Cook slowly until thick. Serve in a bowl with barbecue or fried shrimp.

constructed in 1907 and surrounded by beautiful live oaks, dahoon or swamp hollies, and exotics including Chinese pistachio and tung trees. Opposite the courthouse at 1709 Reynolds is the Mahoney-McGarvey House, known as one of the finest examples of Carpenter Gothic architecture in Georgia.

Newcastle Street. This commercial corridor houses many shops and businesses in nineteenth century Victorian buildings, including the Ritz Theater at 1530 Newcastle, which was built in 1898 as the Grand Opera House. Old City Hall, 1212 Newcastle, was designed by noted architect Albert S. Eichberg and constructed in 1890, and it features an impressive example of Richardsonian Romanesque architecture. During the hurricane of 1898, floodwaters rose to the bottom of its first floor windows.

Lovers' Oak, located at the intersection of Prince and Albany streets. According to local legends, this 900-year-old oak has served as a meeting place for lovers since Indian times. The tree trunk is 13 feet in diameter, and 3 feet from the ground it branches into 10 limbs measuring 12 to 30 inches in diameter.

LODGING IN BRUNSWICK

Motels. Most people who spend the night in Brunswick stay in a chain motel located out by Interstate 95 on their way to somewhere else. Brunswick offers no fewer than 21 choices at Exits 7A/36A, 7B/36B, and 8/38. Here are some reliable options: **Hampton Inn**. Exit 7A/36A. Located near Cracker Barrel and Shoneys. *Moderate. (800) 368-2189.* **Holiday Inn**. Exit 7B/36B. Newly renovated, free full breakfast, coffee makers in rooms, lunch buffet. *Moderate. 264-4033.* **Ramada Inn**. I-95. Exit 7A/36A. With 210 rooms, this is largest motel in Brunswick. Newly renovated, free HBO, in-room coffee, room service, putting green, lounge. *Moderate. 264-3621.*

Bed and Breakfasts. Brunswick's B&Bs are located in the Old Town Historic District:

The Marshes of Glynn

Sidney Lanier made several visits to Brunswick where he was inspired to write several marsh poems, including *Sunrise* and *Marshes of Glynn*. The final stanza of the latter goes as follows:

"And now from the Vast of the Lord will the waters of sleep
Roll in on the souls of men,
But who will reveal to our waking ken
The forms that swim and the shapes that creep
Under the waters of sleep?
And I would I could know what swimmeth below when the tide comes in
On the length and the breath of the marvelous marshes of Glynn."

Brunswick Manor. 825 Egmont Street. Four rooms to choose from here. A full breakfast and high tea included. *Moderate. 265-6889*. **McKinnon House**. 1001 Egmont Street. Three rooms in a restored Queen Anne style home featuring furnishings from Charleston and New Orleans. *Moderate. 261-9100*. **Rose Manor Guest House**. 1108 Richmond Street. Six rooms available here. Gourmet breakfast and afternoon high tea with harpist included. *Moderate. 267-6369*.

CAMPGROUNDS IN GLYNN COUNTY

Four campgrounds are found in Glynn County; one is on the Altamaha River, one is on Blythe Island, one is near shopping, and the last one is on Jekyll Island. **Altamaha Regional Park**. 1605 Altamaha Park Road. 45 campsites and full hookup sites, boat rentals, bait, swimming hole, picnic facilities, boat ramp, fishing, camp store, showers, laundry, wilderness surroundings. From I-95, take Exit 7A/36A, go north approximately 15 miles on US 341; at Everett City go right; campsite is 3 miles east on Altamaha Park Road. *(800) 281-9322*. **Blythe Island Regional Park and Campground**. 6616 Blythe Island Highway. Features 96 campsites and RV camping with full hookups including cable TV. Lake swimming and fishing, archery range, picnic tables, showers, laundry, marina, nature trail, bike trail, primitive sites available. Marina provides access to South Brunswick River. From I-95, take Exit 6/29, US 17 south; GA 303 north, 3 miles on the right. *(800) 343-7855*. **Golden Isles R&R**. 531 Walker Road. 44 full hookups and tent sites. Cable TV, beauty shop, camp store, showers, laundry. Shopping and restaurants nearby. From I-95, take Exit 8/38 onto the Golden Isles Parkway. Turn left at the second traffic light. *265-5794*. **Jekyll Island Campground**. North Beachview Drive. 220 campsites and RV camping on 18 wooded acres. Restrooms, showers, laundry, camp store, bike rentals, plus Jekyll Island attractions. From I-95, take Exit 6/29 to Jekyll Island. Go north on Beachview Drive to campground. *(800) 841-6586*.

Little St. Simons Island, St. Simons Island, & Sea Island

Little St. Simons is a privately owned barrier island with 10,000 acres of maritime forest, beaches, and tidal marshes. St. Simons is Georgia's most populated barrier island, with more than 14,000 residents calling it home. To the east of St. Simons is Sea Island, which serves as a resort and home for the rich.

Wolf Island National Wildlife Refuge

ALTAMAHA SOUND

BUTTERMILK SOUND

Five Pound

ALTAMAHA

Egg Island

RIVER

95

17

405

25

Exit 9/42 — Broadfield

New Hope

Butler Point

The Hampton River Club Marina

Old House Road

North End Road

95

Glynco Jetport

2

Pine Island

1

Little Simons Island

Beach Road

Exit 8/38

17

25

St. Simons Island

HAMPTON RIVER

South End Road

ATLANTIC OCEAN

Spur 25

Golden Isles Pkwy

Lawrence Road

German Village

3 **4**

Sea Palms Golf & Tennis Court

Harrington

Frederica Road

303

Cypress Mills

MACKAY RIVER

5

Glynn Haven

Sea Island Road

Sea Island Drive

Sea Island

17

25

F.J. Torras CSWY

Jewtown

Frederica Road

Sea Island Golf Club

Brunswick

ST. SIMONS SOUND

BRUNSWICK RIVER

1	Little St. Simons Island Housing Compound
2	Taylor's Fish Camp
3	Fort Frederica National Monument
4	Christ Church
5	Ebo Landing
	St. Simons Island
	Sea Island
	Little St. Simons Island
	Trail
	Marsh

Ref: Delorme Georgia Atlas and Gazetteer

RESTAURANTS IN BRUNSWICK

Out by Interstate 95 are predictable favorites with familiar names. The following local restaurants are peculiar to Brunswick and offer a variety of food choices. **Jinright's Seafood House**. 2815 Glynn Avenue (US 17). If you like your seafood fresh and fried, you'll like this venerable restaurant located near the causeway to St. Simons. Open for lunch and dinner, 7 days a week. *Moderate. 267-1590.* **The Oyster Box**. 2129 Glynn Avenue (US 17). This locals' joint is the place to go for affordably priced fresh oysters shucked before your eyes. The chicken wings aren't bad either. Located right at the St. Simons Causeway. Serves lunch and dinner. Closed Sunday. *Moderate. 264-3698.* **Spanky's**. 1200 Glynn Avenue (US 17). Fresh seafood daily is served overlooking the marshes of Glynn, along with other standard bar fare. Outside dining is available. Entertainment on weekends. Serves lunch and dinner. *Moderate. 267-6100.* **Wilson's Seafood Restaurant**. 3848 Darien Highway. "A Seafood Festival Every Night!" boasts this restaurant, which serves all-you-can-eat dinners Tuesday through Saturday 5–10, with meals of catfish, gator tail, seafood and steaks, and prime rib on Fridays and Saturdays. *Moderate. 267-0801.* **Willie's Wee-Nee Wagon**. 3599 Altama Avenue (across from Coastal Georgia Community College). The name says it all. Famous burgers, hot dogs, fish, Polish sausage, chili, steaks, boneless chops, southern iced tea. Serves lunch and dinner. Closed Sunday. *Inexpensive. 264-1146.* **The Georgia Pig**. I-95/US 17 S, Exit 6/29. Brunswick may have the highest per capita number of barbecue joints in the country. It's hard to pick the best; this is the most famous one. Serves lunch and dinner. *Inexpensive. 264-6664.* (*See also* Two Way Fish Camp, page 214.)

Little St. Simons Island

[Fig. 19] If nature lovers were allowed to design the perfect sea island resort, they would come up with Little St. Simons Island, a privately owned barrier island that combines 10,000 acres of pristine maritime forest, beach, and tidal marsh with everything one might want in outdoor recreation, accommodations, and meals. Located northeast of St. Simons, this quiet hideaway offers bird-watching, hiking, biking, horseback riding, beachcombing, swimming, fishing, canoeing, boating, and interpretive programs with trained naturalists. With guests limited to 30 visitors a day, each has 333 acres of unspoiled barrier island all to themselves, which is ample space to restore one's senses and replenish one's soul. While the cost of visiting the island is not inexpensive, the memories gained may be priceless.

Measuring 6 miles long by 2 to 3 miles wide, the island's diverse habitats, located in a relatively small area, allow visitors to enjoy lots of bird and wildlife watching in a short time. Guests can hike, bike, boat, or be driven to various sites where they can identify some of the 220 species of birds known to visit the island. Or they can observe some of the island's exotic game animals, such as European fallow deer (*Dama dama*). Rare species nest on the beaches, including least terns, Wilson's plovers, and black-necked stilts. The island is the best place in Georgia to see long-billed curlews. One guest identified more than 100 species in one day. Freshwater ponds host the last of the ruling reptiles, the alligator, along with migrating ducks and wading birds in the shallower areas. The shell-littered beaches are popular nesting sites for threatened loggerhead sea turtles, which bury an average of 36 nests each year. Armadillos, seen rustling through the underbrush, may be the most commonly seen animal on the island. Offshore and in the tidal creeks are dolphins and river otters, and endangered right whale calving grounds are located just off Little St. Simons Island's beaches.

The island's 3,500 acres of uplands have a mix of tree species, including old examples of slash and loblolly pine, along with live and laurel oaks, sweetgum, cabbage palm, and American holly. Cedar is very common, especially near Indian shell middens found on the island. The shells decompose, creating a soil pH preferred by cedars. Saw palmetto thrives in the understory, and yaupon holly, wax myrtle, and muscadine vine are common plants. The live oaks support a healthy assemblage of Spanish moss, resurrection fern, bubblegum lichen, and the rare greenfly orchid. Marshes buffer the western side of the island, separated from St. Simons Island by the Hampton River. On the eastern side of the island, a causeway is needed to reach the beach, providing dry passage over tidal creeks and marsh that are new to the island since 1869. Little St. Simons Island has grown tremendously since that time due to the increased load of sediment washing up on its shoreline from the Altamaha River. Post–Civil War Georgia had its Coastal Plain forests extensively logged, which released millions of cubic yards of topsoil into its waterways.

Off the island's northern end are Egg and Little Egg islands, important nesting sites for rare terns and part of the Wolf Island National Wildlife Refuge. Off the southern end is Pelican Spit, another important "bird island" that recently has come under state protection. Certain species of shore and sea birds nest in large colonies directly on the ground and require remote, isolated nesting sites such as Pelican Spit. Royal and Caspian terns, avocets, pelicans, cormorants, and many other birds can be observed on this island. On Pelican Spit, the southwestern beach, Hampton River Beach, northeastern spit, and ocean-facing beach are open for recreational use. The restricted area, which is marked with signs, includes the interior dunes and the southeastern spit.

Little St. Simons Island's Indian middens testify to its importance as a hunting and fishing site for Mocama Indians. The first European owner was Samuel Ougspourger, a Swiss colonist from South Carolina, who purchased the island from King George II, in 1760, and eight years later sold it to his grandson Gabriel Maniqualt. The next owner of the island was Major Pierce Butler, the most successful and famous plantation owner on the Georgia coast (see Butler Island, page 205). He owned Butler Island near Darien, Hampton Plantation at Butler's Point, St. Simons Island, as well as Little St. Simons Island. The sea island plantations on Little St. Simons Island and St. Simons grew cotton, and Butler Island grew rice. Eventually, the island passed into the hands of Butler's grandson, Pierce Butler II, who was married to English actress and writer Fanny Kemble.

Her book, *Journal of a Residence on a Georgian Plantation in 1838-39*, described visits to Little St. Simons Island and the cotton plantation called Five Pound, which she described as "a fearful-looking stretch of dismal, trackless sand" and "the swamp Botany Bay of the plantation" where misbehaving slaves would be banished, whipped, and raped. (Five Pound is located at the westernmost portion of the island.) Kemble wrote about visiting slave Quash's house, the remains of which can be seen on the northwestern end of the island today.

The plantation had to cope with many natural disasters such as hurricanes, yellow fever epidemics, and wars. The island was invaded during the War of 1812, and Butler's slaves were seized and released into freedom. After the Civil War, the plantation culture went into decline, and the island reverted to a more natural state. In the early 1900s, O.F. Chichester of the Eagle Pencil Company visited the island and bought it from Fanny Kemble's daughter Francis Butler Leigh for the cedar stocks, used to make pencils. After cutting the cedars and shipping them to sawmills in St. Simons, the deed was transferred to Emil, then Philip Berolzheimer in 1908. The New York family used the island as a private vacation home and hunting plantation, and built the beautiful hunting lodge in the middle of the island at Mosquito Creek. After 40 years of service in the family pencil business, Philip Berolzheimer retired to work in New York politics. He served as city park commissioner and held other city posts, and became a member of the Tammany Society. In the 1920s, Philip and seven other city bosses visited the island, calling themselves "the bandits," and made a flag to represent their backroom political group: an arc of eight ducks with a running stag in the middle. Today, this serves as the island's logo.

Ownership and control of the island passed to the Berolzheimers' children, Charles and Helen, in the 1940s. In 1979, the Berolzheimers decided to open the island to the general public as a private nature preserve/resort. Today, travelers are treated to the same sea island rustic luxury that has welcomed many famous persons, at this one-of-a-kind treasure among resorts.

Trails: 15 miles of trails, 7 miles of beach.

Directions: Little St. Simons Island is reached by private ferry from the north end of St. Simons Island at Hampton River Club Marina. From Brunswick, cross F. J. Torras (St. Simons) Causeway to St. Simons Island. Go left on Sea Island Road. At Frederica Road, go left (north). At fork, go right on Lawrence Road and follow signs to Hampton River Club Marina. The ferry departs at 10:30 a.m. and 4:30 p.m. daily.

Activities: The 10,000-acre island, 7-mile beach, and labyrinth of tidal creeks are available to the guest for the following activities: nature study, hiking, bird-watching, fishing, canoeing, kayaking, boating, beachcombing, biking, horseback riding, picnicking, wildlife observation, and interpretive programs.

Facilities: The island resort offers 13 guest rooms, all with private baths and air conditioning, in five cottages, some with fireplaces, from the 1917 Hunting Lodge to the 1980s Cedar Lodge. Swimming pool. Resort offers boats, bikes, fishing gear, and horses for use by guests. Library and naturalists are available to assist in nature study. Gourmet

St. Simons Coast

St. Simons offers a wide variety of coastal activities in a beautiful natural setting
of sprawling moss-draped live oaks, green-gold salt marsh, and sandy beaches.

1 Fort Frederica National Monument

2 Christ Church

3 F.J. Torras Causeway

4 Gascoigne's Bluff/ Epworth by the Sea

5 Retreat Plantation/ Sea Island Golf Club

6 Avenue of Oaks

7 Neptune Park, Fishing Pier and Village, St. Simons Visitor Center

8 St. Simons Lighthouse and Museum of Coastal History

9 St. Simons Beach

10 Massengale Park

11 East Beach and historic Coast Guard Station

12 Gould's Inlet Park

13 Bloody Marsh Monument

14 Ebo Landing

Marsh

southern meals are served family style three times a day in the Hunting Lodge. Staff will prepare picnic lunches and special meals such as oyster roasts, crab boils, full moon beach picnics, and sunset barge cruises. Classes offered in boating. Only 30 people are allowed to visit the island at any time. Guests can visit for the day, overnight, a weekend, or a week. The entire island can be rented for corporate events.

Fees: Call (888) 733-5774 for rates, which include all meals and activities.

Closest town: St. Simons Island.

For more information: The Lodge on Little St. Simons Island, PO Box 21078, St. Simons Island, GA 31522. Phone (888) 733-5774.

St. Simons Island

[Fig. 19, Fig. 20] St. Simons is Georgia's most popular and extensively developed island, offering a wide variety of coastal activities in a beautiful natural setting of sprawling moss-draped live oaks, green-gold salt marsh, and sandy beaches. The Manhattan-sized barrier island located across from Brunswick is more popular with those who appreciate the beauty and climate of the sea islands, but require a great variety of lodging, restaurants, shopping, and sightseeing options. While St. Simons is Georgia's most populated barrier island, with more than 14,000 residents calling it home, the island has been developed with care to preserve much of its natural charms. Community life has been predom-

Retreat Plantation's majestic Avenue of Oaks.

inant on the island, as it has been the site of several Indian villages, Spanish missions, English settlements, antebellum plantations, and posh resorts. Today, sightseers can tour a historic lighthouse, church, and national monument, or cruise the island's expensive neighborhoods and gawk at opulent mansions. Outdoor recreation offered on the island includes biking, beachcombing, fishing, crabbing, kayaking, bird-watching, historic touring, golfing, and tennis.

The feel of St. Simons Island is distinctly different from Georgia's two other developed islands, Tybee and Jekyll. St. Simons feels quieter, older, and more upscale, with proud residents spending lots of money on landscaping and homes. St. Simons has been a family-oriented town but is now experiencing a second wave of growth. Boomers who grew up visiting the island have come back to buy second homes or relive their summer childhood experiences with their children.

For the most part, the island developed from sediments deposited from the Altamaha

River and the action of rising and lowering seas during the Pleistocene Age, 25,000–35,000 years ago. This makes St. Simons much older and more diverse in plants and animals than its Holocene neighbors to the north and east, Little St. Simons Island and Sea Island, which developed 5,000 years ago. St. Simons's East Beach is a Holocene fragment that has migrated from the north to fuse with the older part of the island. At the island's northern end is the Hampton River, the marshes of Little St. Simons Island, and the Altamaha Sound. Off the southern end are St. Simons Sound and the northern end of Jekyll Island.

Including St. Simons's marshlands, the island measures 27,630 acres, of which 12,300 are uplands, making St. Simons the largest barrier island in Georgia (Cumberland Island has more uplands, but less total area). Ten percent of St. Simons (East Beach) is of Holocene age. Its 4 miles of beach are comparable to Tybee Island.

The first human activity on St. Simons dates back thousands of years. A shell ring on Sapelo Island contains pottery shards more than 4,500 years old, and there's no reason to believe that Indians didn't use St. Simons's lush hunting grounds and fertile waters as they did on other Georgia barrier islands that existed at that time. When Europeans arrived at St. Simons in the 1500s, they found a Mocama Indian village named Guadalquini—the original name of St. Simons Island—on the south end of the island near the lighthouse. Here, the Spanish established a mission called *San Buenaventura de Guadalquini*, which operated from 1605–1684. At the northern end of the island near Cannon's Point from 1661–1684 was the Spanish mission *Santo Domingo de Asao/Talaje*, which had be relocated from Darien. The island gets its name from a short-lived Yamassee Indian village known as *San Simon*, which was established near Fort Frederica by refugees during the late 1660s to 1684. English settlers anglicized the name to St. Simons.

In 1597, an Indian uprising resulted in the deaths of four Franciscan priests and one brother, known by history as the Georgia Martyrs. (A relief of the martyrs hangs in the St. Williams Church on St. Simons.) One priest, Father Velascola, was executed on St. Simons Island. The Spanish tried to re-establish their missions, but by 1680, they had retreated from Georgia to St. Augustine, Florida, leaving behind a greatly reduced population of Indians, who had suffered under Spanish rule. In 1670, the British founded a settlement at Charleston and started to expand their territory into Georgia, building Fort King George at Darien in 1721. This began a period of territorial dispute over the coast of Georgia, termed the "debatable land." In 1733, Gen. James Edward Oglethorpe founded the English settlement of Savannah, and two years later, he established Fort Frederica and Fort St. Simons on the island, which was seen as a provocation by the Spanish. He also built a fort in Darien and settled the area with Scottish Highlanders who would become part of his fighting force.

In 1739, Britain declared war on the Spanish, called the War of Jenkins' Ear. The Battle of Bloody Marsh on St. Simons resolved the conflict in the new southern colonies. Fort Frederica, having served its military purpose, went into decline and in 1758, most of it was destroyed by fire, and the town never recovered. (*See* Fort Frederica National Monument, page 243 and the Battle of Bloody Marsh, page 238.)

Artists and St. Simons and Sea Island

Resort areas have always attracted artists, and St. Simons and Sea Island are no exception. Many writers, singers, painters, and designers have lived or vacationed on the island, a haven for restoring their creative juices. The most beloved artist in St. Simons's history is Eugenia Price, who wrote many historical novels about St. Simons, Savannah, the Georgia coast, and Florida. Price died in 1996 and was buried at Christ Church, resting with many of the characters featured in her books. Perhaps the most brilliant artist to live in the area was playwright Eugene O'Neill, who had a house on Sea Island from 1931 to 1936. He was visited by many celebrities of the stage and literary world, including Lillian Gish, Somerset Maugham, and Sherwood Anderson. O'Neill wrote his only comedy, *Ah, Wilderness!* while at Sea Island and made notes for *Long Day's Journey Into Night*.

After the American Revolution, the island was transformed into 14 plantations that grew sea island cotton. Most of St. Simons's live oaks were cut down to clear land for farming and supply valuable timber for American warships, such as the USS *Constitution*. The iron of Old Ironsides consisted of tough live oak planking. The oaks seen today on St. Simons are generally under 100 years old. A lighthouse was built in the early 1800s, signaling the importance of the harbor of Brunswick.

Most of the plantations were experiencing declines from exhausted soil, insect damage, and poor market conditions when the Civil War arrived in 1860, ending their free source of labor and dealing a final blow to the agricultural enterprises. A Confederate fort was built to guard the St. Simons sound, but it was abandoned and destroyed along with the lighthouse by retreating Rebels.

Lumber mills dominated the next period of activity on the island, from 1870 to 1900. A new lighthouse was built. Across the South, northern timber companies were rapidly cutting down southern forests. The companies used large rivers to transport the logs, and the most important river in Georgia was the mighty Altamaha. St. Simons's strategic location at the mouth of that river resulted in four lumber mills and massive docking facilities being built along Gascoigne Bluff on the Frederica River. The raw logs were cut into lumber and loaded onto great schooners and shipped around the world.

The depletion of Georgia's forests led to the end of this period. While the sawmills were busy, the island started developing a resort industry near the Village of St. Simons, with a new pier and grand hotel built on the southeastern end in the 1880s, accessed by ferry. Beach houses and summer cottages sprung up around the area of the pier village to the King and Prince Hotel.

The construction of a causeway in 1924 between Brunswick and the island spurred additional residential and resort development that continues to this day. A causeway was also built to Long Island, which was renamed Sea Island by the Sea Island Company. The company opened the resort hotel known worldwide as The Cloister in 1928, and developed the long, sandy island into a posh residential community (*see* Sea Island, page 252). Not only did it develop Sea Island, but the company also built a golf club on the remains of Retreat Plantation at the south end of St. Simons Island. The company's effect on the island continues with new developments on the northern end of St. Simons and Hawkins Island.

During World War II, the U.S. Navy used McKinnon Airport as a home base for torpedo bombers, and the King and Prince for a radar training school and quarters for officers. More important, the military improved the island's roads and airport and built a much-needed sewer system, which gave the island a better infrastructure to support the subsequent development boom of the 1950s and 1960s.

Like most islands, one of the main attractions of St. Simons is the beach. Its sandy shore is limited to the southeastern end, as Little St. Simons Island and Sea Island to the north and east receive most of the natural deposits accumulating from the natural sand-sharing system. The beach has experienced the natural changes expected of a sandy barrier island. While some sections have grown, others have shrunk. Huge chunks of the beach have been removed by storms, including Hurricane Dora in 1964, which washed out to sea several homes and large sections of Postell Avenue and Beachview Drive. President Lyndon Johnson ordered the placement of a seawall composed of huge granite boulders known as the Johnson Rocks, which has halted the landward erosion. The south end of Sea Island and East Beach have grown from additional deposits of sand.

With their beaches eroding (and accumulating) at various sites around the southern end of the island, St. Simons residents have been debating the necessity of expensive beach preservation or renourishment programs. Heated political battles have been waged and millions of dollars spent in efforts to keep—or not keep—the beach from migrating away from the island. While the beach is important to resorts and tourism-related businesses, some locals oppose action to renourish their beaches, believing it is better to let nature take its course. Some of these locals, dubbed "bridge burners," are less than sympathetic to tourists who clog their roads, and would like to see all development halted and the bridge burned so no one else is allowed on their beloved island. St. Simons has been trying to cope with the demands of its popularity, which has more than doubled the island's population since 1980, raising property taxes and straining the island's water, sewer, and transportation infrastructure. Despite the opinions of some grumpy locals, growth has not ruined St. Simons, and there is still much to see and do on the beautiful island.

VIRGINIA CREEPER
(Parthenocissus quinquefolia)

St. Simons: Southwestern End

▩ F. J. TORRAS CAUSEWAY

[Fig. 19, Fig. 20(3)] In 1924, the F. J. Torras Causeway was completed to St. Simons Island, and today makes the island one of only four Georgia barrier islands connected to the mainland. From Brunswick, the causeway crosses 4 miles of marsh and five tidal rivers. The high spans over the Mackay and Back rivers provide a fantastic view of the marshes of Glynn. The causeway joins the island at Gascoigne's Bluff on the Frederica River. This section was the site of nineteenth century lumber mills. On the right is Golden Isles Marina Village, and on the left are Gascoigne Bluff/Epworth Methodist Center and St. Simons Boating and Fishing Club. In the river across from the religious center are three marsh islands, created from ballast stones unloaded in the river from European vessels that would then fill their holds with cotton or lumber for the Old World. Over time, the rocky mounds have filled with soil and developed into marsh islands, supporting saltcedar (*Tamarix gallica*), an exotic species that resembles red cedar and was unintentionally brought over by the boats.

Fishermen have two locations to try their luck for inshore prey: the Back River Fishing Pier and McKay River Fishing Pier. Both are located below the causeway near their namesake river.

BIKING THE CAUSEWAY

The 4.3-mile protected bikeway that runs next to the causeway is a glorious way to view some of the most superlative salt marsh on the entire Atlantic coast. The spans above the Mackay and Back rivers are two of the few "hills" cyclists will encounter on the coast, but the view is worth the effort. Besides, after enjoying the panorama from a 65-foot high bridge above the MacKay River, cyclists can coast down the other side.

Trail: 4.3-mile protected, paved biking trail that runs next to the causeway.

▩ GOLDEN ISLES MARINA VILLAGE/ST. SIMONS BOATING & FISHING CLUB

From dugout canoes to million dollar yachts, Gascoigne's Bluff has moored many a ship seeking safe harbor at St. Simons Island. Found here today are two marinas that serve the intracoastal waterway—Golden Isles Marina Village, a complex of marina offerings on a marsh island off the causeway, and the quieter St. Simons Boating and Fishing Club, located on the bluff. **Golden Isles Marina** has floating docks, gas and oil, showers, laundry facilities, food and drinks, marine supplies, hardware, boat repair, and overnight and long-term dockage. Restaurants with a marsh view (Dockside Grill & Raw Bar, 638-4100, St. Simons Brewing Company, 638-0011) and shops are within walking distance. Here you will see everything from luxurious yachts to shrimp boats. The marina hosts the annual Golden Isles Kingfish Classic each summer, which draws hundreds of anglers. 206 Marina Drive (St. Simons Island Causeway). *634-1128*. St. Simons Boating and Fishing Club on the west side of the

GLASSWORT
(Salicornia sp.)
A common species of the high marsh, this halophyte can withstand the high salt concentrations found on salt pans.

island at Gascoigne's Bluff has gas and oil, food and drinks, electric hoist, bait and tackle, and overnight and long-term storage. 1000 Arthur Moore Drive. *638-9146.*

▓ GASCOIGNE'S BLUFF/EPWORTH BY THE SEA

[Fig. 20(4)] This beautiful bluff at the foot of the causeway where it meets St. Simons Island has seen more than its share of history. It has been an Indian settlement, the site of the most beautiful plantation on the island, the headquarters of a Spanish invasion, the source of timber stocks that were used to build the first ships of the U.S. Navy, and today a Methodist Conference Center.

Oaks, cedars, and shrubs dominate the bluff, who features a small park and Epworth By The Sea Methodist Conference Center. The area is open to the public, which can tour the beautiful woodlands, gardens, slave cabins, and Methodist retreat and museum. A Georgia champion southern red cedar (*Juniperus salicicola*) is found here, with a 15.5-foot circumference, 60-foot height, and 74-foot crownspread. Bird watchers should look for gray kingbirds during the summer and white ibis during winter.

Originally an Indian settlement, Gascoigne's Bluff, pronounced "Gas´ co-neeze," was named for Captain James Gascoigne, commander of the man-of-war *Hawk,* which convoyed the two ships bringing settlers to Fort Frederica in 1736, including John and Charles Wesley and German Salzburgers and Moravians. Gascoigne established the headquarters for Georgia's naval forces here along with a plantation. It was at this site that Spaniards landed during their unsuccessful invasion of Georgia during the War of Jenkins' Ear in 1742.

Today, the bluff has many beautiful old live oaks, but none as old as the ones that were cut on the island in 1794 and sent to shipyards in the North to build the first vessel of the U.S. Navy. Trees that grew near here supplied the sturdy lumber used in the famed American warship, USS *Constitution,* or Old Ironsides. When the ship was restored in 1927, many of the original live oak timbers were considered sound enough to last another half century.

During the plantation era, this area had a wharf that was part of the sea island plantation of Charleston merchant James Hamilton. Developed in 1793, the plantation was described four decades later by Fanny Kemble as "by far the finest place on the island." Two tabby slave cabins remain from this period, and were given to the Cassina Garden Club in 1931. Placed on the National Register of Historic Places in 1988, the two structures are probably the best examples of slave quarters on any of Georgia's developed islands. (Another slave building is located on the Epworth By The Sea property.)

From 1874–1902, several great sawmills lined the bluff, cutting raw cypress and longleaf pine logs into timber, which was loaded onto boats and shipped to all parts of the world, including New York, where timber cut here was used to build the Brooklyn Bridge. The ballast islands located off the bluff are a measure of the amount of naval activity that took place here. A community developed in the area that was called "The Mills" disappeared when Georgia's vast timber stocks were exhausted.

John and Charles Wesley, founders of the Methodist Church, visited St. Simons Island and Fort Frederica in March of 1736. In 1949, the South Georgia Conference of the Methodist Church decided to purchase 43.53 acres of the Hamilton Plantation at a bargain price from the Sea Island Company for a Methodist conference center. Bill Jones of the Sea Island Company supported Moore's efforts because he wanted St. Simons to maintain a family atmosphere. Jones believed St. Simons, like many seaside resorts, was at risk at being overtaken by bars and nightspots, which would hurt the value and status of Sea Island. Jones supported many church building activities believing they would inhibit this kind of growth. Under the leadership of Bishop Arthur J. Moore, a group of nine laymen, including Bill Jones, raised the needed $40,000 to purchase the site. On July 25, 1950, in the style of John and Charles Wesley, Moore preached under the live oaks, and named the site "Epworth" for the Wesleys' English village, and "By The Sea" for the coastal surroundings. In 1962, the site was designated an official Methodist shrine. The Arthur J. Moore Methodist Museum and Library opened in 1965 and became the official depository for the conference's archival records.

In 1844, the Methodist church divided into two branches in a dispute over the church position on slavery. The two reunited in 1939 and merged with another church branch in 1968 to become the United Methodist Church. Epworth By The Sea has several historic tabby slave buildings that have endured from the Hamilton Plantation period and are open to the public.

The museum features a mix of St. Simons and Methodist history, including handwritten letters by John Wesley and a life-size wax statue of Bishop Arthur J. Moore. The library has 6,000 volumes that can be used to do historical, genealogical, and scholarly research.

Epworth By The Sea is open to people of all denominations, offering 218 rooms, 12 apartments, 36 meeting rooms, and a banquet hall that can hold 400. There is an athletic field, lighted tennis courts, a youth gym, and two fishing piers.

Directions: From Brunswick, cross F.J. Torras Causeway to St. Simons Island. Follow Demere Road to entrance to Epworth By The Sea, located close to the causeway.

Activities: Historic touring, religious study, museum, nature study, bird-watching, tennis.

Facilities: Park, lodging, tennis courts.

Fees: Museum and sight-seeing is free. Call 638-8688 for lodging availability and rates.

Closest town: St. Simons Island.

For more information: Epworth By The Sea, PO Box 20407, 100 Arthur Moore Drive, St. Simons Island, GA 31522. Phone 638-8688.

▩ RETREAT PLANTATION/SEA ISLAND GOLF CLUB

[Fig. 20(5)] One of the most famous sea island cotton plantations, Retreat Plantation, is today one of the best golf courses in Georgia, if not the U.S. Cotton grown here commanded record prices in Liverpool markets. Course developers were careful to retain much of heritage of the plantation, and visitors can drive the approach and view the breathtaking Avenue of Oaks planted almost 150 years ago. Golf is available to guests of The Cloister (*see* Sea Island, page 252) or members of the club.

The Sea Island Company purchased the property after the King family could no longer support the plantation that flourished in antebellum days, and opened the Sea Island Golf Course in 1929. James Spalding, the man who brought sea island cotton to southern plantations, purchased Retreat Plantation in 1786. According to Thomas Spalding, his father James grew the first sea island cotton, also known as long-staple, black seed, or Anguilla cotton, in the spring of 1787 "upon the banks of a small rice field on St. Simons Island."

Thomas Spalding, who inherited his father's estate in 1794, built Orange Grove on St. Simons Island, a replica of Oglethorpe's residence of Orange Hall in Fort Frederica. In 1802, Spalding sold the plantation for $10,000 to Major William Page, a friend of Major Pierce Butler, and relocated to Sapelo Island.

The Pages established a productive cotton plantation and became one of the richest families in the South. Page's only daughter, Anna Matilda, married Thomas Butler King, a young lawyer from Massachusetts. Like many other wealthy planters, he spent much of his time on politics, while Anna Matilda continued managing the successful cotton plantation, along with beautiful gardens of roses, specimen trees, rare shrubs, and shell walkways. Many famous guests and statesmen experienced the Page's Southern hospitality, including wildlife artist John James Audubon.

Today, the approach to the excellent 36-hole golf course borders the original oak-lined avenue—a beautiful, sun-dappled green tunnel planted in 1850 by Anna Matilda—that led to the cotton fields located in the area of the airport. Also located on the property are the ruins of a two-and-a-half story, 10-room slave hospital, a tabby barn used as a clubhouse, and a small cemetery used by slaves and their descendants since 1800, including Neptune Small (*see* Neptune Park, page 235). Another relic of Retreat Plantation is a slave cabin located at the corner of Frederica and Demere roads.

Directions: From the causeway go right on Kings Way to Retreat Avenue. Turn right to Avenue of Oaks.

For more information: Sea Island Golf Club, Frederica Road at Kings Way, St. Simons Island, GA 31522. Phone 638-5118 or The Cloister, Sea Island, Georgia, 31561. Phone (800) SEA-ISLA.

St. Simons: Village Area & Southeastern End

The Village area of St. Simons, located at the southern end of the island at Mallery Street and Ocean Boulevard, is the best place to start your visit of the island. From here, one can visit the historic lighthouse, fish or crab off the pier, hold a picnic, start a bike tour of the island, walk the beach, browse one of the village shops, or eat in one of St. Simons's finer restaurants. This part of the island is developed and busy; nonetheless, the natural setting is quite beautiful, with large live oaks shading the view of the shimmering St. Simons Sound and Jekyll Island beyond. Shrimp boats are seen trafficking between offshore shrimping grounds and their harbor in Brunswick. Walking north on the beach, a lesson can be learned in the ephemeral character of barrier island sand, while observing a variety of shorebirds feeding on amphipods and fish in the intertidal areas and inlets. In many areas, homes perched practically on top of rip-rap rocks appear ready to fling themselves into the ocean. In other areas, dunes have been allowed to endure and support the fascinating plant and animal communities that populate the dynamic area between beach and forest.

NEPTUNE PARK, FISHING PIER & VILLAGE, ST. SIMONS VISITOR CENTER

[Fig. 20(7)] Neptune Park, located between the village and lighthouse, is St. Simons's most popular park, where visitors can picnic, take a trolley tour of the island, fish off the pier, stroll on the pathway, or relax on a bench. Here visitors may listen to the cackling of iridescent boat-tailed grackles in the live oak canopies, or the screech of begging seagulls, or the noble silence of brown pelicans perched on the pier. One might want to examine finned trophies that lie gasping in buckets, if local fishermen have been lucky angling the deep currents that flow past the pier. The beach is best explored at low tide, when one might find whelks, horseshoe crabs, and sand dollars.

The park's name is not in honor of Neptune, the god of sea, but Neptune Small, a slave that belonged to the Thomas Butler King family of Retreat Plantation, today the site of Sea Island Golf Course. During the Civil War, Small accompanied one of the Kings' sons, who was killed during the Battle of Fredericksburg. Small retrieved the body from the battleground and bore it back to Savannah under very difficult circumstances. The family buried the son at Christ Church, and Small chose to return to Virginia to accompany another son for the rest of the bloody conflict. After the war, Small was given a plot of land on the plantation, located at the park, and he continued to work for the King family as a free man. When he died in 1907, he was buried in a small graveyard on Retreat Plantation.

Two exceptionally large live oaks are found shading the park, where visitors can use picnic tables, a playground, miniature golf, and benches and lounge chairs for contemplative views of sparkling St. Simons Sound. Neptune Park Casino has a public swimming pool open during summer. A 1.5-hour trolley tour leaves from here to other points of interest on the island, but some may prefer to see it under their own steam by using the biking/jogging path. The fishing pier is open to fishing, crabbing, and shrimping.

The village got its start in the 1870s resort period, when vacationers traveled from the mainland on steamships. Most of the early historic buildings of St. Simons were destroyed by fire. The St. Simons Hotel was built in 1888 near Massengale Park, which was linked to the pier by mule-drawn trolley. The grand structure, large enough to host 300 guests, was destroyed by fire in December of 1898. The New St. Simons Hotel was built at the same location in 1910, but in 1916, it too burned. Nonetheless, St. Simons continued to be popular with vacationers, and four other hotels were established near the pier, including the Bellevue, which was renamed St. Simons Hotel.

The third St. Simons Hotel, located at the end of the pier, was replaced by the first Casino Building, which burned in 1934. The area started to develop more rapidly with the building of the causeway in 1924, and more visitors opted to become year-round residents. With a growing population, a village of small shops and businesses was able to flourish year-round by the 1950s, and by 1960, the resident population was 3,199. Today, the village is the focal point of commercial and tourist activities on the island. The St. Simons Visitor Center is located in the second Casino Building at the northern end of Neptune Park and offers a complete assortment of visitor facilities and information, including a library, restrooms, a theater playhouse, and an outdoor bandstand. For information on restaurants, lodging, and night life, see page 248.

Directions: From Brunswick, cross F.J. Torras Causeway. Go right on Kings Way to Ocean Boulevard. At Mallery Street, turn right to village and public parking.

Activities: Historic touring, picnicking, bird-watching, miniature golf, swimming, fishing, crabbing, beachcombing.

Dates: Visitor center is open 7 days a week from 9–5.

Facilities: Visitor center, park, picnic tables, parking, swimming pool, restrooms, biking/jogging trails, lighthouse and museum, beach.

Fees: A fee is charged for the trolley tour, Neptune Casino Swimming Pool, and miniature golf.

Closest town: St. Simons Island.

For more information: St. Simons Island Chamber of Commerce, Neptune Park, St. Simons Island, GA 31522. Phone 638-9014. The Links Miniature Golf, phone 638-0305. St. Simons Island Casino Swimming Pool, phone 638-2877.

ST. SIMONS LIGHTHOUSE AND MUSEUM OF COASTAL HISTORY

[Fig. 20(8)] Perhaps the most beautiful and recognizable landmark on the Georgia coast is the St. Simons Lighthouse, a much-visited, photographed, and beloved monument to the island's nautical history. On a clear day, the climb of 129 steps to the top of the 104-foot gleaming white tower allows perhaps the most glorious view to be experienced on the Georgia coast. The keeper's cottage, where the museum is located, is believed to be the oldest brick structure in Glynn County. It was built of Savannah grey brick with Georgia heart pine floors in 1872, and is on the National Register of Historic Places. The museum is furnished with antiques that belonged to the old families of St. Simons, including one early nineteenth century secretary from Retreat Plantation.

The first structure built in the area of the lighthouse was Delegal's Fort, built in spring of 1936 by troops from South Carolina. It was replaced in 1738 by Fort St. Simons, which was destroyed by retreating Spanish troops after their defeat in the Battle of Bloody Marsh in 1742. The area became a plantation owned by John Couper, who sold 4 acres for $1 to the Federal government for the construction of a lighthouse. In 1807, James Gould of Massachusetts was hired to build the first lighthouse. Although the original specifications called for brick, Gould used tabby, a cheap, durable "coastal concrete" made of equal parts oyster shells, lime, sand, and water. He built a 75-foot octagonal tower, 25 feet in diameter at the base

TIGER SWALLOWTAIL
(Papilio glaucus)
This butterfly takes its name from its yellow wings with black tigerlike stripes.

tapering to 10 feet at the top. The top 12.5 feet were constructed of brick, and supported a 10-foot-high, 8-foot-diameter iron lantern equipped with oil lamps suspended by chains. An 8-foot-thick base supported the weight of the structure. In 1810, Gould was appointed first keeper by President James Madison, and was paid $400 a year until his retirement in 1837. The lantern was originally powered by whale oil, but when the majestic animals were hunted to near extinction, lighthouses switched to kerosene. St. Simons Island author Eugenia Price wrote a historical novel about Gould's efforts, titled simply *The Lighthouse*, which was the second installment in her trilogy about St. Simons Island.

In 1857, the lights of the lighthouse were greatly improved when it was fitted with a third-order, double-convex lens, which can cast a beam 18 miles. This improvement was to be short-lived, however, because of the arrival of the Civil War in 1860. Stationed at Fort Brown, a wooden bastion near the lighthouse to protect St. Simons Sound, were the Macon artillery troops and six field guns. In 1862, when Union warships blockaded the Georgia coast, the Confederates decided to abandon St. Simons, and before leaving, they dynamited the lighthouse and burned Fort Brown so they would not aid their enemy. The ruins of this first lighthouse are found on the complex grounds east of the tower.

After the Civil War, the Federal government decided a new lighthouse was needed on St. Simons Island. Hired to design and build the lighthouse and keeper's house was noted Irish-born architect Charles Cluskey. He designed a graceful, 104-foot, round tower and a nine-room, two-story Victorian house for the keeper. The architectural details not only enhance the beauty of the house but also draw the eye upward to the lighthouse. Cluskey died of malaria a year before he was able to see his work finished in 1872. In 1876, the keeper's house was upgraded and a speaker's tube linking the house with the top of the tower was added. A fire-proof brick oil house measuring 9 feet by 11 feet that could hold

450, 5-gallon oil cans was constructed next to the lighthouse in 1890. This building's purpose became obsolete when the kerosene lamp was replaced by an electrical one in 1934. When the last lighthouse keeper retired in the 1950s, the U.S. Coast Guard fully automated the lighthouse. Today, the Fresnel lens is illuminated by a 1,000-watt mogul lamp, which rotates once a minute.

In 1972, the Coastal Georgia Historical Society took over the unused keeper's house, restored it to its original design, and opened it to the public. A series of renovation and restoration activities continued on the tower and complex until 1984, when visitors were allowed to climb to the top of the lighthouse.

Today, the romantic lure of the lighthouse is irresistible on a foggy night, as the light sweeps slowly out into the night, comforting sailors in the sound and reassuring residents in the community that part of their heritage remains intact for future generations to appreciate.

Directions: From Brunswick, cross F.J. Torras Causeway. Go right on Kings Way to Ocean Boulevard. At Mallery Street, continue to 12th Street. Turn right and proceed to lighthouse and museum.

Activities: Historic touring, museum,

Dates: Open Monday through Saturday 10–5, Sunday 1:30–5. Closed selected holidays.

Facilities: Lighthouse and museum, gift shop.

Fees: A small fee is charged for admission.

Closest town: St. Simons Island.

For more information: Coastal Georgia Historical Society, 101 12th Street, St. Simons Island, GA 31522. Phone 638-4666. Museum of Coastal History, PO Box 21136, St. Simons Island, GA 31522.

BLOODY MARSH MONUMENT

[Fig. 20(13)] This small park provides a panorama of the eastern marshes of St. Simons Island, while it informs the visitor of the Battle of Bloody Marsh. Though it was a relatively small engagement, the outcome had a tremendous influence on the future course of Georgia. An exhibit explains the engagement and a plaque honors Oglethorpe's resolve to keep the Georgia territory in the hands of the British empire.

Geologically, the high ground of the park is the Pleistocene (35,000 years ago) shoreline of St. Simons Island, which existed before Sea Island and East Beach were formed to the east 5,000 years ago. The "Bloody Marshes" filled the lagoon created by the younger, sandy barriers. Marsh species display zonation, with live oaks on the highest, driest ground, cedar at the woodland edge, and marsh elder and groundsel trees by the edge of the marsh, going down to saltwort, glasswort, bunch grass (*Spartina bakeri*), salt meadow cordgrass (*Spartina patens*), and needlerush. Wading birds, such as herons and egrets, are observed fishing the shallower open waters of the marsh, which drain into Postell Creek and enter the ocean at Gould's Inlet.

In 1739, Britain declared war on the Spanish, called the War of Jenkins' Ear. Jenkins was an English smuggler who had his ship boarded by the Spanish off the Florida coast. When the Spanish couldn't find any contraband, Jenkins testified to the English House of Commons, one of the officers grew angry and sliced off his ear. This outraged England, which had been spoiling for a fight with Spain for years. In the vulnerable southern colonies of America, Oglethorpe decided to act first, and laid siege to Spanish-held St. Augustine in 1740, but he was unsuccessful. Two years later, the Spanish sailed past the guns of Fort St. Simons and landed near Gascoigne's Bluff with approximately 2,000 men supported by 50 ships. Flanked and outmanned, Oglethorpe abandoned Fort St. Simons and withdrew his 900 troops along Military Road toward Fort Frederica.

The first action of the day occurred within sight of Fort Frederica at Gully Hole Creek, where a force of Scottish Highlanders, English Rangers, and Indians led by Oglethorpe repulsed an advancing regiment of 200 Spaniards, causing them to retreat. Back in camp, the Spanish commander and governor of Florida, Manuel de Montiano, learning of the defeat, sent several hundred troops up the military road to cover the retreat. Meanwhile, Oglethorpe's men waited in ambush near the road, and at the last possible moment, the Scots and English rangers opened fire on the unprepared Spanish troops, causing anywhere from 100 to 500 casualties, depending on whose account one believes. The marshes reportedly "ran red with blood." The Spanish returned to the south end, and after contemplating the situation for a week, destroyed Fort St. Simons, boarded their ships, and left the Georgia coast for good, ensuring that Georgia and the territories to the north would be of British heritage and speak the English language. The military clash passed into the history books as the Battle of Bloody Marsh.

Directions: From Brunswick, cross F.J. Torras Causeway. Go left on Demere Road. Bloody Marsh Monument is located on the left after the Demere/Frederica intersection.

Activities: Historic touring, bird-watching, nature study.

Dates: Visitor center is open 7 days a week from 8–4.

Facilities: Park, exhibit shelter, audiotape.

Fees: None.

Closest town: Brunswick.

For more information: Administered by Fort Frederica National Monument, National Park Service, Route 9, Box 286-C, St. Simons Island, GA 31522. Phone 638-3639.

The Beaches of St. Simons

St. Simons Island's beaches are limited to the southern end of the island in a band stretching 4 miles from Gould's Inlet on the eastern side to King Creek on the southwestern side. The beaches have experienced tremendous changes since the beginning of the island's recorded history, and continue to erode and accrete as a response to the effects of wind, waves, tides, and storms. Taylor Schoettle's study of the beaches in *A Naturalist's Guide to St. Simons Island* is an excellent primer on the subject. Not many sea turtles nest on St. Simons Island for reasons not entirely understood but probably due to the island's mix of currents, sand quality, width of beach, rock seawalls, beach orientation, and development. From 1994–1998, an average of only one sea turtle has nested on St. Simons a year, compared with 74 on Sea Island, which has roughly the same length of beach.

ST. SIMONS BEACH

[Fig. 20(9)] St. Simons Beach, the area between the King and Prince Beach Resort and fishing pier, through the years has been assaulted by currents, tides, and storms and has eroded significantly. If not for the placement of the Johnson Rocks in 1964, naturalist Taylor Schoettle believes the beach would have retreated all the way to the brick county buildings behind Neptune Park. In the 1920s, the beach extended out to the wings of the present pier, and the old pier extended the length of the new pier from that spot. In the 1920s, people could drive their cars on the beach from the pier to the King and Prince, something that would be unthinkable today. At low tide, beachcombers can walk to the King and Prince, but at high tide, much of the beach is submerged as waves crash on the seawall known as the Johnson Rocks.

Destroying a large portion of St. Simons Beach was Hurricane Dora in 1964. South of the King and Prince, the hurricane snatched beachfront homes into the Atlantic, tore out the middle section of Beachview Drive, and obliterated Postell Avenue, which ran parallel to Beachview one block closer to the ocean. Two small fragments of Postell at 12th Street at the southern end and between Myrtle and Cedar streets at the northern end are evidence of the power of tropical storms. A small gurgling artesian well on the beach south of 9th Street once was found in the backyard of a beachfront home. Today, it is used by thirsty shorebirds or children playing in the gurgling spring.

This part of the island's beach is most vulnerable to erosion for a variety of reasons. Perhaps the main reason is that in front of Neptune Park in the sound is a 70–80 feet deep trench with fast-moving currents.

MASSENGALE PARK

[Fig. 20(10)] Massengale is a popular and busy public park, where the smells of grilled hamburgers and hot-dogs mix with the happy shouts of playing children. Because of its extensive use, it has the worn look of a public park. Nevertheless, it provides access to the southern end of East Beach, and visitors who head north from here will experience the best beach the island has to offer. The sand is hard-packed and suitable for biking.

The park came about due to philanthropy by the Sea Island Company, which was in the process of limiting public access to its beaches and wanted to provide a public beach area for St. Simons residents, but not on Sea Island. The Sea Island Company bought the property in 1945 in an attempt to get the state to build a state park, but it was deemed too small, and the state instead purchased Jekyll Island. In 1955, the Sea Island Company donated the property to Glynn County for the park.

The woodlands of the park and East Beach, supporting live oaks and pines, are remnants of the maritime forest on the Holocene fragment of St. Simons. Because of the younger, poorer soil, this forest is much less diverse, compared with the mid-island forests that are growing on richer, Pleistocene soils found west of Bloody Marsh.

Directions: From Brunswick, cross F.J. Torras Causeway. Go left on Demere Road to East Beach Causeway. After crossing the causeway, go right on Ocean Boulevard. Massengale Park is on the left.

Activities: Beachcombing, picnicking, biking, bird-watching, nature study.

Dates: Open daily 7 a.m.–10 p.m.

Facilities: Park, picnic tables, restrooms, showers.

Fees: None.

Closest town: St. Simons Island.

For more information: St. Simons Island Chamber of Commerce, Neptune Park, St. Simons Island, GA 31522. Phone 638-9014.

EAST BEACH AND COAST GUARD STATION (COASTAL ENCOUNTERS NATURE CENTER)

Tourism and Beaches

America's largest industry is travel and tourism. It accounts for $746 billion of the gross national product, produces $47 billion in tax revenues, employs 14.4 million people, and grows at the rate of 343,000 new jobs annually. Beaches are the leading tourist destination in the U.S. with 85 percent of tourist revenues spent in coastal states. The loss of beaches is perceived by some as an economic threat to tourism, and has lead to federal programs to protect and reclaim beaches at taxpayer expense. At Miami Beach, $6 billion worth of real estate towers over 10 miles of disappearing beach, which has been restored several times, the last effort costing $60 million. Some oppose such activities, claiming that the public's money shouldn't be spent to restore beachfront to private property. An average of $30 million is spent a year on beach restoration, or around $1 million a square mile.

[Fig. 20(11)] The historic Coast Guard Station is home to the St. Simons division of Coastal Encounters Nature Center. This excellent nonprofit organization is dedicated to adult and child education about Georgia's precious coast. Programs include barrier island ecology walks, kayak excursions in the marsh, boating with naturalists, summer science camps, and other field trips. Inside the station are touch tanks and aquariums featuring local marine species. Another branch of Coastal Encounters is located on Jekyll Island (*see* Coastal Encounters Nature Center, page 263). A group is working on a plan to open a maritime museum in the historic station as well.

The beach here has accreted considerably since the 1950s. Wood Avenue runs behind the old shoreline, showing how much the area has grown. The area north of the Coast Guard Station has grown the most on the island and has extensive dune meadow and shrub communities that are interesting to study for plant succession relative to beach and dune formation. Extensive shoals display the effects of longshore currents carrying sand south from Little St. Simons Island and Sea Island meeting cross currents from Gould's

Inlet and northern currents of the sound. Worries about recent erosion at the area known as East End, however, where condos have been built near "new" beach, has led to an application for a seawall to protect this recent development.

Directions: From Brunswick, cross F.J. Torras Causeway. Go left on Demere Road to East Beach Causeway. After crossing causeway, Coast Guard Station is on right.

Activities: Beachcombing, picnicking, biking, bird-watching, nature study, special programs.

Dates: Closed temporarily to walk-in visitors. Reservations for groups only.

Facilities: restrooms, showers at beach.

Fees: Beach access is free; Coastal Encounters programs charge various fees.

Closest town: St. Simons Island.

For more information: Coastal Encounters Nature Center, 100 S. Riverview Dr., Jekyll Island, GA 31527. Email: coastalencounter@mindspring.com Phone 635-9102.

🦝 GOULD'S INLET PARK

[Fig. 20(12)] A small park located at 15th Street and Bruce Drive provides a great view of the best birding spot on the island, recognized by its selection to the Colonial Coast Birding Trail. This inlet separates East Beach, a Holocene fragment of St. Simons south of the inlet, from Sea Island to the north. The bar and inlet are good examples of Georgia's barrier island-estuarine interface. The inlet and sand bars are constantly moving, changing shape, preventing vegetation from becoming established, and creating a resting place for many species of birds, as well as a feeding site for certain species. Resident birds seen here include laughing and herring gulls, willets, American oystercatchers, black skimmers, brown pelicans, black skimmers, and royal terns. During warm weather, including fall and spring migration periods, bird watchers may identify black, sandwich, gull-billed, common, and Caspian terns; black-bellied, semi-palmated, and Wilson's plovers; reddish egrets, marbled godwits, whimbrels, ruddy turnstones, sanderlings, red knots, and western sandpipers. Cold-weather birds include black-bellied and piping plovers; black-backed, and ring-billed gulls; Caspian and Forster's terns; red-backed dunlins; and red-breasted mergansers.

As the southern part of Sea Island has grown, the northern end of East Beach has lost 1,640 feet of land since the Civil War, according to Schoettle. As you walk or bike south on East Beach toward Coast Guard beach, the homes fall away from the shore, due to the growth of the beach since 1930. These homes used to be beachfront property. They still are, but they are located much farther from the water.

Fishermen sometimes try their luck on Gould's Inlet Dock, where tidal pulses attract many species of fish and other marine animals.

Directions: From Brunswick, cross F.J. Torras Causeway. Go left on Demere Road to East Beach Causeway. After crossing causeway, go left on Ocean Boulevard. Turn right at 15th Street and Gould's Inlet Park is straight ahead.

St. Simons: the Northern Half

🔲 EBO LANDING

[Fig. 19(5), Fig. 20(14)] The murky, haunted waters of Ebo Landing are where a group of West African slaves chose mass drowning rather than submit to a life of slavery. In May of 1803, a group of Igbo (the "g" is silent) tribesmen, captured in Igboland (now Nigeria), rebelled as their boat neared the shore in Dunbar Creek, a tributary of the Frederica River. The story goes that led by an Igbo chieftain, the proud tribesmen resolutely marched into Dunbar Creek, chanting an Igbo hymn, and trusting their God Chukwu instead of submitting to slavery in the New World. Survivors were taken to Cannon's Point Plantation, where the story was recounted and passed down to become a well-known legend. Some say that on quiet nights, the ghosts can be heard chanting in the marsh.

Directions: Ebo Landing, now private property, can be seen from a distance. Travel east on Sea Island Road from the causeway, pass Hawkins Island, and look north just before crossing the small bridge at Dunbar Creek. If you get to the Frederica-Sea Island Road intersection, you've gone too far.

🔲 FORT FREDERICA NATIONAL MONUMENT

[Fig. 19(3)] Visitors who want a full picture of Georgia's founding must visit this serenely beautiful national park, an archeological site that quietly tells the story of a British settlement that successfully defended the colony in wartime, but quickly reverted to nature in times of peace. Reclaimed by historians, today it is the enchanting site of an excellent park and museum with many stories to tell about Georgia's colonial past. Shaded by some of the island's oldest live oaks, the historic site overlooks the winding Frederica River and windswept marshes of Glynn, which murmur past the silent ruins of the eighteenth century ghost town.

Naturalists will enjoy viewing wildlife in the park and adjacent marsh. Live oaks estimated to be between 100 and 200 years old dominate the site,

Fort Frederica National Monument.

accompanied by laurel oaks, pecans, red cedar, cabbage and sago palms, and holly. Most impressive may be the century-old giant muscadine grapevine, located near the town gate, and a tremendous loblolly pine, located across the moat from the barracks ruins. Wildlife in the park includes pileated, downy, and red-bellied woodpeckers, songbirds, deer, raccoon, armadillos, and flying squirrels. The marsh is home to alligators, river otters, and a variety of shore and wading birds.

Gen. James Edward Oglethorpe, long regarded as the founder of Georgia, first visited the area in 1734 and selected the site of an abandoned Indian field for the fort's future location. Strategically located on a modest bluff overlooking a tidal tributary of the Altamaha River, the site enjoyed natural defenses that made it virtually impregnable against enemy attack. Both the river and the town were named Frederica, in honor of Frederick Louis, Prince of Wales, the only son of Britain's King George II.

The arrival of Oglethorpe with 116 settlers in March 1736 marked Fort Frederica's birth. As the southern-most settlement in British North America, it guarded not only St. Simons Island, but the entire colony of Georgia against the Spanish in Florida. The settlement of Frederica consisted both of a town laid out in a grid pattern much like Savannah and a fort to defend the approaches on the Frederica River. The town consisted of 84 lots, 60 by 90 feet, divided into two wards by orange tree-lined Broad Street. Settlers built palmetto huts to provide temporary shelter, but these were soon replaced by regular wooden-frame structures and even more substantial two-and three-story houses made of brick and tabby. Oglethorpe built the only house he ever owned in Georgia, Orange Hall, a short distance away.

Prominent among Frederica's early residents were two Anglican ministers, John and Charles Wesley, perhaps best remembered for their role in establishing the Methodist Church. Charles Wesley, who later wrote more than 6,000 hymns, including *Hark the Herald Angels Sing*, served as Oglethorpe's secretary and Frederica's first minister. John Wesley paid five brief visits to Frederica between April 1736 and January 1737 to preach and minister to the needs of the people there.

A moat and two wooden palisades separated the star-shaped earthen fort from the town. In its final form, it consisted of an officer's quarters, a powder magazine, two storehouses, and a blacksmith shop where the armorer of the regiment worked. A spur battery supporting six or seven cannons, including several 18-pounders, projected into the river. Although the town was not initially fortified, following the outbreak of war between Britain and Spain in 1739, a six-foot deep moat and two ten-foot high cedar palisades were built surrounding it. Fort Frederica was connected to a sister fort on the south end of St. Simons Island by the Military Road, a narrow path that led through the island's dense forests.

On a trip home to Britain in 1737, Oglethorpe secured command of a 630-man regiment of regulars, the 42nd Regiment of Foot. These soldiers added muscle to Georgia's defense and made Frederica Georgia's first military town, many years before Columbus, Warner Robins, or Hinesville came into being. The money the soldiers spent became the lifeblood of Frederica's economy, providing many of its citizens with their principal source of income. At its peak, 400 to 500 people called Frederica home, which had attained the appearance of an English village.

Wartime activity at Frederica culminated in the summer of 1742 when Spain, retaliating for a British attack on St. Augustine, Florida two years earlier, launched a full-scale military invasion of the Georgia colony. Comprising approximately 1,500 soldiers and a fleet of thirty-six ships, Spanish forces had reason to be confident in the success of their mission to destroy the colony. Although safely landing their entire army on St. Simons Island on July 5-6, 1742, the Spanish did not bargain on the spirited British resistance that they encountered. In two battles that occurred on July 7, Gully Hole Creek and Bloody Marsh, the British managed first to surprise their opponents amidst the island's dense foliage and then repulse them entirely despite their superior numbers, thereby effectively ending more than a century of rivalry over the territory (*See* Bloody Marsh Monument, page 238).

Following the formal restoration of peace between Spain and Britain in 1748, Frederica's military role ceased. Its garrison was disbanded and many of the townspeople, now lacking a source of income, moved away. Largely abandoned by the mid-1750s, the town's destruction was completed by a fire of unknown origin in 1758.

With Fort Frederica all but forgotten in the years to follow, the effort to preserve its ruins began at the turn of the twentieth century. A group of local citizens led by historian Margaret Davis Cate saw their efforts rewarded in 1936 when Congress officially established the national monument. The park was formally dedicated in 1945.

Touring Fort Frederica today, one can wander the old streets, view house foundations, and read signs that explain the significance of each site. Still visible is the foundation of the Hawkins-Davison House where John Wesley encountered the wrath of Mrs. Beatre Hawkins, who attacked him with a pistol and a pair of scissors. He made good his escape, but not before she had bit him and torn his shirtsleeve with her teeth. The trace outline of the fort still guards the Frederica River as it flows to the sea. Although erosion over the years removed much of the original earthworks, recent stabilization of the riverbank has brought a halt to that process. Still standing despite the ravages of time is only a remnant of the large tabby fort, a silent witness to the former grandeur of British imperial ambitions in North America.

Directions: From Brunswick, take the F.J. Torras Causeway to St. Simons Island. Turn left on Sea Island Causeway and follow it to the intersection of Frederica Road. Make another left on Frederica Road and drive approximately three miles to the park entrance.

Activities: Historic touring, nature study, bird-watching.

Dates: The park visitor center is open daily, except Christmas, from 9 a.m. to 5 p.m. The park grounds are open 8 a.m. to 5 p.m.

Facilities: Visitor center and museum, film, exhibits, taped tour, special events, guided tours by reservation, restrooms, gift shop.

Fees: Admission is $4.00 a vehicle or $2.00 a person on foot, bike, or with a noncommercial bus tour.

Closest town: St. Simons Island.

For more information: Fort Frederica National Monument, Route 9 Box 286-C, St. Simons Island, GA 31522. Phone 638-3639.

▒ CHRIST CHURCH

[Fig. 19(4), Fig. 20(2)] A must see for anyone visiting St. Simons Island is Christ Church, a charming house of worship nestled in a peaceful, quiet glade of the oldest live oaks on the island. The church, adjacent graveyard, and nature walk across the road are well worth an hour of contemplation of the spiritual and natural world.

Not only are the live oaks amazing, but the visitor is also treated to excellent examples of magnolia, sweetgum, crape myrtle, dogwoods, azaleas, yucca, and cedar. Growing on the live oaks are Spanish moss, resurrection fern, lichens, and orchids. Woodpeckers, flickers, and sapsuckers are commonly observed birds.

The gabled, white-framed church is the second oldest Episcopal church in Georgia and the fourth oldest church in the state. Famous hymn-writer and Methodist founder

Christ Church is the fourth oldest church in Georgia.

Charles Wesley preached to settlers and Gen. James Oglethorpe under a large live oak near the church on his first Sunday on St. Simons in 1736. After two months, Charles Wesley returned to England after encountering trouble with parishioners. His brother, John, took over clerical duties until he also left, "with an utter despair of doing good there" in 1737. Taking over religious responsibilities were George Whitefield and others until Frederica was abandoned around 1766. In 1808, the congregation was given a grant of 108 acres, and in 1820 a church was built. It served the St. Simons community until the Civil War, when Union forces stationed on the island used it as a headquarters, nearly destroying the building. They smashed the organ, broke the windows, burned the pews, and used the altar as a chopping block. In 1884, the church was rebuilt by the Reverand Anson Green Phelps Dodge Jr., who became the central character in Eugenia Price's *The Beloved Invader*, the first book of her trilogy on St. Simons Island. His church is cruciform in design, with a trussed Gothic roof, wooden interior, and beautiful stained glass windows illustrating the life of Christ.

The beautiful graveyard contains many of the famous names of St. Simons and Georgia history, and is like a walk back in time. Eugenia Price and many of the people she based her stories on are buried here.

Across the street is Woodland Walk, a short nature trail to the Wesley Memorial—a large Celtic cross—in the woods. In spring, the blooming azaleas are gorgeous. On this trail, visitors will see a second growth forest of pine, bay, and oaks, and in wetter areas red maple, sweetgum, blackgum, and red bay. At the entrance is a large, ancient muscadine vine.

Directions: From Brunswick, cross F.J. Torras Causeway. Go left on Demere Road. Follow Demere to Frederica intersection. Go left on Frederica, and drive 4.75 miles north to church on left. Parking on right.

Activities: Historic touring, nature walk, religious study.

Dates: Open daily 2–5 during summer, 1–4 daily during winter.

Facilities: Historic church, cemetery, and Woodland Walk park across the street.

Fees: Donation requested.

Closest town: St. Simons Island.

For more information: Christ Church Episcopal, 6329 Frederica Road, St. Simons Island, GA 31522. Phone 638-8683.

TAYLOR'S FISH CAMP

[Fig. 19(2)] This small marina offers a glimpse into St. Simons's recent past, when it was a sleepy community of fewer than 5,000 people. The marina is reached by heading north on Lawrence Road, where travelers will see second-growth forest and many historical markers that tell the stories of plantations and settlement on the northern end of St. Simons, most of which is owned by the Sea Island Company. The entrance to Taylor's Fish Camp is on Cannon's Point Road, the right fork off Lawrence road 3 miles north of the turnoff to Fort Frederica. A drive down a sandy road leads past a tabby slave cabin on the left, which currently is being used as an art studio by Peggy Buchan, who paints coastal scenes in oils and acrylics (phone 638-5731). The movie *Conrack*, based on the book *The Water is Wide* by Pat Conroy, was filmed near the sleepy marina, and the ruins of the schoolhouse featured in the movie are located nearby. The marina provides access to the Hampton River and features a hoist, ramp, bait and tackle, and refreshments. For more information, phone 638-7690.

HAMPTON RIVER CLUB MARINA

[Fig. 19] With access to the Hampton River and a full slate of amenities, Hampton River Club Marina has everything you need for a saltwater fishing experience or nature tour. Travelers to Little St. Simons Island leave from here. It is located at the north end of the island. Go north on Frederica and go right on Lawrence Road. Where the road splits, go left until the road ends at the marina. Dry storage and wet slips, hoist and fork lift launching, boat rentals, gas and diesel, bait and tackle, charter fishing and nature tours, and general boat repairs. Open 7 days a week from 7-7. Phone 638-1210.

St. Simons Island Lodging, Restaurants, Night Life, and Activities

While other areas of St. Simons Island have developed commercial sections, the main action is near the village. Located here are a wide variety of excellent restaurants, bars with entertainment, and small shops, along with the beach and many of the more popular tourist attractions of the island. Lodging options are conveniently located within walking distance of all the commercial offerings. A short distance away along East Beach, several excellent lodging options are found, including the historic King and Prince Beach and Golf Resort, and nearby in the Ocean Boulevard area are some of the more popular eating establishments and shops on the island.

▨ LODGING NEAR THE VILLAGE AND EAST BEACH

King and Prince Beach and Golf Resort. 201 Arnold Road. The most famous lodging on St. Simons Island is this resort located on East Beach. This King and Prince is a survivor, having withstood numerous fires, hurricanes, and wars. It started modestly in the 1930s as a private beach club, and has evolved and grown several times since then. It has been rebuilt several times after fires, and managed to hang on to its beach after being assaulted many times by natural forces. Today, it has 139 rooms, 42 villas, two restaurants, a lounge, one indoor pool and four outdoor pools, four tennis courts, bicycles, and golf privileges at the Hampton Club on the north end of the island. *Moderate to expensive. (800) 342-0212.* **Sea Gate Inn.** 1014 Ocean Boulevard. The Sea Gate Inn is an oceanfront getaway with an informal atmosphere. Bedrooms, efficiencies, and suites offered. Swimming pool. *Moderate. (800) 562-8812.* **St. Simons Inn by the Lighthouse.** 609 Beachview Drive. Within convenient walking distance of the village and other attractions. Be sure to ask for one of the 34 rooms that have a view of the lighthouse. *Moderate. 638-1101.* For additional lodging, call the Brunswick and the Golden Isles Visitors Bureau at (800) 933-2627. Numerous condos and homes are available to rent, handled by more than a dozen rental companies. Call the Brunswick and the Golden Isles Visitors Bureau for a complete listing, phone (800) 933-2627, or try your luck with the following: THE Management Company, phone (800) 627-6850; Golden Isles Realty, phone (800) 337-3106; Parker-Kaufman Realtors, phone (888) 227-8573; Georgia Coast Realty, phone (800) 639-1144.

▨ RESTAURANTS AND NIGHT LIFE ON ST. SIMONS ISLAND

Except for Savannah, St. Simons has the best restaurant offerings on the Georgia coast. Chain restaurants have yet to move in and dominate the island, and a wide variety of at least 50 local options will satisfy even the most discriminating tastebuds. Some restaurants have outdoor seating where you can watch the world walk by as you gobble your grouper sandwich. In general, most restaurants are in the Village area or the Redfern area, with a few favorites scattered around the island.

VILLAGE AREA

Dressner's Village Café. 223 Mallery Street. This is a locals' favorite that serves breakfast all day, and claims to have the "best hamburger in the Golden Isles." Breakfast and lunch. *Inexpensive. 634-1217.* **The Fourth of May Café and Deli**. 444 Ocean Boulevard. Another locals' hangout that features delicious Southern cooking with the meat and two-vegetable daily special that rarely disappoints. Huge salads, delicious cornbread, and fresh vegetables, while locals sit spinning yarns. The deli stays busy. Lunch and dinner. *Moderate. 638-5444.* **Blanche's Courtyard**. 440 Ocean Boulevard. A St. Simons's mainstay, with hand-cut steaks and seafood prepared any way you like it, all in an interesting décor. Entertainment on Saturdays. Dinner. *Moderate. 638-3030.* **Blue Water Restaurant**, 115 Mallery. Delicious seafood dishes (and beef, poultry, lamb, and pork) with a New Orleans accent. *Moderate. 638-7007.* **CJ's Italian Restaurant.** 405 Mallery Street. Some believe this small eatery has the best Italian food on the island. Lunch (seasonally) and dinner. *Moderate. 634-1022.* **J. Mac's Island Restaurant and & Jazz Bar**. 407 Mallery Street. Fine dining here, with mouth-watering creations ranging from sautéed lobster and shiitake mushroom appetizers to gorgonzola-stuffed angus beef tenderloin dinners. Dinner. *Moderate to expensive. 634-0403.* **Mullet Bay**. 512 Ocean Boulevard. With a fun, coastal-Caribbean atmosphere, this casual seafood restaurant also is a popular social gathering spot in the village. Lunch and dinner. *Moderate. 634-9977.*

Live Oaks and the Georgia Coast

While the live oak already serves as Georgia's official state tree, if one tree was selected to represent just the Georgia coast, it would have to be *Quercus virginianan*. The live oak earns its name from the fact that it appears to retain its leaves year-round, thus always be "live." Actually, the tree drops its leaves on its own schedule from October to April. The live oak's timber is resistant to rot and weathering, and was prized for shipbuilding in the nineteenth century for its toughness and odd shape that could be fashioned into key elements of ship design. Today, its twisted, tough grain makes it unpopular as lumber: Just try splitting a log with an ax. Live oaks thrive in poor, sandy soils of the Coastal Plain of the southeastern Atlantic and Gulf states, and have a shallow, spreading root system. The tree grows very quickly, causing some to overestimate the age of a favorite live oak on their property. The favorite saying is that live oaks spend 100 years growing, 100 living, and 100 years dying. As you travel the coast, you may notice that live oaks take many shapes, from more spindly oaks with a pruned, thick canopy in a maritime forest, to the singular specimens that grow huge, spreading trunk-sized branches in more open areas. The largest live oak in Georgia is near Baptist Village, Waycross. It is 86 feet high, has a trunk diameter of 10 feet and a 143-foot crown, which shades almost half an acre.

The following establishments are good places for cold drinks and entertainment. **Brogen's**. 200 Pier Alley. This is a sports bar, featuring good burgers, wings, and salads, and a great deck where you can watch the sun set while nursing a cold drink. Lunch and dinner. *Inexpensive to moderate. 638-1660.* **Coconut Willie's**. 121 Mallery Street. A ten-year-old bar and grill that offers good fried seafood sandwiches, burgers, salads, seafood pasta, and mixed drinks. Lunch and dinner. *Moderate. 634-6134.* **Island Rock Café**. 303 Mallery Street. This is a bar and grill with outdoor seating that also features live entertainment. Lunch and dinner. *Moderate. 638-0245.* **Rafters**. 315½ Mallery Street. Music is the attraction at this blues club, as well as a full raw-bar menu of oysters, clams, mussels, and crawfish, along with deli sandwiches. Ribs on Wednesdays. Dinner. *Moderate. 634-9755.*

EAST BEACH AREA

A short distance from the village at the intersection of Ocean Boulevard and Arnold Road are several restaurants popular with residents and tourists. **Chelsea**. 1226 Ocean Boulevard. The food here is delicious, ranging from prime rib to seafood and pasta specials. Dinner served 7 days a week. *Moderate to expensive. 638-2047.* **Crab Trap**. 1209 Ocean Boulevard. A St. Simons tradition that serves the basic fried seafood classics. Dinner. *Moderate. 638-3552.* **The King and Prince Beach and Golf Resort.** 201 Arnold. Not only fine lodging, but fine dining as well, with classic seafood and beef dishes. Live piano music on weekends and extensive Sunday brunch. Breakfast, lunch and dinner. *Moderate to expensive. 638-3631.*

REDFERN AND RETREAT VILLAGES AND ELSEWHERE

Crab Happy & Co. 260 Redfern Village. This is where you go to eat steamed blue crabs. All you can eat crab specials are offered and a seafood buffet on Sunday. Lunch and dinner. *Moderate. 634-8899.* **Marsh Point Bar and Grill.** 253 Redfern Village. Creative cuisine with martinis and a marsh view. Lunch and dinner. *Moderate. 634-2351.* **The Redfern Café**. 200 Redfern Village. Special seafood, veal, lamb, and pasta dishes. Dinner. *Moderate to expensive. 634-1344.* **Allegro Garden Room and Cafe**. 2465 Demere Road. Two separate dining rooms, one more casual than the other, offer inspired creations such as bourbon glazed quail, lobster taquitos, Colorado lamb, and Moroccan spiced pork tenderloin. Dinner. *Moderate. 638-7097* (Garden Room), *638-6097* (Café).

These three popular restaurants are old mainstays and worth a visit: **Alfonza's Olde Plantation Supper Club.** 171 Harrington Lane. You will certainly find something to order at this popular restaurant. *Moderate. 638-9883.* **Bennie's Red Barn**. 5514 Frederica Road. This popular restaurant dates back to 1954, making it the oldest family-owned restaurant on the island. Its long-running success is due to hospitality and great meals featuring fresh seafood and wood-fire grilled steaks. Entertainment Wednesday–Saturday. Dinner. *Moderate. 638-2844.* **Frederica House**. 3611 Frederica Road. Seafood and steaks in a log cabin. Dinner. *Moderate. 638-6789.*

Village Creek Landing. 526 S. Harrington Road. For a very casual, low-country affair, where you can either buy bait or eat it, try this restaurant located at Village Creek Landing Marina. Choices are limited to fried fish, oysters, shrimp, or scallops, or steamed shrimp by the pound, but the beer's cold and the view of the "bloody" marsh from the deck is inspiring. Dinner. *Inexpensive. 634-9054.* For other restaurants, see Golden Isles Marina, page 231.

BIKING AND JOGGING ON ST. SIMONS ISLAND

St. Simons is an excellent island to view from the seat of a bike, where cyclists can get fresh air as they enjoy the charming homes and beautiful landscaping of the island. Extensive, marked bike paths lead from Brunswick over the causeway to the island, where the cyclist can choose from a network of paths leading to most of the island's popular sites. It's best to stay on the paths, as the traffic can get fierce. The hard-packed beach, from Massengale Park to Gould's Inlet, is another safe area to ride, if you don't mind fighting the wind at times or getting sand on your bike. All the trails double as jogging paths for those who want a more strenuous workout.

GOLF AND TENNIS RESORTS ON ST. SIMONS ISLAND

St. Simons has the best golf and tennis offerings on the Georgia Coast. The best action occurs at these four resorts: **The Sea Island Golf Club and St. Simons Island Club**. Owned and operated by the Sea Island Company, these 36- and 18-hole semiprivate golf clubs have different fee structures and availability to the public based on whether golfers are guests of the Cloister Hotel. Call for details. Sea Island: phone 638-5118. St. Simons: phone 638-5130. **Sea Palms Golf and Tennis Resort**. This resort on 800 acres has furnished villas, tennis, rental bikes, two pools, children's programs, restaurant, and 27 holes of golf. Phone (800) 841-6268. **The Hampton Club** is the newest course on the island, featuring 18 holes in the beauty of the coast. Located at the northern end of the island. Golf packages are available through the King and Prince. Phone 634-0255.

KAYAKING, SAILING, SCUBA DIVING, AND NATURE TOURS

The leading outfitter on this part of the Georgia coast is **Southeast Adventure Outfitters**, which offers a full range of outdoor expeditions geared for timid to courageous coastal explorers. 313 Mallery Street. *638-5225.* **Barry's Beach Service.** 420 Arnold Road, rents sailboats, kayaks, wind surfers, boogie boards, as well as providing sailing instruction and nature tours. *638-8053.* **Island Dive Center**, at Golden Isles Marina, provides scuba instruction and charters. *638-6590.*

Sea Island

[Fig. 19, Fig. 20] Guarding St. Simons to the east is Sea Island, a thin Holocene barrier island that serves as a resort and home for the rich. Founded in the Roaring Twenties by Sea Island Company owners Howard Coffin and Alfred (Bill) Jones Sr., the island boasts a world-famous resort, The Cloister Hotel, and a resident community of grand estates with carefully manicured lawns and gardens. The public is allowed to drive the public roads of the island and take a stroll through the hotel, but access to the beach is unfortunately limited to residents and guests. However, if you can afford to stay at The Cloister Hotel, the world is indeed your oyster, with 54 holes of golf, 17 tennis courts, a spa, two pools, four restaurants, horseback riding, shooting school, sailing, biking, nature tours, dance lessons, scuba lessons, surf and deep-sea fishing, and 4.5 miles of beach offered for your pleasure.

Sea Island, 5 miles long by 2 miles wide (including marsh), consists of 2,000 acres of marsh, dunes, beach, and developed maritime forest, of which roughly 750 acres are uplands. To the west of the island is extensive salt marsh fed by the Black Banks River, which flows to the ocean at Gould's Inlet at the southern end, and Village Creek, which flows out to the Hampton River, which separates Sea Island's northern end from Little St. Simons Island. The vegetation on the island is a carefully tended combination of introduced and native species, including some ancient live oaks and pines. The north end is the site of Ocean Forest Golf Club. The south end is the only area left in a relatively natural state. At the extreme north end are a series of old dune ridges and accompanying lowlands made up of brackish marshes and bogs. Migrating sands have created a sandy shoal that extends eastwardly and Pelican Spit, an important haven for migrating birds including terns, pelicans, and avocets. In 1846, English geologist Sir Charles Lyell found 30 varieties of shells, which is still possible to do today. The southern end of the island is a recurved spit that continues to grow toward St. Simons and has developed a narrow shrub zone and extensive interdune meadow. Gould's Inlet at the southern end is an excellent bird-watching site (*see* Gould's Inlet, page 242). Sea Island is also a favorite nesting site for threatened loggerhead turtles, with a 10-year average of 66 nests a year, almost twice as many as Little St. Simons Island to the north.

The island was relatively untouched wilderness when the Sea Island Company purchased it. The first to own Sea Island was James Mackay, a soldier who fought alongside Oglethorpe in his Florida campaign and Battle of Bloody Marsh, and commander of Fort Frederica. After his death, Fifth Creek Island, as it was known, passed through the hands of several of St. Simons plantation owners, including James Hamilton and James Couper. Couper raised cattle here and used it as a hunting retreat. In the 1920s, a group of businessmen bought the island from heirs and subdivided it, hoping to start a beach development. They in turn sold it to a Brunswick group, which sold it to Howard Coffin for $349,485.17 on July 15, 1926.

Sea Island and The Cloister are the brainchild of business geniuses Howard Coffin

and his young cousin, Alfred W. (Bill)
Jones Sr. The Sea Island Company is not
only the biggest developer of Sea Island but
St. Simons as well, with two golf courses
and new construction on Hawkins Island
and several thousand acres on the northern end of the island at Cannon's Point
and Taylor's Fish Camp. Coffin and Jones
have had a tremendous impact on the
Georgia coast, with Coffin's influence
ending with his death in the 1930s and
Jones's influence continuing to this day as
his son and grandson continue his legacy
of conservation and wise development.

Horseback riding on Sea Island.

Coffin made millions as chief engineer
at the Hudson Motor Company in Detroit in the early 1900s, and while attending an
automobile race in Savannah fell in love with the Georgia coast. He first purchased and
developed Sapelo Island as a hunting preserve, cattle ranch, and seafood cannery (*see*
Sapelo Island, page XX). He became interested in St. Simons Island as a resort area after a
causeway was built to the island in 1924. In 1926, Coffin purchased a portion of Retreat
Plantation and started exploring Long Island, which he purchased, renamed Glynn Isle
then Sea Island, and began developing an exclusive resort. At the time the resort was
built, the island lacked electricity, water, and telephone service.

Coffin was a visionary developer. He would conceive a project, draw up the plans,
arrange for financing, and then turn it over to the energetic Bill Jones, who would make
it happen. To design The Cloister, Coffin hired famous Palm Beach architect Addison
Mizner, who designed the hotel in a Spanish-Mediterranean style. It opened on October
12, 1928. With the death of Coffin's beloved wife Matilda, the stock market crash of 1929,
and the following Great Depression, Coffin was forced to sell his Sapelo Island assets to
R.J. Reynolds Jr. to hold onto Sea Island. In the 1930s, Coffin spent much of his time
trying to keep his empire together. Depressed and in poor health, Coffin killed himself
with a rifle in 1937. He was buried with Matilda in Christ Church Cemetery.

Bill Jones was left to struggle for the survival of Sea Island, which after much sacrifice
and hard work turned a profit for the first time in 1941, and became one of the few five-
star resorts in America. (For the complete story, read *This Happy Isle* by Harold H.
Martin.) The list of famous people who have visited and vacationed at the resort is long
and illustrious and includes U.S. Presidents Coolidge, Hoover, Eisenhower, Ford, and
Carter. George Bush honeymooned there, as have 36,000 other couples. The asphalt spine
of the island, Sea Island Drive, divides 36 blocks of spectacular homes.

Perhaps more important than Jones's creation of Sea Island was his influence through
a variety of philanthropic and business dealings in the preservation of many other coastal

areas of natural and historic importance. One could say his fingerprints are on Jekyll Island, Sapelo Island National Estuarine Sanctuary, and Fort King George. On St. Simons, he was responsible for the preservation of Fort Frederica and Retreat Plantation and its Avenue of Oaks, and was involved in the creation of Massengale Park and Epworth By The Sea, selling the property to the Methodist Conference for a bargain price. The Sea Island Company also donated the land for McKinnon Airport and the St. Simons sewage treatment plant. Jones also was instrumental in the creation of Cumberland Island National Seashore, persuading the Mellon Foundation to provide $7.5 million for the purchase of major tracts of Cumberland, which had fallen into the hands of the developer of Hilton Head. No fewer than seven churches on St. Simons have benefited from Jones's donations of land on which to build.

The Cloister has some peculiarities that make it distinctive, such as dress codes for its dining rooms and tennis courts. This isn't the place to walk through the lobby in dripping wet swim trunks. Besides, you never know who you might meet—perhaps a famous movie star, artist, or politician.

Directions: From Brunswick, cross F.J. Torras Causeway. Go left on Demere Road. Follow Demere to Sea Island Road on left. Go left on Sea Island Road and follow road to island.

Activities: The public is limited to sight-seeing from Sea Island's public roads. Guests of The Cloister have a full range of activities available to them, including golf, tennis, swimming, biking, sailing, kayaking, fishing, horseback riding, shooting school, beachcombing, and nature study.

Dates: The Cloister and island are open to the public daily. Beaches closed to general public.

Facilities: The Cloister offers 286 rooms, 4 restaurants, 3 golf courses (36-hole Sea Island Golf Club, 18-hole St. Simons Island Club), 17 tennis courts, a spa and health club, 2 pools, sea kayaks, a skeet shooting course, bikes, and riding stables. Lessons offered in golf, tennis, riding, fishing, sailing, shooting, and dancing. Nature tours are also offered.

Fees: Call (800) SEA-ISLA or 638-3611 for rates. The Cloister accepts most major credit cards.

Closest town: Sea Island.

For more information: The Cloister, Sea Island, GA 31561. www.seaisland.com Phone (800) SEA-ISLA or 638-3611. For private and cottage rentals call Sea Island Cottage Rentals, phone 638-5112.

DINING ON SEA ISLAND

The Cloister Main Dining Room is almost as famous as the resort, serving classic five-course dinners with an emphasis on the freshest local seafood, along with black angus beef, lamb, and veal. Jacket and tie is required. *Expensive. 638-5111.*

Jekyll Island State Park

[Fig. 21] The state of Georgia owns Jekyll Island, one of only four Georgia barrier islands reachable by car, where authorities attempt to maintain a delicate balance between preserving the island's natural qualities and offering a full plate of outdoor recreational opportunities. The 5,700-acre island, with 8 miles of beach and 4,400 acres of uplands, supports every kind of natural community found on a Georgia barrier island, thus creating an outdoor classroom for the study of island flora and fauna. Several sites on the causeway and island are on the Colonial Coast Birding Trail. Also located on the island is the 200-acre Jekyll Island Club National Historic District, where the richest and most powerful men in America built an exclusive, winter hideaway from the demands of their businesses. The natural beauty of the island, the historic district, golf, tennis, and biking are the main attractions of the island, located only 6 miles from Brunswick and 10 miles from Interstate 95.

While there are not as many lodging, restaurant, or shopping options as on Georgia's other developed islands, there are fewer residents and development is limited to one-third of the island, producing a wilder experience. About 20 miles of trails are available to hikers, joggers, and bikers, where they can experience firsthand the beautiful native flora and fauna of Georgia's beaches, dunes, maritime forests, marshes, creeks, and salt flats. Because the island is a state park, a small parking fee is charged at the entrance to the island. Not as tacky as Tybee, or sumptuous as St. Simons and Sea Island, this island with controlled development and outstanding natural areas might be just right for you.

Jekyll, a relatively small island measuring 7 miles long and 1.5 miles wide, consists of both Pleistocene and Holocene components, which has affected natural communities on the island as well as developmental patterns. The richer, older Pleistocene soils (35,000 years old) support a greater diversity of species and attracted farming and timbering activities during the plantation period of the island's recent history. The younger, Holocene soils (5,000 years old), found at the northern end past Clam Creek and at the southern end in the form of dunes and sloughs of a recurved spit, are eroding southward. Under normal conditions, the northeastern end would feature extensive shoals, but sands migrating from islands to the north are trapped by a man-made trench, which allows large ships into Brunswick harbor. The northeast end features a beautiful boneyard beach, where a maritime forest of live oak is being undercut by currents and tides. At the south end, developing dune systems make a living laboratory for plant succession.

From eastern beach to western marsh, the mix of natural communities supports an impressive array of animal species. Atlantic bottle-nosed dolphins are commonly observed surfacing for air in Jekyll Creek, and deer and raccoons are abundant. Over the last 10 years, the beaches of Jekyll have provided critical nesting grounds to an average of 100 threatened sea turtles a year. Shells and marine creatures wash up on the beaches, such as knobbed whelks, mermaid purses, horseshoe crabs, and whelk egg cases.

Biking on Jekyll Island is a popular activity.

Several species of marine creatures are found living in the intertidal zone such as ghost shrimp, mole crabs, and coquina clams. At the base of the primary dunes, quarter-sized holes are evidence of ghost crabs, which feed on tiny organisms in the wrack at night. Freshwater ponds, including those on the golf courses, are refuges for alligators, turtles, frogs, and snakes. Bird life is abundant across the island, including many shorebird, waterfowl, and songbird species. Woodpeckers and owls are observed in the woodlands, and hawks and vultures are seen gliding on warm currents in the sky.

Like Georgia's other barrier islands, shell mounds are evidence that the island was a popular hunting ground for Indians on the coast. However, during the Spanish mission period from 1560 to 1680, Jekyll Island had no major Indian settlements and consequently the Spanish never established a mission there. (Earlier histories supply Jekyll with an Indian name, an Indian village, and a Spanish mission, but new research proves these accounts are wrong.) The original Indian name for the island is lost to history. The Spanish called it *Isla de Ballenas*, which translates to "whale island," referring to the fact that the waters in this area were (and are to this day) breeding grounds for right whales.

During the 1600s and first half of the 1700s, Georgia became known as "the debatable land" as Spain and England struggled to control the new territory. England sent Gen. Oglethorpe and 114 colonists to Georgia to establish a foothold. Oglethorpe established towns and fortifications along the coast, including Savannah, Darien, and Frederica on St. Simons.

Oglethorpe named Jekyll Island in honor of his friend Dr. Joseph Jekyll who was the greatest contributor to the new colony. On Jekyll Island, Oglethorpe established a forward observation post commanded by Maj. William Horton. Horton grew rye and hops on 222 acres for the purpose of brewing beer for English soldiers. Rum was forbidden in the new colony, but beer was not. Ruins of Horton's brewery can still be seen on the island today.

Not wanting his enemy to see his Frederica fortifications, Oglethorpe used Jekyll as a neutral meeting ground for English and Spanish negotiations. After the Battle of Bloody Marsh on St. Simons in 1742, the Spanish relinquished their claims on Georgia, but stopped on Jekyll first and destroyed Horton's home. Horton rebuilt, but left the island in 1748 for a new plot of ground near the Ogeechee River.

After Horton's death, the island passed through several hands before being bought by the colorful Frenchman, Christopher Poulain du Bignon, who had fought with American patriots during the Revolutionary War. The du Bignons, in partnership with four other French families, settled Sapelo Island first, but when the partnership dissolved in 1793, du Bignon and several other families purchased Jekyll Island. Eventually, du Bignon became sole owner of the island and it remained in his family's possession for nearly a century.

The du Bignons planted sea island cotton on much of the 3,000 acres of Pleistocene soil, which was much more fertile than the soil of Holocene portions of Jekyll. The older portions of the island were also logged for their live oak timber, and today have recovered in a mix of pines, younger oaks, and mixed hardwoods. The Holocene portions were left relatively untouched. The slave-holding du Bignons became wealthy plantation owners until the Civil War ended the plantation era in the South.

The last slaves brought to America from Africa landed on Jekyll Island in 1858, when the 114-foot racing schooner *Wanderer* unloaded its illegal cargo here. The importation of slaves had been outlawed, but great profit lay in smuggling human cargo to the South. The *Wanderer* picked up 490 slaves on the West Coast of Africa and sailed to Georgia, where the Charleston, South Carolina ship owner received as much as $600 per slave. Ironically, the slave ship was seized during the Civil War by Union forces, fitted with guns, and used to fight for black freedom during the war.

In 1886, du Bignon's grandson John sold the island for $125,000 to the Jekyll Island Club, a group of the wealthiest, most powerful men in the country, ushering in the most well-known chapter in the island's history. The club's membership boasted some of the most famous names of American enterprise: Morgan, Vanderbilt, Astor, Gould, Rockefeller, McCormick, Baker, Biddle, Whitney, Armour, Crane, Goodyear, Pulitzer, Macy, and Bliss. This group's interest in Jekyll sparked interest from other wealthy businessmen who purchased Wassaw, Ossabaw, St. Catherines, Sapelo, and Cumberland islands for personal hunting grounds and winter retreats.

The millionaires built a village of beautiful cottages and a nine-hole golf course. Because they owned the entire island and their activities only impacted one-tenth of it,

Jekyll Island Club Hotel.

the major effect on Jekyll was to preserve the island for 60 years while other islands, such as Tybee and St. Simons, were being developed as residential islands.

The Great Depression of the 1930s, World War II, and the advent of income taxes made Jekyll much less attractive to the millionaires, who sold the island to the state in 1947 for $675,000 to become a new state park. A causeway and bridge were completed in December 1954, allowing much greater public access. Today, the Jekyll Island Authority manages the island, where 65 percent is left in a more or less natural state (including parks and picnic grounds), and the other 35 percent is developed, including motels, a convention center, residences, businesses, public golf courses, and a water park. Some 800 people live on the island in privately owned residences. They have a 99-year lease on their land from the Jekyll Island Authority, which is transferable if the residence sells, but no more property is available for housing.

Activities on the island range from scheduled nature walks to gliding down a water slide. Visitors and vacationers will be well entertained by Jekyll's golf, tennis, biking, horseback riding, fishing, camping, historic touring, beachcombing, and bird-watching. Offered in stores on the island is a highly recommended field guide to Jekyll Island titled *A Guide to a Georgia Barrier Island*, by Taylor Schoettle, which makes an excellent companion to this volume and is able to go into greater detail.

For more information: Jekyll Island Convention and Visitors Bureau, PO Box 13186, Jekyll Island, GA 31527. Phone (877) 453-5955.

Jekyll Island: Southern Area

▓ JEKYLL ISLAND CAUSEWAY AND JOINTER CREEK

[Fig. 21] Most people view causeways as something to quickly travel across on the way to their destination. But nature lovers might want to slow down on their way to Jekyll for some outstanding wildlife viewing opportunities. The causeway crosses 4,000 acres of *Spartina* marsh and adjoining mud flats on Jointer Creek to the south, which support many animal species. At low tide, the mud flats of Jointer Creek, located 1.8 miles south of the causeway on US 17, are some of the best places to view roseate spoonbills between July and September, as well as wood storks, great blue herons, and great egrets. Look out for rare diamondback terrapins, which cross the road between April and July and are frequently squashed by vehicles.

The land supporting the causeway hosts salt-tolerant coastal shrub species such as wax myrtle, sea oxeye, marsh elder, and exotic pink and white oleander. The causeway at dusk might be the best place on the Georgia coast to view marsh rabbits. The gray berries of wax myrtles provide important food energy to thousands of migrating tree swallows, which are one of the most glorious sights of the coast. Tree swallows fly in large groups and look from a distance like a swarm of graceful bees. They are identified by their white belly. Avocets and plovers have been seen in the mud flats behind the Jekyll Island Visitors Center, along with many other species of birds. Seaside sparrows are heard singing in spring, and secretive clapper rails and willets inhabit the marsh. Whimbrels and long-billed curlews are unusual migrants in the winter. Birds observed perching on wires and poles include osprey, red-tailed hawks, kestrels, and peregrine falcons.

Binoculars are a great aid for wildlife watching in the marsh, and remember to use great caution while viewing wildlife on the causeway because of the hazard of fast-moving traffic. Fishermen angling for inshore prey use Jekyll Creek Pier on the Jekyll Island Causeway near the bridge.

Directions: From Brunswick, travel south on US 17, cross Sidney Lanier Bridge. At causeway, turn left toward Jekyll Island. For Jointer Creek mud flats, go straight from turnoff 1.8 miles to site.

▓ SOUTH DUNES PICNIC AREA, GLORY BOARDWALK, AND SOUTH BEACH

If you are looking for a good place to picnic and enjoy the beach near a fascinating and beautiful maritime and dune forest of live oaks, then South Dunes Picnic Area [Fig. 20(12)] is for you. Protected by a 20-foot back dune, the well-equipped picnic area has two boardwalks, numerous picnic tables and shelters, and public bathrooms with showers for those spending a day at the beach. The series of dune ridges fronting the picnic area supports several interesting natural communities, including an older, wind-sheared live oak and shrub forest, along with a re-establishing shrub-interdune meadow. Wildlife observed here includes songbirds in the forest and shorebirds on the beach, raccoons in the park, and deer south of the park where the forest ends and a beach meadow begins. Freshwater ponds support frogs, turtles, snakes, and an occasional alligator. The boardwalks provide glimpses into the dune communities without disturbing them. Insect repellant is highly recommended in this area.

Today, it is much better understood, but unfortunately not entirely practiced, that one should not disturb a dune community by trampling or picking the plants found there. In the past, the area was assaulted by beach-lovers whose foot traffic up and down the dunes caused tremendous erosion. Dune plants hold the sand in place, and when they are killed the sand is liberated, causing a domino effect. Tons of freed sand migrated southward on Jekyll and to the north end of Cumberland Island, burying healthy forests and shrub communities. In 1983, a beach restoration project formed new primary dunes with bulldozed sand, installed snow fences, planted sand-trapping plants, and built two boardwalks over the dunes. After crossing the oak-shrub forest on the boardwalk, naturalists may want to examine the natural progress of the dune communities that are the results of these reclamation activities and compare species diversity here with less disturbed, more established shrub-meadow zones. The live oak forest is most interesting, as it shows the shrubbing effect. Notice that regardless of whether the tree's base is located near the top or the bottom of the dune, it grows up to the shearline created by the prevailing winds from the ocean.

Directions: From Brunswick, travel south on US 17, cross Sidney Lanier Bridge. At causeway, turn left toward Jekyll Island. Continue across Ben Fortson Parkway to dead end. Go right. Picnic Area is marked on left.

Activities: Picnicking, swimming, fishing, bird-watching, beachcombing, and nature study.

Dates: Open daily.

Facilities: Picnic tables, restrooms, showers, shelters at Picnic Area.

Fees: None.

Closest town: Jekyll Island.

For more information: Jekyll Island Convention and Visitors Bureau, PO Box 13186, Jekyll Island, GA 31527. Phone (877) 453-5955. For rental information call 635-3400.

GLORY BOARDWALK AND SOUTH BEACH

[Fig. 21(11)] Known as the Glory Boardwalk, this footway was built by the producers of the movie *Glory*, who filmed the climactic battle scene of the classic Civil War movie on Jekyll's beach. This provides easy access to the progression of natural communities in five dune ridges that lead to the beach on Jekyll's southern Atlantic side. The beaches of the southern end of Jekyll, in an arc from the Atlantic side, past St. Andrews Sound, and to the western side of the island to the St. Andrews Picnic Area, are regarded as the best places for shell collecting and wildlife observation on the island, especially during the winter. The South Beach area is regarded as one of the best sites on the Georgia coast for bird-watching during migratory periods. Saltwater fishing is excellent here as well. Access is available at the Glory Boardwalk, the

4-H boardwalk farther south, and a boardwalk located at the end of Macy Lane.

Crossing the Glory Boardwalk, the nature observer will travel from the shrub forest zone of oaks, willows, buckthorn, hercules club, and other woody plants into the shrub zone of wax myrtle and groundsel, then into an extensive beach meadow zone of camphorweed, yucca, Russian thistle, and various grasses. Each dune is like the rings of a tree, with the older communities closest to the parking lot and the youngest closest to the beach. The swales between the dunes trap water and provide important freshwater sites for wildlife. Rabbit, raccoon, and deer tracks are observed in the muddier portions of sloughs. Traveling south on the beach, eroded scarps expose older, clay soils in layers below younger sands, suggesting the former existence of an ancient salt marsh. For clays to settle out, they need a calmer body of water. Like all barrier islands, the sands of Jekyll remain in transition.

The shifting shoals in the intertidal area, along with the shrub dune and marsh transition areas of South Beach, are popular with many bird species that roost and feed here. Identified here are a variety of gulls (laughing, ring-billed, and herring), terns (royal, Caspian, and Forster's), and sandpipers. Brown pelicans and double-crested cormorants are very common during all seasons. Plovers, turnstones, avocets, godwits, curlews, dowitchers, willets, stilts, and oystercatchers are observed resting or feeding in the intertidal area during migratory seasons. As the beach becomes marsh, more wading birds are seen, including wood storks and a variety of herons and egrets. Migratory birds of prey, including kestrels, peregrine falcons, and merlins hunt the South Beach area, and rattlesnakes populate the interdune areas.

Directions: Glory Boardwalk is reached by driving 0.5 mile south of water tower to Jekyll Island Soccer Complex gate. Turn left and drive toward beach to boardwalk. South Beach area extends in an arc around to St. Andrews Picnic Area on the western side of island. It can be accessed at the end of Macy Lane and St. Andrews Drive. A boardwalk here provides access to the beach.

Activities: Picnicking, swimming, fishing, bird-watching, beachcombing, and nature study.

Dates: Open daily.

Facilities: Handicapped accessible boardwalk to beach at Glory Boardwalk.

Fees: None.

Closest town: Jekyll Island.

For more information: Jekyll Island Convention and Visitors Bureau, PO Box 13186, Jekyll Island, GA 31527. Phone (877) 453-5955. For rental information call 635-3400.

ST. ANDREWS PICNIC AREA

[Fig. 21(10)] With views of Jekyll Sound, St. Andrews Picnic Area rests on a bluff where several dramatically different natural communities come together. Fronting the bluff is a narrow inlet beach, which runs north from the tip of Jekyll to the picnic area where it ends at a marsh creek. On the bluff at the picnic area is a mixed forest of live oaks, red cedars, and loblolly pines that are being undercut by erosion from fast and deep tidal currents carrying a rich soup of marine life. Locals are often seen pulling seine nets attempting to snare shrimp, crabs, flounder, and mullet. Out in the sound, gleaming Atlantic bottlenosed dolphins are commonly seen surfacing for air. Going south, the trees give way to buckthorn shrubs and dune grasses. The dune ridges reveal the fingerprints of a recurved spit. This mix of natural communities produces an edge effect preferred by many species.

The live oaks of the picnic area harbor many plants on their branches and trunks worth examining, including lichens, resurrection fern, and Spanish and ball moss. Ball moss (*Tillandsia recurvata*) is a tropical cousin of Spanish moss that is more commonly observed in the Caribbean. It has a coarser texture and tends to clump in balls.

Directions: From Brunswick, travel south on US 17, cross Sidney Lanier Bridge. At causeway, turn left toward Jekyll Island. Turn right on South Riverview Drive and continue to picnic area on right.

Activities: Picnicking, swimming, fishing, bird-watching, beachcombing, and nature study.

Dates: Open daily.

Facilities: Picnic tables, restrooms, beach.

Fees: None.

Closest town: Jekyll Island.

For more information: Jekyll Island Convention and Visitors Bureau, PO Box 13186, Jekyll Island, GA 31527. Phone (877) 453-5955.

MID-ISLAND NATURE TRAIL

[Fig. 21(13)] This short but interesting nature trail that crosses the southern end of the island allows access to mid-island forest habitat and the wildlife it supports. This area can be inundated with water during wet seasons and insect repellant is strongly recommended. Bikes are allowed on the trail, but nature lovers may prefer to enjoy the surroundings at a slower pace.

Hikers cross a dune ridge before descending into a lower area of mixed maritime forest of live oak, pine, and cedar. The understory is populated with saw palmetto, wax myrtle, sparkleberry, and beautyberry. Muscadine vines, with their grapelike fruit, cling to trees and shrubs. Very interesting are 15-foot-tall saw palmettos, noticed by naturalist and author Taylor Schoettle, that grow nearly as upright as a tree about 35 yards from the entrance. Palmettos, with their fan-shaped leaves, usually creep along the surface of the ground. As the hiker approaches Riverview Drive, the canopy opens up and pine, cedar snags, and cabbage palms are more prevalent. Here the quiet observer may see deer, turkeys, or quail that remain from the island's service as a hunting plantation for the rich. At the end of the trail, walk north to a freshwater marshy area where marsh plants and frogs are common.

Trail: 0.2 mile one-way made of shells and dirt. Trailhead is across from Summer Waves waterpark on the west and between the Holiday Inn and Ramada on the east.

Directions: From Brunswick, travel south on US 17, cross Sidney Lanier Bridge. At causeway, turn left toward Jekyll Island. Cross Ben Fortson causeway, and turn right on South Beachview Drive. Trailhead is between Holiday Inn and Ramada. Park in either parking lot.

COASTAL ENCOUNTERS NATURE CENTER

[Fig. 21(9)] If Jekyll Island is an outdoor classroom, the teachers are based out of here. Coastal Encounters Nature Center has two centers, one on St. Simons in the historic Coast Guard Station and one here in the location of the closed Waterskipark. The work done here is extremely valuable if you love the Georgia coast. Environmental education plays an important role in generating understanding and political support for protection of Georgia's sensitive natural areas.

The Jekyll center has 12 aquariums featuring local wildlife, including baby loggerheads, and many nature programs geared for children and adults. Travelers with an interest in the island's natural history and environments should stop in and get acquainted with the animals and programs. Summer science camp for children age 7–12 helps open younger minds to the world around them with hands-on educational programs. Other programs include stargazing, family boat trips, all-ages beach and marsh ecology walks, and kayak excursions with experienced biologists that are a great way to learn coastal ecology. (*See* also Nature Tours and Sea Turtle Watches on Jekyll Island, page 271.)

The Coastal Encounters Jekyll office fronts a 17-acre man-made lake that was part of the 1968 effort to build a marina on the island. The lake was to be used to osmotically kill unwanted saltwater organisms on the hulls of yachts, and the marina site, located south of the lake, was dredged to create a 36-acre marina for yachts. However, nature is hard to control, and silt quickly filled in the marina site and salt water seeped into the freshwater lake. The lake was then used as a waterpark, where tourists were pulled on water skis by a towing contraption.

Today, the lake is home to alligators, snakes, frogs, turtles, and fish such as croaker and drum. Raccoons and deer are local residents. Wading birds commonly seen feeding in the shallower areas of the pond include egrets, herons, and wood storks. Many types of migrating

PIGNUT HICKORY
(*Carya glabra*)

Jekyll Island

The 5,700-acre island, with 8 miles of beach and 4,400 acres of uplands, supports every kind of natural community found on a Georgia island, thus creating an outdoor classroom for the study of the island flora and fauna.

Brunswick

341

27

Andrews
Island

17

Brunswick
Port of
Entry

25

Sydney
Lanier
Bridge

520

BRUNSWICK RIVER

Jointer
Island

St. Simons Island

ST. SIMONS SOUND

ATLANTIC OCEAN

N

North End Beach

1

2

Clam Creek Rd

3

Claflin

Maurice

4

Riverview Drive

Beachview Drive

Jekyll
Island

Old Plantation

Capt. Wylly Rd

Jekyll Island Causeway

520

5

7   13

6

Shell Rd.

14

JOINTER CREEK

JOINTER CREEK

JEKYLL CREEK

Fortson Pkwy

8

Mountain St

S. Beachview

9

Black
Hammock

LITTLE SATILLA RIVER

JEKYLL
SOUND

10   11

12

South
Beach

ST. ANDREW SOUND

1	Fishing Pier
2	Clam Creek Picnic Area
3	Jekyll Island Campground
4	Horton Ruins & Trails
5	Jekyll Island Authority (Crane Cottage)
6	Jekyll Wharf Marina
7	Jekyll Island Club Historic District
8	Jekyll Harbor Marina
9	Coastal Encounters Nature Center
10	St. Andrews Picnic Area
11	Glory Boardwalk
12	South Dunes Picnic Area
13	Mid-Island Nature Trail
14	Duck Pond Bike Path
~	Marsh

Ref: Delorme Georgia Atlas and Gazetteer

waterfowl rest on the surface. A nature walk is found on the property and is used in the educational programs.

Directions: From Brunswick, travel south on US 17, cross Sidney Lanier Bridge. At causeway, turn left toward Jekyll Island. Continue across causeway. After collection station, turn right on South Riverview Drive. Coastal Encounters is on the right.

Activities: Nature programs, hiking, kayaking.

Dates: Open daily.

Facilities: Aquariums, lake, nature trail.

Fees: Small donation requested.

Closest town: Jekyll Island.

For more information: Coastal Encounters Nature Center, 100 South Riverview Drive, Jekyll Island, GA 31527. Email: coastalencounter@mindspring.com Phone 635-9102.

JEKYLL HARBOR MARINA

[Fig. 21(8)] Seen on the right as you cross the causeway is Jekyll's most fully equipped marina. The restaurant, **SeaJay's**, is located here, as well as boat rentals, food and drinks, gas and oil, bait and tackle, forklift hoist, diesel, telephone, pool, spa, showers, laundry, picnic area, and rental bikes. Located down Harbor Road off South Riverview Drive. Phone 635-3137.

Jekyll Island: Historic District and Northern Area

THE JEKYLL ISLAND CLUB NATIONAL HISTORIC DISTRICT

[Fig. 21(7)] History buffs will enjoy the 200-acre Jekyll Island Club National Historic District, a collection of 33 buildings constructed by America's richest families from the late 1800s to early 1900s. Some buildings are open for overnight stays and tours, or have been converted into shops. Judging by early photos, the area is probably more beautiful today than at any time in its past as the landscaping has had time to grow in, with beautiful live oaks festooned with Spanish moss, 100-year-old cabbage palms, pines, flowering oleander, and azaleas.

The club was established to provide a pressure-free retreat where millionaires and their families could enjoy outdoor recreation such as hunting, fishing, golfing, tennis, boating, swimming, and biking during winter months. Driving newfangled motorcars on the beach was another popular activity. Between 1886 and 1928, members built "cottages," which were more like mansions, in styles ranging from informal Shingle to formal Italian Renaissance Revival with expensive furnishings and indoor swimming pools and tennis courts. This was the period in American history of rapid industrialization, when vast fortunes were being made and income tax had yet to be invented. Members such as Morgan, Vanderbilt, Astor, Gould, Rockefeller, McCormick, Baker, Biddle, Whitney, Armour, Crane, Goodyear, Pulitzer, Macy, and Bliss controlled one-sixth of the entire U.S. economy. Rest and relaxation may have been the goal, but the club members managed to conduct some business including the development of the Aldrich Plan in 1910, which led to the formation of the Federal Reserve System. In 1915, the island participated in the first transcontinental telephone call across the U.S. In 1899, a secret meeting was held with U.S. President William McKinley and his rival, the speaker of the house, to determine who would be president in the next election. A Brunswick reporter learned the details of the meeting and wired it around the world, which broke up the meeting and caused a political scandal. McKinley won re-election and Thomas Reed was ousted as speaker.

At the height of its popularity, the village was a self-sufficient compound that was supported by artesian wells, an electric power generator, and an infirmary with an on-call doctor. A seasonal staff maintained game on the island, and chefs used the island's gardens, dairy, oyster beds, fishing grounds, and terrapin pens. The stock market crash of 1929 started an era of decline for the club, which closed after 55 years during World War II and was purchased by the state. In 1979, the area was designated a National Historic District, and historic preservation of the cottages is ongoing.

The area and cottages have many fascinating features and stories to tell that are beyond the scope of this book. It is recommended that history buffs visit the Jekyll Island Museum and take a tour of the district, which includes several interesting shops and art galleries. The tram tours are twice a day, take an hour and a half, and include access to three historic buildings. The area can be walked or biked for those who want to explore the area on their own. Some of the buildings are available for rent by large groups. The museum is located in the Club Stables on Stable Road. See lodging and restaurants on Jekyll Island for information about the Grand Dining Room and Jekyll Island Club Hotel.

Directions: From Brunswick, travel south on US 17, cross Sidney Lanier Bridge. At causeway, turn left and cross causeway to Jekyll Island. After collection station, follow signs to the historic district. Turn right onto Stable Road and proceed approximately 0.5 mile to Museum Visitors Center on right.

Activities: Historic touring, shopping, biking.

Dates: Historic district is open daily to the public.

Facilities: Lodging, restaurants, restrooms, shops, museum. (See lodging and restaurants on Jekyll Island, page 270.)

Fees: Rates vary. Call phone numbers listed below.

Closest town: Jekyll Island.

For more information: Museum Visitor Center/Tours: phone 635-2762. Carriage Tours: phone 635-9500. Historic Structure Rental: phone 635-2119. Jekyll Island Welcome Center, PO Box 13186, Jekyll Island, GA 31527. Phone (877) 453-5955.

JEKYLL WHARF MARINA

[Fig. 21(6)] Of Jekyll's two marinas, this is the historic wharf built in 1886 by the island's millionaires for their expensive yachts. J.P. Morgan, who anchored his 304-foot *Corsair II* in the channel, was asked about the cost of this fine pleasurecraft, which generated his famous reply, "If you have to consider the cost you have no business with a yacht." The wharf is located in the historic district off Pier Road. A seafood restaurant, **Latitude 31**, offers "fine dining in a casual atmosphere" on the wharf. Open for dinner. Phone 635-3800. Amenities offered here are gas and oil, floating docks, food, soft drinks, and ice. Phone 635-3152.

DUCK POND BIKE PATH

[Fig. 21(14)] A less than 1-mile path connecting the historic district with the Ben Fortson Parkway is popular with bird watchers and naturalists. The trail runs from the intersection of Shell and Stable roads to beyond the gas station on Ben Fortson Parkway. Passing through marsh and oak-pine forest, the path runs on top of an old dike for a view of marshes and uplands until it ends at a road that connects with the parkway. The first part of the trail, according to Schoettle, runs along the natural border of the Pleistocene uplands to the north and the intermittent wetlands of the Holocene recurved-spit system to the south. Duck Pond, to the east, is a dike-controlled pond that was created by the millionaires for duck hunting. Because of the variety of habitats, the area is good for wildlife watching. Look for alligator "slides," where mashed down marsh grasses reveal the activities of these ancient reptiles.

Trail: 1-mile path.

Directions: On Ben Fortson Parkway, look for trail head on left just past gas station.

CLAM CREEK PICNIC AREA, FISHING PIER, NORTH END BEACH, HORTON RUINS, AND NORTH BEACH PICNIC AREA

[Fig. 21(2)] In a beautiful natural setting of woodlands, beach, inland salt marsh, and marsh hammock, this area offers one of three picnicking facilities on the island with a covered fishing pier that extends out into St. Simons Sound. Bird watchers, bikers, and hikers have much to explore in this area, which is conveniently located near Jekyll's campground and historic ruins to the south. Horseback rides also start from here.

Clam Creek Road winds through a young mixed oak-saw palmetto forest along the top of an old dune ridge that separates Jekyll's western salt marshes from the meandering Clam Creek. This thin peninsula is a Pleistocene fragment that is threatened by oxbows from Clam Creek to the north. The fishing pier extends from the end of the picnic area into the Brunswick River and St. Simons Sound. Container ships entering the Brunswick Harbor pass close to the pier, evidence of the proximity of the artificially deep channel. Structures have been sunk nearby to create a more suitable habitat for fish species. Fishermen catch flounder, trout, crabs, and other species here [Fig. 21(1)]. The bridge over Clam Creek is another popular spot for fishermen who seek fish, crab, and shrimp that travel the currents between the marsh and Brunswick River. Sharks are caught off the northern end of the island. On the beach, seining is popular, and the nets pull in a variety of species, including flounder, mullet, croakers, hogchokers, whiting, menhaden, pompano, and seatrout, as well as invertebrates such as blue crabs, white and brown shrimp, whelks, oyster drill, and jellyfish.

A hiking/biking path goes north from the end of the picnic area, crosses Clam Creek, and splits into two trails that cross land that is a remaining fragment of Holocene dunes that have been eroding southward. Each trail is approximately 1 mile in length. The northernmost trail, suitable for hiking, follows along North End Beach before turning south along the southern border of a second marsh and continuing to the northeastern side of the island.

North End Beach, best walked at low tide, shows dramatic evidence of erosion, with the exposed roots of dead, decorticated oaks and pines producing a boneyard beach that wraps around to the eastern side of the island. The oaks have flat root mats and the pines have deep, vertical roots. During storms, the heavier oaks tend to tip over and remain, while the pines snap off at the roots and are carried off by the tides. Off the north end is the Brunswick shipping channel, which is annually dredged to allow deep-draft container ships to enter Brunswick Harbor. Geologists believe the dredged channel is responsible for the loss of more than 1,000 feet of beach since the early 1900s when dredging began. Sand drifting southward from islands across the sound is trapped in this channel rather than renourishing the northern beaches. The result is erosion with no accretion, and the Holocene fragment with its natural communities continues to adapt and change.

After North End Beach, the path turns south to border a marsh that experiences poor tidal circulation, thus supporting high marsh and marsh border flora that is less tolerant of salt water, such as the yellow aster-flowered sea oxeye and dark needle rush. On the other side of the marsh, which is accessible by beach during lower tides, is a fascinating and beautiful boneyard beach that reveals the erosion that has occurred on the northern end of the island.

The southern trail, suitable for biking, follows the eastern side of Clam Creek to the North Beach Picnic Area. The bike path follows the marsh, where one can observe alligators, otters, deer, and snakes, along with bird life such as egrets, herons, painted buntings, yellow-throated warblers, clapper rails, and kingfishers. The path dissects some pine and cedar hammocks that are havens for wildlife, before reaching the North Beach Picnic Area. This site was closed in 1986 due to erosion problems. Today, it is the best example of a boneyard beach on a developed island off the Georgia coast. Some exploration will reveal how currents and tides are stripping away soil and undercutting and killing a maritime forest that tumbles onto the sands to create a beautiful boneyard beach. If the erosion continues, Clam Creek will connect with the Atlantic on the eastern side and create an island out of the Holocene northern portion of Jekyll.

Trail: One trail leaves from the north end of Clam Creek and splits to become two trails, each about 1 mile long. Both connect with the abandoned North Beach Picnic Area located north of Villas By The Sea. The northernmost trail is more suitable for hiking, the southernmost trail is best for biking.

Directions: From Brunswick, travel south on US 17, cross Sidney Lanier Bridge. At causeway, turn left toward Jekyll Island. Continue across Ben Fortson Parkway to dead end. Go left. Clam Creek Picnic Area, Fishing Pier, and North End Beach are located on the north end of island on right. The abandoned site of the North Beach Picnic Area is on the eastern side of the island, just past Villas By The Sea.

Activities: Picnicking, swimming, fishing, bird-watching, beachcombing, and nature study.
Dates: Open daily.
Facilities: Covered fishing pier, picnic tables, nature trail. Campground is across the street.
Fees: None.
Closest town: Jekyll Island.
For more information: Jekyll Island Convention and Visitors Bureau, PO Box 13186, Jekyll Island, GA 31527. Phone (877) 453-5955.

HORTON RUINS AND TRAIL

[Fig. 21(4)] One-half mile south of Clam Creek Road on the eastern side of North Riverview Drive are the remains of the Horton House. The two-story tabby structure, one of the oldest in the state, was built in 1742 after Horton's original structure was destroyed by retreating Spanish, who had just been defeated by Oglethorpe in the Battle of Bloody Marsh. An exceptionally large red bay occupies the northwest corner of the house. Across the street in a peaceful setting of cedars, oaks and pines is the du Bignon family cemetery. The du Bignons owned the island for nearly a century before selling it to the Jekyll Island Club millionaires. Major Horton Road, on the north side of the property, connects with Beachview Drive on the eastern side of the island. This road becomes a trail that passes freshwater sloughs and a pond open to freshwater fishing.

Horton Ruins.

Maj. William Horton served as forward lookout on Jekyll Island for Gen. James Oglethorpe during the British colonial period. Horton, who commanded English forces after Oglethorpe returned to England, is best known for having the first brewery in Georgia, the ruins of which are seen south of this site on the western side of Riverview Drive.

Trail: 1-mile.
Directions: From Brunswick, travel south on US 17, cross Sidney Lanier Bridge. At causeway, turn left toward Jekyll Island. Continue across Ben Fortson Parkway to dead end. Go left. Horton House Ruins and trailhead are on left past Clam Creek Picnic Area.

LODGING ON JEKYLL ISLAND

The most famous lodging on the island is the **Jekyll Island Club Hotel**, located in the historic district on the marsh side of the island. Built in 1886, the hotel features turn-of-the-century charm with modern amenities. In 1985, the four-story Queen Anne–styled clubhouse of the megarich was refurbished to the tune of $17 million—25 times more than what the entire island sold for in 1947. The hotel has to be the croquet capital of Georgia. *Moderate to expensive. (800) 535-9547.*

Other lodging on the island is located along Beachview Drive, which provides easy access to the beach. Most of the following motels are moderately priced and offer rooms with views of the ocean, bike rentals, golf and tennis packages, swimming pools, restaurants, and lounges. Some also offer villas with multiple bedrooms and kitchens. Ask for amenities when you call. **Clarion Resort Buccaneer**, *(800) 253-5955*; **Comfort Inn Island Suites**, *800-204-0202*; **Days Inn Oceanfront Resort**, *(800) 325-2525*; **Holiday Inn Beach Resort**, *(800) 7-Jekyll*; **Beachview Club**, *800-299-2228*; **Jekyll Inn**, *(800) 736-1046*; **Ramada Inn**, *(800) 835-2110*; **The Seafarer Inn & Suites**, *(800) 281-4446*; **Villas By The Sea Resort Hotel and Conference Center**, *(800) 841-6262*. For home rentals, call **Jekyll Realty Company**, *635-3301* or **Parker-Kaufman Realtors**, *635-2512*.

RESTAURANTS AND NIGHT LIFE ON JEKYLL ISLAND

One of the attractive characteristics of Jekyll is the lack of billboards and tacky restaurants lining the roadways—no McDonald's here. This doesn't mean the island doesn't have anywhere to eat. It's just that the island's restaurants are not very obvious because most are built into resort hotels. Night life is somewhat limited as well to hotel lounges.

The most famous, expensive, and best restaurant on the island is the **Grand Dining Room** at the Jekyll Island Club Hotel. The dramatic, colonnaded dining room is indeed grand, with a huge fireplace and view of the swimming pool, and the shine and sparkle of silver and crystal. Service is excellent as hungry diners are served low-country cuisine featuring Georgia fish, shrimp, and quail along with veal and beef options. Informal dress is allowed for breakfast and lunch, but jackets requested for men at night. *Moderate to expensive. 635-2600.* A more casual and limited low country option for lunch is **SeaJay's Waterfront Café & Pub**, located in the Jekyll Harbor Marina. Here you can get the low-country boil, Brunswick stew, peel and eat shrimp or a barbecue sandwich. Entertainment on Fridays and Saturdays. *Inexpensive. 635-3200.* **Latitude 31** is a seafood restaurant with a marsh view at Jekyll Wharf. *Moderate. 635-3800.* Other dining options on the island include **Remington's Bar and Grill**, with a Saturday night prime rib and seafood buffet. *Moderate. 635-3311.* **The Italian Fisherman**, features Italian food, seafood, and beef. *Moderate. 635-2531.* **Blackbeard's Seafood Restaurant and Lounge**, fresh local seafood. *Moderate. 635-3522.* **Zachary's Seafood House** serves seafood, steaks, chicken, and sandwiches. *Moderate. 635-3128.*

NATURE TOURS AND SEA TURTLE WATCHES ON JEKYLL ISLAND

During summer, the best night life on the island emerges from the ocean, crawls up on the beach, buries a nest of eggs, and returns to the sea. Many an environmentalist has been born after witnessing the miracle that occurs on the beaches of Jekyll every summer from June to mid-August. Jekyll Island offers nighttime sea turtle watches that let you discover (without disturbing) mother sea turtles building nests on the beach. Any age is welcome with a parent, and children over 12 can participate unattended with parental permission. Call The Sea Turtle Project at 635-2284. Guided boat tours and nature walks on the beach and marsh are also offered. Call 635-9102 for a schedule of events.

BIKING AND HORSEBACK RIDING ON JEKYLL ISLAND

Jekyll is best seen on the seat of a bike, where one can pedal the 22 miles of trails while enjoying the natural beauty of the island. Rentals are available at hotels, the campground, the mini-golf course, the Jekyll Harbor Marina, and other locations. Be sure to ask for a bike map. Horseback riding is a fun and exciting way to see the island. Rides depart from Clam Creek Picnic Area on the north end of Jekyll. Reservations are required. Call 635-9500.

FISHING AND BOATING ON JEKYLL ISLAND

Jekyll Island's beaches are open to surf casting but the best saltwater fishing is on the island's south end at the St. Andrews Picnic Area. Freshwater fishing is allowed at two lakes: one behind the outdoor amphitheater adjacent to the historic district and the one across from Villas By The Sea on the northern end. At the fishing pier at the northern end, anglers catch flounder, trout, and other species. Fishing rods can be rented at **Maxwell's Variety Store**, 16 Beachview Drive, 635-2205, and bait and tackle is available at Jekyll's marinas. For fishing charters, dolphin cruises, and water tours, contact **Jekyll Harbor Marina** at 635-3137 or **Jekyll Wharf/Water Taxi** at 635-3152. See also Clam Creek Picnic Area and Fishing Pier, page 267; Jekyll Harbor Marina, page 265; and Jekyll Island Club National Historic District, page 265.

CAMPGROUNDS ON JEKYLL ISLAND

See Campgrounds in Glynn County, page 221.

GOLF AND TENNIS ON JEKYLL ISLAND

Jekyll Island offers 63 holes of exciting public golf at four courses: **Great Dunes 9**, which retains some of the original holes of the millionaires' course; **Oleander**, an 18-hole gem; **Pine Lakes**, the longest course on the island; and **Indian Mounds**, with wide fairways and spectacular scenery. A driving range, pro shop, and restaurant and lounge are part of the golf complex. For rates and tee times, call 635-2368 (for Great Dunes 9, call 635-2170).

Jekyll Island Tennis Center features 13 clay courts, 7 lighted, for tennis buffs. The center was selected by *Tennis Magazine* as one of the 25 best Municipal Tennis Facilities in the country. Call 635-3154 for rates.

WATERPARKS AND MINIATURE GOLF ON JEKYLL ISLAND

What's the beach without miniature golf and waterslides for the kids? Jekyll truly has it all. Miniature golf: phone 635-2648. Summer Waves Waterpark: phone 635-2074.

Camden County and St. Marys

The major attractions in fast-growing Camden County are Cumberland Island National Seashore, the St. Marys National Historic District, and Crooked River State Park. Visiting Cumberland Island requires boat transportation. Having a tremendous economic impact on the area and open to occasional tours is the Kings Bay Naval Submarine Base, home of the technologically advanced Trident nuclear submarine fleet. The county also boasts three good-eating festivals: the Woodbine Crawfish Festival, the Kingsland Catfish Festival, and the St. Marys Rock Shrimp Festival (See Appendix D).

ST. MARYS

[Fig. 22] A quaint river town perched on Buttermilk Bluff, St. Marys has served as the location of an Indian village, colonial settlement, and, more recently, a U.S. Naval base. One of the oldest towns in Georgia, it boasts a national historic district and functions as the embarkation point for Cumberland Island. Visitors may want to first buy tickets for their Cumberland Island trip, then spend time in the historic district until it's time to board the ferry.

Some historic accounts say St. Marys was the site of a Timucuan Indian village, *Tlathlothlaguphta*, which translates to "rotten fish." It is believed that French Captain Jean Ribault visited this village in 1562 and sailed up the St. Marys River, which he named the Seine. In 1568, the Spanish founder of St. Augustine, Pedro Menendez de Aviles, established a mission on Amelia Island called Santa Maria de Guadeloupe.

During the Revolutionary War, the British established a fort on Point Peter called Fort Tonyn, which controlled the southern part of Georgia for two years. Built at the junction of Peter Creek and the St. Marys River in 1776, the fort was repeatedly attacked by American forces and eventually abandoned.

In 1787, Jacob Weed, owner of a 1,672-acre tract of land near the river, sold shares of the property to 19 other shareholders for $38, which entitled them to four blocks of high land, marsh property, and a share of the commons. Surveyor James Finley laid out the town the next year and it still has the same configuration and uses many of the original 20 founders' names. First named Saint Patrick, it was changed in 1792 to Saint Marys, an anglicized version of the Amelia Island mission name.

While Florida was under the control of the Spanish from 1783–1821, St. Marys prospered as the southernmost seaport in the U.S., as many agricultural and timber products were shipped from tidewater plantations and timberlands located upstream. Shipbuilding and sawmills were important industries. Several historic buildings survive from this period, including the 1801 Clark home, visited by Aaron Burr and General Winfield Clark, and the First Presbyterian Church, the third oldest church in Georgia, built in 1808.

Other early settlers of this region were French Acadians, who were driven from their Canadian homelands in the middle of the eighteenth century. Their names are found on tombstones in historic Oak Grove Cemetery.

As a border town, St. Marys occasionally suffered raids from the south by smugglers and hostile Indians who were encouraged by the Spanish in Florida. One local legend tells how smugglers stole a horse, carried it to the belfry of the First Presbyterian Church, and tied a bell rope around the horse's neck. The horse tried to free

Pecans and St. Marys

The pecan tree, a fixture in Southern agriculture, cooking, landscape, and culture, had its beginnings in St. Marys. Captain Samuel F. Flood found pecan nuts floating at sea and brought them home to St. Marys in 1840. His wife and a neighbor planted the nuts, and they produced large, heavy mast-bearing trees. From these nuts, more trees were planted and eventually pecan trees spread across the southeastern states. These trees have led to other varieties grown on farms across the Sunbelt. Today approximately 150,000 tons are grown annually in the U.S., worth millions of dollars.

itself, causing the bell to ring and diverting the town's attention from the activities of smugglers who were trying to avoid payment of duty on their goods. During the War of 1812, the town was attacked and captured by the British, who occupied the town until they learned the war was over.

St. Marys was abandoned during the Civil War, after which the town went into general decline due to the devastation of the southern economy. Adding to the town's stagnation were inland railroads, which successfully competed with shipping as a mode of transporting goods. The town was helped when it became the county seat from 1871 to 1923, then started to flourish when a large pulp mill was built in the 1940s, bringing better wages to locals. The selection of Kings Bay as a submarine base for the U.S. Atlantic Trident fleet gave the community a tremendous economic boost that continues today. The creation of the Cumberland Island National Seashore in the 1970s and the growth of ecotourism have brought additional prosperity to Camden County during the 1980s and 1990s, making it one of the fastest growing areas in the U.S. St. Marys is now known as "The Gateway to Cumberland Island."

ST. MARYS NATIONAL HISTORIC DISTRICT, WELCOME CENTER, WATERFRONT AND PIER, CUMBERLAND FERRY

[Fig. 22(1)] The National Historic District, recognized in 1976, has more than 30 buildings and an old cemetery. Bounded by Alexander and Norris streets, Waterfront Road, and Oak Grove Cemetery, the history lover will find much of interest in the nineteenth and early twentieth century homes located here. Of special interest is the

St. Marys Welcome Center (Orange Hall).

beautiful Orange Hall, built in 1829, which houses the St. Marys Welcome Center. Historic site tours begin at Orange Hall. Across the street is the graceful First Presbyterian Church, built in 1808. Start your tours from the St. Marys Welcome Center. On the waterfront are the St. Marys Pavilion, Fishing Dock, and Boat Ramp, as well as the National Park Service building and dock where nature lovers book trips on the *Cumberland Queen* to Cumberland Island (*see* Cumberland Island, page 279). Fishing and crabbing is allowed from the pier.

Directions: I-95 to Exit 2/3. Go east on GA 40 to St. Marys Street. Go right on Osborne. Welcome center is located at corner of Conyers and Osborne.

Activities: Historical touring, fishing, tours of historic district. Ferry to Cumberland Island.

Facilities: Museum, restrooms, historic district, fishing pier, gift shop.

Dates: Open Monday through Saturday 9–5, Sundays 1–5.

Closest town: St. Marys.

For more information: Orange Hall/St. Marys Welcome Center, PO Box 1291, St. Marys, GA 31558. Phone 882-4000.

ST. MARYS SUBMARINE MUSEUM

[Fig. 22(2)] Located on the St. Marys Waterfront, the Submarine Museum tells the story of the invention, development, and military record of the submarine. Military and naval buffs will appreciate the storehouse of models, displays, exhibits, plaques, movies, and other memorabilia relating to the stealthy fighting ships. A working periscope allows viewers to spy on the St. Marys River area, and one section commemorates the eight submariners who received the Medal of Honor. Situated across from the Cumberland Island Ferry, the museum provides an interesting diversion for tourists waiting to depart or just returning from Cumberland Island.

Dates: Open Tuesday through Saturday 10–4, Sunday 1–5.

Facilities: Restrooms, gift shop.

Fees: A small fee is charged for admission.

For more information: St. Marys Submarine Museum, 102 St. Marys Street West, St. Marys, GA 31558. Phone 882-2782.

St. Marys & Camden County Lodging, Camping, and Restaurants

LODGING IN ST. MARYS/CAMDEN COUNTY

Two bed and breakfasts and one hotel are great places to stay in the quaint historic district. **The Riverview Hotel**, 105 Osborne Street, built in 1916, has a funky charm that would not be out of place in New Orleans or Key West. One expects to see Hemingway leaning over the veranda telling fish stories to a friend in the street. An excellent restaurant, Seagles, is located in the building, and you only have to cross the street to fish off the pier or board the Cumberland Ferry. A small lounge is a great place to rest your sore legs and nurse your sunburn after an expedition on Cumberland. Be sure to ask for a room that opens out on the veranda. *Moderate. 882-3242.* Two B&Bs within walking distance of each other in the historic district are good alternatives to the Riverview Hotel. I recommend reviewing both before making a decision. **Spencer House Inn**, 200 Osborne Street, was built in 1872 by Capt. William T. Spencer and was regarded as the finest hotel in St. Marys and southeast Georgia. It has a veranda and 14 beautifully furnished rooms, each with private bath. *Moderate. 882-1872.* **The Goodbread House**, 209 Osborne Street, is a smaller, 1870s historic home with an eclectic charm. All the rooms offered here have fireplaces and private baths. *Moderate. 882-7490.*

Chain motel lodging and many chain restaurants are found along GA 40 (also known as Kingsland-St. Marys Road), at Exit 2/3 and Interstate 95. There are at least 12 choices here, including **Best Western**, *(800) 728-7666*; **Comfort Inn**, *729-6979*; **Holiday Inn**, *(800) 322-6866*; and **Quality Inn & Suites**, *729-4363*. (*See* Crooked River State Park, page 276.)

Cabin Bluff, run by the Sea Island Company of The Cloister fame, is a rustic retreat on the Cumberland River that has a view of Cumberland Island to the east and 50,000 acres of natural surroundings to the west. The retreat features the historic main lodge and six cabins that can host up to 32 people, who have hunting, fishing, horseback riding, and other outdoor recreation offerings at their beck and call. A 3,000-square-foot conference center is available to those who want to pretend they are working. The property was owned and developed by Detroit automobile millionaire Howard Coffin, who developed Sapelo and Sea Island. It was used as a hunting preserve by Coffin's Cloister and Sapelo guests, until he went broke in the 1930s and was forced to sell it to the Brunswick Pulp and Paper Company in order to hold onto Sea Island. Sight-seeing is available aboard the *Zapala*, one of the first gasoline yachts built before World War I. Coffin had the boat built to his specifications, which resulted in a 124-foot vessel, weighing 159 gross tons with a cruising speed of 15 knots. *Expensive. (800) 732-4752.*

CAMPGROUNDS IN ST. MARYS/CAMDEN COUNTY

Near Interstate 95, one option is located at Exit 3/7 with access to Harriett's Bluff and Cabin Bluff, and two options are located at Exit 1/1. **King George RV Resort**, Exit 3/7, West Harriett's Bluff. New clubhouse, pull throughs, full hookups, bathhouse, fishing in Crooked River. *(800) 852-1206.* **Country Oaks Campground & RV Park**, Exit 1/1, 0.25-mile west, general store, water and sewer, pull throughs, laundry, bathhouse. *729-6212.* **K.O.A. Campground**, Exit 1/1, West Scrubby Bluff Road. Daily, weekly, monthly rentals, daily cabin rentals. Full hookups, country store, laundry, bathhouse, and pool. *(800) KOA-3232.* (*See also* Crooked River State Park, below.)

RESTAURANTS IN ST. MARYS/CAMDEN COUNTY

Several good choices are found in the St. Marys historic district that are convenient to the Cumberland Island Ferry. **Seagles Waterfront Café**. 105 Osborne St. Located inside the Riverview Hotel is a charming restaurant that uses fresh local seafood in its delicious recipes. Rock shrimp, which are caught in boats located steps away, are served fried, blackened, grilled, or in Rock Shrimp Diane, which features rock shrimp sautéed in Cajun spices and mushrooms served over pasta. If fish is your fancy, try the lemon butter grouper, a fresh filet of grouper sautéed in a lemon butter sauce topped with grilled pecans. Open Monday through Saturday for dinner. *Moderate. 882-4187.* **Trolleys Food and Spirits**. 104 W. St. Marys. This is a casual, wings-nachos-burgers kind of place, with a deck across from the ferry and river. *Inexpensive. 882-1525.* **Lang's Marina Restaurant**. 307 W. St. Marys Street. Enjoy fried shrimp and other seafood dishes with a view of the marsh. Lunch and dinner. Tuesday-Saturday. *Moderate. 882-4432.* If you are tired of seafood, a very good Georgia barbecue choice just off I-95 is **Jack's Famous Wood-Cooked Bar-B-Q**. If smoke is pouring out of the building, then pull in for some tasty pork, ribs, chicken, or smoked turkey. Jack Sutton for 30 years has used a combination of live oak and hickory for true low-country flavor. The Brunswick stew is homemade and delicious. Open for lunch and dinner 7 days a week. *Inexpensive.* Two locations: Exit 3/7 (Harriet's Bluff) next to Shell Station, *729-1500*; and Exit 4/14 (Woodbine) near Sunshine Plaza, *576-4073.*

Crooked River State Park

[Fig. 18(5), Fig. (22(5)] Crooked River is a 500-acre state park that is popular for saltwater fishing, boating, and camping. Fishermen try their luck for speckled trout, channel bass, sheepshead, drum, and striped bass in the Crooked River, or navigate 8 miles downstream to the Cumberland Sound. The less ambitious can fish, crab, or shrimp from the dock. Naturalists looking for a place to relax before riding the ferry to Cumberland Island may want to consider this well-equipped state park, that features 60 tent, trailer, and RV sites, 11 cottages, along with a swimming pool, miniature golf, playground, and nature trail for antsy youngsters. Hikers can explore the roughly 2-miles of nature trails, which wind through a mix of natural communities including pine-palmetto, live-oak hammock, and marsh that support a variety of wildlife. Birding is good here, and the park is on the Colonial Coast Birding Trail. Picnic sites offer a refreshing panorama of the marsh and river, where wildlife is observed performing their prehistoric roles in the rich estuarine zone. Motionless blue herons stalk marine life in shallower waters, and bottlenosed dolphins hunt the deeper currents for menhaden. A historic site located on the approach to the park boasts the oldest industrial ruins in the state.

Two nature trails begin as one near cottage 11, then split into two loops, each with its own distinct natural environment. A spur trail off one trail leads into marsh. Both coastal and woodland species of birds may be observed on the trails. From the trailhead, hikers walk through a mixed oak community with palmetto, bracken ferns, and wax myrtle. A sign pointing to the left marks the Sempervirens Trail, which leads into a mature live oak maritime forest, with Spanish moss, palmetto, wax myrtle, and muscadine. (*Sempervirens* is Latin for "everliving.") Large magnolias are evident, as well as occasional hickory, sweet gum, and pine. During summer, painted buntings and Eastern blue birds are seen in this subtropical broadleaf forest.

A spur off this loop leads to the *Spartina* coastal marsh, where marsh and wading birds such as clapper rails, blue herons, and great egrets may be observed on the ground, and gulls, terns, and osprey are spotted in the air. Deer, squirrels, and armadillos are the most common mammals, but quiet observers may spot a feral hog, bobcat, or fox.

The second nature trail, the Palmetto Trail, loops off the first and winds back to the trailhead, exposing hikers to a second type of coastal forest comprising southern pine and palmetto. Longleaf pine forests once covered the Coastal Plain of the southeastern U.S., but logging and fire suppression removed this predominant, fire-dependent ecosystem, which today is found only in a few relictual patches. This part of the park is not a pure example of that natural environment. Longleaf and slash pine are the dominant trees, and palmetto grows profusely in the understory. Fox squirrels, which prefer longleaf pine forests, are seen in this area, as well as threatened gopher tortoises that dig burrows in the sandy soil. If you hear a loud rustling sound in the palmetto thickets, it's probably an armadillo, an animal that has expanded its range into Georgia from Florida. White-tailed deer are also very common.

Located approximately 3 miles from the gate of the park on Spur 40 are the John H. McIntosh Tabby Sugar Works ruins. John Houstoun McIntosh, born in 1773 in McIntosh County, was greatly influenced by agrarian genius Thomas Spalding of Sapelo Island, and he established two plantations in Camden County to grow sugar cane, the most famous being New Canaan. He built the mill in 1825, and it was called the first

FOX SQUIRREL
(*Sciurus niger*)
This is the largest tree squirrel in the U.S., with black fur and a white face.

Cumberland Island

Reached by ferry from St. Marys, Cumberland Island offers much to explore, including deserted beaches, sun-dappled maritime forests, shimmering freshwater lakes, golden marshes, and grand historic ruins.

SATILLA RIVER

CUMBERLAND RIVER

Lighthouse (abandoned)

Little Cumberland Island

Union Carbide Road

Forestview

INTRACOASTAL WATERWAY

The Settlement

High Point

Shellbine

North Cut Road

Union Carbide Road

Cabin Bluff

Brickhill Bluff

BRICKHILL RIVER

Table Point

Main Road

CROOKED RIVER

Plum Orchard

Yankee Paradise

ATLANTIC OCEAN

5

Hickory Hill

N

Spur 40

Stafford

The Chimneys

CUMBERLAND SOUND

Stafford Beach

1	St. Marys National Historic District, Welcome Center, Waterfront and Pier, Cumberland Ferry
2	St. Marys Submarine Museum
3	Sea Camp Dock
4	Dungeness Dock
5	Crooked River State Park
	Private Property
	Cumberland Island

Greyfield

Kings Bay Naval Station

4 Sea Camp Beach

40

Dunge-ness Ruins

3

St. Marys

1 **2**

Refuge Boundary

ST. MARYS RIVER

Pelican Banks

ST. MARYS ENTRANCE

Ref: Delorme Georgia Atlas and Gazetteer

Amelia Island

horizontal sugar mill worked by cattle. After his death, the plantation was sold to Colonel Hallowes, who changed the plantation's name to Bollingbrook. He continued sugar production, and also used the mill as a starch factory during the Civil War.

Trails: The 1.5-mile Palmetto Trail and 0.5-mile Sempervirens Nature Trail are connecting loops, leading from cottage 11.

Directions: I-95 to Exit 2/3. Go east on GA 40 approximately 4 miles. Turn left at Kings Bay Road. Proceed 4 miles to Kings Bay Submarine Base. Turn left at base entrance onto Spur 40 and proceed 2.5 miles to park entrance.

Activities: Fishing, boating, camping (primitive, intermediate, recreational vehicle), hiking, picnicking, shrimping, crabbing, canoeing, biking, miniature golf, nature study, historical touring, guided tours by prior arrangement.

Facilities: Boat ramp and fishing dock, 60 combination tent, trailer, and RV sites, full hookups, picnic tables, grills. 2 comfort stations with showers, toilets, electrical outlets, and laundry. 11 cottages with kitchens, fireplaces, heat and air conditioning. (Visitors may want to ask for one of the cottages that are located on the bluff overlooking the river.) Pioneer campground for organized groups and scouts. 5 picnic shelters and 1 group shelter. Historic site (sugar mill ruins), swimming pool, miniature golf, playground.

Dates: Open 7 days a week 7 a.m.–10 p.m.

Fees: Separate fees for camping, cottages, and pool. Parking fee for all vehicles. Call for fees: 882-5256. Camping reservations 30 days in advance; cottage reservations maximum 11 months in advance, recommended 60 days in advance. Phone 882-5256.

Closest town: St. Marys.

For more information: Crooked River State Park, Georgia Department of Natural Resources, 3092 Spur 40, St. Marys, GA 31558. Phone 882-5256. Reservations: Phone (800) 864-7275.

Cumberland Island National Seashore

Travelers looking for an experience of a lifetime should put beloved Cumberland Island at the top of their list. A national treasure, Cumberland Island is the most accessible of Georgia's "wild" barrier islands, and offers an unforgettable adventure for anyone who makes the journey. Reached by ferry from St. Marys, the island has much to explore, including deserted beaches, sun-dappled maritime forests, shimmering freshwater lakes, golden marshes, and grand historic ruins. With visitation limited to 300 people a day, hikers can experience the tranquility and solitude that is the hallmark of a visit to Cumberland.

Established as a national seashore in 1972, the island's scenic, historic, and natural qualities are protected and managed by the National Park Service from the northern tip of Little Cumberland Island to Pelican Banks on the southern end. Adding to the island's

Feral horses are a common sight on Cumberland Island.

protection was the designation of a large, central tract of forest and beach as a national wilderness in 1982. Small parts of the island still remain in private hands, and political struggles continue over the management and development of the island as a whole. While debates continue into the new millennium concerning historic preservation of crumbling properties, the use of motor vehicles, and other issues great and small, it appears that nothing can seriously threaten the beauty of Cumberland.

Cumberland is frequently described as the largest barrier island on the Georgia coast, an assertion that is both true and false. It certainly has the longest beach, with 17.5 miles, and the most upland acreage with 15,100, but it is third in acreage when marshlands are included in the total, with 23,000 acres on Cumberland, 25,000 acres on Ossabaw, and 27,630 acres on St. Simons. Roughly 90 percent of Cumberland is of Pleistocene age—approximately 35,000 years old. As an older island, Cumberland has richer soils and more diverse flora. The 10 percent of the island that is Holocene, or 5,000 years old, ranges from the eastern beach and dunes to the southern knob of the island. The island fronts the shoreline of Camden County, and off the northern end are St. Andrew and Jekyll sounds, fed by the Satilla River, and Jekyll Island. At its southern end are Cumberland Sound, fed by the St. Marys River, and Amelia Island.

Cumberland Island is larger than Manhattan Island, so there is much to explore. The island has two docks (each with a visitor center), a developed campground, and four primitive campgrounds. Roads traverse the island and are used as hiking trails. The ruins of Dungeness at the southern end are the most popular and easily accessed, but other historic structures are interesting to view, including Plum Orchard, which is open on Sundays, and First African Baptist Church at the northern end. Those looking for creature comforts in their lodging have one choice: Greyfield Inn.

CUMBERLAND ISLAND'S NATURAL FEATURES

Cumberland Island is not pristine, untouched wilderness. Its live oaks were cut for ship timbers, and land was cleared to grow sea island cotton and southern yellow pine. But the island has regenerated from many of these activities. Three major natural communities dominate the island with distinctly different assemblages of plants and animals: The western salt marsh, mid-island maritime forest, and eastern beach each have natural features that are fascinating to investigate.

The rich salt marsh is the first natural community visitors will encounter on their way to the island. Scientists believe marshlands are the most productive land acres on earth, and play a vital role in the nutrient cycle of the estuary. Not only do they decay and add nutrients to the food cycle of the marsh, but also trap river sediments and detritus flushed through the marsh by a combination of river currents and tides and act as a protective nursery for a wide variety of marine creatures. While the marsh appears to be a one-dimensional hedge that some giant has neatly pruned flat, it actually is teeming with creatures small and large. With their wealth of nutrients, marshlands support large populations of shellfish, fish, plants, and bird life. Raccoons, birds, and other animals come down from uplands to feed on crabs and shellfish, fiddler crabs scurry across mud flats, eating decaying vegetation, and wading birds are seen stalking fish and marsh creatures. Atlantic bottlenosed dolphins swim in the tidal rivers.

From the dock, the visitor can hike into an upland forest of oaks, pines, cedar, and saw palmetto. Most beautiful are the maritime forests of salt-pruned live oaks, draped in Spanish moss and muscadine vines, which form an unbroken green canopy that protects the visitor from the harsh rays of the sun. Raccoons can be observed resting on a soft garden of resurrection and shoelace ferns, mosses, and lichens that grow on the bent, trunk-sized limbs. Songbirds such as prothonotary warblers, cardinals, and yellow-throated and northern parula warblers flit from branch to branch in the denser foliage. Palmettos, with their fan-shaped leaves, add to the exotic, tropical feeling of the forest. Other trees making up the island's forests include willow oak, laurel oak, magnolia, red bay, cabbage palm, American holly, and several kinds of pines: slash, loblolly, pond, and longleaf. Deer, turkeys, squirrels, and armadillos are frequently seen crossing the sandy roads on the island. The quiet observer may catch a glimpse of the recently reintroduced bobcat.

In the lower areas between the older dune ridges are freshwater and brackish ponds where alligators, frogs, snakes, turtles, minks, and otters spend a large part of their lives. Cottonmouth snakes are common. The ponds serve as an important oasis for a wide variety of bird, mammal, and amphibian species that travel to the source of fresh water. The shallow, 83-acre Whitney Lake is one of the largest freshwater lakes on Georgia's barrier islands.

As one breaks out of the green dome of the forest onto the dunes and beach, it takes a moment to adjust to the blinding light reflected off the white sands of the dunes. Only the toughest plants, such as Russian thistle, sea oats, beach elder, and orach, have adapted to survive the shifting sands, salt spray, fierce winds, and desiccating sun of the dune and beach. One thing they can't survive is grazing by Cumberland's popular feral horses, which destroys the stability of the dunes and causes erosion. Dunes on Cumberland can be spectacular, with some as high as 40 feet. At the wrack line, ghost crabs pick over marsh reeds and other detritus that has floated in at high tide. Closer to the wash line, small creatures such as worms, mole crabs, and ghost shrimp live in burrows in the sand. Thousands of sandpipers, sanderlings and other shorebirds dodge waves as they probe for these tasty tidbits. During raptor migration in October, bird watchers may see a variety of hawks and peregrine falcons. Soaring above the beach and dunes may be vultures, hawks, and bald eagles. The entire island is on the Colonial Coast Birding Trail, as more than 277 species of birds have been identified on Cumberland Island. The island's long, deserted beaches are the most attractive on the Georgia coast to loggerhead turtles, which have averaged 198 nests a year in the last 10 years.

CUMBERLAND ISLAND'S HUMAN HISTORY

Archeologists believe Indians used Cumberland as a hunting and fishing ground as far back as 4,000 years ago. During the time of European colonization, at least seven Moca-ma Indian villages were located on the island, and 11 were located on the mainland opposite the island. When the Spanish arrived in 1566, they named the island *San Pedro* and constructed a garrison and mission at the southern end of the named *San Pedro de Mocama*, which remained in operation from 1587 to 1660. Another Spanish mission on Cumberland was Puturiba, which operated from 1595–1597. An additional mission was relocated from the North Newport River to the northern end of Cumberland from 1670–1684 named *San Phelipe*.

The Indians they met called the island *Missoe*, their word for sassafras. This name didn't last long after English Gen. James Oglethorpe arrived at the Georgia coast. Turning the custom upside down, the island was named by an Indian for an Englishman. Toona-howi, the young nephew of Chief Tomochichi who visited England with Oglethorpe, suggested the island be named for William Augustus, the 13-year old Duke of Cumber-land. An additional honor was a fort erected at the southern point of the island called Fort William, of which no trace remains today. Here Oglethorpe also established a hunting lodge he called Dungeness. At the northern end of the island, Oglethorpe built Fort St. Andrews, and for a decade a small village named Berrimacke existed near the fort. The forts were built to defend English settlements to the north from the Spanish in Florida. After defeating the Spanish in Battle of Bloody Marsh in 1742, the need for the forts evaporated, and the forts were abandoned and the village disappeared. The sea claimed Fort William, and most signs of Fort St. Andrews have been obliterated by time. In the 1760s, the island was divided into royal grants but saw little activity. When naturalist William Bartram visited the island in 1774, the island was mostly uninhabited.

Plum Orchard is an 1898 Georgian-revival mansion open to tours.

Development of the island started in earnest after the American Revolution. Plantation owners cut and sold live oak and pine timber; grew corn, cotton, rice, and indigo on the rich soils; and raised cattle, hogs, and horses that ranged freely across the island. Perhaps the largest and most productive plantation in the region was Stafford Plantation, an 8,000-acre tract that remains in private hands today.

One of the most famous estates on the Georgia coast was Dungeness, owned by Revolutionary War hero Gen. Nathanael Greene, who commanded the Southern Department of the war. While he owned Mulberry Grove Plantation near Savannah, he also planned to build a huge mansion on Cumberland Island near the site of Oglethorpe's Dungeness hunting lodge. He died in 1786 before he was able to complete his plans. His wife, Catherine, remarried 10 years later to Phineas Miller, and they followed through on Greene's designs, building a huge, four-story tabby mansion on top of an Indian shell mound. The mansion, with 6-foot thick walls at the base, featured four chimneys and 16 fireplaces, and was surround by 12 acres of gardens. Catherine Miller's charm and beauty were legendary, and she was a favorite ballroom partner of George Washington and "Mad" Anthony Wayne. She is credited with inspiring inventor Eli Whitney with the idea of the cotton gin when she flicked lint from his machine with her handkerchief and remarked that it needed a brush. Dungeness was the scene of many special social galas where statesmen and military leaders enjoyed the Millers' hospitality. When the island was briefly occupied during the War of 1812, the British used Dungeness as their headquarters. Here a British captain named John Fraser met and eventually married a southern belle named Ann Couper, who was a member of the family that owned Cannon's Point plantation on St. Simons.

In 1818, Gen. "Lighthorse" Harry Lee, Revolutionary War hero and old friend of Nathanael Greene, came ashore at Cumberland Island. He was in failing health and was returning from the West Indies when he asked to be taken to his old friend's estate of Dungeness. After a month of illness, he died on March 25 and was buried on the island. His son, Confederate Gen. Robert E. Lee, had a tombstone placed over the grave and visited his father's final resting place several times. In 1913, Harry Lee was moved to Lexington, Virginia, to lie beside his famous son, but the gravestone was left on Cumberland Island.

From 1820 to 1838, a lighthouse operated on the southern end of Cumberland. The year a new one was established on Little Cumberland, the lighthouse on Big Cumberland was moved to Amelia Island, where it stands today.

The plantation economy was dealt a deathblow with the Civil War, and Dungeness deteriorated and the family moved away. Slaves were rounded up by the Union Army and moved to Amelia Island, but some returned to Halfmoon Bluff on the northern end in an area known as The Settlement. Freed slaves may have been the cause of the fire of 1866 that destroyed the historic mansion, and another legend tells the story of Cumberland plantation owner Robert Stafford burning the quarters of his former slaves after they refused to work for him after gaining their freedom.

The island remained abandoned until the 1880s, when Pittsburgh millionaire Thomas Carnegie, brother of Andrew, acquired the Dungeness property for use as a winter retreat. On the foundations of the Greene-Miller-Shaw Dungeness, the Carnegies built an even grander mansion in 1884. The third Dungeness, at its peak, was a 59-room turreted Scottish castle, with a pool house, squash court, and golf course, and 40 other buildings that accommodated a staff of 200. Thomas died around the time the mansion was finished, but his widow, Lucy, and their nine children continued to develop Cumberland. Lucy purchased 90 percent of the island and she and her heirs built Cumberland's most famous buildings, including Greyfield, Stafford, and Plum Orchard. Dungeness remained occupied off and on until 1959, when it tragically burned. Greyfield is a private inn and Plum Orchard, an 1898 Georgian-revival mansion, is administered by the National Park Service.

As the island passed down to successive generations of Carnegies, the heirs were confronted with what to do with their isolated property. In 1955, the National Park Service identified Cumberland Island and Cape Cod as the two most significant natural areas on the Atlantic and Gulf coasts. This increased awareness of the island, but little action was taken. In 1969, Hilton Head developer Charles Fraser, who wanted to create a similar development on Cumberland Island, purchased one-fifth of the island. When he started to bulldoze a 5,000-foot airport runway on the northern end, alarms were set off in the environmental community, which knew it was now or never to save the island. The Georgia Conservancy played a historic role in helping to push through a bill introduced by Congressmen Bill Stuckey and Bo Ginn that established Cumberland Island as a national seashore, signed by President Nixon in 1972. Most of the Carnegie heirs decided the island should remain a wilderness and worked toward that goal by selling to the federal government. The Mellon Foundation donated $7.5 million to buy up property on the island, including Fraser's tract, which then was deeded to the federal government, and most of the island became part of the park system.

Subsequently, heated debate has taken place for more than 25 years on how the National Park Service should manage the island, with residents, conservationists, and developers taking a variety of positions. How many people should be allowed on the island? What amenities should be built to accommodate tourists? Should a causeway be built to allow heavy visitation? The Georgia Conservancy also weighed in heavily on the anti-development side, which has preserved the island's natural qualities. Today, the general management plan has settled many of these issues, with limits on the number of tourists and vehicle use by residents.

A new burst of publicity occurred for Cumberland Island when John F. Kennedy Jr. married Carolyn Bessette at the First African Baptist Church on the northern end of the island in September, 1996. Maintained by the National Park Service, this simple one-room frame structure, with 11 handmade pews, and three windows on each side, was built in 1937 to replace a cruder 1893 structure. The wedding party stayed at the Grey-field Inn, which was built in 1900.

▓ VISITING CUMBERLAND ISLAND

Most visitors ride the ferry from the waterfront docks at Cumberland Island National Seashore Visitor Center located in St. Marys. The 45-minute trip down the St. Marys River and across Cumberland Sound is part of the Cumberland experience. No supplies are available on the island so visitors must bring all supplies with them. Drinking water is available at the visitor center, the ranger station, the museum, and Sea Camp Beach Campground. Campers who come for multiple-day visits cannot use the ferry for resupply. All trash must be packed off the island. Visitors will want to bring food, drinks, insect repellant, comfortable walking shoes, and rain gear. The island can get hot, so sunglasses, suntan lotion, and a hat are recommended. A camera preserves memories of your visit.

Snacks, beverages, and souvenirs are available on the *Cumberland Queen* ferry, which leaves the island at 10:15 a.m. and 4:45 p.m. CAUTION: If you miss the last ferry, you are stuck on the island or must arrange a charter for your return trip.

The ferry stops first at Dungeness Dock [Fig. 22(4)] at the southern end and then heads north to the Sea Camp Dock [Fig. 22(3)] located less than 1 mile away. At either site, a park ranger gives an orientation to the island and tells visitors about scheduled history and nature walks and beach seinings. Dungeness Dock is located close to the Carnegie ruins and 1 mile from the beach. Sea Camp Dock is located 0.5 mile from Sea Camp Beach Campground. Hand-drawn carts are available to transport equipment to the campgrounds. Campers who want to use one of the four other primitive campsites have to make reservations, receive their campground assignment at Sea Camp Beach Campground, then hike to their assigned campground, which can be up to 10.6 miles from Sea Camp Dock. On the first Sunday of each month, the ferry also travels to Plum Orchard for an additional fee.

Group charters are available for 46 to 120 people, with a sliding rate scale for larger groups. Trips to Plum Orchard are available to groups for an additional charge.

HIKING ON CUMBERLAND ISLAND

If you want to enjoy the island, hiking is not only the best option but also the only option. Most of the hiking trails are narrow, sandy roads that pass by many natural and historic features. Maps are essential and should be picked up from the National Park Service at the St. Marys visitor center. While most of the island is national park, some private estates still remain on the island, and the hiker should know where they are at all times and respect private property. Trespassing on private property is strictly prohibited. Hikers are allowed to cross private property on major trails.

The most popular day hike on the island is a 3.5-mile loop that starts at Dungeness Dock, goes southeast to the Dungeness Ruins, then crosses to the beach. From here hikers walk up the beach to Sea Camp Beach Campground, then cross over to Sea Camp Dock, where they catch a ride back to the mainland or walk the River Trail to Dungeness Dock, making a circle. For first-time visitors, this is a predictable but rewarding hike.

The impressive ruins of Dungeness speak to the glory of the 1890s. A small tabby house west of Dungeness is all that remains of the Greene-Miller-Shaw estate. Built around 1800, it is believed to be the oldest structure on Cumberland. Used originally as the gardener's cottage, it was later remodeled by the Carnegies and used as a business office. Other attractions include the recreation house, the carriage house, and the Greene-Miller cemetery, which includes the graves of Catherine Green Miller, her daughter Louisa Shaw, and her husband James. Lighthorse Harry Lee once was buried here. The South Point Trail leads to freshwater ponds that may feature wading birds or waterfowl such as green-winged teal and American black ducks. The mud flats are excellent sites for observing sandpipers, plovers, and whimbrels.

The Main Road, also known as Grand Avenue, links the south end with the north end and passes by maritime forest thick with saw palmetto and stands of loblolly, slash, and longleaf pine. Many hikers use the quieter Parallel Trail, unused by vehicles, to reach Stafford Beach. Hikers pushing farther north use the Main Road or the beach. Trails leading off the Main Road lead to the beach and historic buildings such as Plum Orchard, a 20-room mansion built in 1900 with an indoor swimming pool and squash court. The home is being renovated and is open to tours on Sundays. The Duckhouse Trail leads from Plum Orchard past Yankee Paradise Campground to the beach, where migrating sands are burying the Carnegies' hunting lodge. This trail crosses part of the Sweetwater Lake complex, where a pond cypress, rare on the island, grows among sawgrass marsh species found in the Everglades. Duckweed grows in mats in sloughs, and red maples, willow, and blackgum are common tree species. Many wading birds nest in this series of small lakes.

Heading north, the Lost Trail connects to the Roller Coaster Trail, which follows old dune ridges to Lake Whitney. Sloughs support cordgrass, sawgrass, water willow, and marsh mallow. Otter and mink are seen in this area. At the northern end on the western side are ruins of the Cumberland Wharf, used by steam-boats that carried vacationers from Brunswick and St. Simons to the Cumberland Island Hotel, which hosted guests from 1870 to 1920. Continuing around the north end from the wharf, hikers will find the First African Baptist Church.

Trails: More than 50 miles of backcountry trails.

CAMPING ON CUMBERLAND ISLAND

All camping is limited to seven days. The developed campground at Sea Camp Beach has restrooms, cold showers, and drinking water. The beach is located nearby. Campfires are permitted at Sea Camp, but only dead and downed wood may be used. Trash must be packed out. Quiet hours are enforced between 10 p.m.–6 a.m. None of the backcountry sites—Brickhill Bluff, Yankee Paradise, Hickory Hill, or Stafford Beach—have any facilities. Stafford Beach is a nonwilderness campsite located 3.5 miles from Sea Camp, and is suggested for novice backpackers and those wanting easy access to the beach. Wilderness camping is located at Hickory Hill (5.5 miles away), Yankee Paradise (7.4 miles), and Brickhill Bluff (10.6 miles). Backcountry campsites have wells nearby; the water should be treated. There are no restrooms, so bury waste in the top 6 inches of soil, but never within 50 yards of a water source. Campfires are not permitted in the backcountry, but portable stoves are allowed. If you plan to camp, you must have both a camping reservation and permit. Obtain permits from the Sea Camp Visitor Center. Camping reservations are made by calling 882-4335 Monday through Friday, 10 a.m. to 4 p.m. All campers should load their equipment on the ferry before other tour passengers board and unload it at the island after day visitors have disembarked. If you do not appear for the boat as scheduled and do not call, your boat and camping reservations will be cancelled 15 minutes before your scheduled departure time.

FISHING ON CUMBERLAND ISLAND

Fishing is allowed on the island, and Georgia fishing laws apply. Many anglers try surf casting or fish in one of the freshwater lakes of the island. Lake Whitney is known for good fishing.

YUCCA OR SPANISH BAYONET
(Yucca sp.)
May through July, yuccas send up a 6-foot stalk with flowers at the end

LODGING ON CUMBERLAND ISLAND

Greyfield Inn. Box 900 Fernandina Beach, Florida 32035. This 1900 Carnegie home, with 13 rooms, offers the only accommodations on the island. Filled with antiques and island grandeur, it was turned into an inn in 1968. Price includes meals, transportation, naturalist tours, and bike rentals. *Expensive. (904) 261-6408.*

ACCESS AND FERRY INFORMATION

Most visitors to Cumberland Island arrive by ferry from the waterfront docks at the Cumberland Island National Seashore Visitor Center located in St. Marys. The mainland visitor center is where you can make reservations for the ferry or campsites at Sea Camp Beach Campground. Backcountry camping assignments are issued at Sea Camp Visitor Center. The St. Marys visitor center has maps and guidebooks to aid the traveler. The ferry is daily, except from October 1 to February 28, when the ferry does not operate on Tuesdays and Wednesdays. The ferry does not transport cars, bicycles, or pets. Mainland departure times are 9:00 and 11:45 a.m.; the island departures are 10:15 a.m. and 4:45 p.m. You can make ferry reservations up to six months in advance by calling 882-4335 between 10 a.m. and 4 p.m., Monday through Friday. Fully paid reservations are refundable if cancelled 14 days prior to departure, with a cancellation fee of 16 percent per ticket. No refunds are made within 13 days of sailing. Full refunds will be made if the ferry is cancelled at the captain's discretion due to mechanical problems or severe weather. Rain and cloudy conditions will not cancel sailings and no refunds will be made. If you miss the last ferry from the island, you must charter a boat for the return trip.

Directions: From Interstate 95, take Exit 2/3, and travel 10 miles east on GA 40 to visitor center. Parking is allowed nearby.

Activities: Hiking on 50 miles of backcountry trails, fishing, camping (primitive, intermediate), bird-watching, picnicking, swimming, nature study, historical touring, guided tours by prior arrangement.

Facilities: 1 developed campground, Sea Camp Beach, has 16 sites and accommodates 60 people. Restrooms, drinking water, and cold showers available here. 4 backcountry sites, with well water, are available elsewhere on the island. Bathrooms are available at the Ice House Museum at Dungeness Dock, Sea Camp Visitor Center at Sea Camp Dock, and at Dungeness ruins.

Dates: Seashore is open 7 days a week.

Fees: Separate fees for ferry and campsites. Call for fees and reservations. Camping reservations can be made six months in advance, but 60 days recommended.

Closest town: St. Marys.

For more information: Ferry and camping reservations are made by calling 882-4335 Monday through Friday, 10 a.m. to 4 p.m. or write Superintendent, Cumberland Island National Seashore, PO Box 806, St. Marys, GA 31558.

Little Cumberland Island

[Fig. 22] At the north tip of Cumberland Island is Little Cumberland Island, a 2,400-acre tract that is separated from the big island by Christmas and Brockington creeks. Though part of the Cumberland Island National Seashore, Little Cumberland Island is privately owned and not open to visitors without an invitation. With 1,600 acres of uplands, this Holocene island is larger than Sea Island, but has less beach with approximately 2.5 miles of sand. There are 100, 2-acre lots where development is allowed, but only 36 homes have been built. Little Cumberland has monitored sea turtle nesting since 1964, longer than any other island on the Georgia coast. Unfortunately, the island has seen drastically reduced numbers of turtle nests, declining from an average of 151 in the 1970s to an average of 44 in the last 10 years, for reasons that are not entirely clear to scientists.

Little Cumberland Island and the historic communities known as the Settlement and High Point located just across the creek on Big Cumberland form the north end. This area has a separate history from the south end because the two were located 18 miles away from each other. The northenders' commercial and social activities were influenced by their proximity to St. Simons and Brunswick, while the southenders were influenced by the settlements of St. Marys and Fernandina.

Most interesting on Little Cumberland Island is the Little Cumberland Lighthouse, the southernmost beacon on the Georgia coast. Owned and maintained by the Little Cumberland Island Association, the 60-foot-tall lighthouse, 22 feet at the base tapering to 11 feet at the top, began operation in June of 1838. The light featured a stationary lantern that contained 14 lamps. Also known as the St.

WILD TURKEY
(Meleagris gallopavo)
A popular game bird in the South, wild turkeys grow to 4 feet tall.

Andrews Lighthouse, it was improved in 1867 with a third order Fresnel lens. In 1873, imperiled by the encroaching Atlantic, the base was fortified by a brick wall and oyster shells. In 1915, the Lighthouse Service deactivated the lighthouse.

For more information: Little Cumberland Island Association, PO Box 3127, Jekyll Island, GA 31527.

Satilla River

The Satilla River is a true blackwater stream, born in river swamps of the Coastal Plain and flowing 260 winding miles before emptying out into St. Andrew Sound on the Georgia coast. The Alabaha and Little Satilla rivers are the main tributaries, adding to the 3,530-square-mile watershed drained by the Satilla River. Blackwater rivers flow through a narrow floodplain carrying a high organic, low sediment load. Decaying vegetation produces tannic acid, which creates the signature burgundy red color that gives the river its "blackwater" designation. Adding to the Satilla's silvery, reflective beauty are the adjoining swamplands and bottomland forests that buffer the course of the river as it winds between glistening white sand banks. As the river approaches its lower reaches, it broadens and loses its canopy of trees. Below US 17 (at Woodbine), the river widens and becomes tidally influenced and the surrounding vegetation consists of marsh. It was near this area that many famous large rice plantations were developed, including Belleview, Fairfield, and Refuge plantations.

The river's name comes from Saint Illa, the name of an officer of the Spanish Army, which was later shortened and corrupted to Satilla. In early times, the Satilla was known for abundant game, and fur trappers tried their skills along the riverbanks. A pre-Revolutionary War fort, known as Burnt Fort, is located where the GA 252 bridge crosses the Satilla. The name comes from a local legend that a fort once was built there by South Carolinians from 1715–1725, which later burned. Burnt Fort Station was built in 1793 by Capt. James Randolph, who the next year commanded a squad of dragoons to defend Camden County from Creek Indian attacks.

Wildlife common along the banks of the river includes raccoons, opossums, armadillos, deer, squirrels, ducks, and wild turkeys. A study of the river's insect fauna revealed a great abundance and diversity of stoneflies, mayflies, dragonflies, dobsonflies, caddisflies and beetles, which are supported by submerged decaying vegetation such as snags and roots. Fishermen seek the river's largemouth bass, crappie, redbreast, and bluegill. Warmouth, channel catfish, bowfin, chain pickerel, and American eels share the river with softshell and hardshell turtles, cottonmouths, and alligators.

Flora surrounding the river is determined by the degree and duration of submergence. In wetter areas, the river flows through cypress and gum swamps. Drier areas support water oak, laurel oak, sweetbay, red maple, and pine. Swamp blackgum are common. In the understory are titi, black titi, and an azalea (*Rhododendron canescens*), which produces beautiful floral displays in spring. Many of the higher, sandy plateaus have been converted to monoculture pine plantations.

Magnolia Bluff, a virgin hardwood tract, is one of Georgia's prized botanical areas. It is found 1 mile north of Burnt Fort on the river, and is renowned for its very mesic (wet) seepage bluff forest that supports a strange assemblage of flora species, including 500-year-old magnolias growing side by side with floodplain species such as cypress and water hickory.

CANOEING AND CAMPING ON THE SATILLA RIVER

The Satilla is a peaceful, slow-moving river that creates feelings of tranquility and mystery in its wilder sections. Unfortunately, the river is interrupted by farmlands and pine plantations developed right up to the river, which can disturb the sense of isolation and remoteness on the river. The novice canoeist will feel comfortable on the slow-moving Satilla. Camping can be excellent on the white point bars found on the inside turns of the river, or on the higher bluffs that go up to 50 feet above the river in the upper reaches and 8 feet in the lower reaches. Of interest to historians is Burnt Fort, located where the river flows under the GA 252 bridge (*see* page 290).

Another approach to canoeing the Satilla is to launch a boat in the Little Satilla River Wildlife Management Area and paddle down to the Satilla River. The Little Satilla River flows past extensive swamps, with clay banks instead of the characteristic white sand banks of the Satilla.

Suggested canoe trips on the Satilla River: US 82 to GA 15/121, 15.7 miles. GA 15/121 to US 301, 26.8 miles. US 301 to US 84, 20.2 miles. US 84 to GA 252 (Burnt Fort), 35.3 miles. GA 252 to US 17 (Satilla River Waterfront Park), 24.5 miles. Little Satilla: US 84 to intersection with Satilla River at Oak Grove Church on GA 110 south of Needmore, 30 miles.

SATILLA RIVER WATERFRONT PARK

[Fig. 3(5)] Established in 1980 on the banks of the beautiful Satilla River in Woodbine, this well-equipped park provides access to the upper reaches of the river. The Crawfish Festival, featuring locally raised "mudbugs," is a popular event held in the park the last weekend in April. Located on the southeastern side of the US 17 bridge, the park's facilities include a boat ramp, 2 docks, picnic tables and shelters, and restrooms.

For more information: Phone 576-3211.

LITTLE SATILLA WILDLIFE MANAGEMENT AREA

This 16,934-acre wildlife management area borders both sides of the Little Satilla River and its extensive river swamps in Pierce and Wayne counties. The WMA is a popular site for hunting deer, turkeys, raccoons, and opossums. Hikers should only contemplate visiting this wildlife management area when it is not hunting season and must give notice to the forest supervisor. Contact the Wildlife Resources Division, Georgia Department of Natural Resources for hunting seasons.

Directions: Located 8 miles east of Patterson on US 32. Turn left from the main road into the area at the entrance sign.

For more information: Wildlife Resources Division, Georgia Department of Natural Resources, Fitzgerald, GA 31750. Phone 423-2988.

St. Marys River

Born in the Okefenokee and Pinhook swamps, the waters of the St. Marys River appear indecisive, flowing south, then east, then north, then finally east past the town of St. Marys to Cumberland Sound. The St. Marys River, a blackwater stream that drains 1,500 acres, winds 125 river miles to reach the sea only 50 miles from its birth. The main impediment is Trail Ridge, the Pleistocene dune line that helps create the Okefenokee Swamp and forces the St. Marys to make its tortuous journey south before reaching a gap and flowing to Cumberland Sound. The serene, beautiful river serves as the state line between Georgia and Florida, making the unmistakable "toe" in the southeastern portion of the state.

Mariners went out of their way to obtain the tea-colored water of the St. Marys, which was prized for its chemical qualities. Decaying vegetation produces tannic acid, giving the water its burgundy color and also acting as a preservative that would keep the water fresh for two years.

At the Okefenokee origin of the river, called the North Prong, the narrow river reflects images of stately moss-draped baldcypress, tupelo, and Ogeechee lime trees that line its banks. Trees in the channel become less prevalent as it moves away from the bog swamp, and the river picks up volume and becomes more winding after it meets the Middle Prong of the St. Marys, which has made the journey from Pinhook Swamp and Osceola National Forest. Swamp forests of water-tolerant species dominate the surrounding floodplain, which supports an abundance of palmettos and tropical species. White sand bars add to the beauty of the river and provide intimate camping spots.

Quiet and observant paddlers may see swamp bears, deer, bobcats, raccoons, armadillos, opossums, and otters. Shy alligators, turtles, and snakes sun themselves before sliding into the dark, reddish waters. Frogs are more frequently heard than seen, singing their love songs in spring. Bird life is abundant, and vultures, osprey, hawks, and owls are year-round residents. Cruising above the water channels are kingfishers, as well as Mississippi and swallowtail kites, which are seen in spring. During migratory periods, songbirds flit across the river channel in front of the boat. Unsubstantiated reports of panther sightings are relatively common. Fishermen pursue the river's largemouth bass, crappie, redbreast, and bluegill.

Along the bottom of the toe, the South Prong joins the river and it turns toward Folkston. From the origin in the Okefenokee to St. George, the St. Marys River is a docile, narrow stream that is at its most wild and undisturbed character. As the canoeist approaches Traders Hill and Folkston, the river's banks rise to more than 7 feet, and the natural surroundings are increasingly disturbed by encroaching agriculture and powerboat traffic. Canoeists may want to explore some of the tributaries feeding the St. Marys, such as Spanish Creek a few miles north of Traders Hill. (Folkston once was the location of a Spanish mission, San Lorenzo de Ibihica, from 1620–1656.) East of Folkston, the canoeist starts to sense the influence of tides, and the river cuts deeper into its channel.

Below US 17, the river's scenery becomes marsh and canoeists must contend with tides as they paddle to St Marys.

CANOEING AND CAMPING ON THE ST. MARYS RIVER

The river is appropriate for the novice, with the biggest dangers being deadfalls in the upper reaches and strong tides in the lower parts. There are many points of access for planning a variety of experiences, a short trip, overnighter, or weeklong trip. Camping is available on sand bars and high bluffs, but canoe-campers should get permission before camping on private property.

Suggested canoe trips on the St. Marys River: GA 94 (Moniac) to FL 120, 5.14 miles. FL 120 to GA 23, 12.4 miles. GA 23 to Stokes Bridge, 9.6 miles. Stokes Bridge to GA 94 (St. George), 13.7 miles. GA 94 (St. George) to Traders Hill Recreation Park, 27.5 miles. Traders Hill Recreation Park to White Springs Landing (Camp Pickney Park), 7.7 miles. White Springs Landing (Camp Pickney Park) to US 17, 26.3 miles. US 17 to St. Marys Waterfront Dock, 16.8 miles.

TRADERS HILL RECREATION PARK

[Fig. 23(9)] Once a fort and settlement, Traders Hill today is a 32-acre recreation park on the banks of the St. Marys River where visitors can launch a boat, camp, fish, swim, or enjoy the natural beauty of the river. It is close to the Okefenokee Swamp National Wildlife Refuge. When human activity is at a minimum, the park can be an excellent bird-watching site, with a variety of wading and woodland species seen in the waters and trees in the park.

First known as Fort Alert, an Indian trading post, it was renamed Traders Hill and was a thriving center of trade about 1755 and was designated the county seat when Charlton County was formed in 1854. The county seat was moved to Folkston in 1901.

Facilities: 12 full hookups, RV and tent campsites. Showers, dumping station, picnic tables.

Directions: From Folkston, go south on GA 23/121 approximately 5 miles to park entrance on left.

For more information: Traders Hill Recreation Park, phone 496-3412.

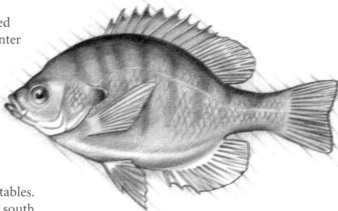

BLUEGILL
(Lepomis macrochirus)
This freshwater fish is the most common sunfish in the U.S.

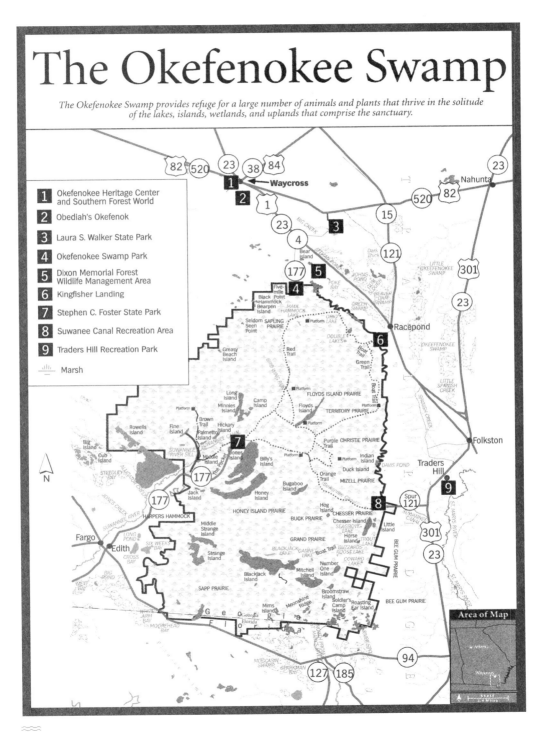

The Okefenokee Swamp

The Okefenokee Swamp provides refuge for a large number of animals and plants that thrive in the solitude of the lakes, islands, wetlands, and uplands that comprise the sanctuary.

1 Okefenokee Heritage Center and Southern Forest World

2 Obediah's Okefenok

3 Laura S. Walker State Park

4 Okefenokee Swamp Park

5 Dixon Memorial Forest Wildlife Management Area

6 Kingfisher Landing

7 Stephen C. Foster State Park

8 Suwanee Canal Recreation Area

9 Traders Hill Recreation Park

Marsh

Area of Map

The Okefenokee Swamp

[Fig. 23] If you fly across Georgia and look down on the landscape, it appears that almost every acre of the state is under some kind of development. Roads, towns, cleared patches of farmland, and rows upon rows of pine trees seem to fill every available patch of land. Then, at the last minute before arriving at the coast, you look down and it appears the hand of man has been stayed: Below you are 700 square miles of wet, green wilderness, known as the Okefenokee Swamp, the largest peat producing bog swamp in North America.

A national treasure, the vast and mysterious Okefenokee Swamp provides refuge for a large number of animals and plants that thrive in the solitude of the lakes, islands, wetlands, and uplands that make up the sanctuary. As one of the largest and most significant wetland complexes in the United States, the Okefenokee has its own peculiar mix of natural environments, wildlife, and human mythology. Visitors to the swamp can hear the prehistoric bellow of ancient reptiles, the raucous call of the sandhill crane, and the garrulous chorus of frogs in spring. The natural setting is a strange and beautiful mosaic, from a maze of towering cypresses growing out of the mirrorlike waters in some areas of the swamp to vast prairie grasslands in other sections.

Visiting the swamp can be somewhat confusing. There is no one park you go to that offers the entirety of the Okefenokee experience. Visitors have four choices of parks, each with their own set of natural qualities and recreation opportunities. Three parks are located on the eastern side of the swamp, and one park is located on the southwestern side. Because of the size of the swamp, visiting the full complement of parks requires some driving because one must travel around the perimeter of the wetland, which is larger than the interior of Interstate 285 or all the barrier islands of Georgia combined. The most popular activities in the swamp are sightseeing, boating, and fishing.

On the southwestern side near Fargo is Stephen C. Foster State Park, which marks the headwaters of the Suwannee River and is popular for its cypress swamps and fishing. North of the swamp near Waycross is Laura S. Walker State Park, which comprises the natural communities that are characteristic of the swamp's margin. Not quite the swamp experience that some may expect, it nonetheless offers picnicking, camping, golfing, and a lake for water recreation. West of the park and south of Waycross is the Okefenokee Swamp Park, which is geared for the visitor who would rather see alligators, snakes, and bears in captivity rather than search them out in the wilds. This is a quick and easy way to see the typical environments and wildlife of the swamp without investing too much trouble or time. Farther south near Folkston is Suwannee Canal Recreation Area, a Federal park near that failed venture that today provides water access to the more typical prairie environment of the swamp. Highlights here are nature boardwalks, historic sites, fishing, boating, and nature observation. Other attractions around the swamp include a large hunting area and two museums dedicated to the swamp's historical and natural heritage. Full details on these attractions follow.

AMERICAN ALLIGATOR (Alligator mississippiensis) A survivor from the age of reptiles, the American alligator builds nests and lays 30 to 70 oblong eggs.

THE OKEFENOKEE SWAMP'S NATURAL FEATURES

In the 1770s, naturalist William Bartram correctly observed that the swamp was a "terrestrial paradise" and "great source of rivers" and that Creek Indians considered the "Ouaquaphenogaw" a "most blissful spot of the earth." In 1902, naturalist Roland M. Harper wrote that the swamp "must be seen to be appreciated…there is nothing else exactly like it in the world." In modern times, photographs of the swamp taken by satellite far above the earth show it as an obviously distinct greenish-yellow shape in the southeastern corner of the state.

What the Indians appreciated long before European naturalists and high tech space-craft is that the Okefenokee is a very unusual and special ecosystem. Unfortunately, for many years swamps were not prized by colonizing Europeans, who believed them to be wastelands that need to be drained, cut out, and planted with crops. Today we know better, but much of the general public still has a negative image of swamplands as dark, scary jungles where evil lurks. Nothing could be further from the truth.

The Okefenokee Swamp is a vast mosaic of natural communities, some looking like the stereotypical cypress swamp, and others looking more like a treeless prairie of wet grass. From aerial photography, scientists have identified approximately 20 different major habitat types that form the patchwork known as the Okefenokee. Much of the swamp has never been visited by man.

The dimensions of the swamp are huge. While scientists debate its actual boundaries, most agree that its watershed is more than 1,400 square miles and the swamp is roughly 700 square miles, including wetlands in Florida. The national wildlife refuge is 396,315 acres of which 353,981 acres are part of the wilderness preservation system. Rainfall—50 inches a year—supplies 70 to 90 percent of the water in the swamp, with some small springs adding to the total. Depth of the water ranges from 2 to 9 feet. Water drains in from the northwestern side of the swamp and collects in a 435,000-acre basin. Eighty-five percent of the water flowing out of the swamp is carried by the Suwannee River, which rolls to the Gulf coast, and the remainder is carried by the St. Marys River to the Atlantic coast. While water is a main element of the Okefenokee, only 1,000 acres of the swamp are open water areas, consisting of some 60 lakes, gator holes, and watercourses.

Geologically, the swamp is a newborn, with the oldest peat estimated to be 8,000 years old. Approximately 200,000 years ago, the Atlantic Ocean covered the swamp. As the climate cooled during subsequent ice ages, sea level dropped, and as the seas receded, high dunes formed at various shorelines. Around 140,000 years ago, a giant dune line known as Trail Ridge was formed, stretching from Starke, Florida to Jesup, Georgia. This ridge, which makes up the eastern edge of the swamp, acted as a dam to southeastern flowing rivers, causing water to pool behind the ridge or flow around it to gaps in the ridge. The Satilla River flows through one such gap, while the St. Marys River is forced south before reaching a gap, where it moves east then north and east to the Atlantic Ocean.

Underlying the Okefenokee is a saucer-shaped basin with a firm sand floor that is elevated between 128 and 103 feet above sea level. The top layer of sand is from the Pleistocene Age only 2 million years ago. Below these sands at depths ranging form 30 to 110 feet are 6-million-year old sands of the Pliocene epoch. On top of the sand floor is a bed of peat that ranges from a thin layer to more than 20 feet in depth. The peat gives the swamp much of its character; its name, much of its landscape, and its unique water. The word Okefenokee is an Indian word translated to mean "land of the trembling earth." The swamp produces vegetation faster than it can decay. As vegetation dies and sinks, it slowly decomposes, producing methane gas. When enough gas is produced, peat mats will break away from the bottom and float to the water's surface in what is called a blowup. Plants will colonize this blowup, creating a new entity called a battery. Eventually, larger and sturdier trees become established on the battery giving birth to an island. Walking on these batteries and islands, which may be floating, is literally and figuratively like walking on a waterbed. Hence the name "land of the trembling earth."

The peat, when mixed with fresh water, creates the acidic, tea-colored, reflective waters of the Okefenokee that are internationally famous. With a pH of 3.7 (a neutral pH is 7, with higher values alkaline), the chemistry of the water affects every living form in the swamp. It is also delicious to drink, and sailing ships used to go out of their way to fill their stores with the waters from the St. Marys River, which would remain fresh during long journeys.

Floral communities of the swamp consist of pine uplands; forested wetlands of bay, cypress, and blackgum; scrub-shrub wetlands; and mixed aquatic bed and emergent wetland natural habitats. The ecosystem is fire dependent, with a high lightning frequency. Fires generally burn lightly, considering the wet nature of the swamp. Natural succession here goes from prairie, to cypress swamp, and finally to blackgum or bay swamp. Fire prevents the last stage from happening, keeping the swamp at the cypress stage as cypress is fire-tolerant but blackgum and bays, normally understory trees, are not. Dry peat is very combustible. When vast forests of cypress were cut out from the swamp—

SANDHILL CRANE

(Grus canadensis) These large cranes have spectacular calls and elaborate dances they perform during courtship.

425 million board feet—in the first third of the 1900s, bay and blackgum shot up to replace the cypress trees. The building of a dam near Stephen C. Foster State Park has kept the swamp unusually wet, which has affected the frequency and strength of fires in the swamp in ways still not totally understood.

Today, the swamp has roughly 70 tree islands that make up 10 percent of the swamp. The signature cypress forest occupies around 25 percent. Approximately 20 percent of the swamp is prairie, consisting of grasses and sedges, moss, ferns, and rushes. Emergent plants such as golden club, pickerelweed, and yellow-eyed grass are characteristic plants of the prairie. Blue flag irises add splashes of lavender. And roughly 33 percent of the swamp is scrub-shrub, with evergreen, leathery leafed shrubs such as dahoon holly and fetterbush dominating the landscape. The rest of the swamp is mixed pine uplands.

One fascinating aspect of the Okefenokee's flora are the carnivorous plants that have adapted to the swamp's low nitrogen and phosphorus content. Carnivorous plants have evolved the skill of surviving in nutrient-poor conditions by luring, trapping, and digesting animals. This specialization gives them the advantage of living in impoverished areas with little crowding from other plants. In the swamp, beautiful hooded pitcher plants (*Sarracenia minor*), golden trumpets (*Sarracenia flava*), sundews (*Drosera intermedia*), and bladderworts (*Utricularia purpurea*) use varying strategies for finding meals.

Because the swamp is young, the diversity of its flora and fauna is relatively low and no endemics have been found—no Okefenokee pocket gopher. However, many species thrive because it is such an immense refuge with an absence of roads, providing sanctuary not found in smaller parks. Identified in the refuge have been 232 species of birds, 42 species of mammals, 58 species of reptiles, 32 species of amphibians, and 34 species of fishes.

Some particular fauna of the swamp should be mentioned. Of course alligators and snakes are the two most feared animals associated with the swamp. Okefenokee's alligator population has rebounded since the animal received federal protection in the 1970s, and today about 12,000 alligators make their home here, a conservation success story. Their bellows in spring may be the most remarkable sound made by a North American animal. With 36 species of snakes, 5 of them poisonous, the swamp is serpent heaven. The most common poisonous snake is the water-loving cottonmouth. Other venomous snakes include the Eastern diamondback, pygmy rattler, canebrake rattler, and coral snake. The likelihood of getting bitten by a snake is greatly overrated, with the vast majority of snakebites occurring as a consequence of people picking up snakes. Nonetheless, they can be deadly so visitors should avoid disturbing them.

Maybe the most beautiful snake of the swamp is the rare rainbow snake, which has an iridescent black body with red stripes running its length and brilliant yellow along its lower sides. Also found in the swamp is the federally threatened Eastern indigo snake, the longest native snake in the U.S. growing to more than 8 feet.

Florida naturalist Archie Carr wrote that there are only three great animal voices remaining in the southeastern U.S.: the "jovial lunacy of the barred owl…the roar of the alligator…(and) the ethereal bugling of the sandhill crane." All three are heard in the swamp and all three will stop you in your tracks. Certainly the dinosaur rumble of the alligator can be imagined, as can the hoot of an owl, but the voice of the "watchman of the swamp" is unlike anything you've ever heard. Sandhills are the largest birds in the swamp, standing 4 feet tall with a 7-foot wingspan, and they have a cypress gray body and red forehead. They mate for life and nest in open places where trees do not block their keen vision.

Approximately 30 warblers have been identified in the swamp, including the prothonotary warbler (*Protonotaria citrea*), a bird that is characteristic of southern swamplands, where its bright, golden-orange plumage is conspicuous in the dark cypress swamps. It nests in the refuge and has a loud ringing "sweet-sweet-sweet-sweet" song.

Many species of waterfowl use the wet areas during the winter, including mallards, ring-necked ducks, wood ducks, black ducks, coots, green-winged teal, and mergansers. Anhingas are a common sight, perched on a stump with their wings outstretched. The water turkey, as it's also called, swims in the water preying on fish, and then must dry its wings before it can fly.

The most commonly observed white wading bird in the swamp is the white ibis (*Eudociums albus*), with its orange curved bill and orange legs, but many other wading birds can be seen including herons, egrets, and wood storks. Osprey, hawks, vultures, and eagles are soar the skies looking for food. In the woodlands, wild turkeys, owls, and red-headed and red-cockaded woodpeckers make their homes.

Adding to the sounds of the swamp are the more than 20 frog and toad species, each with its distinctive song. On a rainy summer night, visitors may hear up to 12 different frog species singing their particular songs.

The more commonly seen of the 50 mammals of the swamp are white-tailed deer, foxes, feral hogs, raccoons, and armadillos. Nine species of bats can be observed eating

GOLDEN CLUB
(Orontium aquaticum)
An emergent perennial with a golden-yellow, clublike spadix.

insects as the sun goes down. Round-tailed muskrats are common in the prairies. Bobcats are widespread and plentiful, but very shy. Floyds Island is a great place to see a bobcat. Otters are more frequently seen in colder months when alligators are less active. Of special mention is the largest mammal of the swamp, the Florida black bear (*Ursus americanus floridianus*). This subspecies, called a "hog bear" and smaller than the bears found in the Great Smoky Mountains National Park, weighs approximately 150 pounds and numbers around 500 animals. They are hunted during a six-day period once a year.

The insect life of the swamp is fascinating and plays an important role in nutrient cycling. Scientists have estimated that 12 to 40 percent of the forest canopy is consumed by insects, primarily butterflies and moths. Hordes of iridescent and harmless dragonflies are seen perched on tree trunks, warming themselves in the sun's rays. On the lily pads are fishing spiders (*Dolomedes*), which do not spin webs to capture prey but eat insects that have fallen into the water. The beautiful, orb-weaving golden-silk spider (*Nephila clavipes*) females have golden bodies and legs with conspicuous tufts of black hair on the first and last pair of legs. The male is small and drab colored. Large colonies of these spiders can be found in shaded woodlands near watercourses.

THE OKEFENOKEE SWAMP'S HUMAN HISTORY

Shell middens found in the swamp are evidence of Indian activities in the Okefenokee, where the earliest artifacts date back 4,000 years. The earliest record of European inhabitation of the swamp shows it occurred from 1620–1656 when the Spanish established a mission named Santiago de Oconi at the headwaters of the St. Marys River.

When naturalist William Bartram traveled in the swamp in the 1770s, he recorded an old Indian legend he heard about the swamp. A band of Indians, hunting in the swamp, had seen a "terrestrial paradise" on the banks of an enchanted island surrounded by a beautiful lake, and as they tried to reach it, they only became lost in the confusing labyrinth of the swamp. They were at the point of perishing when a group of beautiful Indian maidens mysteriously appeared and shared food with them and helped them find their way home. Subsequent groups of Indians tried to find the hidden paradise but never could locate it. Bartram guessed that the swamp might have hidden a remnant population of Yamasees, who sought asylum from the fury of their enemies, the Creeks.

FRAGRANT WATERLILY
(Nymphae odorata)
A beautiful white flower with yellow stamens and round, flat, floating leaves that are green on top and purplish-red underneath.

What Bartram believed true of the Yamasees came true of other displaced Indian tribes, such as the Creeks and Seminoles, who used the swamps as a reliable hiding place when Europeans settled the Georgia coast. It is believed that the great Seminole Indian Osceola spent time in the Okefenokee. In the 1820s, Chief Billy Bowlegs led his Indians against white homesteaders near and in the swamps. In 1838, General Charles Floyd, son of the famous Indian fighter John Floyd, searched the swamp for Billy Bowlegs but never found him. Billy led his Indians to the Everglades, where he and his men became part of the Seminole tribe. Two of the largest islands in the swamp are named for Billy and his pursuer.

In the 1850s, when it was obvious Indians had abandoned the swamp, homesteaders moved in to claim their piece of it. These isolated and independent families, such as the Chessers on Chesser Island and the Lees on Billys Island, raised families and livestock, grew crops, and established a unique culture all their own.

PICKERELWEED
(Pontederia cordata)

The Chessers' homestead is preserved and open to tour at Suwannee Canal Recreation Area, and remnants of the Lees' homestead are found on Billys Island, accessed at Stephen C. Foster State Park.

The swamp has suffered two major insults to its ecosystem, the first in the 1890s. Captain Henry Jackson and a group of investors purchased 238,120 acres of the swamp for $63,101.80, and began a venture to build a canal that would drain the swamp into the St. Marys River, which would allow for easy access to cypress trees and rice, cotton, and sugar cane farms. This became known as "Jackson's Folly." Convict labor, large steam shovels, and gold miners from North Georgia started digging a trench from the swamp toward Trail Ridge and westward toward the swamp's prairies. Fortunately, the drainage effort failed after three years. In 1894, a sawmill was built at Camp Cornelia, and some of the country's first uses of industrial forestry were attempted, using steam-powered skidders and logging pullboats. The sawmill produced over 7 million board feet of lumber. The company hoped to make enough profits on the lumber to continue the drainage project. Fortunately, there was a glut of lumber and it was unable to operate profitably. Jackson died of appendicitis in 1895, and his father took over. The company went into receivership in 1897 and was sold to lumberman Charles Hebard of Philadelphia in 1901. Today, the canal serves as the principal waterway into the heart of the swamp.

The second major insult occurred from 1909 to 1927, when the Hebard Cypress Company did its best to cut out the swamp's cypress and pine forests. Roughly 2,000

A canoe trail in the Okefenokee Swamp.

people eventually were at work in the swamp in lumbering or turpentining activities. The company built a network of elevated trams across the swamp to get to the magnificent cypresses, some over 1,000 years old. They headquartered on Billys Island, which became a company boom town that supported 600 residents, two motels, a movie theater, a grocery store, a school, churches and a "juke joint." Although the company was unable to clear-cut the swamp, it was able to remove 425 million board feet of timber, said to be enough to build 42,000 homes. Tens of thousands of railroad crossties were cut. The depletion of the resource and onset of the Depression slowed the logging efforts, and the Hebards sold the property to the Federal government, which ended this era.

During the Depression, the Federal government examined a proposal to build a canal across the swamp that would connect the Atlantic with the Gulf. This alarmed a naturalist who loved the swamp and its swamper community. Francis Harper was introduced to the swamp in 1912 when he was 25 years old and a junior member of a Cornell University biological team. His fascination with the swamp grew, and he returned many times to continue his explorations of its flora and fauna and swampers. In 1935, he built a cabin on Chesser Island.

With the canal project threatening to destroy the swamp, Harper moved to convince President Franklin D. Roosevelt to make the swamp a national wildlife refuge. Lucky for the swamp, Harper's wife, Jean, had worked as a tutor to Roosevelt's children. The

Harpers' personal relationship with Roosevelt helped their appeal get heard, and in 1937, the Federal government purchased the Okefenokee and made it a national wildlife refuge. In 1974, most of the refuge received protection as a national wilderness area. Ironically, this forced Harper's beloved swampers off their property forever. Harper had collected their folklore for years with the intention of publishing a book, but died at the age of 84 before finishing his work. A book based on Harper's notes was published posthumously called *Okefinokee Album*, by Delma E. Presley.

In the early 1950s, several droughts dried the swamp to combustible conditions. In 1954 and 1955, terrible fires swept through the swamp and surrounding uplands, burning more than half a million acres. This caused alarm among many conservation and forestry groups, who asked Congress to build a dam near the western side of the swamp to keep it in wet conditions. The sill, which was built in 1957, keeps the swamp unnaturally wet in the area of the river and has resulted in further debate about the management of the swamp and the effect of fires on its natural system.

The latest threat to the swamp occurred in the late 1990s, when the DuPont Corporation purchased the mineral rights to Trail Ridge with the intention of strip-mining the ancient dune for valuable titanium deposits. Scientists believe such a drastic alteration of the landscape that backs up the waters of the swamp may destroy it forever. Opposition to the plan is fierce but the issue remains unresolved as this book goes to press.

The Okefenokee Swamp: Waycross Area

▒ OBEDIAH'S OKEFENOK

[Fig. 23(2)] This quirky site offers a look at the swamper's life in the 1800s. Obediah Barber, born in 1825, was one of the first settlers on the northern boundary of the swamp. A backwoods naturalist, he loved the creatures and plants of the swamp, and became a famous outdoorsman whose Bunyanesque exploits in the Okefenokee earned him the title of King of the Swamp. One story tells how he was attacked by a black bear. Unarmed, Barber grabbed a piece of wood and beat the bear into submission. Apparently, he was equally hard on his women, as he was married three times and fathered 20 children. During the Civil War, he supplied beef to the Confederate Army. He died in 1909 at the age of 84. This homestead features his mid-1800s cabin, several farm buildings, a nature trail, animal exhibits, and a general store.

Directions: Going north on US 1 South, go west on US 82 (GA 520) to Gilmore Street. Turn left onto Gilmore, and follow street to Swamp Road. Go left on Swamp Road. Obediah's Okefenok is on left.

Activities: Historical touring.

Facilities: Restrooms, short nature trails.

Dates: Open Tuesday through Saturday.

Fees: A small admission fee is charged.

Closest town: Waycross.

For more information: Obediah's Okefenok, PO Box 423, Waycross, GA 31502. Phone 287-0090.

OKEFENOKEE HERITAGE CENTER AND SOUTHERN FOREST WORLD

[Fig. 23(1)] Located 2 miles west of Waycross, the Okefenokee Heritage Center features exhibits on life in and around the swamp. Indian culture and local history are documented through artifacts and displays. Southern Forest World is an interpretive center that tells the story of southern forestry and includes exhibits on timbering skills and naval stores operations that had a tremendous economic impact on the Georgia coast.

Directions: Both are located on North Augusta Avenue. Take Business US 1 (State Street) north to W. Blackshear Avenue. Turn left on W. Blackshear Avenue, and travel 4 blocks to attractions on the left.

Activities: Historical touring.

Facilities: Museum, restrooms.

Dates: Open 7 days a week.

Fees: A small admission fee is charged.

Closest town: Waycross.

For more information: Okefenokee Heritage Center, 1460 North Augusta Avenue, Waycross, GA 31503. Phone 285-4260. Southern Forest World, 1440 North Augusta Avenue, Waycross, GA 31503. Phone 285-4056.

LAURA S. WALKER STATE PARK

[Fig. 23(3)] Laura S. Walker is one of those all-things-to-all-people state parks, with a full range of facilities and recreation opportunities located near the Okefenokee Swamp Park and Dixon Memorial Forest Wildlife Management Area. Camping, swimming, boating, golfing, and picnicking are all popular activities here. During hunting season, sportsmen stay here for easy access to Dixon Memorial Forest. Campers may want to consider staying in the 306-acre park at night while they explore the various attractions related to the Okefenokee during the day. An 18-hole golf course is located here. During warmer months, insect repellant is recommended at this site.

In reality, the park is not in the Okefenokee/Suwannee/St. Marys watershed: Its waters flow north to the Satilla River and the Atlantic coast. The terrain, flora, and fauna, however, are characteristic of the Okefenokee Swamp's boundary landscape. Animals seen here include deer, bobcats, alligators, and gopher tortoises, along with fascinating carnivorous sundew and hooded pitcher plants. The lake, created by an impoundment, is stocked with common game fish such as largemouth bass and bream.

Built in the 1930s by the Works Progress Administration (WPA), the park was named for Mrs. Laura Singleton Walker, a writer, teacher, and civic leader who supported conservation long before it was popular to do so.

The Big Creek Nature Trail, located across GA 177 from the campgrounds, is a good place for early morning birding and to learn about Coastal Plain flora and fauna. The easy trail loops around to Big Creek, the dammed brook that creates Walker Lake, before heading back to the trailhead. At the beginning of the trail, the habitat is typical Coastal Plain pinelands, with longleaf pines, laurel oaks, bluejack oaks, palmetto, sparkleberry, perfoliate rattleweed, and honeysuckle vines. Mounds of white sand tip off gopher tortoise (*Gopherus polyphemus*) burrows, a sign of a sandhill area. The threatened gopher tortoise is a large reptile that is adept at digging underground chambers that are in turn used by a community of animals, including Eastern indigo snakes, gopher frogs, and diamondback rattlesnakes. It is the existence of the latter that has been the cause of suffering for gophers tortoises at the hand of man. Snake hunters, who search the Georgia woods for rattlesnakes for rattlesnake roundup events and to make snakeskin souvenirs and clothing, pour gasoline down the burrows to flush the serpents out, which kills a community of animals dependent on the protection of this sandy den.

Farther along the trail, hikers approach a wetland area identified as a Carolina bay. These mysterious, round depressions are the only natural lakes in Georgia, believed to be created by meteors, according to one theory, or gale force winds, another theory. (Georgia's other lakes are created by dams on rivers.) Most Carolina Bays are large and hard to reach due to the swamp wetlands that surround their borders. They are found in the Coastal Plain and can be identified by looking at a map for teardrop-shaped lakes. This area has some of the natural components of a Carolina bay. In this swampy area, hikers will find tupelo, sweet gum, live oaks, and laurel oaks, with wax myrtle and titi shrubs occupying the midstory. The trail returns to cutover pinelands that are undergoing succession.

Trail: The Big Creek Nature Trail is a 1.3 mile loop.

Directions: Exit I-95 at Exit 6/29. Go west on US 82 to GA 177. Go south on GA 177 for 2 miles to park.

Activities: Camping, boating, canoeing, swimming, golfing, picnicking, hiking. Interpretive programs by prior arrangement. Special events scheduled annually.

Facilities: 120-acre lake, boat ramp and dock, canoes, 44 campsites (primitive, intermediate, group, RV), 2 bathhouses, laundry, restrooms, swimming pool, 250 picnic tables, 2 screened shelters, 18-hole golf course.

Dates: Open 7 days a week.

Fees: A small fee is charged for parking. Separate fee for camping and golf. Reservations recommended for campsites on weekends, holidays, and during hunting season.

Closest town: Waycross.

For more information: Laura S. Walker State Park, 5653 Laura Walker Road, Waycross, GA 31503. Phone 287-4900.

DIXON MEMORIAL FOREST WILDLIFE MANAGEMENT AREA

[Fig. 23(5)] At 38,464 acres, this wildlife management area is the third largest in the state. Popular for hunting deer, bears, turkeys, small game, raccoons, and opossums, Dixon Memorial Forest sits like a cap just north of the Okefenokee National Wildlife Refuge. Primitive camping is allowed in the forest, but many choose to stay at Laura S. Walker State Park located nearby. Hikers should only visit this wildlife management area when it is not hunting season and must give notice to the forest supervisor. Contact the Wildlife Resources Division, Georgia Department of Natural Resources for hunting seasons.

Directions: From Waycross go south on US 1 for approximately 8 miles to GA 177. Turn left and follow signs to check station.

For more information: Wildlife Resources Division, Georgia Department of Natural Resources, Fitzgerald, GA 31750. Phone 423-2988.

OKEFENOKEE SWAMP PARK

[Fig. 23(4)] This park offers quick, easy, and safe access to the Okefenokee Swamp experience, suitable for all members of the family. A network of trails and boardwalks wind through animal exhibits in the park, where visitors can familiarize themselves with the flora and fauna of the swamp—or stop at a snack bar for an ice cream cone. Animals highlighted here are young and adult alligators (some grown to impressive size), bears, deer, otters, turtles, and snakes. The swamp here consists mainly of young tupelo and cypress, surrounded by pine flatland.

The park is leased by a nonprofit organization from the U.S. Fish and Wildlife Service, and is located in the national wildlife refuge, so uncontrolled wildlife makes an appearance, including otters, water snakes, and migratory birds. Wading bird rookeries can be sighted with binoculars. Boat tours, interpretive exhibits, lectures, wildlife shows, wilderness walkways, a 90-foot observation tower, a pioneer homestead, and a Seminole Indian village all combine to educate and highlight the Okefenokee Swamp. Don't miss the Serpentarium. The more adventurous can rent a canoe and head out on the boat trails by themselves.

Directions: Exit I-95 at Exit 6/29. Go west on US 84 to GA 177. Go south on GA 177 for 11 miles to park.

Activities: Wildlife viewing, bird-watching, hiking, boat tours, canoeing, museum, picnicking, interpretive programs.

Facilities: Museum, animal exhibits, hiking trails, picnic areas, restrooms, gift shop, snack bar.

Dates: Open 7 days a week. Extended hours during summer.

Fees: An admission fee is charged. Separate charges for boat rental and tours.

Closest town: Waycross.

For more information: Okefenokee Swamp Park, Inc., Waycross, GA 31501. Phone 283-0583.

▨ KINGFISHER LANDING

[Fig. 23(6)] Many wilderness canoeists and campers start their journey at Kingfisher Landing, which offers a boat ramp into the northern reaches of the swamp. The red and green canoe trails begin here (*see* Suwannee Canal Recreation Area, below). The grounds of this site are worth exploring for plant and animal species found in the swamp. Of interest to historians is abandoned railroad equipment located south of the trailhead, a silent reminder of the logging and peat moss gathering activities that occurred in the swamp. The vegetation growing over, around, and through the rusty equipment testifies to the perseverance of nature.

Fishing is allowed here but is subject to regulations governing the wildlife refuge. Call 496-7836 for details.

Directions: From Waycross, go 20 miles south on US 1/23 toward Folkston. After GA 121/Racepond, go 2.5 miles. Go right to Kingfisher Landing.

Activities: Fishing, wilderness canoeing and camping.

Facilities: Primitive restroom, parking.

Dates: Open 7 days a week.

Fees: Wilderness canoeing and camping by reserved fee permit only. See Suwannee Canal Recreation Area.

Closest town: Waycross.

For more information: Suwannee Canal Recreation Area, U.S. Fish and Wildlife Service, Okefenokee National Wildlife Refuge, Route 2, Box 338, Folkston, GA 31537. Phone 496-3331 for canoe-camping reservations.

Folkston Area: Suwannee Canal Recreation Area

[Fig. 23(8)] This park is one of two that offers a wilderness adventure in the refuge. Visitors can explore the swamp on their own by car, bike, boat, or on foot, or take a guided nature tour offered from the concessionaire. Suwannee Canal Recreation Area, located on the eastern side of the swamp, was known for years as Camp Cornelia, the scene of "Jackson's Folly." Thanks to the captain's failed canal-building efforts, sightseers have excellent water access to the eastern prairies of the Okefenokee Swamp.

On the upland portion of the park, the lazy can drive the 4.5-mile Swamp Island Drive. Cyclists may want to bike to trailheads and hike from there. Recommended is the 4,500-foot boardwalk to Seagrove Lake and the 50-foot Owl's Roost Tower where quiet observers may see the endangered Florida sandhill crane during winter and early spring. Other trails lead through pine flatlands typical of the swamp's boundary. At the boat basin, a concession offers guided boat tours, motorboats, canoe, and bicycle rentals as well as supplies and souvenirs. A popular activity is wilderness canoeing and camping on the area's 120 miles of canoe trails. Yellow and orange wilderness canoeing trails begin and end here.

The canal penetrates 11 miles into the heart of the Okefenokee, where boaters can access Chesser, Grand, and Mizell prairies, the swamp's most extensive open areas. These shallow, flooded marshlands are covered with waterlilies, neverwet, pipewort, ferns, maidencane, and a variety of sedges and grasses. During late spring and early summer, visitors will hear the dinosaur rumblings of male and female alligators, and wading birds are very common. The park is on the Colonial Coast Birding Trail established by the Georgia Department of Natural Resources.

Of interest to historians is the Chesser Island Homestead, the authentic homesite of the Chesser family for almost 100 years. The family's cabin and grounds are open to tour. An Indian mound is located nearby. Other attractions include Swamp's Edge Information Center, with exhibits, books, and information on the Okefenokee, and a picnic area.

Fishing is a popular activity, with largemouth bass, bluegill, warmouth, catfish, and pickerel being the most common catches. No live fish may be used as bait, and boats are limited to 10 horsepower engines.

Trails: Sometimes trails are closed for repair or other reasons. Canal Diggers Trail, 0.55 mile; Songbird Trail, 0.97 mile; Peckerwood Trail, 0.17 mile; Chesser Island Homestead Trail, 0.49 mile; Deerstand Trail and Tower, 0.53 mile; Boardwalk to Owl's Roost Tower and Seagrove Lake, 1.5 miles round-trip. Canoe trails range from 12 miles to 55 miles.

Directions: From I-95 take Exit 2/3. Go west on GA 40 to Folkston. Turn south onto GA 23/121 and proceed 7 miles. Turn right onto Spur 121 and drive 4 miles to the recreation area.

Activities: Hiking, biking, canoeing, boating, fishing, picnicking, boat tours, interpretive programs, historic exhibits, special events. Wilderness canoeing and camping by reserved fee permit only. For guided tours, ask the concessionaire for approved outfitters.

Facilities: Boat and canoe rentals, gift shop, snack bar, visitor information center with nature exhibits, picnic areas, marked canoeing and walking trails, boardwalk, photo blinds, observation platform, restrooms.

Dates: Open 7 days a week, with seasonal hour changes. Closed Christmas Day.

Fees: An admission fee is charged. Separate fees for boat rental and tours.

Closest town: Folkston.

For more information: Suwannee Canal Recreation Area, U.S. Fish and Wildlife Service, Okefenokee National Wildlife Refuge, Route 2, Box 3330, Folkston, GA 31537. Phone 496-3331 for canoe reservations or 496-7836 for other information. Refuge concession: Carl E. Glenn Jr. Route 2, Box 3325, Folkston, GA 31537. Phone (800) 792-6796.

Fargo Area: Stephen C. Foster State Park

[Fig. 23(7)] On the western side of the swamp is an 80-acre state park that provides access to the heart of the Okefenokee. Named for the songwriter who penned *Swanee River*, Stephen C. Foster offers wilderness adventures to the headwaters of the Suwannee, or an excursion to Billys Island, site of an Indian village (500 A.D.), the Lee Homestead (1853), and a town that supported Hebard Cypress Company's logging efforts (1908-27).

The state park is one of the few in the country located inside a national wildlife refuge. From Fargo, visitors drive 17 miles along the Suwannee River then out a curving, upland peninsula known as The Pocket, which ends at Jones Island. Inside the park, there is a pioneer camping area, a tent and trailer area, cottages, an interpretive center, picnic facilities and shelters, and a boat basin. Boat tours leave from here with entertaining programs covering the swamp's natural and human history. Or you can rent a canoe or motor boat, grab a map, and head out on your own adventure. A store offers food and beverages, fishing supplies, and information about the swamp. This is the only park that offers drive-up camping inside the refuge. Wilderness canoeing and camping expeditions begin and end here as well.

An interesting mix of habitats is encountered in this part of the swamp, including blackwater lakes, blackgum, bald and pond cypress swamps, bay islands, and lily and golden club prairies. Baldcypress (*Taxodium distichum*) prefer wet areas with moving waters, such as streams and rivers, and are recognized by shallow, furrowed bark that peels off in thin, flaky strips, and needles borne singly in 2 rows on slender green twigs. Pond cypresses (*Taxodium ascendens*) prefer lakes and ponds and are recognized by their thick, deeply furrowed bark and shorter, scalelike leaves.

The western portion of the swamp is popular with fishermen. A river sill built in 1957 and a natural sand ridge keep the waters unnaturally high around the river. The most common catches are bluegill, warmouth, catfish, bowfin, and pickerel. No live fish may be used as bait, and boats are limited to 10 horsepower engines. The Trembling Earth Nature Trail begins and ends near the boat basin, forming a 1.5-mile loop of trail and boardwalk through pinelands and swamp. Interpretive brochures are available in the office. A museum offers interpretive displays on the swamp's ecosystem and wildlife.

Trails: 1.5-mile Trembling Earth Nature Trail.

Directions: From I-95 take Exit 6/29, and go west on US 82 to Waycross. Continue west on US 84 to Homerville. Turn left on US 441 and proceed south to Fargo. Turn left at GA 177 and proceed to park entrance.

Activities: Canoeing, boating, fishing, camping, hiking, biking, picnicking, boat tours, interpretive programs, special events.

Facilities: Boat and canoe rentals, gift shop, snack bar, museum (open 8 a.m. to 5 p.m.), 3 group picnic shelters, marked canoeing and walking trails, restrooms, children's playground. Camping: 9, 2-bedroom cottages with heat and air conditioning, kitchen, utensils, and linens. Reservations can be made up to 11 months in advance by calling 637-5274. Two camping areas have a total of 66 tent and trailer sites with water and electrical hookups. Each campsite has a picnic table and grill, and each camping area has a comfort station with hot showers, toilets, and washer-dryers. Primitive camping is available to organized groups. Be sure to purchase groceries before arriving at the campsite. The brown, red, green, and orange canoeing-camping trails begin and end here.

Dates: Open 7 days a week, with seasonal hour changes.

Fees: An admission fee is charged. Separate charges for boat rental and tours.

Closest town: Fargo.

For more information: Stephen C. Foster State Park, Georgia Department of Natural Resources, Route 1, Fargo, GA 31631. Phone 637-5274.

WILDERNESS CANOEING-CAMPING IN THE OKEFENOKEE SWAMP

An excellent way to experience the Okefenokee is to go on a canoe-camping trip. Trips range in length from two to five days, and paddlers leave from Suwannee Canal Recreation Area, Stephen C. Foster State Park, or Kingfisher Landing and follow marked trails to platforms or island campsites. This is a popular activity, especially during the cooler months, and reservations may be hard to get. Trips may be reserved no earlier than two months in advance, so call refuge headquarters (496-3331) when it opens at 7 a.m. exactly two months in advance of the desired reservation date. With little current flow and obstructions in the form of peat blowups, canoeists must paddle the entire way, which can get strenuous with hot sun and the wind blowing in your face. Mosquitoes are generally not a problem except after dark from April to October.

For more information: Suwannee Canal Recreation Area, U.S. Fish and Wildlife Service, Okefenokee National Wildlife Refuge, Route 2, Box 3330, Folkston, GA 31537. Phone 496-3331 for canoe reservations or 496-7836 for other information.

LODGING AND CAMPING NEAR THE OKEFENOKEE SWAMP

One of the best options is to use cabins or campsites that are available inside the refuge at Stephen C. Foster State Park. Laura S. Walker State Park also offers campsites. Those looking for more predictable chain motels can stay near the northern end of the swamp in Waycross. Phone 283-3742 for list of options. Those looking to stay closer to Stephen Foster State Park but outside the park may want to consider **The Gator Motel** in Fargo, which is short on luxury but remains an inexpensive and dog-eared classic. *637-5445.*

Folkston has reliable chain lodging, which puts visitors near the Suwannee Canal Recreation Area. Phone 496-2536 for list of options. A more charming choice is **The Inn at Folkston Bed and Breakfast** at 509 West Main Street, Folkston. Genna and Roger Wangsness run a warm and comforting B&B in a recently restored and decorated 1920s bungalow. They offer Okefenokee Swamp tour packages and can help guests find nature-oriented activities. Campgrounds on the eastern side include Traders Hill Park (*see* page 293), and Okefenokee Pastimes, phone 496-4472. The latter also rents bikes and kayaks.

░ RESTAURANTS NEAR THE OKEFENOKEE SWAMP

Okefenokee Restaurant. US 1, Folkston. Rub elbows with locals in this popular small restaurant that is a fixture in the area. Open for breakfast, lunch and dinner. Closed Sunday. *Moderate. 496-3263.*

The Suwannee River

Beginning as a blackwater river in the Okefenokee Swamp, the river of musical legend emerges below the sill and flows 240 miles southwest to the Gulf of Mexico to the town of Suwannee. In Florida, the river is joined by Georgia's beautiful blackwater Alapaha and Withlacoochie rivers, before it receives tremendous volumes of clear spring water from underground springs. The Santa Fe River is the last major tributary that enters the Suwannee before it reaches the Gulf. The upper reaches, in the swamp and below the sill, are the best areas for canoeing. A permit, which is required to portage the sill, can be obtained by calling the Okefenokee National Wildlife Refuge.

The river remains isolated and pristine in its upper sections, where canoeists will pass shallow, white sandy banks and forests of baldcypress bearded with Spanish moss, blackgum, sweetbay, magnolia, pine, and palmetto. Wildlife is as abundant as in the refuge.

The Suwannee River begins officially 2 miles north of the boat basin entrance from Stephen C. Foster State Park at the confluence of the East and Middle forks at the northern end of Billys Island. Compulsive canoeists can paddle north then turn around so they can say they started at the beginning, or just turn left out of the boat basin and start down the river for 5 miles to the sill. In a few miles, canoeists reach the River Narrows, which it does, surrounded by a heavily logged area of baldcypress stumps, blackgum, fetterbush, and smilax vines. After winding through the narrow channel, paddlers reach prairie and then the river narrows again, in an area lined with blackgum, before eventually reaching the river sill.

Below the sill, the Suwannee becomes a river and flows 17 miles to Fargo, where there is a public boat ramp and small park. Between the refuge and Fargo, 2 miles below the sill on the eastern bank is Griffis Fish Camp, phone 637-5395, which offers camping and takeout for a fee. From Fargo, the river winds 20 miles through beautiful wilderness, crossing the state line before reaching the next best takeout site at Florida Highway 6.

The Suwannee River is well known due to the songwriting talents of Stephen C. Foster, who also wrote *Beautiful Dreamer, Camptown Races, Jeannie with the Light Brown Hair*, and *My Old Kentucky Home* from 1844 to 1864. *Swanee River* is also known as *The Old Folks at Home*. He apparently never visited the river he made famous. An alcoholic, he died poor at the age of 38 in the charity ward at New York's Bellevue Hospital.

Suggested Canoe Trips: Stephen C. Foster State Park to Griffis Landing, 8 miles; Stephen C. Foster State Park to Fargo, 20 miles; Fargo to Florida Highway 6, 20 miles.

Appendices

A. Fish Camps and Marinas

BONA BELLA MARINA

SERVICES PROVIDED: Drive-Up Boat Launching, Dock Space (West Slips), Boat Rentals, Bait Available, Fishing Gear Available, Boat Fuel Available, Ice Available, Food & Drinks Available, Floating Boat Dock, Fish Cleaning Table, Restrooms

DRIVING DIRECTIONS FROM INTERSTATE-95: Take Exit 17 east on I-16 for 7.8 miles to Exit 35. Take 37th Street Connector Exit for 0.6 mile to 37th Street. Turn left (west) on GA 204 for 0.8 mile to Abercorn Street. Turn right and continue west on GA 204 for 0.3 mile to U.S. 80. Turn left (east) for 2.2 miles to Skidaway Road. Turn right 1.0 to LaRoche Avenue. Turn left 0.9 mile to Jasmine Avenue. Turn left and immediately bear right on Livingston Avenue for 4.0 miles to marina. Facility provides hoist lift launching (8,000 lb). Phone (912) 355-9601.

BULL RIVER YACHT CLUB

SERVICES PROVIDED: Dock Space (West Slips), Charter Fishing, Bait Available, Boat Fuel Available, Ice Available, Food & Drinks Available, Floating Boat Dock, Fish Cleaning Table, Restrooms

DRIVING DIRECTIONS FROM INTERSTATE-95: Take Exit 17 east on I-16 for 7.8 miles to Exit 35. Take 37th Street Connector Exit for 0.6 mile to 37th Street. Turn left (west) on GA 204 for 0.8 mile to Abercorn Street. Turn right and continue west on GA 204 for 0.3 mile to U.S. 80. Turn left (east) 8.6 miles to club entrance located on right. Facility does not provide launching. Phone (912) 897-7300.

CHIMNEY CREEK FISH CAMP

SERVICES PROVIDED: Drive -Up Boat Launching, Dock Space (West Slips), Dry Boat Storage, Lodging/Camping On Site, Charter Fishing, Bait Available, Fishing Gear Available, Boat Fuel Available, Ice Available, Food & Drinks Available, Floating Boat Dock, Fish Cleaning Table, Boat Wash-Down Area, Restrooms

DRIVING DIRECTIONS FROM INTERSTATE-95: Take Exit 17 east on I-16 for 7.8 miles to Exit 35. Take 37th Street Connector Exit for 0.6 mile to 37th Street. Turn left (west) on GA 204 for 0.8 mile to Abercorn Street. Turn right and continue west on GA 204 for 0.3 mile to U.S. 80. Turn left (east) for 14.8 miles to D.A.V. Road. Turn right 0.3 mile to marina located on left.

Facility provides hoist lift launching (6,000 lb). Phone (912) 786-9857.

COFFEE BLUFF FISH CAMP

SERVICES PROVIDED: Drive -Up Boat Launching, Dock Space (West Slips), Dry Boat Storage, Bait Available, Fishing Gear Available, Boat Fuel Available, Ice Available, Food & Drinks Available, Floating Boat Dock, Fish Cleaning Table, Boat Wash-Down Area, Restrooms

DRIVING DIRECTIONS FROM INTERSTATE-95: Take Exit 16 east on GA 204 for 8.9 miles to Holland Drive. Turn right 0.5 mile to White Bluff Road. Turn right 3.2 miles to marina at end of road. Note that White Bluff Road becomes Coffee Bluff Road. Facility provides hoist lift launching (4,000 lb). Phone (912) 925-9030.

DELEGAL CREEK MARINA

SERVICES PROVIDED: Dock Space (West Slips), Charter Fishing, Bait Available, Fishing Gear Available, Boat Fuel Available, Ice Available, Floating Boat Dock, Fish Cleaning Table, Restrooms

DRIVING DIRECTIONS FROM INTERSTATE-95: Take Exit 16 east on GA 204 for 10.4 miles to Montgomery Crossroads. Turn right 1.2 miles to Waters Avenue. Turn right 5.2 miles to security gate. Note that Waters Avenue leads into Whitefield Avenue then into Diamond Causeway leading to Skidaway Island. Enter security gate and request information to marina. Facility does not provide launching. Phone (912) 598-0023.

FOUNTAIN MARINA

SERVICES PROVIDED: Dock Space (West Slips), Dry Boat Storage, Bait Available, Fishing Gear Available, Boat Fuel Available, Ice Available, Food & Drinks Available, Floating Boat Dock, Fish Cleaning Table, Boat Wash-Down Area, Restrooms

DRIVING DIRECTIONS FROM INTERSTATE-95: Take Exit 17 east on I-16 for 7.8 miles to Exit 35. Take 37th Street Connector Exit for 0.6 mile to 37th Street. Turn left (west) on GA 204 for 0.8 mile to Abercorn Street. Turn right and continue west on 204 for 0.3 mile to U.S. 80. Turn left (east) 3.2 miles to River Drive. Turn right 0.2 mile to marina located on left. Facility does not provide drive-up launching (9,000 lb). Phone (912) 354-2283.

HOGAN'S MARINA

SERVICES PROVIDED: Drive-Up Boat Launching, Dock Space (West Slips), Dry Boat Storage, Charter

Fishing, Bait Available, Fishing Gear Available, Boat Fuel Available, Ice Available, Food & Drinks Available, Floating Boat Dock, Fish Cleaning Table, Boat Wash-Down Area, Restrooms

DRIVING DIRECTIONS FROM INTERSTATE-95: Take Exit 17 east on I-16 for 7.8 miles to Exit 35. Take 37th Street Connector Exit for 0.6 mile to 37th Street. Turn left (west) on GA 204 for 0.8 mile to Abercorn Street. Turn right and continue west on 204 for 0.3 mile to U.S. 80. Turn left (east) 4.9 miles to Johnny Mercer Blvd. Turn right 2.9 miles to Wilmington Island Road. Road to marina located immediately on right after turning onto Wilmington Island Road. Facility provides hoist and fork lift launching (15,000 lb). Phone (912) 897-3474.

ISLE OF HOPE MARINA
SERVICES PROVIDED: Drive-Up Boat Launching, Dock Space (West Slips), Boat Rentals, Charter Fishing, Bait Available, Fishing Gear Available, Boat Fuel Available, Ice Available, Food & Drinks Available, Floating Boat Dock, Fish Cleaning Table, Boat Wash-Down Area, Restrooms

DRIVING DIRECTIONS FROM INTERSTATE-95: Take Exit 17 east on I-16 for 7.8 miles to Exit 35. Take 37th Street Connector Exit for 0.6 mile to 37th Street. Turn left (west) on GA 204 for 0.8 mile to Abercorn Street. Turn right and continue west on 204 for 0.3 mile to U.S. 80. Turn left (east) 2.2 miles to Skidaway Road. Turn right for 1.0 to LaRoche Avenue. Turn left for 3.4 miles to Bluff Road. Right on Bluff Road 0.4 mile to marina. Facility provides hoist lift launching (8,000 lb). Phone (912) 354-8187.

LANDINGS HARBOR
SERVICES PROVIDED: Drive-Up Boat Launching, Dock Space (West Slips), Dry Boat Storage, Charter Fishing, Bait Available, Fishing Gear Available, Boat Fuel Available, Ice Available, Food & Drinks Available, Floating Boat Dock, Fish Cleaning Table, Boat Wash-Down Area, Restrooms

DRIVING DIRECTIONS FROM INTERSTATE-95: Take Exit 16 east on GA 204 for 10.4 miles to Montgomery Crossroads. Turn right 1.2 miles to Waters Avenue. Turn right for 5.2 miles to McWhorter Drive. Note that Waters Avenue leads into Whitefield Avenue then into Diamond Causeway leading to Skidaway Island. Turn left on McWhorter Drive for 1.7 miles to the Landings security gate located on right. Enter security gate and request information to marina. Facility provides fork lift launching (8,000 lb). Phone (912) 598-1901.

LEE SHORE MARINA
SERVICES PROVIDED: Dock Space (West Slips), Floating Boat Dock

DRIVING DIRECTIONS FROM INTERSTATE-95: Take Exit 17 east on I-16 for 7.8 miles for Exit 35. Take 37th Street Connector Exit for 0.6 mile to 37th Street. Turn left (west) on GA 204 for 0.8 mile to Abercorn

Street. Turn right and continue west on 204 for 0.3 mile to U.S. 80. Turn left (east) 4.9 miles to Johnny Mercer Blvd. Turn right for 2.7 miles. Lee Shore Marina is located on the right just past bridge. Facility does not provide launching. Phone (912) 897-1154.

MARLIN MARINA
SERVICES PROVIDED: Drive-Up Boat Launching, Dock Space (West Slips), Charter Fishing, Bait Available, Fishing Gear Available, Ice Available, Food & Drinks Available, Floating Boat Dock, Fish Cleaning Table, Boat Wash-Down Area, Restrooms

DRIVING DIRECTIONS FROM INTERSTATE-95: Take Exit 17 east on I-16 for 7.8 miles for Exit 35. Take 37th Street Connector Exit for 0.6 mile to 37th Street. Turn left (west) on GA 204 for 0.8 mile to Abercorn Street. Turn right and continue west on 204 for 0.3 mile to U.S. 80. Turn left (east) 16.6 miles to Jones Avenue located on Tybee Island. Turn right 1.3 miles to 14th Street. Turn right 0.3 mile to Chatham Avenue. Marina located across Chatham Avenue to the left. Facility provides hoist lift launching (4,000 lb). Phone (912) 786-7508.

PALMER JOHNSON
SERVICES PROVIDED: Dock Space (West Slips), Boat Fuel Available, Ice Available, Food & Drinks Available, Floating Boat Dock, Restrooms

DRIVING DIRECTIONS FROM INTERSTATE-95: Take Exit 17 east on I-16 for 7.8 miles for Exit 35. Take 37th Street Connector Exit for 0.6 mile to 37th Street. Turn left (west) on GA 204 for 0.8 mile to Abercorn Street. Turn right and continue west on 204 for 0.3 mile to U.S. 80. Turn left (east) for 3.2 miles to River Drive. Turn right 0.6 mile to marina located on left. Facility does not provide drive-up launching (300,000 lb). Phone (912) 352-4956.

RIVERWATCH MARINA,
(FORMERLY AMBOS MARINA)
SERVICES PROVIDED: Dock Space (West Slips), Dry Boat Storage, Charter Fishing, Fishing Gear Available, Boat Fuel Available, Ice Available, Floating Boat Dock, Fish Cleaning Table, Boat Wash-Down Area, Restrooms

DRIVING DIRECTIONS FROM INTERSTATE-95: Take Exit 17 east on I-16 for 7.8 miles for Exit 35. Take 37th Street Connector Exit for 0.6 mile to 37th Street. Turn left (west) on GA 204 for 0.8 mile to Abercorn Street. Turn right and continue west on 204 for 0.3 mile to U.S. 80. Turn left (east) for 3.2 miles to River Drive. Turn right 0.3 mile to marina located on left. Facility does not provide drive-up launching (25,000 lb). Phone (912) 354-4133.

SAIL HARBOR MARINA
SERVICES PROVIDED: Dock Space (West Slips), Ice Available, Food & Drinks Available, Floating Boat Dock, Restrooms

DRIVING DIRECTIONS FROM INTERSTATE-95:
Take Exit 17 east on I-16 for 7.8 miles for Exit 35. Take 37th Street Connector Exit for 0.6 mile to 37th Street. Turn left (west) on GA 204 for 0.8 mile to Abercorn Street. Turn right and continue west on 204 for 0.3 mile to U.S. 80. Turn left (east) for 4.9 miles to Johnny Mercer Blvd. Turn right 2.9 miles to Wilmington Island Road. Turn right for 1.2 miles to marina entrance on right. Facility does not provide launching. Phone (912) 897-2896.

🦐 SAVANNAH BEND MARINA
SERVICES PROVIDED: Dock Space (West Slips), Dry Boat Storage, Charter Fishing, Bait Available, Fishing Gear Available, Boat Fuel Available, Ice Available, Food & Drinks Available, Floating Boat Dock, Fish Cleaning Table, Boat Wash-Down Area, Restrooms
DRIVING DIRECTIONS FROM INTERSTATE-95:
Take Exit 17 east on I-16 for 7.8 miles for Exit 35. Take 37th Street Connector Exit for 0.6 mile to 37th Street. Turn left (west) on GA 204 for 0.8 mile to Abercorn Street. Turn right and continue west on 204 for 0.3 mile to U.S. 80. Turn left (east) and drive 3.8 miles. Take first left turn past Wilmington River Bridge. Follow narrow paved road for 0.2 mile to Marina. Facility does not provide drive-up launching (12,000 lb). Phone : (912) 897-3625.

🦐 TIDEWATER BOAT WORKS
SERVICES PROVIDED: Dock Space (West Slips), Dry Boat Storage, Boat Fuel Available, Ice Available, Floating Boat Dock, Fish Cleaning Table, Restrooms
DRIVING DIRECTIONS FROM INTERSTATE-95:
Take Exit 17 east on I-16 for 7.8 miles for Exit 35. Take 37th Street Connector Exit for 0.6 mile to 37th Street. Turn left (west) on GA 204 for 0.8 mile to Abercorn Street. Turn right continue west on 204 for 0.3 mile to U.S. 80. Turn left (east) for 3.0 miles to Mechanics Avenue. Turn left 0.5 mile to end of road. Marina located on right. Facility does not provide drive-up launching (50,000 lb). Phone (912) 352-1335.

🦐 TUTEN'S FISH CAMP
SERVICES PROVIDED: Drive-Up Boat Launching, Dock Space (West Slips), Bait Available, Ice Available, Food & Drinks Available, Floating Boat Dock
DRIVING DIRECTIONS FROM INTERSTATE-95:
Take Exit 17 east on I-16 for 7.8 miles for Exit 35. Take 37th Street Connector Exit for 0.6 mile to 37th Street. Turn left (west) on GA 204 for 0.8 mile to Abercorn Street. Turn right and continue west on 204 for 0.3 mile to U.S. 80. Turn left (east) for 2.2 miles to Skidaway Road. Turn right 1.0 miles to LaRoche Avenue. Turn left .26 mile to marina located on left. Facility provides hoist lift launching (3,000 lb). Phone (912) 355-8747.

🦐 YOUNG'S MARINA
SERVICES PROVIDED: Drive-Up Boat Launching, Dock Space (West Slips), Dry Boat Storage, Ice Available, Floating Boat Dock, Boat Wash-Down Area, Restrooms

DRIVING DIRECTIONS FROM INTERSTATE-95:
Take Exit 17 east on I-16 for 7.8 miles for Exit 35. Take 37th Street Connector Exit for 0.6 mile to 37th Street. Turn left (west) on GA 204 for 0.8 mile to Abercorn Street. Turn right and continue west on 204 for 0.3 mile to U.S. 80. Turn left (east) for 4.9 miles to Johnny Mercer Blvd. Turn right 2.9 miles to Wilmington Island Road. Turn right 0.6 mile to marina entrance on right. Facility provides hoist lift launching (4,000 lb). Phone (912) 897-2608.

BRYAN COUNTY

🦐 FT. MCALLISTER MARINA
SERVICES PROVIDED: Drive-Up Boat Launching, Dock Space (Wet Slips), Dry Boat Storage, Charter Fishing, Bait Available, Fishing Gear Available, Boat Fuel Available, Ice Available, Food & Drinks Available, Floating Boat Dock, Fish Cleaning Table, Boat Wash-Down Area, Restrooms
DRIVING DIRECTIONS FROM INTERSTATE-95:
Take Exit 15 east on GA 144 for 6.6 miles to GA SPUR 144. Turn left 3.1 miles to Marina located on left side of road. Facility provides hoist lift launching (24,000 lb). Phone (912) 727-2632

🦐 KILKENNY FISH CAMP
SERVICES PROVIDED: Drive-Up Boat Launching, Dock Space (Wet Slips), Dry Boat Storage, Bait Available, Fishing Gear Available, Boat Fuel Available, Ice Available, Food & Drinks Available, Floating Boat Dock, Fish Cleaning Table, Boat Wash-Down Area, Restrooms
DRIVING DIRECTIONS FROM INTERSTATE-95:
Take Exit 15 east on GA 144 for 12.5 miles to Kilkenny Road. Turn left 2.9 miles until payment ends. Follow dirt road for 0.1 mile to fish camp. Facility provides hoist lift launching (4,000 lb). Phone (912) 727-2215

LIBERTY COUNTY

🦐 HALF MOON MARINA
SERVICES PROVIDED: Drive-Up Boat Launching, Dock Space (Wet Slips), Dry Boat Storage, Bait Available, Fishing Gear Available, Boat Fuel Available, Ice Available, Food & Drinks Available, Floating Boat Dock, Fish Cleaning Table, Boat Wash-Down Area, Restrooms
DRIVING DIRECTIONS FROM INTERSTATE-95:
Take Exit 13 east on GA 38 for 7.3 miles to Kings Road. Turn right 1.2 miles to Azalea Road. Turn right 0.1 mile to marina located on right. Facility provides hoist lift launching (8,000 lb). Phone (912) 884-5819.

🦐 YELLOW BLUFF FISH CAMP
SERVICES PROVIDED: Drive-Up Boat Launching, Dock Space (Wet Slips), Dry Boat Storage, Charter Fishing, Bait Available, Fishing Gear Available, Boat Fuel

Available, Ice Available, Food & Drinks Available, Floating Boat Dock, Fish Cleaning Table, Boat Wash-Down Area, Restrooms

DRIVING DIRECTIONS FROM INTERSTATE-95: Take Exit 13 east on GA 38 for 9.8 miles to Yellow Bluff Road. Turn right 0.2 mile to fish camp. Facility provides hoist lift launching (4,500 lb). Phone (912) 884-5448.

MCINTOSH COUNTY

BELLE BLUFF MARINA
SERVICES PROVIDED: Drive-Up Boat Launching, Dock Space (Wet Slips), Dry Boat Storage, Lodging/Camping on Site, Charter Fishing, Bait Available, Fishing Gear Available, Boat Fuel Available, Ice Available, Food & Drinks Available, Floating Boat Dock, Fish Cleaning Table, Boat Wash-Down Area, Restrooms
DRIVING DIRECTIONS FROM INTERSTATE-95: Take Exit 11 south on GA 57 for 1.0 miles to U.S. 17. Turn left (north) 2.2 miles to Pine Harbor Road. Turn right 0.1 mile and then turn left on Shellman Bluff Road. Drive 3.0 miles to Belle Hammock Road. Turn right 1.6 miles to Belle Bluff marina sign. Follow dirt road to left for 0.2 mile to marina. Facility provides hoist lift launching (7,000 lb). Phone (912) 832-5323.

DALLAS BLUFF MARINA & CAMP
SERVICES PROVIDED: Drive-Up Boat Launching, Dock Space (Wet Slips), Lodging/Camping on Site, Charter Fishing, Ice Available, Floating Boat Dock, Fish Cleaning Table, Boat Wash-Down Area, Restrooms
DRIVING DIRECTIONS FROM INTERSTATE-95: Take Exit 11 south on GA 57 for 1.0 miles to U.S. 17. Turn left (north) 2.2 miles to Pine Harbor Road. Turn right 0.1 mile and then turn left on Shellman Bluff Road. Drive 6.8 miles to stop sign. Turn left and follow road for 1.7 miles to Dallas Bluff Marina sign. Turn right at sign and follow road for 0.1 mile to marina. Facility provides hoist lift launching (4,000 lb). Phone (912) 832-5116.

FISHERMAN'S LODGE
SERVICES PROVIDED: Drive-Up Boat Launching, Charter Fishing, Bait Available, Fishing Gear Available, Boat Fuel Available, Ice Available, Food & Drinks Available, Floating Boat Dock, Fish Cleaning Table, Boat Wash-Down Area, Restrooms
DRIVING DIRECTIONS FROM INTERSTATE-95: Take Exit 11 south on GA 57 for 1.0 miles to U.S. 17. Turn left (north) 2.2 miles to Pine Harbor Road. Turn right 0.1 mile and then turn left on Shellman Bluff Road. Drive 6.8 miles to stop sign. Turn right toward Southerland Bluff then immediately take first road on left and drive 0.2 mile to Broro River Bluff. Turn right drive 0.3 mile to marina. Facility provides hoist lift launching (11,000 lb). Phone (912) 832-5162.

MCINTOSH ROAD & GUN CLUB
SERVICES PROVIDED: Drive-Up Boat Launching, Boat Rentals, Charter Fishing, Bait Available, Fishing Gear

Available, Boat Fuel Available, Ice Available, Food & Drinks Available, Floating Boat Dock, Fish Cleaning Table, Boat Wash-Down Area, Restrooms

DRIVING DIRECTIONS FROM INTERSTATE-95: Take Exit 10 south on GA 251 for 1.2 miles to U.S. 17. Turn right (south) 0.9 mile to GA 99. Turn left (north) 4.4 miles to Blue-N-Hall Park sign on right. Turn right and follow dead end road to marina. Facility provides hoist lift launching (6,000 lb). Phone (912) 437-4677.

PINE HARBOR MARINA
SERVICES PROVIDED: Drive-Up Boat Launching, Dock Space (Wet Slips), Dry Boat Storage, Bait Available, Fishing Gear Available, Boat Fuel Available, Ice Available, Food & Drinks Available, Floating Boat Dock, Fish Cleaning Table, Boat Wash-Down Area, Restrooms
DRIVING DIRECTIONS FROM INTERSTATE-95: Take Exit 11 south on GA 57 for 1.0 miles to U.S. 17. Turn left (north) 2.2 miles to Pine Harbor Road. Turn right 2.7 miles to Belle Hammock Road. Turn onto Belle Hammock Road for 0.1 mile then turn right on Pine Harbor Marina Road for 0.2 mile to marina. Facility provides hoist lift launching (6,000 lb). Phone (912) 832-5999.

SHELLMAN BLUFF FISH CAMP
SERVICES PROVIDED: Drive-Up Boat Launching, Chart Fishing, Bait Available, Fishing Gear Available, Boat Fuel Available, Ice Available, Food & Drinks Available, Floating Boat Dock, Fish Cleaning Table, Restrooms
DRIVING DIRECTIONS FROM INTERSTATE-95: Take Exit 11 south on GA 57 for 1.0 miles to U.S. 17. Turn left (north) 2.2 miles to Pine Harbor Road. Turn right 0.1 mile and then turn left on Shellman Bluff Road. Drive 6.8 miles to stop sign. Turn right toward Southerland Bluff then immediately take first road on left and drive 0.2 mile to Broro River Bluff. Turn right on bluff road and drive 0.2 mile to camp. Facility provides hoist lift launching (7,000 lb). Phone (912) 832-4331.

SHELLMAN BLUFF MOTEL
SERVICES PROVIDED: Dock Space (Wet Slips), Lodging/Camping on Site, Floating Boat Dock, Fish Cleaning Table
DRIVING DIRECTIONS FROM INTERSTATE-95: Take Exit 11 south on GA 57 for 1.0 miles to U.S. 17. Turn left (north) 2.2 miles to Pine Harbor Road. Turn right 0.1 mile and then turn left on Shellman Bluff Road. Drive 6.8 miles to stop sign. Turn right toward Southerland Bluff then immediately take first road on left and drive 0.2 mile to Broro River Bluff. Turn left on bluff road and drive 0.1 mile to marina. Facility does not provide launching. Phone (912) 832-5426.

GLYNN COUNTY

BLYTHE ISLAND REGIONAL PARK MARINA
SERVICES PROVIDED: Drive-Up Boat Launching,

Dock Space (Wet Slips), Lodging/Camping On Site, Bait Available, Fishing Gear Available, Boat Fuel Available, Ice Available, Food & Drinks Available, Floating Boat Dock, Fish Cleaning Table, Boat Wash-Down Area, Pier With Hand Railings, Wheelchair Accessible, Restrooms, Picnic Tables, Children's Playground

DRIVING DIRECTIONS FROM INTERSTATE-95: Take Exit 6 south on U.S. 17 for 0.6 mile to GA 303. Turn right (north) 3.6 miles to park entrance. Turn right into park entrance, drive 1.2 miles to marina. Facility provides hoist lift launching (8,000 lb). Phone (912) 261-3805.

BRUNSWICK LANDING MARINA
SERVICES PROVIDED: Dock Space (Wet Slips), Dry Boat Storage, Charter Fishing, Bait Available, Boat Fuel Available, Ice Available, Food & Drinks Available, Floating Boat Dock, Fish Cleaning Table, Restrooms

DRIVING DIRECTIONS FROM INTERSTATE-95: Take Exit 7 south on U.S. 341 for 3.7 miles to marina located on right. Facility does not provide drive-up launching (100,000 lb). Phone (912) 262-9264.

BRUNSWICK MARINA
SERVICES PROVIDED: Drive-Up Boat Launching, Dock Space (Wet Slips), Dry Boat Storage, Bait Available, Boat Fuel Available, Ice Available, Food & Drinks Available, Floating Boat Dock, Fish Cleaning Table, Restrooms

DRIVING DIRECTIONS FROM INTERSTATE-95: Take Exit 8 south on Spur 25 (North Golden Isles Expressway) 4.3 miles to U.S. 17. Turn right (south) 2.4 miles to marina located on left. Facility provides hoist lift launching (4,500 lb). Phone (912) 265-2290.

CREDLE'S FISH CAMP
SERVICES PROVIDED: Drive-Up Boat Launching, Dock Space (Wet Slips), Bait Available, Fishing Gear Available, Ice Available, Food & Drinks Available, Floating Boat Dock, Fish Cleaning Table, Boat Wash-Down Area, Restrooms

DRIVING DIRECTIONS FROM INTERSTATE-95: Take Exit 6 north on U.S. 17 for 3.0 miles. Look for Credle's sign on right. Turn right on dirt road and drive 0.3 mile to camp. Facility provides hoist lift launching (6,000 lb). Phone (912) 261-1935.

GOLDEN ISLES MARINA
SERVICES PROVIDED: Dock Space (Wet Slips), Charter Fishing, Boat Fuel Available, Ice Available, Food & Drinks Available, Floating Boat Dock, Fish Cleaning Table, Restrooms

DRIVING DIRECTIONS FROM INTERSTATE-95: Take Exit 8 south on Spur 25 (North Golden Isles Expressway) 4.3 miles to U.S. 17. Turn right 1.7 miles to the Torras Causeway leading to St. Simons Island. Turn left (east) 4.2 miles. Marina located on right before crossing Frederica River Bridge. Facility does not provide launching. Phone (912) 634-1128.

HAMPTON RIVER CLUB MARINA
SERVICES PROVIDED: Drive-Up Boat Launching, Dock Space (Wet Slips), Dry Boat Storage, Boat Rentals, Charter Fishing, Bait Available, Fishing Gear Available, Boat Fuel Available, Ice Available, Food & Drinks Available, Floating Boat Dock, Fish Cleaning Table, Boat Wash-Down Area, Restrooms

DRIVING DIRECTIONS FROM INTERSTATE-95: Take Exit 8 south on Spur 25 (North Golden Isles Expressway) 4.3 miles to U.S. 17. Turn right 1.7 miles to the Torras Causeway leading to St. Simons Island. Turn left (east) 4.4 miles to Sea Island Road. Turn left 3.1 miles to Frederica Road. Turn left 2.2 miles to Lawrence Road. Turn right 6.7 miles to Hampton Marina sign. Turn right 0.2 mile to marina. Facility provides hoist and fork lift launching (9,000 lb). Phone (912) 638-1210.

JEKYLL ISLAND HISTORIC (WHARF) MARINA
SERVICES PROVIDED: Dock Space (Wet Slips), Boat Rentals, Charter Fishing, Bait Available, Fishing Gear Available, Boat Fuel Available, Ice Available, Food & Drinks Available, Floating Boat Dock, Fish Cleaning Table, Lighted or Night Fishing, Restrooms

DRIVING DIRECTIONS FROM INTERSTATE-95: Take Exit 6 north on U.S. 17 for 5.0 miles to Jekyll Island Causeway (GA 50). Turn right 6.5 miles to River View Drive (south). Turn left and make a U-turn back west on GA 50. Drive back toward Toll Booth to River View Drive (north). Turn right 0.5 mile to wharf. Wharf and parking located on left. Facility does not provide launching. Phone (912) 635-2891.

ST. SIMONS ISLAND BOATING AND FISHING CLUB
SERVICES PROVIDED: Drive-Up Boat Launching, Dock Space (Wet Slips), Dry Boat Storage, Charter Fishing, Bait Available, Boat Fuel Available, Ice Available, Floating Boat Dock, Fish Cleaning Table, Boat Wash-Down Area, Restrooms

DRIVING DIRECTIONS FROM INTERSTATE-95: Take Exit 8 south on Spur 25 (North Golden Isles Expressway) 4.3 miles to U.S. 17. Turn right 1.7 miles to the Torras Causeway leading to St. Simons Island. Turn left (east) 4.4 miles to the Sea Island Road. Turn left 0.2 mile to Hamilton Drive. Turn left 0.2 mile to marina. Facility provides hoist lift launching (8,000 lb). Phone (912) 638-9146.

TAYLOR'S FISH CAMP
SERVICES PROVIDED: Drive-Up Boat Launching, Charter Fishing, Bait Available, Floating Boat Dock, Fish Cleaning Table, Boat Wash-Down Area, Restrooms

DRIVING DIRECTIONS FROM INTERSTATE-95: Take Exit 8 south on Spur 25 (North Golden Isles Expressway) 4.3 miles to U.S. 17. Turn right 1.7 miles to the Torras Causeway leading to St. Simons Island. Turn left (east) 4.4 miles to the Sea Island Road. Turn left 3.1 miles to Frederica Road. Turn left 2.2 miles to Lawrence Road. Turn right 3.0 miles to Cannon Point Road. Turn right at Taylor's

Fish Camp sign and follow road to camp. Facility provides hoist lift launching (2,000 lb). Phone (912) 638-7690.

TROUPE CREEK MARINA
SERVICES PROVIDED: Drive-Up Boat Launching, Dock Space (Wet Slips), Dry Boat Storage, Bait Available, Fishing Gear Available, Boat Fuel Available, Ice Available, Food & Drink Available, Floating Boat Dock, Fish Cleaning Table, Boat Wash-Down Area, Restrooms
DRIVING DIRECTIONS FROM INTERSTATE-95: Take Exit 8 south on Spur 25 (North Golden Isles Expressway) 1.0 miles to Walker Road. Turn left 2.2 miles to U.S. 17. Turn left (north) 0.3 mile to Yacht Road just past small bridge. Turn right 0.6 mile to marina. Facility provides hoist lift launching (8,000 lb). Phone (912) 264-3862.

TWO-WAY FISH CAMP
SERVICES PROVIDED: Drive-Up Boat Launching, Dock Space (Wet Slips), Dry Boat Storage, Lodging/Camping On Site, Charter Fishing, Bait Available, Fishing Gear Available, Boat Fuel Available, Ice Available, Food & Drink Available, Floating Boat Dock, Fish Cleaning Table, Boat Wash-Down Area, Lighted or Night Fishing, Restrooms
DRIVING DIRECTIONS FROM INTERSTATE-95: Take Exit 9 north on GA 99 for 1.2 miles to U.S. 17. Turn left (north) 1.3 miles to entrance to marina. Before crossing Altamaha River Bridge, turn right 0.3 mile to marina. Facility provides hoist and fork lift launching (12,000 lb). Phone (912) 265-0410.

VILLAGE CREEK LANDING
SERVICES PROVIDED: Boat Rentals, Bait Available, Ice Available, Food & Drink Available, Floating Boat Dock, Fish Cleaning Table, Restrooms
DRIVING DIRECTIONS FROM INTERSTATE-95: Take Exit 8 south on Spur 25 (North Golden Isles Expressway) 4.3 miles to U.S. 17. Turn right 1.7 miles to the Torras Causeway leading to St. Simons Island. Turn left (east) 4.4 miles to Sea Island Road. Turn left 3.1 miles to Frederica Road. Turn left 1.7 miles to Harrington Drive. Turn right 0.9 mile to end of road. Facility does not provide launching. Phone (912) 634-9054.

CAMDEN COUNTY

HICKORY BLUFF MARINA
SERVICES PROVIDED: Drive-Up Boat Launching, Dock Space (Wet Slips), Charter Fishing, Bait Available, Fishing Gear Available, Boat Fuel Available, Ice Available, Food & Drinks Available, Floating Boat Dock, Fish Cleaning Table, Boat Wash-Down Area, Restrooms
DRIVING DIRECTIONS FROM INTERSTATE-95: Take Exit 5 east on Dover Bluff Road for 1.7 miles to Hickory Bluff Road. Turn left 0.8 mile to Hickory Bluff Marina. Facility provides hoist lift launching (8,000 lb). Phone (912) 262-0453.

LANG'S MARINA
SERVICES PROVIDED: Dock Space (Wet Slips), Charter Fishing, Bait Available, Ice Available, Food & Drinks Available, Floating Boat Dock, Restrooms
DRIVING DIRECTIONS FROM INTERSTATE-95: Take Exit 2 east on GA 40 for 9.3 miles to St. Marys Street. Turn right 0.2 mile to marina located on left. Facility does not provide launching. Phone (912) 882-4452.

OCEAN BREEZE MARINA & CAMP
SERVICES PROVIDED: Drive-Up Boat Launching, Dock Space (Wet Slips), Lodging/Camping On Site, Charter Fishing, Bait Available, Fishing Gear Available, Boat Fuel Available, Ice Available, Food & Drinks Available, Floating Boat Dock, Fish Cleaning Table, Boat Wash-Down Area, Restrooms
DRIVING DIRECTIONS FROM INTERSTATE-95: Take Exit 5 east on Dover Bluff Road for 2.4 miles to Ocean Breeze Drive. Turn left 0.5 mile to marina. Facility provides hoist lift launching (4,000 lb). Phone (912) 265-8280.

WARMOUTH
(Lepomis gulosus)

LONGEARED SUNFISH
(Lepomis megalotis)

The warmouth can be identified by a combination of three characteristics: short anal fins, three anal spines, and teeth on the toungue. Longears have long, upward turned opercular lobes.

B. Books And References

A Birder's Guide to Georgia, edited by Kenneth Turner Blackshaw and Joel R. Hitt, Georgia Ornithological Society, Cartersville, GA, 1992.

A Guide to a Georgia Barrier Island, by Taylor Schoettle, Watermarks Publishing, St. Simons Island, GA, 1997.

A Guide to the Georgia Coast, by The Georgia Conservancy, edited by Gwen McKee, Longstreet Press, Atlanta, GA, 1993.

A History of Fort Screven Georgia, by James Mack Adams, JMA2 Publications, Tybee Island, GA, 1998.

A Naturalist in Florida: A Celebration of Eden, by Archie Carr, Yale University Press, Vail Ballou Press, Binghamton, NY, 1994.

A Paddler's Guide to Southern Georgia, by Bob Sehlinger and Don Otey, Menasha Ridge Press, Birmingham, AL, 1980.

An Introduction to Coastal Zone Management, by Timothy Beatley, David J. Brower, Anna K. Schwab, Island Press, Washington, DC, 1994.

Chew Toy of the Gnat Gods: Reflections on the Wildlife of the Southeast Coast, by Bruce Lombardo, Cherokee Publishing Company, Atlanta, GA, 1998.

Early Days on the Georgia Tidewater: The Story of McIntosh County and Sapelo, by Buddy Sullivan, McIntosh County Board of Commissioners, Darien, GA, 1997.

From Beautiful Zion to Red Bird Creek: A History of Bryan County, Georgia, by Buddy Sullivan, Bryan County Board of Commissioners, Richmond Hill, GA, 1999.

Georgia Historical Markers—Coastal Counties, by Kenneth W. Boyd, Cherokee Publishing Company, Atlanta, GA, 1991.

Georgia's Land of the Golden Isles, by Burnette Vanstory, University of Georgia Press, Athens, GA, 1956.

Georgia Place-Names, by Kenneth Krakow, Winship Press, Macon, GA, 1975.

Georgia Wildlands: A Guide to Lands Protected by The Nature Conservancy of Georgia, edited by Suzanne Burger, The Nature Conservancy of Georgia, Atlanta, GA, 1996.

Georgia Wildlife Viewing Guide, by Jerry McCollum, Betsie Rothermel, and Chuck Rabolli, Georgia Wildlife Press, Conyers, GA, 1996.

Historic Tybee Island, by Margaret Godley, The Tybee Museum Association, Tybee Island, GA, 1988.

Journal of a Residence on a Georgia Plantation in 1838-1839, by Frances Anne Kemble, Brown Thrasher Books, University of Georgia Press, Athens, GA, 1984.

Little St. Simons Island on the Coast of Georgia, by Junius Rochester, Little St. Simons Press, Little St. Simons Island, GA, 1994.

Major Butler's Legacy: Five Generations of a Slaveholding Family, by Malcolm Bell, University of Georgia Press, Athens, GA, 1987.

Portrait of an Island, by Mildred Teal and John Teal, Brown Thrasher Books, University of Georgia Press, Athens, GA, 1997.

St. Catherines: An Island in Time, by David Hurst Thomas, Georgia History and Culture Series, Georgia Humanities Council, Atlanta, GA, 1988.

St. Simons Memoir, by Eugenia Price, Lippincott, Philadelphia, PA, 1978.

Ten Years on a Georgia Plantation Since the War, by Frances Butler Leigh, Beehive Press, Library of Georgia, Savannah, GA, 1992.

The Civil War in Georgia: An Illustrated Traveler's Guide, by Richard J. Lenz, Infinity Press, Watkinsville, GA, 1995.

The Curious Naturalist, National Geographic Society, Washington, DC, 1991.

The Georgia Trilogy: Bright Captivity, Where Shadows Go, Beauty From Ashes; The St. Simons Trilogy: Lighthouse, New Moon Rising, The Beloved Invader; The Savannah Quartet: Savannah, To See Your Face Again, Before the Darkness Falls, Stranger in Savannah; The Florida Trilogy: Don Juan McQueen, Maria, Margaret's Story, by Eugenia Price, various publishers.

The Jekyll Island Club, by Tyler E. Bagwell, Arcadia Publishing, Charleston, SC, 1998.

The Life of the Seashore, by William H. Amos, McGraw-Hill, New York, NY, 1966.

The Natural Environments of Georgia, by Charles H. Wharton, Bulletin 114, Department of Natural Resources, Atlanta, GA, 1978.

The Ogeechee, by Jack Leigh, The University of Georgia Press, Athens, GA, 1986

The Okefenokee Swamp, by Francis Russel, The American Wilderness/Time-Life Books, NY, 1973.

The Seaside Naturalist, Deborah A. Coulombe, Fireside Press, Simon & Schuster, New York, NY, 1992.

This Happy Isle: The Story of Sea Island and The Cloister, by Harold H. Martin, Sea Island Company, Sea Island, GA, 1978.

Tideland Treasure, by Todd Ballantine, Deerfield Publishing, Hilton Head Island, SC, 1983.

Travels of William Bartram by William Bartram, edited by Mark Van Doren, Dover Publications, New York, NY, 1921.

C. Coastal Golf Courses

Black Creek, Pembroke, 18 holes, semiprivate, 858-4653.

Willowpeg, Rincon, 18 holes, semiprivate, 826-2092.

Southbridge Golf Club, Savannah, 18 holes, semiprivate, 651-5455.

Henderson Golf Club, Savannah, 18 holes, public, 920-4653.

Mary Calder Golf Club, Savannah, 9 holes, semiprivate, 238-7100.

Savannah Inn & Country Club, Savannah, 18 holes, semiprivate, 897-1615.

Bacon Park, Savannah, 27 holes, public, 354-2625.

Sapelo Hammock Golf Club, Sutherland Bluff, McIntosh County, 18 holes, public, 832-4653.

Glynco Golf Course, Brunswick, 9 holes, public, 264-9521.

Golden Isles Golf Center, Brunswick, 9 holes, public, 264-1666.

Sea Island Golf Club, St. Simons Island, 36 holes, semiprivate, 638-5118.

St. Simons Island Club, St. Simons Island, 18 holes, semiprivate, 638-5130.

Sea Palms, St. Simons Island, 27 holes, semiprivate, 638-9041.

Hampton Club, St. Simons Island, 18 holes, semiprivate, 634-0255.

Jekyll Island Golf Club, Jekyll Island, 63 holes, public, 635-2368.

Folkston Golf Club, Folkston, 18 holes, public, 496-7155.

Laurel Island Links, Kingsland, 18 holes, public, 729-7277.

Osprey Cove, St. Marys, 18 holes, semiprivate, 882-5575.

D. Annual Events

Before making plans to attend an event, please call to verify dates as they are subject to change.

ONGOING ACTIVITIES

First Saturday Festival, Savannah, March–December. Phone 234-0295.
Tybee Island Pier Entertainment, Tybee Island 2nd Saturday, February–December. Phone 786-5444.
Brunswick Harbor Market, 1st Saturday, January–December. Phone 262-6934.

JANUARY

Annual Bluegrass Festival, Jekyll Island, Jan. 1–3. Phone 635-3636.

FEBRUARY

Annual Georgia Heritage Celebration, Savannah, Feb. 1–12. Phone 897-3773.
Revolutionary War Re-enactment Battle, Fort Morris Historic Site, Liberty County, 1st weekend. Phone 884-5999.
Savannah Irish Festival, Savannah, 2nd weekend. Phone 234-8444.
Sandhill Crane Awareness Day, Okefenokee National Wildlife Refuge, Folkston, 2nd week. Phone 496-7836.
Mardi Gras, St. Marys, Saturday before Ash Wednesday. Phone 882-6200.
Savannah on Stage International Arts Festival, Savannah, last weekend in February, 1st week in March. Phone 236-5745.

MARCH

Spring Fling, Okefenokee Swamp Park. Phone 283-0583.
Spring Encampment at Fort King George, Darien, March 3rd weekend. Phone 437-4770.
Annual Jekyll Island Art Association Art Festival, Jekyll Island, 2nd weekend. Phone 635-3920.
St. Patrick's Day Parade, Savannah, March 17. Phone 233-4804.
Annual Tour of Homes and Gardens, St. Simons Island, 3rd Saturday. Phone 638-3166.
Blessing of the Fleet, Darien, Last weekend. Phone 437-4192.
Great Azalea Kayak Races, Melon Bluff, Midway. Phone 884-5779.

APRIL

April Fools Road Run, Savannah Exchange Club Fairgrounds, 1st weekend. Phone 285-9235.
Annual Savannah Tour of Homes and Gardens, Savannah, late March or early April. Phone 234-8054.
Great Golden Easter Egg Hunt, Jekyll Island, Saturday before Easter. Phone (800) 433-0225.

Festival of Colors, Okefenokee Heritage Center, 3rd week. Phone 285-4260.
Annual NOGS Tour of the Hidden Gardens, Savannah, 3rd weekend. Phone 238-0248.
Earth Day Festival, St. Simons Island, 3rd Saturday. Phone 638-0221.
Darien Annual Tour of Homes, Darien, 3rd weekend. Phone 832-6282.
Night In Old Savannah, Savannah, 3rd weekend. Phone 650-7846.
National Wildlife Weekend and Art Festival, Okefenokee National Wildlife Refuge and Suwannee Canal Recreation Area, Folkston, 3rd weekend in April. Phone 496-7836.
Annual Crawfish Festival, Woodbine, last weekend. Phone 576-3211.
"Sink the Standard" Festival, Melon Bluff, Midway, last weekend. Phone 884-5779.

MAY

Savannah Seafood Festival, Savannah, 1st weekend. Phone 234-0295.
Scottish Games and Highland Gathering, Savannah, 2nd weekend. Phone 369-5203.
Haborfest and Blessing of the Fleet, Brunswick, 2nd weekend. Phone 265-4032.
Spring Tour of Historic Gardens, Savannah, 2nd weekend. Phone 234-1810.
Annual Seaside Fine Arts Festival and Georgia-Sea Island Heritage Festival, St. Simons Island, 3rd weekend. Phone 638-8770.

JUNE

Country by the Sea Music Festival, Jekyll Island, 1st weekend. Phone (800) 841-6586.
Free Fishing Weekend and Youth Fishing Tournament, Okefenokee National Wildlife Refuge, Folkston, 1st weekend. Phone 496-7836.
Savannah Blues Festival at City Market, Savannah, 1st weekend. Phone 232-4903.
Tunis Campbell Festival, Darien, 4th Saturday. Phone 437-3900.

JULY

America's Sail Tall Ship Festival, Savannah, July 2–5. Phone (800) 444-2427.
Cannons Across the Marsh, Fort King George, Darien, July 4. Phone 437-4770.
Sunshine Festival, St. Simons Island, July 4–5. Phone 638-8771.

AUGUST

Georgia Sea Island Festival, Neptune Park, St. Simons Island, 2nd weekend. Phone 262-6934.
Annual Beach Music Festival, Jekyll Island, last Saturday in August. Phone (800) 841-6586.

SEPTEMBER

Labor Day Catfish Festival, Kingsland, 1st weekend. Phone (800) 433-0225.
Sapelo Island Cultural Day, Sapelo Island, 3rd weekend. Phone 485-2126.
Savannah Folk Music Festival, Savannah, 3rd weekend. Phone 927-1376.
The Confederate Civil War Soldier, Fort McAllister, Richmond Hill, 1st Saturday. Phone 756-2676.

OCTOBER

Coastfest, Brunswick, 1st weekend. Phone 264-7218.

Oktoberfest on the River, Savannah, 1st weekend. Phone 234-0295.

Revolutionary War Re-enactment, Fort Morris State Historic Site, Liberty County, 1st weekend. Phone 884-5999.

Rock Shrimp Festival, St. Marys, 1st Saturday. Phone (800) 868-8687.

St. Marys Fine Arts Festival, St. Marys, 1st weekend. Phone 882-6200.

Pogo Festival, Waycross, 1st weekend. Phone 283-3742.

Timberland Jubilee, Homerville, 1st Saturday. Phone 487-2360.

Okefenokee Festival, Folkston, 2nd weekend. Phone 496-2536.

Savannah Greek Festival, Savannah, 2nd weekend. Phone 236-8256.

The Fort By Candlelight, Fort King George, Darien, 3rd weekend. Phone 473-4770.

Okefenokee Festival/Chesser Island Homestead Open House, Okefenokee National Wildlife Refuge, Folkston, 2nd weekend. Phone 496-7836.

Golden Isles Annual Arts Festival, St. Simons Island, 2nd weekend. Phone 638-8770.

Halloween Night Festival, Okefenokee National Wildlife Refuge, Folkston, last Friday in October. Phone 496-7836.

NOVEMBER

Annual Crafts Festival and Cane Grinding, Oatland Island Education Center, Savannah, 2nd Saturday. Phone 897-3773.

Holiday Lights—A Celebration of Community, Brunswick and the Golden Isles, Thanksgiving Friday until Jan. 1st. Phone 265-0620.

Drums Along the Altamaha, Fort King George, Darien, 2nd weekend. Phone 437-4770.

Cane Grinding, Obediah's Okefenok, Waycross, last Saturday in November. Phone 287-0090.

Thanksgiving Weekend Wild Turkey Day, Melon Bluff, Midway. Phone 884-5779.

DECEMBER

Annual Christmas Tour of Homes, Savannah, 1st weekend. Phone 234-1810.

St. Marys Candlelight Tour of Homes, St. Marys, 2nd weekend. Phone 882-6200.

The Guyton Tour of Homes, Brunswick, 2nd Saturday. Phone 754-3301.

The Annual Winter Muster, Fort McAllister, Richmond Hill, 2nd weekend. Phone 756-2676.

Christmas at the Reynolds Mansion, Sapelo Island, 2nd and 3rd weeks. Phone 427-3224.

E. Environmental and Historic Preservation Organizations

Coastal Conservation Organization of Georgia, PO Box 60366, Savannah, GA 31420. Phone (912) 920-2300.

Coastal Georgia Historical Society, P.O. Box 21136, St. Simons Island, GA 31522.

The Georgia Conservancy, 1776 Peachtree Street NW, Suite 400 South, Atlanta, GA 30309. Phone (404) 876-2900. Coastal Office: 428 Bull Street, Savannah, GA 31401. Phone (912) 447-5910.

Georgia Wildlife Federation, 1930 Iris Drive, Conyers, GA 30094-5046. Phone (770) 929-3350.

The Nature Conservancy of Georgia, 1401 Peachtree Street NE, Suite 236. Atlanta, GA 30309. Phone (404) 873-6946.

The Wilderness Society, 1447 Peachtree Street NE, Suite 812, Atlanta, GA 30309. Phone (404) 872-9453.

The William Bartram Trail Conference, 431 East 63rd Street, Savannah, GA 31405.

Tybee Island Historical Society, PO Box 366, Tybee Island, GA 31328. Phone (912) 786-5801.

ANHINGA
(Anhinga anhinga)

The anhinga, also called the snakebird and water turkey, has a commonly observed habit of perching with its wings outstretched, which some believe is the bird's attempt to dry its wings. The bird spends a lot of time in the water, where it hunts fish, frogs, and even small alligators. It swims with its snakelike head and neck above the surface.

F. Glossary

Amphipod—A crustacean of the order Amphipod including the sand fleas and beach hoppers. There are 3,000 species of amphipods.

Anadromous—Migrating from sea water into fresh water to spawn, as salmon or shad.

Brackish—Salty, but less so than sea water.

Calcium carbonate—$CACO_3$, a widely distributed compound occurring in nature as limestone and marble as well as being a component of invertebrate exoskeletons.

Crustacean—Animals that wear a segmented shell and have segmented legs are arthropods, such as insects and crustaceans. Crustaceans are arthropods that live in the water and breathe by gills, such as lobsters, barnacles, crabs, and shrimps.

Detritus—Decomposed plant and animal matter that has been worked to sediment size through the action of water and sand.

Diatoms—One-celled algae with cell walls of silica that make up the first links in aquatic food chains.

Ebb tide—The movement of the tidal current away from shore; a decrease in the height of the tide.

Ecosystem—A biological community existing in a specific physical environment.

Epiphyte—A plant growing on another plant such as Spanish moss.

Estuary—Brackish-water areas influenced by the tides and located where the mouth of a river meets the sea.

Habitat—Where an animal lives; its natural home.

Halophyte—A plant that can tolerate salty soils.

Hammock—An island in a marsh.

Inlet—An opening through which ocean waters enter and leave an enclosed body of water, such as a sound, bay, or marsh.

Interstitial—Pertaining to the organisms that live between sand grains or in other minute spaces.

Intertidal zone—The zone along the shore between high and low tide marks.

Littoral—Pertaining to the seashore, especially the intertidal area.

Neap tide—Lowest range of the tide, occurring at the first and last quarter of the moon.

Niche—The place where an organism lives and the activities it carries out.

Pelagic—The division of the ocean that includes the whole mass of water; it is divided into the neritic zone (water depth 0–600 feet) and the oceanic zone (water deeper than 600 feet).

Plankton—Aquatic organisms that float at the mercy of the currents or have limited swimming abilities.

ppt—Parts per thousand.

Salt marsh—An area of soft, wet land periodically flooded by salt water.

Spring tide—Tide of maximum range occurring at the new and full moon.

Zooplankton—Animal plankton.

F. Index